Psychology for Social Work

PSYCHOLOGY FOR SOCIAL WORK

A Comprehensive Guide to Human Growth and Development

Emma Zara O'Brien

First published 2016 by
PALGRAVE

Palgrave in the UK is an imprint of Macmillan Publishers Limited, registered in England, company number 785998, of 4 Crinan Street, London, N1 9XW.

Palgrave Macmillan in the US is a division of St Martin's Press LLC, 175 Fifth Avenue, New York, NY 10010.

Palgrave is a global imprint of the above companies and is represented throughout the world.

Palgrave® and Macmillan® are registered trademarks in the United States, the United Kingdom, Europe and other countries.

ISBN 978–1–137–57662–0

This book is printed on paper suitable for recycling and made from fully managed and sustained forest sources. Logging, pulping and manufacturing processes are expected to conform to the environmental regulations of the country of origin.

A catalogue record for this book is available from the British Library.

A catalog record for this book is available from the Library of Congress.

Printed in China

To my son Ultan D. O'Brien, my father Brian O'Brien
And in memory of Nancy Twamley

CONTENTS

LIST OF ILLUSTRATIONS

Figures

Tables

ACKNOWLEDGEMENTS

I wish to thank all those who supported me in the writing of this book in giving their time and expertise. A particular word of thanks to Dr Paula Faller and Garett Evers. The support of my son Ultan has been invaluable. Many thanks to all those involved in bringing the book to production.

chapter

1 INTRODUCTION

CHAPTER OUTLINE

- Life happens
- What is social work?
- Psychology
- Factors
- Specialities in psychology
- Finally – the structure of the book

This chapter will be relatively short compared with other chapters. Its purpose is to introduce some basic ideas and concepts in psychology and to outline the structure of the book. Psychology as a discipline will be examined, including its history, its different perspectives and its goals. Social work and its definition will be examined as will the role of psychology in social work. A brief explanation of the different specialities within psychology is given at the end of the chapter. This book is meant to introduce students who have little or no knowledge to some of the fundamental tenets and concepts in psychology that are relevant to social work and its practice. This chapter is an introductory one, outlining some basic premises and ideas from psychology; its goal is to familiarise you with the field of psychology.

LIFE HAPPENS

Even the monkeys fall out of the trees.

– Old Japanese proverb

I'm very fond of this proverb as it reminds me that 'life' happens! The proverb tells us that sometimes we go off the tracks or get sidelined. Monkeys sometimes fall out of trees even though it is not their 'natural' behaviour; people can be similarly unfortunate or unpredictable. This is what appeals to me every time I think of this proverb; that 'stuff' happens, events can sidetrack us and we can end up in situations we never imagined. It's a good lesson in humility, I think.

Those of us who work in the arena of social work encounter people who are vulnerable, people who need support. Yet how do we support them to ensure the best outcomes possible? I originally stumbled into psychology because I was curious as to how some people were able to overcome extreme adversity and have successful lives, while others were not. Why the different outcomes? There are no easy answers – I doubt there will ever be answers that are conclusive – but the quest to understand human behaviour is a fascinating one. The question of how we become who we are is not recent; it has exercised the minds of humans since they could reason. Before we look at that and other issues pertinent to the study of psychology, we should address what is meant by social work and the relationship between psychology and social work.

WHAT IS SOCIAL WORK?

The social work profession promotes social change, problem solving in human relationships and the empowerment and liberation of people to enhance well-being. Utilising theories of human behaviour and social systems, social work intervenes at the points where people interact with their environments. Principles of human rights and social justice are fundamental to social work.

All social workers need: Knowledge
Skills
Values

In this book we will be looking at knowledge from a psychological perspective, through choosing theories and concepts relevant to social work, and considering some of the skills required. In terms of values', the following piece outlines what is considered the value base of social work.

Value base of social workers

The value base of social work is clearly defined within the International Federation for Social Workers (IFSW) International Policy on Human Rights (1996):

Social workers serve human development through adherence to the following basic principles:

i) Every human being has a unique value, which justifies moral consideration for that person.
ii) Each individual has the right to self-fulfilment, to the extent that it does not encroach upon the same right of others; and has an obligation to contribute to the well-being of society.
iii) Each society regardless of its form should function to provide the maximum benefits for all its members.
iv) Social workers have a commitment to principles of social justice.
v) Social workers have the responsibility to devote objective and disciplined knowledge and skill to work with individuals, groups, communities and societies in their development and resolution of personal–societal conflicts and their consequences.
vi) Social workers are expected to provide the best possible assistance without discrimination on the basis of gender, age, disability, colour, social class, race, religion, language, political beliefs or sexual orientation.

Lalor and Share (2009) list the following as important areas to social work and care: working in partnership, marginalisation or disadvantage, children and their families and people with disabilities, those who are homeless, those with addiction, older people and recent immigrants.

Psychology is, at its most simplistic, the study of the human mind and behaviour. The link is clear between (applied) psychology, which strives to understand, explain and improve people's lives, and social work, which involves working with people, particularly those who are vulnerable and have 'needs' that require support. So what exactly is the potential role of psychology in social work?

The role of psychology in social work

Seligman and Csikszentmihalyi (2000, p. 1) articulate their vision for the role of psychology in shaping people's lives and improving them:

> At this juncture, the social and behavioural sciences can play an enormously important role. They can articulate a vision of the good life that is empirically sound while being understandable and attractive. They can show what actions lead to well-being, to positive individuals, and to thriving communities. Psychology should be able to help document what kinds of families result in children who flourish, what work settings support the greatest satisfaction among workers, what policies result in the strongest civic engagement and how people's lives can be most worth living.

Until recently, psychologists concerned themselves only with how people survive and endure adversity. Seligman identifies the emphasis in psychology on the study of psychopathology, when people develop maladaptive behaviours and become 'mentally unwell'. Seligman states that most psychologists have 'scant knowledge of what makes life worth living'. He eloquently identifies the potential that psychology has to benefit the field of social work through improving the lives of others. Throughout this book the role of psychology within social work will become clear, from psychological theory to informed evidence-based interventions. So what is psychology?

PSYCHOLOGY

The historical perspective

Throughout history there have been attempts to understand what makes us human, what shapes our thoughts and behaviour. Religion played an early part in attempting to unravel human behaviour; for example, there was the Christian assertion of 'original sin', the idea that people are born flawed and susceptible to undesirable behaviour. Philosophers added to the debate as the centuries unfolded. John Locke, for instance, suggested that a person was born a 'blank slate' or '*tabula rasa*' and that life experiences shaped the person we became. Jean-Jacques Rousseau, in contrast to the Christian view, believed in the innate goodness of humans striving to reach their full potential. Of course, these arguments are best left to theologians and philosophers, but the study of psychology is really not much different in that, put simply, it attempts to gain understanding of humans, their development and behaviours.

What is psychology?

Psychology is the study of people: how they think, act, react and interact. Psychology is concerned with all aspects of behaviour and the thoughts, feelings and motivations underlying behaviour. In their search for the causes of diverse forms of behaviour, psychologists take into account biological, psychological and environmental factors. Psychology is different from psychiatry, which requires a medical degree and historically concerns itself with mental illness from a biological perspective.

The history of psychology

Within the history of psychology several approaches have been used to gain a greater understanding of human behaviours, beginning in the early 1800s with:

Introspection: As the name indicates this approach relied on 'inspection' where an individual would be asked to report on their feelings and thoughts. William James, considered one of the forefathers of psychology, was an exponent of this method, as was William Wundt.

Psychodynamics: Originating in the late 1800s, this movement is best known through the work of Freud. It placed emphasis upon the 'unconscious' mind, believing that a person had awareness of only a fraction of his thoughts and mental processes. Freud believed that unconscious urges were responsible for behaviour. Techniques such as hypnosis and dream analysis were used to access these unknown recesses of the mind. While many are critical of Freud as we will see in Chapter 4, arguably his belief that early experiences affect later development still remains popular.

Behaviourism: This approach was very popular in America in the 1920s. Those best known for their work in this field are Skinner and Pavlov. Behaviourists believed that, while the inner workings of the mind could not be observed, a person's behaviour could. Their work still has some relevance in the area of learning and behaviour modification.

Humanism: This approach was, it could be argued, a reaction against the behaviourist picture of a human as almost a robot merely responding to outside influence (external stimuli) or the Freudian image of humans driven by their unconscious urges. Humanists such as Carl Rogers and Abraham Maslow promoted the view that within a person is an active desire to reach their full potential, or 'self-actualisation'. Their work has been important in the area of personality, counselling and person-centred practice.

Socio-cultural: No person is an island. We are social creatures and this perspective recognises this and suggests that our thoughts and behaviours are influenced through our interactions with others. Importantly, it highlights how we are embedded in the culture we are raised or live in and, how the views of that culture in turn influence us. In the past, psychology tended to look at the individual to gain a greater understanding of them, without looking outside of the person to gauge external influences on them. The socio-cultural approach examines how culture is transmitted to the members of a society and investigates the differences and similarities of people from differing cultures.

Social Constructionism: Social constructionism emphasises how contextual, linguistic, and relational factors combine to determine the kinds of human beings that people will become and how their views of the world will develop. Knowledge is negotiated between people within a given context and time frame. Social Constructionism proposes that reality is socially negotiated. This leads to questions such as 'what is mental illness', 'what is disability', 'what is woman', fundamentally every construct or concept is informed or constructed by social knowledge. You may come across the term 'constructivism'; this can cause confusion due to its similarity to 'constructionism'. Perhaps the simplest way of distinguishing constructionism is as a sociological description of knowledge, while constructivism is a psychological description of the cognitive processes and structures at an individual level, how the person perceives their world. In Chapter 10 this concept is discussed in greater depth. Constructionism is pivotal to social work, highlighting the influence of cultural and social norms on attitudes and behaviour, which in turn feed into issues of equality and diversity.

Scientific: The predominant approach within psychology at present is the scientific method, or science of behaviour. This approach is less interested in human behaviour *per se*, focusing instead on *why* that behaviour occurs. Thus, if a child exhibits aggressive behaviour the psychologist would not focus on the behaviour itself but rather would want to know why the child is behaving in such a fashion. Methods of research (methodology) include statistics and experiments.

Recent developments in psychology

Dissatisfaction has been voiced regarding the use of the scientific approach within psychology as critics claim that it cannot capture the complexity of human behaviour. More recent developments have been seen in psychology and social work through the emergence of approaches which challenge the status quo of existing theories. Reactionary approaches include that of community, feminist and critical psychology; let's take a look.

Critical psychology encompasses a range of approaches, challenging and critiquing mainstream psychology's assumptions that help sustain unjust political, economic and societal structures. With social justice at its core, it finds resonance with social work approaches which aim to promote social justice. In Chapter 7 we will discuss the anti- and post-psychiatry movements and their critique of mental health. In Chapter 10 we will examine the arguments of critical psychology. Dennis Fox and Isaac Prilleltensky are the best known advocates of this movement.

Feminist psychology, as in the case of critical psychology, questions the influence of unjust structures in maintaining the status quo, but feminist psychology focuses on the role of gender in subjugating women. This movement originated in the 1960s with the growing reaction against stereotypes and discrimination faced by females. In psychology it is associated with a backlash against Freud's psychoanalytic movement and in particular his concept of penis envy and hysteria (believed to be a disorder of the womb). This inherent discrimination harmed women and excluded them from an equal place within society and caused them to be labelled as 'mad' if they did not conform to societal norms and beliefs about what 'woman' is. Feminist psychology recognises the role of gender stereotypes within psychological beliefs, diagnoses and therapies and attempts to challenge them. In Chapter 5, Carol Gilligan's Critique of Kohlberg's theory of moral development hinges on its exclusion of gender, she further argues that many theorists, including Kohlberg, have ignored women when developing theories explaining human development. Gilligan argues that for gender to either facilitate or hinder, gender must first be recognised in psychological development.

Transcultural psychiatry – psychiatry differs from psychology. Psychiatrists are medically trained doctors and traditionally have a particular interest in the biological aspects of 'mental illness'. Transcultural psychiatry, like critical psychiatry, aims to look outside the individual in understanding different factors that influence a person. Transcultural psychiatry is interested in the role of culture in 'mental illness'; this can range from how cultures perceive mental illness to cultural factors that may affect the individual's mental health.

BLACK PERSPECTIVES

According to Robinson (2007, p. 11) the common experiences of black people form the framework for developing a black perspective which challenges the '... racist and stereotypic, weakness-dominated and inferiority-oriented conclusions about black people. This perspective is interested in the psychological well-being of black people and is critical of oppressive research paradigms and theoretical formulations that have a potentially oppressive effect on black people. Black psychologists (mainly in the US) have presented alternative perspectives on black child development'. Robinson reflects that mainstream psychology has chosen in large part to ignore the research of black academics. Robinson concludes that social workers with an understanding of the black frame of reference are better equipped to develop and offer 'more accurate and comprehensive explanations of black child development'.

CROSS-CULTURAL PERSPECTIVE

As with the Black Perspective, cross-cultural psychology questions the ethnocentrism of mainstream psychology's Euro-American approach. Segall et al. (as cited in

Robinson 2007, p. 12) define cross-cultural psychology as 'the scientific study of human behaviour and its transmission, taking into account the ways in which the behaviours are shaped and influenced by social and cultural forces'.

> **Community psychology** examines individuals within their social world. Community psychology explores social issues and how they influence individuals, groups and society at large.

Despite all these critiques, the degree to which psychology and psychiatry have embraced a more social justice position is questionable. Arguably, mainstream psychology has been slow to critique assumptions or attitudes that may in fact be maintaining unhealthy or harmful beliefs and practices.

WHAT DO YOU THINK?

Which approach in psychology do you feel has the most to offer social workers? Do you think aspects of psychology have and can perpetuate beliefs and assumptions that are detrimental to principles of social justice?

While we have seen the approaches and new directions in psychology change and adapt, the goals of psychology remain constant and reflect arguably a more empirical and scientific direction.

The goals of psychology

1. to *describe* how people and other animals behave
2. to *understand* the causes of these behaviours
3. to *predict* how people and animals will behave under certain conditions
4. to *control* behaviour through knowledge and control of its causes.

Terminology

Terminology can wane and change with each new concept or theory introduced in psychology. It is helpful early on to define and clarify the core terms you will encounter in this book. Terminology can be intimidating; throughout the book an effort is made to explain terms in accessible languagep the following are terms used repeatedly in psychology and social work.

Term	**Definition**
Theory	Describes, explains or predicts certain phenomenon
Method	Specifies what to do when faced with certain phenomenon
Perspective	A way of viewing or understanding certain experience based on words and principles
Model	A theory or method depicted logically or graphically

Finally, while we are in the mode of defining or outlining basic terms and concepts often found within psychology, we should take this opportunity to overview 'factors' as they frequently appear in the book.

FACTORS

So what is a factor?

A factor at its simplest is something that influences or produces a result or outcome

An individual's health, development and well-being are shaped by a range of factors, such as the individual's characteristics, family characteristics, and the broader social, economic and physical environments which the individual inhabits. In Chapter 4 we will look at the work of Bronfenbrenner and his ecological theory, which is a fantastic framework to understand the layers of influences and their potential interaction in affecting development and outcomes.

Factors can be either 'risk' or 'protective' and can affect all areas of an individual's life throughout the lifecycle. Added to this is our recognition that experiences early in life affect later development: that the early years are a critical and sensitive period that can have massive ramifications throughout the remainder of a child's life.

Risk factors are factors that can have an adverse impact on an individual person or their immediate and distal (distant) environments and that have a potentially negative influence on their development or behaviour. Often where you have one risk factor you are more likely to see others, for example, children born with low birth weight (biological risk) may also be born to mothers with low education levels and who live in poverty (psychosocial risks). This phenomenon is sometimes called 'double jeopardy'. The more risk factors that accumulate; the longer these factors last and the more severe the factor, the greater the impact on the individual and their development.

Offset against this are protective factors that operate in a similar fashion to risk factors in that, to put it simply, the more you have, the better 'protected' you are and the more likely you are to enjoy better outcomes. Intervention programmes all operate by targeting children, families and individuals who are vulnerable for a variety of reasons by putting in place support mechanisms. These programmes are protective in and of themselves and their ideology reflects the need to target at-risk populations by increasing protective factors to offset risk factors and, thus, improve outcomes.

Throughout the book, factors will be discussed together with their relationship to a particular topic or aspect of development. In Chapter 6 factors related to disability are examined. In Chapter 7 those that impact upon mental illness are overviewed. Within Chapter 8 particular attention is given to psychosocial factors involved in well-being, including poverty, community and ethnicity. It is difficult to capture the interplay between the myriad of risk and protective factors contained within a complex socio-cultural environment and its interaction with the unique characteristics of an individual. It is hoped that this will become apparent throughout the book.

Social workers work in partnership and collaborate with other professionals and stakeholders. The field of psychology is diverse and wide ranging, as you will see in the book; the different specialities reflect this diversity. The following piece outlines the different specialities within psychology.

SPECIALITIES IN PSYCHOLOGY

Clinical psychology is the application of psychological theories, models and research to a range of psychological, psychiatric, mental health and developmental problems. Clinical psychologists provide a variety of services, including assessment, therapy and consultancy services. They work primarily, but not exclusively, in child and/or adult and learning disability services where emotional, behavioural, psychiatric or developmental difficulties are addressed.

Counselling psychology, as a psychological speciality, facilitates personal and interpersonal functioning across the life span with a focus on emotional, social, vocational, educational, health-related and developmental concerns. Therefore, counselling psychologists can be found working in such diverse areas as schools and colleges, industrial workplaces and health services. Counselling psychology encompasses a broad range of practices that help people improve their well-being, alleviate distress and maladjustment, resolve crises and increase their ability to live more highly functioning lives. Counselling psychologists work with people who have experienced a range of emotional and psychological difficulties. These include problems of identity and bereavement, relationship problems, sexual abuse, emotional abuse and neglect.

Educational psychologists deal with the psychological and educational development of people in the education system. This may include students of any age, their parents or guardians and the people who work with them. Their work can involve both assessment and intervention within the education setting. They are also likely to be involved in training and research on related issues.

Forensic psychologists work in a variety of areas, including prisons, probation services, special secure hospitals, rehabilitation units and in private practice. Responsibilities include the assessment of offenders prior to sentencing, management of offenders during sentence and in the community upon release, risk assessment and sex offender treatment programmes. Forensic psychologists also act as expert witnesses and give evidence in court.

Health psychology involves an examination of the way in which biological, psychological and social factors affect health and illness. Health psychologists are concerned with studying the relationship between psychological factors (for example, proneness to hostility), social/psychological factors (for example, psychological stress) and illness (for example, heart disease). Areas of practice include health-risk behaviours and developing better ways of helping people to change their behaviours. Health psychologists are also involved in helping individuals to improve their health or to cope with chronic illness or unpleasant medical procedures.

Neuropsychology is the scientific study of brain–behaviour relationships, and the clinical application of that knowledge to human problems. A clinical neuropsychologist is a professional psychologist who applies principles of assessment and intervention based upon the scientific study of human behaviour as it relates to normal and abnormal functioning of the central nervous system.

Occupational (also known as Organisational) psychology involves the study of human behaviour in the workplace. Organisational psychologists recognise the importance of relationships between individuals, organisations and society. Occupational psychology helps organisations to get the best from their workforce and improve the job satisfaction of individual employees. It deals with issues and problems involving people at work by serving as advisors in a variety of organisations.

FINALLY – THE STRUCTURE OF THE BOOK

Before we look at the structure of the book, I would recommend those with no knowledge of psychology to read Chapter 4, which overviews the major theories in psychology and Chapter 5, which is a very comprehensive outline of **Human Growth and Development**, explaining the individual's journey from conception through the life span from the different domains (areas) of development, including physical, cognitive and socioemotional and the different age-related and developmental milestones one may typically see.

Structure of the book

While this is first and foremost a psychology textbook, it has been tailored to focus on material and topics of direct relevance to social work. As psychology and social work are vast and diverse fields, it is not possible to be exhaustive, it is intended to demonstrate the relevance of psychology to social work though explaining psychology and demonstrating how it links to social work.

Chapter 2 The brain and behaviour

Chapter 2 focuses on the brain. With increasing advances in medicine and longevity we are likely to meet people who have brain injury or disease. Exploring the brain and its role in behaviour early in the book will acclimatise you to the more 'biological' aspects within psychology and highlights this area's growing importance. Knowledge of neurology is a helpful addition to the social worker's knowledge base and this chapter will explain brain structures and function, providing examples of how this knowledge is relevant to social work, including case studies.

Chapter 3 Communication and relationships in social work

The centrality of skills is reflected in the inclusion of a Chapter on 'Communication and Relationships in Social Work'. It will aim to introduce 'communication' into this discourse as it is so fundamental within social work; this will be done within the rubric of psychology, for example, communication and social work from an attachment perspective.

Chapter 4 Approaches to psychology

We return to all things psychological in Chapter 4, which seeks to explain some of the major theories within psychology, Teater (2010, p. 6), confirms, 'at the foundation of current social work theory and practice is psychosocial theory', highlighting the importance of theory to the social worker. An emphasis continues in illustrating the relevance of psychological theories to social work, for example, an explanation of Maslow's theory is accompanied with its use in an addiction programme, or learning theory's role in behaviour modification. Hopefully, the applied aspect of this book will enable readers to see the theories from a practice-orientated perspective.

Chapter 5 Human growth and development

Human Growth and Development is tackled in Chapter 5, a large chapter reflecting the range of the life span. Here we will journey from conception onwards and consider the domains of physical, social-emotional and cognitive development. Use of case studies, examples and other tools are used to offer a more applied perspective. Knowledge of the life span is fundamental to those of us who work with people; it not only provides a knowledge base to operate from but allows us insight into the multifactorial nature of human development and the many influences that can shape it.

Here we begin to move from a more general discussion to specific exploration of topics of relevance to social work and its practice, including topics such as disability, abuse, trauma and mental health.

Chapter 6 Disabilities

Disability, its definitions and models are discussed and what we think of disability is challenged. Describing disability will explore the language used in discussing disability – its nuances and how language can have a 'disabling' effect upon an individual. We will than move towards a practical overview of the different categories of disability as they exist, causes, characteristics and some of the interventions engaged in the treatment of different conditions and disorders. Different influences will be explored, including the role of culture and ethnicity, and an ecological approach to understanding disability will be discussed.

Chapter 7 Mental health

Mental health plays a pivotal role in social work knowledge and practice. This chapter examines how we define mental health and the models and classification used within this field. The role of biological, psychological and social factors will bediscussed. Interventions and treatments will be considered, an overview of the main theorists used in therapeutic approaches will be outlined, as will the efficacy of counselling. An 'In focus' section at the end will explore addiction in depth, highlighting the prominent role it occupies within social work practice.

Chapter 8 Well-being and environmental stressors

While the focus of the previous chapter was narrow, dealing with the classification of mental disorders, this chapter explores, in greater depth, well-being and environmental stressors, psychosocial resilience and adversity, and the factors, characteristics and interplay that occur, to include groups vulnerable to mental health problems. Issues such as poverty and how it impacts on development and functioning are explored.

Chapter 9 Abuse and trauma

In this chapter you are introduced to the key aspects of abuse and trauma with the emphasis on the psychological aspects rather than legislation, policy or practice pertaining to social work. We begin with a discussion on the question of intentionality and its role in defining abuse, the different categories of abuse, their characteristics and associated factors will be overviewed. Groups vulnerable to abuse will be examined, such as the increased risk of abuse faced by those with mental illness. Further, an 'In focus' piece on the abuse of disabled children illustrates the varied mechanisms involved. Societal and cultural influences in abuse and its perpetuation are discussed. The final section of this chapter gives greater focus to the perspective of those victimised; topics such as the search for meaning and post-traumatic stress disorder are explored.

Chapter 10 Social psychology – B =f(P,E)

Lewin's famous equation B=f(P,E), that behaviour is a function of the person in the environment, captures the concept that our behaviour reflects, and is a function of, environment. Chapter 10 considers the field of social psychology and how behaviour is a function of the 'person-in-environment'. Sociological perspectives consider the role of society and its effects. Social psychology is often seen as a crossover between psychology and sociology, an interdisciplinary bridge between the two. This chapter examines how people influence our behaviour (social influence), how we think about and perceive our social world (social thinking and social perception) and how we behave towards other people (social relations).

To conclude!

I hope this book will serve as a guide to walk you through some of the most fundamental aspects of human development that have relevance to social work. This book is intended to offer a foundation for further exploration of the topics touched on. Life is akin to a voyage; it can be said that it's not so much the destination that is important as the journey there – I wish you a fruitful one!

chapter

2 THE BRAIN AND BEHAVIOUR

CHAPTER OUTLINE

- Role of the brain
- Functions of the brain
- Structures of the brain
- Brain development across the life span
- Recommended viewing
- Caring for people with dementia

The focus of this chapter is to chart the development of the brain from a neurodevelopmental approach navigating across five periods; infancy, childhood, adolescence, adulthood and the older years. A major theme throughout this chapter will be that of *plasticity*, or the ability of neurons (nerve cells) to change in structure or function. In other words, how the brain reacts and adapts to its changing environment and how experiences, both positive and negative, can shape the developing brain. Before we can fully engage with these issues it is important for the reader to acquire an introductory understanding of the brain, its structure, functions and its role in behaviour and emotions, this will form the first part of the chapter. Once we have established a rudimentary knowledge of the brain itself, we will delve further into each period across the life span, reviewing its distinct development including the potential impact of both positive and negative experiences on the developing brain. Within the sections, topics of particular relevance to the field of social work such as the neuroscience of attachment, its impact on brain development and the consequences to behaviour in relationships will be discussed. Other topics, including trauma and the impact of stress on brain development, are examined. The chapter ends by exploring whether the work of neuroscience is being misrepresented by some proponents of the *First Three Years* movement. This chapter intends to demonstrate to the reader the relevance of neuroscience and knowledge of the brain to social work and its practice, in addition to the 'In focus' pieces, case studies will be utilised.

ROLE OF THE BRAIN

The role of the brain in behaviour has not always been obvious; it took an accident involving a man named Phineas Gage to demonstrate its integral role in regulating our behaviour. Gage worked on the railway lines in America in the mid-1800s. Explosives he planted detonated early causing his tampering iron to enter under his cheekbone and exit through the top of his head as you can see in the image below.

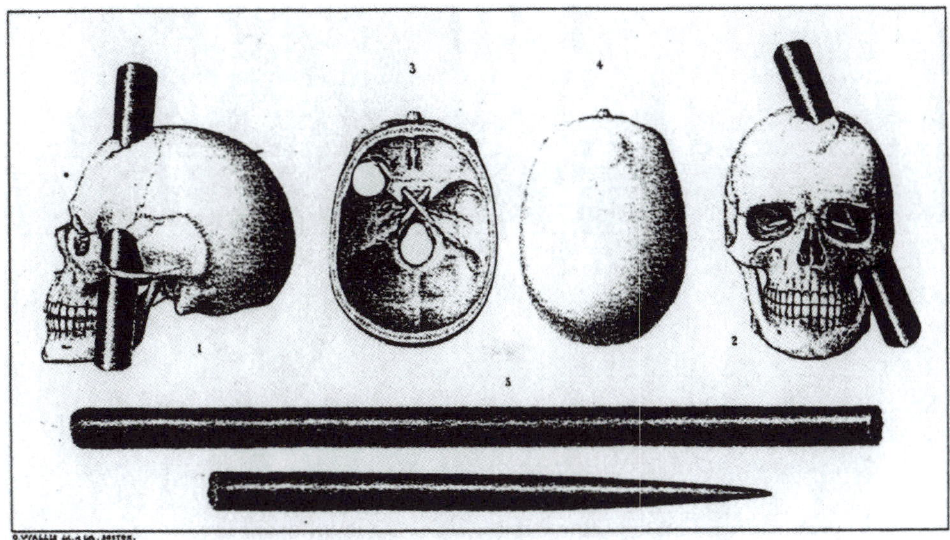

Figure 2.1 The brain of Phineas Gage
Source: H. J. Bigelow (1850)

Amazingly he survived this injury, but most of the front part of his left brain had been destroyed, resulting in a complete change in his personality and behaviour. As his doctor noted, 'Gage was no longer Gage.' Before the accident Gage held the position of foreman and was considered diligent, conscientious and hard-working. Afterwards he became unreliable, nasty, used vulgar language in front of women (considered quite a *faux pas* then) and changed his mind from moment to moment. This dramatic change in behaviour gave the first indication that damage to the brain could affect behaviour, and this is why Phineas Gage holds an important place in the history of the brain. The area of Gage's injury (frontal lobe) is significant because, as you will see, different parts of the brain are responsible for different functions (referred to as **localisation**). Modern day individuals with the same area of brain damage as Gage are affected similarly: they are unable to make effective personal or social decisions and they cannot plan ahead, demonstrating also how emotions are involved in our ability to reason. As a result of the case of Phineas Gage, the role of the brain in human behaviour is now understood to be paramount. The brain is involved in all aspects of development: motor (movement), sensory, cognitive and social.

FUNCTIONS OF THE BRAIN

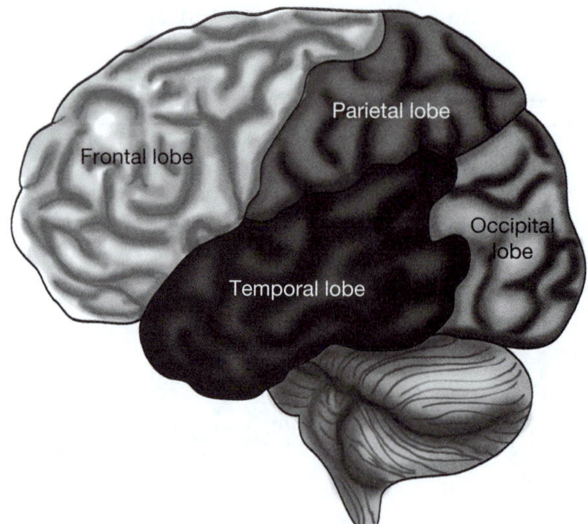

Figure 2.2 The four lobes of the brain

The brain consists of four lobes, which have different locations and functions.

Frontal lobe: located behind the forehead, this is the 'front' of the brain. This lobe does not develop fully until the teen years and its functions include higher forms of thinking, such as reasoning, and also voluntary movements. It is possible to divide the frontal lobe into three distinct zones of functioning:

- **Motor cortex:** responsible for making movements
- **Premotor cortex:** selects the movements
- **Prefrontal cortex:** controls cognitive (thinking) processes so that appropriate movements are selected at the correct time and place. The prefrontal cortex is also responsible for selecting behaviour with respect to context (put plainly, appropriate behaviour). Gage was unable to perform this function. As we will see, the prefrontal cortex has a particular relevance in adolescents' ability to process emotional information and respond.

Frontal lobe damage

Damage to the frontal lobe can result in the following difficulties:

- Loss of ability to solve problems and plan actions may be experienced
- Concentration may be affected; apathy and inattentiveness may be noticed
- A lack of inhibition may occur, including socially inappropriate behaviour and a disregard for the consequences of the behaviour.

Parietal lobe: located behind the frontal lobe, around the top of the head. Its main responsibility is in somatosensory functions. Somatosensory means the sensation of the body and its movement, including sensations of pressure, warmth, cold, vibrations and limb position and movement. The functions of this lobe include processing information about body sensations.

Parietal lobe damage

Features of damage in this area can include:

- Numbness and impaired sensation occurring on the side of the body opposite the area of damage in the brain
- Affected individuals can have difficulty identifying a sensation's location and type (pain, heat, etc.)
- Damage to the right side of this lobe can result in apraxia – a loss of intentional movements. Apraxia results in the inability to perform simple skilled tasks, such as dressing or brushing the hair.

Occipital lobe: located at the back of the brain. One of its main functions is vision, including perception of form, colour and movement.

Occipital lobe damage

The following features are associated with damage in this lobe:

- Visual impairment: this lobe's main function concerns the processing of visual information so that some will be left unable to see, even though the eyes themselves are functioning normally
- Impairment of the ability to recognise familiar objects and faces and to interpret what is seen may occur.

Temporal lobes: located at either side of the brain. They are involved in hearing and enable the processing of speech. The temporal lobes are also involved in the analysis of visual processing, especially recognition of form. Finally, these lobes play a role in long-term memory.

Temporal lobe damage

Damage to these lobes can have the following consequences:

- The ability to recognise sounds and shapes may be impaired
- Memory may be affected; there may be loss of ability to understand language (aphasia)
- Personality changes, such as extreme religiosity and humourlessness, may be noticed.

The brain is not one huge mass; it is divided into two halves or 'hemispheres'. These are connected by a bundle of nerves called the corpus callosum, which allows each half to communicate with the other, thus ensuring that they are working in unison. **Lateralisation** is a term used to describe the specialisation of function in one or the other hemispheres. Put more plainly, it means that one hemisphere can be responsible for a particular function; for example, in most people the left side of the brain is generally responsible for language. However, this does not mean that the right side has no role at all in language – it does, but not the dominant role. It is generally accepted that lateralisation occurs between the ages of 2 and 12.

The nervous system

The main function of the nervous system is as the body's decision and communication centre. It consists of the central nervous system (CNS) and the peripheral nervous system. The central nervous system is made up of the brain and spinal cord. Its main function is to relay information to and from the brain. A healthy nervous system controls movement and coordination of the limbs. The peripheral nervous system consists of nerves. Together, these systems control every part of our daily life: nerves connect the brain to the face, eyes, ears, nose and spinal cord and connect the spinal cord to the rest of the body.

Sensory nerves gather information from the environment through the senses (eyes, ears, etc.) and that information is transmitted to the spinal cord and relayed to the brain. The brain then deciphers the message and fires off a response. Motor neurons (neurons are nerve cells) take the instructions from the brain to the rest of the body. The spinal cord plays an essential role in the relationship between the brain and body as a transmitter, delivering and relaying messages to and from the brain.

We have seen the different lobes of the brain and the role of the CNS in relaying and receiving information to and from the brain. In addition to the lobes of the brain, other structures exist including the outside 'layer' of the brain (the cerebrum) to deep in the brain (limbic system), let's take a look at them.

STRUCTURES OF THE BRAIN

- cerebrum
- cerebellum
- limbic system
- brain stem.

The ***cerebrum***, or cortex, is the biggest part of the brain and is divided into four lobes: frontal, parietal, occipital and temporal, as discussed above. The cerebral cortex is generally associated with higher thinking and brain function. As you might have noticed in the diagram of the brain, the surface of the cortex is wrinkled. If you take a piece of cloth and lay it down flat it will cover an area the size of the cloth; however, if you were to fold the fabric continually upon itself that same piece of cloth would take up a smaller surface area. The same principle can be applied to the brain; by folding in on itself to create this wrinkled surface it has a larger surface area; this allows the brain to have a higher density of neurons, which creates a much more powerful brain.

The ***cerebellum***, or 'little brain' as it is sometimes known, is located deeper in the brain and is associated with regulation and coordination of movement, posture and balance.

The ***limbic system*** is found deep in the cerebrum and is often called the 'emotional brain' as it houses some of our basic emotions, such as rage and happiness. It contains the **thalamus**, which serves as a station receiving sensory information of all kinds (particularly pain and pleasure) and relays it to the cortex; it also receives information from the cortex. Drugs that shut down the thalamus are often used for anaesthetic effects. The **hypothalamus** is a part of the limbic system that helps regulate hormone activity, directs autonomic nervous system functions and influences or manages many critical functions, including sleep. The **amygdala** is a part of the limbic system that plays an important role in motivation and emotional behaviour. In adolescence the prefrontal cortex is not fully matured so when processing emotional information teens use the amygdala; this can result in poor impulse control and difficulties managing emotional responses appropriately. The **hippocampus** is involved in controlling emotion (such as fear or happiness) and instinct (how we respond in certain situations). It is called the hippocampus because it is shaped a bit like a seahorse; 'hippocampus' is Greek for seahorse.

The ***brain stem*** is located at the base of the brain and is responsible for fundamental life functions such as breathing, heartbeat and blood pressure. It is considered the earliest, simplest part of the human brain. Damage to this part of the brain is inevitably fatal as it supports the vital life functions.

Earlier in discussing the case of Phineas Gage the important role played by emotions in our ability to reason was noted, so let's now look at the relationship between emotions and brain function.

Emotions and the brain

Emotions enable us to react to situations – for example, anger or fear will set your heart racing, and feeling happy will make you smile. One of the key areas of the brain that deals with showing, recognising and controlling the body's reactions to emotions is known as the limbic system.

ANIMAL EMOTIONS

The limbic system is often thought of as a primitive part of the brain as it is present in lower mammals and is even found in reptiles, which is why it's nicknamed the 'reptilian brain'. Animals need emotions to survive – they need fear as a trigger to escape predators and aggression to defend their territory, young and food. Charles Darwin thought emotions were merely left over from our animal past. However, we rely on our emotions to make quick, often complex, decisions.

Fear triggers immediate changes in humans just as in other animals – your hair stands on end, your heart beats faster and your body gets ready to either attack or run. When you recognise danger or feel afraid, you are using an area of your brain called the amygdala. People with damage to this area can no longer recognise fear in others.

Anger: danger can make you feel either angry or frightened and both these emotions are triggered by the same part of the brain – the amygdala. The amygdala in turn triggers a response in the hypothalamus, a key area for many of the functions your brain performs 'without thinking', including this 'fight or flight' response.

Happiness: enjoyment triggers areas in your brain known as 'pleasure centres'. They release 'feel-good' chemicals, in particular dopamine. All animals have this reward system, usually triggered by food or sex. However, the system can be affected by drugs, including nicotine and alcohol. At first these act in the same way as 'natural' rewards, producing pleasure. But with increased use the drug is needed to stop unpleasant symptoms that appear when it is not available (withdrawal); these effects contribute to drug addiction.

Brain dysfunction

When the brain becomes damaged it can malfunction in many different ways, depending on the severity and location of the damage and the speed with which the damage progresses. Brain dysfunction can be diffuse (widespread) or localised (confined to a specific area). Causes of diffuse damage include infections, such as encephalitis and meningitis, and lack of oxygen. Localised brain dysfunction can be the result of a brain tumour or disorders, such as stroke, that decrease the blood (and thereby oxygen) supply to a specific area. The following three characteristics of the brain contribute to its ability to compensate for, and recover from, damage:

- Redundancy: many brain functions can be performed in more than one area of the brain
- Adaptation: areas with somewhat overlapping functions can sometimes compensate for lost functions
- Plasticity: certain areas of the brain can adapt to perform new and different functions.

Neuroplasticity refers to the ability of neurons to change in structure and function. It allows the neurons to compensate for injury and disease and most usually to adjust their activities in response to new situations or to changes in their environment. Two areas of interest in the realm of neuroplasticity are the role of early experience on brain development and recovery from brain damage. It should be noted that while the brain maintains some level of plasticity throughout our lives, in the early years the brain is at its most malleable (mouldable). This can be both hugely positive and negative, as we will see later when examining Margot Sunderland's work studying affective neuroscience and in particular how stress can impact the developing brain.

Thus, undamaged areas of the brain can sometimes take over functions previously performed by a damaged area, aiding recovery. A fascinating case exists of a young boy, Nico, who had his right hemisphere removed and yet the other hemisphere took over many of its functions, leaving the boy functioning well.

Box 2.1 Nico: The boy with half a brain

Nico's right hemisphere was removed when he was three in an effort to control his severe and intractable epilepsy. Despite the removal of half his brain, he developed into a bright child with relatively minor physical and mental impairments; he had no significant cognitive or affective (emotional) disorder. It appeared that the left hemisphere had taken over the functioning of the right hemisphere.

Of course, the fact that we know about this case indicates how unusual this level of recovery is, but it does demonstrate the potential capacity of the brain to recover functioning after a trauma or injury to it. Additionally, the fact that he was young was a major factor in his astounding recovery; as we age the brain becomes less able to shift functions from one area to another, functions become more localised (fixed) and therefore the ability for other parts to take over diminishes. Further, certain functions, such as vision, cannot be performed by any other part of the brain and thus damage to these areas generally results in permanent impairment.

In this next section we will explore brain development across the life span. At the end of each life stage an 'In focus' section will examine a topic of particular relevance to that age group. In infancy and childhood we will look at the effects of stress on the developing brain and the role of attachment in shaping brain development. Adolescence and risk-taking behaviour will be discussed, and in adulthood Acquired Brain Injury will be considered, ending in older age with a focus on dementia.

BRAIN DEVELOPMENT ACROSS THE LIFE SPAN

In this section we are going to take a life span approach to exploring brain development from infancy into old age.

Some brain facts:

- The brain weighs about three pounds
- 85 percent of the weight is in the cerebrum, the largest part of the brain
- The brain is made up of 75 percent water
- One side or hemisphere is dominant
- It has no pain receptors, so the brain cannot feel pain
- The brain consolidates memories as we sleep.

The brain at birth weighs 25 percent of its eventual adult weight, and by the child's second birthday the brain will have grown to 75 percent of its adult weight. This gives us some insight into the rapid changes that occur in the brain during the first two years of life. An infant is born with reflexes that diminish as the brain develops and takes over control from these innate reflexes.

The infant brain

An infant is born with all the brain cells it will need; in fact, it is born with more than it needs. As the brain develops it will cut back or 'prune' cells, synapses (cell connections) and pathways it does not need or use. Imagine a city that has hundreds of little roads: it comes to the mayor's attention that some of these roads are not very efficient or are not being used and that an overhaul is needed. So he orders that the inefficient or superfluous roads that aren't contributing to the smooth running of traffic be removed. When this is done the traffic moves more smoothly and quickly as it is easier and clearer to see how to get from one point to another. So, although there are fewer roads, the roads that are left are the ones that work best and ensure traffic flows quickly and efficiently. This is similar to how the brain develops. Pruning away superfluous neural pathways and cells ensures that the brain works more efficiently. Another process that occurs during the first two years of life is myelinisation, when the nerve fibres are insulated, improving and speeding up the nerve impulses.

In terms of early experience and brain development, modern neuroscience argues that our early experiences with primary carers are internalised and become an organising principle throughout our lives (Cozolino, 2002). Our patterns of communicating will be largely shaped by these early experiences with our primary carers. We will explore this issue later when discussing affective neuroscience.

Interestingly the interaction of a child with its environment influences the development of the brain. As discussed in Chapter 1, the brain needs a stimulating environment. If a child is severely neglected, the brain does not develop normally. Pathways for language can be lost if no stimulation or access to language is available to the child. In fact, such a child's brain can weigh significantly less than the brain of an average child of similar age. So as we can see, the child's environment can influence the development of the brain. Yet is it that straightforward? At the end of this chapter we will discuss the current debate focussing on the growing influence of neuroscience in social work. While it is important for social workers to understand neuroscience' how much influence should biologically based arguments have on social work practice? Critics claim that the 'facts' presented by neuroscience as to the impact of neglect on the developing brain have been misrepresented, this reflects a tension between the role of biological versus social arguments, the latter being core to social work. This debate on the role of neuroscience in early interventions will be explored in more depth later.

IN FOCUS: THE USE OF LANGUAGE – NON ACCIDENTAL HEAD INJURY (FORMERLY KNOWN AS SHAKEN BABY SYNDROME)

We've seen how rapidly the brain develops. Young infants have weak neck muscles and are unable to support the weight of their heads. Further, the blood vessels in the developing brain are fragile. For these reasons it is essential that the baby's head is protected and care is taken to prevent falls, and so on. Shaken Baby Syndrome is the result of abuse which involves the violent shaking of an infant, causing damage to the brain. Injuries can include blindness, seizures, developmental delay, brain damage and death. But can language affect how we perceive this syndrome? The Crown Prosecution Service (CPS) issued a directive that the term 'Shaken Baby Syndrome' no longer be used; one reason given was that the term was 'emotive'. This recognises the power of language in constructing a concept or idea and in influencing reactions and attitudes.

THINK ABOUT IT!

Think about the use of language. Are there other terms that you think may be emotive, or even discriminatory? Social constructionism can be found in every facet of life as the example above illustrates. We will revisit this issue again particularly in the chapters on disability and mental health.

Child's brain

While the brain at birth weighs 25 percent of its eventual adult weight, by the child's second birthday the brain will have increased to 75 percent of its adult weight. Clearly this period in a child's life is one of marked growth. It is therefore imperative that this development is supported and the child suitably stimulated to ensure the best outcomes possible. During this period the number and size of nerve endings increase. The process of **myelinisation** continues with a resulting increase in the speed of information transmission between cells; this process occurs by the age of seven and results in a lengthening of attention span. At around three years, the hippocampus matures, allowing the retention of memories before this; according to Carter (2009) few memories are recalled from before this time. Between the ages of 6–13, growth spurts affect brain regions concerned with language and spatial relationships, these changes improved cognitive (thinking) and social development including the ability to read and to make friends.

IN FOCUS: AFFECTIVE NEUROSCIENCE – STRESS AND THE DEVELOPING BRAIN

The idea of who we are, what our sense of self is, is vital to how we conceive of ourselves and others. Early experiences shape the people we become and neurologists are very interested in the role of early experiences and their impact on brain development. We will look at the work of Margot Sunderland of the Centre for Child Mental Health whose interest lies in affective neuroscience, which looks at the relationship between brain development and an individual's emotional content. This informs her work with children who have been traumatised and are suffering the effects of their experiences. She offers some interesting insights into the nature of early experience and how it can shape the brain and the potential ramifications in later life.

According to Sunderland, modern science is now confirming the power of early relationships and their effects on the brain, which are long-lasting. One can think of a child's brain as an ice sculpture which is 'sculpted' through relational interactions for better or worse. Earlier we spoke of the brain's malleability, that is, it is flexible and can be 'shaped' accordingly. Sunderland (2006, p. 27) makes a powerful case for the effects of stress on the developing brain and its long-term consequences for the child:

> The developing brain in those crucial first years of life is highly vulnerable to stress. It is so sensitive that the stress of many common parenting techniques can later upset delicate 'emotion chemical' balances and stress response systems in the infant's brain and body, and sometimes cause actual cell death in certain brain structures .... There is a mass of scientific research showing that quality of life is dramatically affected by whether or not you established good stress-regulating systems in your brain in childhood. One of the most important alarm systems in the lower brain is called the amygdala. One of its main functions is to work out the emotional meaning of everything that happens to you. If the amygdala senses that something threatening is happening to you, it communicates with another structure called the hypothalamus, and this part of the brain actions the release of stress hormones, which can prepare your body for flight or fight .... If you were left in childhood to manage your painful feelings on your own, and without counselling or therapy in later life, your higher brain may not have developed the necessary wiring to be able to perform these wonderful stress- managing functions. As a result, you can stay feeling stressed out for hours and sometimes days and even weeks. This can result in clinical depression.

Sunderland is clearly saying that if children are not met with responsive and attuned relationships in early life, which teach them to manage what she calls the 'big feelings', then the cycle of flight or fight that we experience when we are stressed becomes literally ingrained in the brain; that is, it shapes and sculpts the brain leaving the person unequipped to deal with stressful feelings in later life and in a state of permanent alert. This has devastating effects for later life. Sunderland reports that an individual who has not established effective stress-responsive systems in their brain can suffer from a range of difficulties in later life, including:

- depression
- persistent states of anxiety
- phobias and obsessions
- physical symptoms/illness
- being cut off emotionally
- lethargy and lack of 'get-up-and-go'
- lack of desire and excitement
- lack of spontaneity (p. 32).

Dr Sunderland speaks of the stress response that is triggered within the young, one powerful trigger response can be 'attachment', which at its simplest is a 'long-enduring, emotionally meaningful tie to a particular individual' (Schaffer, 1996). Attachment behaviour is the seeking of protection when anxious, which is triggered by external threats or behaviours. Protection is sought generally from attachment figures who are predominantly parents or guardians early in a child's life. While we will examine attachment in depth in Chapter 4, ask yourself the following: if parenting is implicated in affecting brain development of children does this have practice implications for social work?

WHAT DO YOU THINK?

Does this have implications for social work practice? If it is the case that the brain development of young children can be adversely affected due to unresponsive or poor parenting and these effects can last the child's life span, do we remove children from their families, do we increase interventions and support services or are we over-emphasising this factor and ignoring other ones, such as poverty and other societal structures? Are biological factors more powerful than other types of factors? What do you think?

Of course, another factor that needs to be considered in this debate is 'individual variation', in Chapter 4 we will examine extreme deprivation and the lasting consequences that it has for most of the children who had suffered it. Individual variation acknowledges that every person is unique and the same 'experience' may affect people in different ways, reflecting our own distinct biopsychosocial make-up. Some children were more resilient than others in overcoming such traumas; so what makes the difference in terms of the impact of factors on individuals and how individuals respond? Why is this? As you move through this book keep in mind that factors do not have the same degree of influence or impact on everyone, yet we run the danger of locking ourselves into a self-fulfilling prophecy if we allow ourselves to become deterministic in our thinking.

Adolescence

The brain undergoes a major growth spurt, particularly in the frontal cortex at the front of the brain. You will recall that an infant has far more brain cells, synapses (cell connections) and pathways than it needs and that 'pruning' occurs to cut back the superfluous and inefficient cells and connections. The maturation of the parietal and temporal lobes sees a subsequent improvement in areas including language, spatial, auditory and sensory development, allowing the teen to deal with cognitive and social challenges (Carter, 2009). However, as referred to earlier, the prefrontal cortex does not mature at the same rate. The prefrontal cortex is crucial to planning and understanding the consequences of actions. Further, as alluded to, teens continue to process emotional information through the amygdala, and both these aspects are involved in the poor judgement and impulse control issues that can be seen in adolescents. Dr Giedd elaborates on this.

IN FOCUS: THE TEENAGE BRAIN AND RISK-TAKING BEHAVIOURS

Dr Jay Giedd (2004, pp. 2–9) has discovered that a second wave of synapse formation occurs just before puberty in the prefrontal cortex, whose functions include planning, memory and organisation. A maturing prefrontal cortex increases the teenager's ability to reason, to control their impulses and in general to make better judgements. During adolescence 'pruning' occurs again, with the brain discarding cells that are not stimulated and used. It's similar to the idea of pruning a tree and cutting back the dead or weak branches. It has been argued that the principle of 'use it or lose it' is important during adolescent brain development. If a teenager takes part in sport or plays a musical instrument, the brain connections that are stimulated by these experiences will survive and become 'hardwired' in the brain. If, on the other hand, the teenager watches television most of the day, a different set of cells and connections will be maintained.

Further, an immature prefrontal cortex and its associated functions have been implicated in the risk-taking behaviours seen in some adolescents, as Dr Giedd (2004) explains:

> Now that MRI studies have cracked open a window on the developing brain, researchers are looking at how the newly detected physiological changes might account for the adolescent behaviours so familiar to parents: emotional outbursts, reckless risk taking and rule breaking, and the impassioned pursuit of sex, drugs and rock 'n' roll. Some experts believe the structural changes seen at adolescence may explain the timing of such major mental illnesses as schizophrenia and bipolar disorder. These diseases typically begin in adolescence and contribute to the high rate of teen suicide. Increasingly, the wild conduct once blamed on 'raging hormones' is being seen as the by-product of two factors: a surfeit of hormones, yes, but also a paucity of the cognitive controls needed for mature behaviour.

THINK ABOUT IT!

Do you think biology alone can explain adolescent risky behaviours? What other factors and influences could play a part in teen behaviour? Is culture one of them, and if so, how?

We leave the somewhat choppy waters of adolescent brain development to journey to the adult brain, a period usually not marked by rapid or uneven growth spurts.

The adult brain

Indeed, it is suggested that the brain is not fully mature until 25 years of age. So we can see that as the physical brain develops and matures, we would expect to see the cognitive (thinking) functions increase and mature also. The adult brain has activity patterns reflecting emotional maturity. Processing emotional information activates the frontal lobe much more than in teens, leading to more thoughtful perceptions. The prefrontal cortex is the last area of the brain to mature, and is associated with considering the consequences of actions and reasoning. The hippocampus is only one of the parts of the brain that actually produces neurons in adulthood. The prefrontal cortex is now fully developed, meaning the brain is less reliant on the amygdala to process emotional information. Other areas of the brain that were still developing in adolescence have now been completed.

IN FOCUS: ACQUIRED BRAIN INJURY – ITS IMPACT ON FAMILY LIFE

Acquired brain injury (ABI) is an umbrella term and refers to any injury to the brain that occurs after birth due to trauma or disease. Traumatic Brain Injury (TBI) is a form of ABI occurring due to a sudden blow or jolt to the brain from an accident, fall or assault. Other forms of ABI include infection, tumour and stroke; rehabilitation depends of many factors from social support network to the severity of the damage. ABI can affect an individual at any stage across the life span and is one of the most common causes of disability. As we saw earlier, the brain is involved in all aspects of functioning from physical, intellectual, social and emotional; therefore ABI can affect physical ability, speech, memory and thought process, and psychological functioning and behaviour. Personality, as we saw in the example of Phineas Gage, can be a common though sometimes 'unseen' impairment; personality change and the ability to regulate emotions can be particularly distressing for family members. For the individual, ABI can trigger issues around identity and affect self-esteem; for example, if a parent suffers a brain injury they may be no longer able to work and they may face financial difficulties. It is the ripple effect of ABI that can often be underestimated. For a child who suffers a brain injury, their developmental life path can be fundamentally altered, no longer being able to play with friends or attend their school. We will focus on the impact of ABI on families and their carers and consider the many aspects that can be affected.

According to Linden and Kristiansen (2013), significant strain can be placed on families whose children have suffered ABI due to the long-term care often involved. The authors contend that such strain can lead to the development of mental health problems, financial hardship and social isolation. The role of social support is an important one, providing a protective value in mediating the psychological distress of carers; the absence of social support, however, increases distress over time. Whoever the family member is, ABI can have a profound impact upon the individual and those around them. Consider the impact from both perspectives under the following headings:

Relationships, Support networks, Financial, Mental Health

CASE STUDY 1

Daisy was seven when she was involved in a road traffic accident. She spent several weeks in a coma and her family was told that she had suffered a severe brain injury and may not survive. Daisy was transferred to a specialist treatment centre. She has some awareness but limited communicative abilities, and she is paralysed. Her parents, Susie and Dave, are struggling to cope; they have two younger children and the centre is 50 miles away from their home. In the first month that Daisy was in a coma in the hospital, Susie did not leave her bedside. Susie was working part-time but had to leave in order to stay with her daughter. Dave tried to look after their other two children while Susie was in the hospital with Daisy but had to return to work. The offers of help and support are drying up and Susie feels tremendous guilt as she struggles to make the trip to the centre every day. Dave tries to convince Susie to visit at the weekends as it's putting a strain on the younger two. Financially, things have become difficult with the loss of Susie's job; they find themselves even bickering about the petrol money involved in the daily commute. Dave often expresses that Daisy would've been better off if she hadn't survived and that they've 'lost' the Daisy they knew. Susie feels as if she has lost her Daisy but feels terrible guilt thinking this. Dave's sentiments lead to increasingly bitter rows between them. The other two children, Ben (5 years) and Lily (2 years), are very confused by what has happened. Ben has started wetting the bed and cries for his sister. Neither Susie nor Dave's family lives nearby, although Susie's sister Liz visits every second weekend to help out. Susie looks forward to her sister's visits as she feels she has no one she can talk to as Dave has become increasingly withdrawn.

Using the headings above (Relationships, Support networks, Financial, Mental Health), characterise how this family is functioning. What are the difficulties facing this family, and what are their strengths? Identify any areas that need support or intervention; for example, for 'Support Networks' – does this appear to be an issue for the family? Liz's visits make a big difference to Susie as she feels she has an outlet, so are there other ways to increase the support networks? Perhaps a support group for parents whose child has ABI.

Adults who suffer ABI face similar challenges. Apply the same headings to the following case study:

CASE STUDY 2

Simon was in his mid-40s and a successful lawyer when he suffered a stroke. Though he received treatment quickly he suffered some brain damage, affecting his personality and memory. After a short stay in hospital he returned home; however, his partner Jenny started to notice that Simon wasn't 'quite himself'. Before he had been easy-going and could get along with anyone; now he loses his temper at the drop of a hat. He has rages which include saying really dreadful and vulgar things to her, something he had never done before. Jenny feels as if she's walking on eggshells all the time, afraid of what might set him off. Their teenage children also experience these rages and now avoid their father, choosing to spend time at their friend's houses. Simon returned to work a month after his stroke but, within a few weeks, quit. He struggles to remember basic information, and his frustration at not being able to do his job led to Simon frequently losing his temper with his work colleagues. Jenny feels it's as if he has no brakes at all, uttering whatever comes into his head. They have lost most of their friends due to Simon's outbursts and his discomfort with being around them now he can no longer work. With the loss of Simon's job, the family is sinking into debt, as Jenny's salary is not enough to cover their mortgage. Jenny had hoped that Simon's moods were a temporary effect of the stroke, but six months later, with no improvement, both Jenny and Simon are suffering from depression. The only break Jenny feels she has is when she goes to work. Simon feels he's not a man anymore and that his life is over.

As we can see from the case studies, the effect of ABI on individuals and those around them can be profound; the ripple effect in particular can often not be obvious and yet can have a devastating impact. Unfortunately, I have had experience of several people close to me suffering from ABI. The big things are obvious, such as the fear families face wondering if their loved one will pull through or how badly affected they will be. On some level, at least personally, the hospital was the easy part compared to what came after: the personality change, uncontrolled temper and how relentless it can feel. Yet not to be too negative, there are amazing support services out there that can make a world of difference. It's just important to connect and encourage people to avail themselves of the supports that may be on offer. Before moving on, I have chosen to focus on the impact on families when a loved one suffers ABI. Word count prevents me from being exhaustive, but this in no way should blind you to the impact it has on the individual involved.

RECOMMENDED VIEWING

It can be difficult, particularly when starting out or where we haven't had direct experience of the personality changes that can occur, to understand the impact of them on the person themselves and those around them. The following link contains an interview with a woman and her partner on the effects of her brain damage upon her and her family: www.nhs.uk/Conditions/Subarachnoid-haemorrhage/Pages/Heathersstory.aspx.

Finally, it is important to recognise individual variation in outcomes of ABI. In addition, from a developmental life span approach, the timing of illness or dysfunction can have an impact on a person's overall development through their life span. A person born with brain damage will experience a different impact on their life than someone who acquires a brain injury later in life.

THINK ABOUT IT!

Could the timing of brain injury impact on the individual and their families differently? For instance, if I acquire a brain injury at 11 or 41, would the effects of that differ in terms of impact on my life and those around me. What about being born with a learning disability which affects development across the life span? Research has suggested that differences exist, including in terms of family and financial outcomes.

Compare

A 40-year-old mum of two who works full time and acquires a brain injury to that of a baby born with brain damage. Will differences exist in how it impacts on their lives and those around them? Draw up a list of the different areas of life affected.

Another area to consider is that of 'cohort effects,' which we delve into in Chapter 4, Elder's theory of 'cohort effect' basically considers how social change can affect an individual's life experiences; for example, would the experience of being born in the 1960s with brain damage be different to a child born nowadays with the same condition?

The ageing brain

Particular attention has been given to brain development in the young and, more recently, the old. The 'ageing' brain is a relatively recent phenomenon as we are living much longer than previous generations. This, of course, comes with its own implications; the increasing cost of supporting older people is a fiscal and societal one, and ethical issues pertaining to quality of life is another. We are going to focus on an aspect that can accompany the 'ageing' brain: dementia.

According to Carter (2009, p. 206), 'the natural degeneration of the brain and the nervous system is not caused by disease, and so should not be confused with the pathology of dementia, which is associated with a pattern of specific brain changes. Recent research shows that most neurons actually remain healthy until you die, but brain volume and size decrease 5–10 percent from the ages of 20–90.' As mentioned earlier, the ageing brain is a relatively recent phenomenon in the history of humankind, as in the past most people did not live beyond the age of 50. The biggest threat to successful ageing is loss of mental function – memory, thinking, concentration, learning, problem-solving, alertness, error-proneness, vulnerability to crime/deception, and so on. Changes in these mental abilities occur because the brain changes as we get older, and these alterations may accelerate in the fifties and sixties. In an unfortunate minority of people, they accelerate into dementia. Such difficulties are also linked to other common problems of age – depression, falls and social isolation. Research on the ageing brain has much to catch up on, and the following section reflects much of the research conducted in this area.

Memory

Memory is a function that is located in many parts of the brain; as we get older memory can deteriorate. This, however, is very different from diseases of the brain such as dementia. Further damage to the brain (e.g. a stroke) can also damage the memory function. Generally speaking, left-hemisphere damage leads to verbal memory problems, while damage to the right results in non-verbal (visuospatial) memory problems. Amnesia, put simply, is a failure to remember. There are two types of amnesia: *retrograde* and *anterograde*. Retrograde amnesia is an inability to recall events that occurred prior to the trauma, while anterograde amnesia involves difficulties in learning new material and forming new memories. Anterograde amnesia is far more common than retrograde and can result from a wide range of neurological trauma or insult.

In focus: Dementia

A woman in her early 50s was admitted to hospital because of increasingly odd behaviour. Her family reported that she had been exhibiting memory problems and strong feelings of jealousy. She also had become disoriented at home and was hiding objects. During a doctor's examination, the woman was unable to remember her husband's name, the year, or how long she had been at the hospital. She could read but did not seem to understand what she read, and she stressed the words in an unusual way. She sometimes became agitated and seemed to have hallucinations and irrational fears.

This account relates to the first known case of dementia, presented in the early 1900s. Dementia is an umbrella term for a collection of symptoms that can result from a number of disorders that affect the brain. Those with dementia have significantly impaired intellectual functioning, with a consequent impact on relationships and daily activities. Symptoms can include:

- inability to solve problems
- personality changes, such as agitation, loss of emotional control and hallucinations
- memory loss, though this feature alone is not enough to warrant a diagnosis of dementia.

Doctors diagnose dementia only if two or more brain functions, such as memory, language skills, perception or cognitive skills, including reasoning and judgement, are significantly impaired without loss of consciousness.
Dementia statistics

- By 2015 there will be 850,000 people with dementia in the UK
- There are over 40,000 younger people with dementia in the UK
- There are over 25,000 people with dementia from black and minority ethnic groups in the UK
- Two-thirds of people with dementia are women
- The proportion of people with dementia doubles for every five-year age group
- One-third of people over 95 have dementia
- There are 670,000 carers of people with dementia in the UK.

www.alzheimers.org.uk/statistics

ALZHEIMER'S DISEASE

Alzheimer's disease is the most common cause of dementia in people aged 65 and older. In most people, symptoms of Alzheimer's disease appear after age 60. However, there are some earlyonset forms of the disease, usually linked to a specific gene defect, which may appear as early as age 30. Alzheimer's disease typically causes a gradual decline in thinking abilities, usually during a span of 7 to 10 years. Nearly all brain functions, including memory, movement, language, judgement, behaviour and abstract thinking are eventually affected. Different types of dementia cause characteristic patterns of memory loss because they attack different parts of the brain. In Alzheimer's disease the first area to be affected tends to be the hippocampus, where personal memories are stored. The hippocampus is also involved in remembering one's way around, which is why people with Alzheimer's disease often get lost (Carter, 1998).

Alzheimer's disease is characterised by two abnormalities in the brain: amyloid plaques (clumps of protein found in the tissue between the nerve cells) and neurofibrillary tangles (bundles of twisted filaments found within neurons). These tangles are largely made up of a protein called tau. In healthy neurons, the tau protein helps the functioning of microtubules, which are part of the cell's structural support and deliver substances throughout the nerve cell. However, in Alzheimer's disease, tau is changed in a way that causes it to twist into pairs of helical filaments that collect into tangles. When this happens, the microtubules cannot function correctly and they disintegrate. This collapse of the neuron's transport system may impair communication between nerve cells and cause them to die.

THE BRAIN OF A HEALTHY PERSON AND THE BRAIN OF A PERSON WITH DEMENTIA

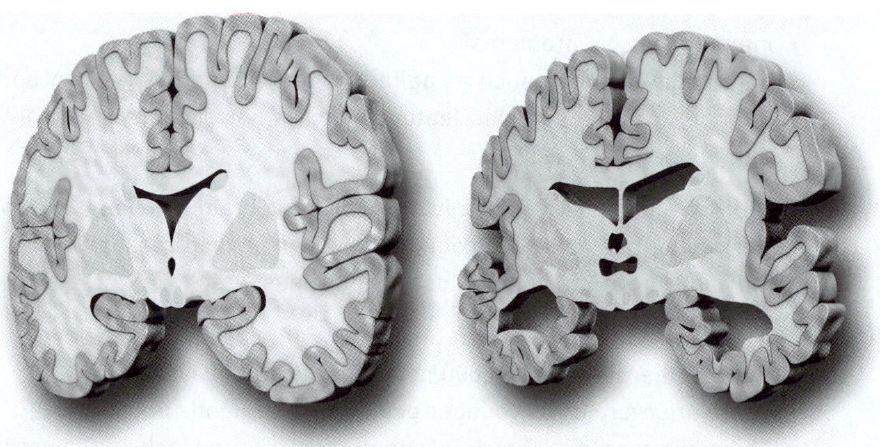

Figure 2.3 The brain of a healthy person and the brain of a person with dementia
Source: National Institute of Aging

In the early stages of Alzheimer's disease, patients may experience memory impairment, lapses of judgement and subtle changes in personality. As the disorder progresses, memory and language problems worsen, and patients begin to have difficulty performing activities of daily living. They may become disoriented about places and times, may suffer delusions (such as the idea that someone is stealing from them or that their spouse is being unfaithful), and may become short- tempered and hostile. During the late stages of the disease, patients begin to lose the ability to control motor functions such as swallowing, bowel and bladder control. They eventually lose the ability to recognise family members and to speak. As the disease progresses it begins to affect the person's emotions and behaviour and they develop symptoms such as aggression, agitation, depression, sleeplessness and delusions. On average, patients with Alzheimer's disease live for 8 to 10 years after they are diagnosed. However, some people live as long as 20 years.

In the following chapter we will explore the role of relationship and communication within social work. Here we will see how a person-centred approach can support clients with dementia.

CARING FOR PEOPLE WITH DEMENTIA

Sometimes when we read the theory and research on dementia it can make for despairing reading, and we wonder what can be done practically to support sufferers. The good news is that there is plenty that we can do. This section examines some research on person-centred care and dementia, and will give you a practical perspective on how best to support clients experiencing the disease.

Person-centred approach

Carl Rogers coined the term 'person-centred' in terms of the therapeutic relationship that should be fostered between client and therapist (see Chapter 4). It puts an emphasis on relationship and focuses on the individual. This approach has become very popular within health and social care, as it places a primary focus on the person, rather than on a disability, a service or some other particular issue. Brooker (2004) relates that the term 'person-centred approach' in the context of dementia was first used by Kitwood to differentiate ways of working with people with dementia that were not framed within a biological and technical model. At the heart of this approach is the recognition of the person with dementia as an individual with rights and a need for sensitive interactions, thus reflecting Rogers's emphasis on the individual and the quality of the relationship. Brooker (2004, p. 219) offers the following four elements as integral to person-centred care:

V **valuing** people with dementia and those who care for them;
I treating people as **individuals**;
P looking at the world from the **perspective** of the person with dementia;
S a positive **social** environment in which the person living with dementia can experience relative well-being.

These elements in turn form a model of person-centred care for people with dementia, as is illustrated below.

Element	Underemphasis	Overemphasis
***V**aluing people with dementia and their carers	Discrimination	Care evangelism
***I**ndividual and being treated as such	Inappropriate assessments	Lots of care plans that that meet needs within a a narrow focus
Looking at the world from the person's ***P**erspective	Priorities of the person not met	Lots of information collated but not implemented
A positive ***S**ocial environment	Poor communication and lack of dementia awareness & skills	Frequent changes in direction as multiple techniques followed and discarded

Source: Brooker, 2004, p.220

This model outlines the outcome when an underemphasis is placed on an element; for example, if the element of 'valuing' the individual with dementia is underemphasised, the result is discrimination. Similarly, it is possible to place an overemphasis upon an element. An overemphasis on 'valuing' has the consequence that we 'talk the talk' but are unable to apply it in our practice. So it is clear that skill and reflection are involved in ensuring not just that the elements within the care-centred model are met but that a balance is struck to ensure best practice outcomes.

Brooker details a number of activities that can be used to meet a care-centred approach in working with people with dementia, including life-story work, reminiscence, creativity, play, doll therapy, pet therapy, sensory therapies and psychotherapy. We will look briefly at one of those activities: reminiscence therapy.

REMINISCENCE THERAPY

Reminiscence therapy is an activity where in the elderly person recalls various experiences from their past life and shares them with others. Through this process it is expected that emotional stability will be promoted and that the elderly person will benefit from being able to share their knowledge and areas of expertise. In the following study, the researchers compared outcomes between reminiscence therapy and general conversation with people with dementia.

Okumura et al. (2008, p. 125) elaborate on the design of their study: 'There were four reminiscence themes: (i) childhood play; (ii) helping with housework; (iii) school memories and (iv) memories centred on the current session'.

The authors conclude that reminiscence therapy performed over a short period of time in closed groups was shown to be more effective than everyday conversations in the treatment of elderly people with dementia. Further, they suggest that (2008, p. 132), 'based on the results of the present study, it is concluded that reminiscence therapy is an effective method of providing care to a wide range of elderly people, including those with dementia. It could be introduced as a part of the daily exchange at care facilities. For example, it may be implemented quickly in group homes with the goal of improving care in accordance with the wishes of elderly with dementia. The present study revealed the usefulness of introducing such therapy over a short period of time.'

It seems only right to end this chapter on the brain with a discussion on the role of neuroscience, and its place, in social work.

IN FOCUS: NEUROSCIENCE AND ITS ROLE IN SOCIAL WORK: IS NEUROSCIENCE BEING MISUSED?

Recommended

Below is a link to a speech given by Iain Duncan Smith, former Conservative party leader and now MP, you can listen to it on the following link:

www.theguardian.com/politics/audio/2010/apr/07/iain-duncan-smith-brain-size

What do you think of this speech? What are the themes that are evident?

- That we can predict what kind of adult a child will become?
- That physical signs exist that support this assertion including the size and capacity of the brain?
- That neuroscience findings support this?

Duncan-Smith's interest in the area of social breakdown and poverty is evident; he founded the Centre for Social Justice, a think-tank, in 2004. Duncan-Smith's interest extends to the realm of neuroscience and the 'first three Years' movement, which recognises the importance of the early years as being critical to development. In 2008, Duncan-Smith and another MP, Graham Allen, produced a policy document *Early Intervention, Good Parents, Great Kids, Better Citizens*, which reflects points made in his speech. In this document a controversial image was used, that of the brain of a 3-year-old child who had suffered extreme neglect and whose brain was significantly smaller compared against that of a 'normal' child.

The imagery used is powerful in suggesting that neglect can impact on the development of the brain leaving it potentially smaller and damaged. You can view this image in Allen and Duncan-Smith's report (2008, p. 59), which references an article by Dr Bruce Perry's, '... what childhood neglect tells us about nature and nurture'. The original provenance of this image is not clear but consensus suggests the smaller brain reflects a child who has suffered extreme neglect (we discuss extreme neglect in Chapter 4). This image represents the extreme of what can happen to the brain in extreme circumstances, but is this 'brain' really applicable to a child in the UK who suffers some form of neglect? In Duncan-Smith and Allen's 2008 report, the implication would seem that it is.

According to the report, 'The brain of an abused or neglected child is significantly smaller than the norm ...' (p. 59) this piece of information is footnoted to three research articles in the references, the first article relates to combat-related post-traumatic stress disorder (PTSD), the second to women with a history of sexual abuse and PTSD and finally to the neurobiology of child abuse. There is no article that refers specifically to 'neglect' alone and its potential relationship to smaller brains. As you will see in Chapter 9 on abuse and trauma, there is a difference between abuse and neglect, at least in intentionality. Of course, that is not to say that the effects of neglect cannot be as devastating of those of abuse or that the two are mutually exclusive. However, ask yourself is it reasonable, let alone good practice, to take one finding on PTSD in adults and then apply it to another area, in this case neglect?

'Give me the child till the age of seven and I will show you the man.' This quote attributed to St Ignatius of Loyola opens Chapter 3 of their report (ibid.). This could be argued as clear determinism. While Early Years is an important time of development and interventions, such as Sure Start, are important, do you agree with Duncan-Smith's arguably deterministic belief?

Of course, I must admit to my bias, I don't agree with deterministic thinking on several levels, including from a social justice perspective. I find the use of the brain image of extreme neglect and its associations unsettling. Dr Perry, who is acknowledged by Allen and Duncan-Smith in their report (2008) as an inspiration and whose work is referred to by them, has been clear in his rejection of how his work has been misinterpreted. Nonetheless it would be wrong to dismiss the contribution neuroscience offers to understanding development and outcomes. Neuroscience as a knowledge base has a role in social work. As we saw, Dr Sunderland's work does suggest that stress may influence the brain and it is common sense that babies respond well to stimulating environments. Yet to contribute to something is quite different than to cause it; individual variation is always involved as is the interplay of a multitude of factors. Further, some factors would appear to have a greater influence in affecting outcomes, particularly poverty as we will explore in Chapter 8. The important thing is for you to make up your own minds based on your personal and practice experience, research and self-reflection.

THINK ABOUT IT!

You have been asked to debate against Iain Duncan-Smith. Research this topic and form counter-arguments that you can use in the debate on the following points:

- Dr Bruce Perry's research shows that young brains are damaged by neglect
- By the age of three years you can predict what kind of adult a child will become
- Early brain development is a more powerful indicator of criminality than poverty.

To get you started, the following URLs represent either side of the argument:

Pro – Allen and Duncan-Smith (2010) *Early Intervention, Good Parents, Great Kids, Better Citizens*

www.centreforsocialjustice.org.uk/publications/early-intervention-good-parents-great-kids-better-citizens.

Against – Dr E. Reader, *A Policy Driven By Prejudice Masquerading As Research*

http://blogs.kent.ac.uk/parentingculturestudies/files/2011/06/A-Policy-Driven-By-Prejudice-Masquerading-As-Research1.pdf.

Both sides! – a series of letters representing a mix of viewpoints

www.theguardian.com/society/2014/apr/29/early-years-interventions-social-justice.

WHAT DO YOU THINK?

Does neuroscience have a place in social work, if not why? If yes, in what fields and to what extent? Support your reasoning.

SUMMARY

By now you should have grasped something of the complexity of the brain and its implication for practice. Having some degree of knowledge and understanding of the brain when working with those who have brain dysfunction of some kind can inform practice. A care-centred approach to working with those with dementia or any other brain disorder or disease should form a fundamental part of daily practice. Finally, what should be apparent from the findings of Dr Sunderland and those who study the effects of early experiences on brain development is the importance of supporting good development in the young to optimise their later outcomes in life.

chapter

3 COMMUNICATION AND RELATIONSHIPS IN SOCIAL WORK

CHAPTER OUTLINE

- Intrapersonal communication and relationships
- Interpersonal (skills and groups)
- Gerard Egan's SOLER technique for active listening
- Communicating with different groups
- Implications for practice – person-centred practice

'The capacity to communicate openly and confidently is a crucial aspect of the social work task.' As Walker (2008, p. 5) suggests, communication skills are identified as a core skill needed by social workers. Another core domain is that of 'contexts and organisations', highlighting the importance of being able to work with others, inter-professionally and with communities as key to the work of social workers. The ability to build relationships and communicate within them is a fundamental skill in social work. This chapter is notionally divided into three parts. Part 1 will focus on 'Intrapersonal Communication' and consider the role of emotional intelligence and reflective function in the acquisition of skills needed by social workers to engage and communicate with themselves, clients and other professionals. Walker (2008) argues that the concept of emotional intelligence or emotional literacy is being increasingly emphasised within education and learning and holds a role for social work practitioners. From here the concept of reflective function and its role in developing awareness will be considered. This section ends with an overview of communication and social work from an 'attachment perspective'. Section 2 focuses on 'Interpersonal Communication', on the actual skills needed and used to engage with others and is followed by an overview of the different elements of communication specific to particular groups, for example, the use of the 'Three Houses' approach when communicating with children is outlined. Other groups, including the elderly and those with disabilities, are also considered, as well as cross-cultural communication. The final section examines 'implications for practice' and includes an in-depth look at person-centred practice, including planning and thinking skills. A taxonomy (scheme of classification) of core condition and skills is outlined as a guide to use in developing greater knowledge and awareness of communication. The chapter ends with an activity on the use of self-awareness in social work.

INTRAPERSONAL COMMUNICATION AND RELATIONSHIPS

How do we put all we have learnt into practice? How can we support those we work with? It can be challenging to attempt to apply what we have learned to real-life situations. We will examine 'emotional intelligence' and the use of 'reflective practice', not only as a way of coping with those anxieties but also to improve your ability to support others through your work. As we embark on working with different groups of people, sometimes in stressful and challenging situations, it can become clear to us that we need specialized knowledge to enable us to be more supportive. It seems obvious that we need to learn new knowledge but what can seem less clear is that we need to acquire new skills, hone existing ones and become self-reflective in a more structured way than we might be used to. Gardner (1983, p. 27) suggests that '... implicit in the development of skills and values is a significant degree of self-awareness. Students and workers must be aware of their own attitudes and values, personal issues that may affect their work with clients, how they relate and present themselves to others'.

Emotional intelligence

We are going to consider these very issues, beginning with emotional intelligence and reflective function. Emotional Intelligence or emotional literacy has been gaining recognition as an essential aspect of developing our ability to self-care and to communicate with and support others. Walker (2008) defines emotional literacy as the:

> practice of interacting with others in ways that build understanding of our own and other's emotions, then using this understanding to inform our actions

5 CORE SOCIAL WORK TASKS

Often, when working with others in a supportive environment, we focus on the needs and feelings of others and pay little attention to our needs and emotions even though our emotions can powerfully impact on our actions towards others and vice versa. So fundamental is emotional intelligence to the work of 'caring' professions that Morrison (2007) places it as central to the following five core social work tasks:

- engagement of users
- assessment and observation
- decision making
- collaboration and cooperation
- dealing with stress

Strongly tied to the concept of emotional intelligence is **reflective function or reflective practice.** Reflective function plays a pivotal role in relationship building and intrapersonal awareness and skills. These concepts of emotional intelligence and reflective practice (function) are integral to the acquisition of skills needed by practitioners to engage and communicate with themselves, clients and other professionals. So what is reflective function and how can we put it to practical use?

Reflective function: communication and social work from an attachment perspective

Jim Walker charts the role of attachment and attachment experiences in early relationships (for attachment theory see Chapter 4) and how these can affect whether communication is effective within social work. Walker suggests that our early relationships form the template for future relationships and that, in the sphere of social work, our ability to communicate and interact effectively with service users is a reflection of these early templates. Therefore, it is essential to be aware of, and reflect on, the feelings and needs not just of service users, but also our own. Walker defines **reflective function** as:

> ... the ability to think flexibly about thoughts and feelings in both oneself and others.

Walker advocates its use as a construct to enable practitioners to improve how they communicate with service users through 'the ability to go beyond immediately known phenomena to give an account of one's own or other's actions in terms of beliefs, desires, plans etc.' (p. 8). Reflective function is more than just empathy, which is concerned with 'other'. It is important that you think about your own emotional reactions to clients and to the work, rather than purely focussing on the client. Walker argues that reflective function forms the foundation of effective communication. An example of a failure of reflective function is to take the position of 'knowing best' and of disregarding others' opinions. Walker explains instances of a failure of reflective function.

REFLECTIVE FUNCTION AND CHILD PROTECTION

Another aspect of the communication process to be aware of in social work practice is in child protection. Walker believes that for the communication process to be effective, both practitioners and agencies need to adopt this approach. He describes the importance of 'reflective function' in the area of child protection, suggesting that breakdowns in communication hamper the delivery of services. He cites the case of Victoria Climbie, who died at the hands of her abusive aunt and the aunt's boyfriend. Lord Laming's report into her death identified that a breakdown in communication between the agencies charged with her protection had contributed to her death. Reflective practice has relevance in the practitioner/service-user interaction but also between agencies. For those studying social work, Walker emphasises the importance of keeping a journal in order to analyse and improve the skills of reflective function.

EXAMPLE OF REFLECTIVE FUNCTION IN CLIENTS

During his work with teenage girls who had been sexually abused he noticed that the girls were very attuned to his emotional state. When Walker asked them how they thought he was feeling they were able to offer an opinion, yet when he reciprocated and asked them how *they* felt, the girls were unable to tell him. Walker surmises that:

> in the process of focusing on other people they seemingly had been unable to retain any focus on their own mental processes; they were completely unaware of their own feelings; ... they had some empathy for my state of mind but nevertheless lacked reflective function and an understanding of their own internal processes. (p. 9)

This particular example is a jarring one; how quickly would any of us have been 'attuned' to the girls' inability to articulate their feelings even though they were highly tuned to others? It takes a level of awareness to recognise that this is happening rather than just seeing the surface of it and believing the girls to be empathic or sensitive. What kind of situations do you think might create young people who are so tuned into the emotional states and needs of others? Having parents with addiction issues or mental health difficulties, or being a young carer where your focus is on another to the detriment of yourself.

THINK ABOUT IT!

How as a practitioner can you become more attuned and aware of this phenomenon? How do you think it is best to respond to your clients' level of attunement and at what point to do you believe it becomes detrimental to their well-being and ability to meet their own needs?

In keeping a journal, how can we use reflection as part of our practice? According to Teater (2010, p. 5), 'Critically reflective practice requires social workers to be both reflective and critical about social work practice.' This process can be undertaken by asking after a social work encounter the following questions:

Reflection

What happened?
How did it compare with previous experience?
How did I do?

Critical reflection

How well did I do?
What could I have done better?
What could I have done differently?

Tip! Keep a diary and record your responses, this is a powerful tool in charting your development and improving your practice. It can also be useful for CPD.

THINK ABOUT IT!

You are dealing with a very difficult client; he is rude and uncooperative despite your best efforts. Perhaps you start to dread dealing with him and spend greater time on other clients who you get on with. By keeping a reflective journal and paying attention to your emotions you might begin to recognise that you have a role to play in this dynamic with the difficult client. Maybe he reminds you (unconsciously – see Freud) of someone from your life with whom you had a difficult relationship. Perhaps if this client has an addiction and you come from a family who also have addiction issues, it can be difficult not to unconsciously bring that into the dynamic with the client. Or perhaps, as we will see later, issues of cultural communication are at play. Reflect on a work situation or client where the experience was enjoyable and, similarly, where it was unpleasant, and identify why you believe you had such differing reactions.

When I was working in a placement I remembered being warned about a particular teen who 'was trouble'. Sure enough on my first day he was disruptive, however I made a conscious effort not to form a judgement and attitude about him. It took patience and perseverance but in time his behaviour improved, though only for me. Yet that was because attitudes had been formed about him based on his behaviour and a judgement made; he was fulfilling that role and was not being given the opportunity to behave differently. We have to be very careful, when we work with others, of our emotions, our attitudes and how they can affect our interactions with others. This is also why anti-discriminatory practice must form a core part of your reflective function and part of a growing awareness of the need to adopt **person-centred practice** when we work with and support clients, as we will see later in the chapter.

While, clearly, communication forms an integral part of our interaction with service users, it is evident that the communication process begins with the practitioner through emotional intelligence and reflective function. At the end of this chapter an activity on the use of self-awareness in social work is presented. Now that we have dealt with aspects of communication and its relationship to social work, let's consider actual communication skills and their use with different groups.

INTERPERSONAL (SKILLS AND GROUPS)

An essential element of social work involves relating to other people. More often than not, many of those we interact with are experiencing difficulties in their lives and as such it is important that you are equipped to relate to them sensitively and supportively. Understanding the origins and manifestations of personal difficulties and distress that people face and, in addition, developing certain communication skills will help you support service users. In this section we are going to explore the different **interpersonal or interactive skills** that can be used to enable effective communication. Before we look at those skills let's consider a theoretical approach that can helps us better understand the interactions we have with others.

The symbolic interactionist perspective

The symbolic interactionist perspective views social meaning as arising through the process of social interaction. Contemporary symbolic interactionism rests on three basic premises:

1. Human beings act toward things on the basis of the meanings that they attach to them.
2. These meanings are derived from, or arise out of, social interaction with others.
3. These meanings may be changed or modified through the processes of interaction and interpretation.

Proponents of this perspective, often referred to as the interactionist perspective, engage in micro-level analysis, which focuses on the day-to-day interactions of individuals and groups in specific social situations. Concepts important for understanding this theoretical approach include meaningful symbols, the definition of the situation, the labelling approach and the looking-glass self.

Meaningful symbols: George H. Mead (1863–1931) insisted that the ongoing process of social interaction and the creating, defining, and redefining of meaningful symbols make society possible. Language is one of the most important and powerful meaningful symbols humans have created, because it allows us to communicate through the shared meaning of words.

The looking-glass self: The looking-glass self refers to the idea that an individual's self-concept is largely a reflection of how he or she is perceived by other members of society (Cooley). Society is used as a mirror to reflect a feeling of self-doubt, self-loathing or self-worth. These important elements of symbolic interactionism contribute to socialisation and the process of becoming human as we establish our personal and social identities.

The labelling approach: this theoretical perspective contends that people attach various labels to certain behaviours, individuals and groups that become part of their social identity and shape others' attitudes about and responses to them.

THINK ABOUT IT!

Using some of the ideas in symbolic interactionism identify how this would impact on interpersonal communication; for example, the use of language, body language or how we dress all affect the communication process. I referred earlier to a boy I had worked with who had been labelled as 'trouble', can symbolic interactionism further explain how this would affect and impact on the interpersonal relationship and communication process?

Before we delve into communication skills, I have a question: Would you describe yourself as a good listener? I used to describe myself as such before I realised that listening is an active skill and yet so many of us treat it as a passive activity, something we just do and don't pay any real attention to. This is 'hearing'; listening is much more active and consuming. Try this exercise; next time you're listening to someone, really concentrate and pay attention to everything they're saying for five minutes. Don't allow your mind to wander to thoughts of what's on the TV tonight! You might be surprised at how tired you feel and, more importantly, recognise that listening takes effort and most of us really aren't the great listeners we think we are. As we consider the following communication skills, it is important that we become more aware and reflective of our own communication style.

WHAT IS A SKILL?

For Cournoyer (1991, p. 3) a skill, from a social work perspective, can be thought of as a 'set of discrete cognitive and behavioural actions that derive from social work knowledge and from social work values, ethics, and obligations; are consistent with the essential facilitative qualities and comport with a social work purpose within the context of a phase of practice'. So let's look at some skills beginning with 'interpersonal' ones.

Interpersonal skills

Communication is an integral part of any professional caring relationship; further, that relationship is a two-way process. There are a range of interpersonal skills that are important in any helpful/caring relationship. These include the following:

- **Listening skills** – the ability to listen is a key interpersonal skill. Active listening involves being able to hear what a person is saying and respond in the most appropriate way (sometimes by not saying anything at all but using non-verbal communication to let the other person know that you hear and understand them). Being perceptive to someone's non-verbal communication is also important (e.g. facial expressions, posture, eye contact and other forms of body language).
- **Being assertive** – this involves being honest about our own wishes, rights and needs and respecting those of others. It involves being able to communicate your own needs without being aggressive or disrespectful towards another person. In some situations we can be more assertive than in others – it depends on the circumstances. Part of being assertive can be the ability to say 'no' to people – sometimes the easier option is to say 'yes' (but then regret it later). Being assertive should never be confused with being aggressive.
- **Being warm and caring** – these create a positive atmosphere in any caring relationship and should always be evident even if there are times (which there will be) when you do not particularly agree with what a client is saying or doing. It does not mean that you convey false warmth towards a person.
- **Being non-judgemental** – this involves being open-minded and also aware of our own beliefs, values, biases and prejudices. This is so important whether you view it from a symbolic interactionist perspective or from an anti-discriminatory or anti-oppressive approach
- **Tolerance and patience** – it is important to be patient and tolerant with clients. Clients may be facing very difficult situations that we may have little knowledge of. It can be easy to become impatient with clients if we feel that they are not making the type of progress *we* might be looking for.
- **Empathy** – the ability to try and put yourself in someone else's position and imagine what it might feel like to be in their situation. Empathy is different to sympathy and asks you to try to see the world through the eyes of another.

- **Acceptance** – accepting a person for who they are and see them as a person no matter what the circumstances. This aspect is central to Carl Rogers's work and development of the person-centred approach as discussed in Chapter 4.

A lot of these skills can be seen in the values of social work; of course, communication is universal and the following are specific or micro skills utilised in the communication process, including listening, questioning, silence and non-verbal behaviour.

Microskills

LISTENING

- use eye contact (where culturally appropriate)
- demonstrate attention (e.g. by nodding)
- offer encouragement (e.g. 'Mm-hmm', 'Yes')
- minimise distractions (e.g. television, telephone, noise)
- do not do other tasks at the same time
- acknowledge the client's feeling (e.g. 'I can see you feel very sad.')
- do not interrupt the client unnecessarily
- ask questions if you do not understand
- do not take over and tell your own 'story'
- repeat back the main points of the discussion in similar but fewer words to check you have understood the client correctly (paraphrase, reflect feelings, clarify, summarise).

As we saw earlier, listening is an interpersonal skill. In terms of the 'behaviour' of listening, active listening is to be aimed for, especially when carrying out an assessment where detail is crucial. Gerard Egan's model for active listening is a popular one and is utilised within social work.

GERARD EGAN'S SOLER TECHNIQUE FOR ACTIVE LISTENING

S: Sit SQUARELY on to the client, preferably at a 5 o'clock position to avoid the possibility of staring.
O: Maintain an OPEN posture at all times: not crossing your arms or legs, which can appear defensive.
L: LEAN slightly in towards the client.
E: Maintain EYE CONTACT with the client without staring.
R: RELAX. This should in turn help the client to relax.

THINK ABOUT IT!

As you can see, Egan's SOLER technique includes a lot of non-verbal cues which we will discuss later. Consider your body language next time you are interacting with a:

- Friend
- Colleague
- Client

Are there differences in your non-verbal cues; what was you emotional content at the time and did this affect your body language? What factors have affected your ability to actively listen: not feeling well or disliking your client perhaps? Become more aware of the different influences that impact on your ability to actively listen and record them in your journal.

Questioning

While listening is integral to communication, questioning is a key skill required by social workers. There are different types of questioning:

- A **closed question**, for example, 'Are you on medication?' limits the response of the client to a one-word answer. Closed questions may not require clients to think about what they are saying. Answers can be brief and often result in the need to ask more questions.
- An **open question** requires more than a one-word answer. Open questions generally begin with 'what', 'where', 'how' or 'when'. They invite the client to continue talking and to decide what direction they want the conversation to take.
- With **leading questions** the counsellor guides the client to give the answer they desire. These questions are usually judgemental. For example 'You do practice safer sex, don't you?', 'Do you agree that you should always use a condom?'

Think of the different contexts where 'closed' questions are more useful. Which type of questioning approach do you use the most, and can you think of scenarios where a leading question might be used?

Silence

- gives a client time to think about what to say
- gives a client space to experience their feelings
- allows a client to proceed at their own pace
- provides a client with time to deal with ambivalence about sharing
- gives a client freedom to choose whether to continue or not

Silence is an interesting communication skill; it almost feels counter-intuitive to think of it as such. Silence can be a powerful tool, however it can be challenging to the practitioner to sit in silence especially when there are 'big' emotions present such as loss or grief. It can be instinctual, almost, to speak and fill the silence as silence can make us feel uncomfortable; we may wish to 'fix' things or offer 'soothing' words even if only to make us feel better and not ineffectual. Have you ever used silence when working? If you have not, or infrequently, reflect on why this is and what might prevent you from doing so. Are there groups or contexts where you feel silence would be inappropriate and why? From an intrapersonal (reflective) perspective I find silence a powerful tool and use it in mindfulness work, allowing me to 'feel' and be 'aware'; this leads to the potential for greater insight.

Non-verbal behaviour

- body language
- gestures
- facial expressions
- posture
- body orientation
- body proximity/distance
- eye contact
- mirroring
- removing barriers (e.g. desks)

Non-verbal interaction is a fundamental, though often overlooked, tool of communication. All of the examples given above are the obvious examples of non-verbal but are there any missing? Mode of dress and the context or place where the interaction is occurring are important aspects. I must admit that being in a hospital affects how I communicate as I associate hospitals with the loss of loved ones. Are there any contexts or places that would make you feel more at ease or more on edge? Trevithick (2000) identifies seven types of non-verbal communication:

- **Chronomics** – timekeeping, such as the likelihood of people being too early or too late, promptness
- **Artificial communication** – the language of the physical setting, such as how the home is arranged and personal presentation, including personal dress, state of clothes
- **Smell** – emotional states communicated through subtle changes in body odour
- **Touch** – handshaking, hugs; these tend to be defined according to situation and the cultural norms
- **Paralinguistics** – cues that depend on hearing and how words are said in terms of their tone, pitch, volume, speed, emphasis, intonation, articulation and intensity
- **Proxemics** – communication through space and distance; the distance people need in order to feel comfortable
- **Body language kinesics –** visual communication through the face, eyes, hands and arms, feet and legs

THINK ABOUT IT!

When you next interact with a client become aware of your 'self' in the interaction, especially your body language and the other types of non-verbal communication types outlined above. Is your body language in sync with your verbal communication; for example, you may greet 'that you're pleased to meet' the individual but your body language may betray your unease with or distrust of the person. In terms of your client, become more attuned to their body language, does it match what they are verbally communicating? Use this exercise as part of your 'reflective function', making note of it in your journal – it can give an invaluable insight!

As this is a psychology book, after all, it would be remiss not to mention Carl Rogers in this chapter. Rogers was an influential figure who challenged the mainstream in psychology with his 'humanist' theory (see Chapter 4). In ending this section on skills in communication, we are going to overview some skills Rogers developed for use in counselling; 'paraphrasing of content, reflection of feeling and reframing'. For ease, I will use the term 'counsellor' when discussing Rogers's skills.

Paraphrasing content and reflecting feeling

These two techniques are rooted in the Rogerian approach to counselling and were used extensively by Carl Rogers. *Paraphrasing content* involves repeating back what the client has said in simple terms so the client knows they are being listened to and heard. *Reflecting feeling* is a similar process except that it focuses on the emotional content of what or how the client is feeling. For example, if I were to say that I had started a new course in college and was finding the work difficult, leaving me crying often, the content aspect of that statement is that I've started college, but the feeling part is that I'm stressed and overwhelmed. A counsellor would paraphrase and reflect this back to me.

Example of reflection of content and feeling

> **Client statement:** I keep expecting my mother to show more interest in me. Time and again I've asked her to come over to see me, but she never does. Yesterday it was my birthday and she did come to visit me, but do you know she didn't even remember it was my birthday. I just don't think she cares about me at all. (Said slowly in a flat tone of voice.)
>
> **Counsellor response:** You're disappointed by your mother's behaviour (or) You feel hurt by your mother's apparent lack of caring.

This technique, as mentioned, let's the client know they are being listened to; it has a dual purpose in allowing you to clarify that you have understood what the client has said to you accurately. Sometimes we think we have picked up on the central issue but in reflecting this back to the client they can clarify that it is a different point that's at the heart of the issue.

Reframing

Each of us has a unique perspective on how we 'view' situations; you and I may see the same event and yet give different descriptions of it, reflecting that our perspective is a product of our beliefs and life experiences. When a client presents a perspective or 'picture', the counsellor will attempt to put a different 'frame' on the 'picture', thus giving them another way of viewing the situation. This is called reframing. Geldard and Geldard (2005, p. 149) explain, 'The idea behind reframing is not to deny the way the client sees the world, but to present them with an expanded view of the world. Thus, if the client wishes, they may choose to see things in a new way.'

Example of reframing

The client has explained that she seems unable to relax because as soon as she turns her back her young son misbehaves and she has to chase after him and punish him. The counsellor has reflected back her feelings about this and now the client is calmer. At this point, the counsellor decides to offer the client a reframe concerning the behaviour of her son.

> **Counsellor reframe:** I get the impression that you are really important to your son and that he wants lots of attention from you.

This statement presents the client with a more positive approach to viewing her son's behaviour; not as an attempt to irritate her but instead as seeking attention from her. Should the client decide to accept this reframe and view her son's behaviour differently, this may bring a new direction to their relationship.

While Rogers developed these skills for use in the counselling interaction, they have been widely adopted in many disciplines as has Rogers's promotion of person-centred values. As you will see in Chapter 4, Rogers believed fervently that we must have respect, empathy and be 'congruent' (or genuine) when interacting with others. These mirror the interpersonal skills listed earlier and marry with social work values. In the next section of this chapter we will consider how different groups of people have different needs and require communication styles to match. As we will see, a purely verbal approach with children is not necessarily the most appropriate or effective way to communicate. Infantilising older people through your style of communicating is equally inappropriate. So let's look at communication with children, those with disabilities and the elderly. The role of culture in communication will also be discussed.

COMMUNICATING WITH DIFFERENT GROUPS

Communication with children

It can be challenging communicating with children; developmental difference and abilities differ across age ranges, affecting children's ability to comprehend questioning or to find the words to articulate feelings and events. In addition, children can be reticent to divulge information about their family situation as the tie between child and parent, reflecting attachment theory, is powerful no matter how deleterious the parenting. This piece on communicating with children will involve more detail than other pieces, although it will only scrape the surface of what is a complex task involving much awareness and many skills on the part of the practitioner.

We will begin by exploring a guide to communicating with children and then a brief overview of the skills needed to communicate effectively with children will be outlined. Finally, the 'Three Houses' model, which includes a case study taken from The Munro Report on Child Protection is presented as one approach that can be used to interact with children.

CHILDREN'S DEVELOPMENT AND IMPLICATIONS FOR COMMUNICATION

As mentioned, childhood encompasses a wide range of developmental stages and capabilities. Language is often included within 'cognitive development' and is tied to brain development; as the brain grows so too does thinking and language ability. As a practitioner, and contained within social work standards, there is an emphasis on knowledge. In order to tailor your approach to communicating with a child it is necessary to understand that child's developmental level to ensure effective communication can occur. For this reason, included here is a link to a detailed developmental guide compiled by UNICEF, which outlines several domains of functioning to allow you to grasp all aspects of capability and better inform your communicative approach. Each age grouping includes 'implications for communication'. While this guide is very useful, its range in ages in each stage is quite vast and you then need to also factor in individual variation and cultural aspects too.

www.unicef.org/cwc/files/CwC_Final_Nov-2011.pdf

THINK ABOUT IT!

Outline the different aspects of development you would need to consider when communicating with a 4 year old and a 13 year old. Discuss how their different levels of development, including cognitive, brain, social and emotional, would impact on their comprehension level and ability to communicate. Would you factor other areas of development as impacting on the communication process? How would these considerations affect your communication approach and style?

After consulting the UNICEF guide, reflect on how you might utilise this knowledge to improve how you communicate with different age groups and what approaches you would use. For instance, would play therapy be appropriate with a 6 year old and with a 15 year old? Drawing, play and art are acknowledged to be useful alternatives, when interviewing children; to a more verbal, formalised approach; indeed these approaches have been integrated into therapy. As Piaget commented, 'Play is the work of childhood', reflecting its centrality to children's development. By using something (play) so core to children, one is more likely to be able to communicate more effectively with them. The following 'Three Houses' model highlights such an approach and is recommended in *The Munro Report* (2011, pp. 30–31).

The Three Houses

The Three Houses tool for interviewing children was first created by Nicki Weld and colleagues in New Zealand and further refined and developed through the efforts of many international practitioners. This tool focuses on interviewing children through their own words and drawings focused on a 'house of worries', 'house of good things' and 'house of dreams'.

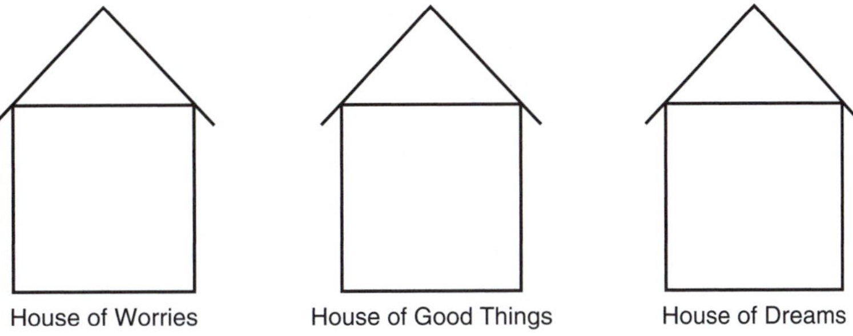

Figure 3.1 The Three Houses

Source: The Munro Review of A Child-Centred System (2011).

Example

A child protection worker had to investigate a domestic violence case involving a mother, her boyfriend and children 'Ramon' (10 years) and 'Stephanie' (7 years). The children had been interviewed twice previously but were very withdrawn, giving very little information. Knowing she needed to do something different, the worker conducted the third interview using the three houses tool.

After the children drew house outlines on three separate blank sheets, she gave the children the choice of which house they would start with. They began by together drawing cold and drafty stables where the boyfriend would often lock them at night together with his aggressive black dog. As the children drew, the worker would write their exact explanations alongside the drawings.

Next the children drew the following in the house of worries:

- Ramon kicking and yelling at the boyfriend – this had never actually happened but it was obvious to the worker that it was important to let Ramon draw this picture;
- on the roof Stephanie drew her mother crying in distress;
- in the roof space Ramon drew his bedroom which he said he hated including a broken window that made the room cold. Stephanie described that she didn't have a bedroom since the boyfriend moved in but had her bed in a corridor;
- a picture of the boyfriend yelling at the children for not finishing a meal; and
- a fork, which he used to stab them if they did not eat their meals. (Ramon showed the worker healing scars on his hand consistent with the tines of a fork.)

The children then went on to create their house of good things, drawing their experience of visiting their father, and then on separate sheets of paper drew separate houses of dreams. Though Stephanie's house of dreams was more colourful, both showed them living with their mother, the boyfriend gone, each house protected by strong doors and guard dogs and them having good food, nice clothes and activities and their own rooms.

With the children's permission, the worker showed the mother the children's drawings, which led the mother for the first time to admit the problems at home. The mother made commitments to leave the boyfriend but unfortunately was not able to and the

Figure 3.2 Child's drawing

Source: The Munro Review of A Child-Centred System (2011)

children were brought into care. Nine months later when the mother was able to separate she came immediately back to the worker to work to get her children back (Taken from Munro (2011, pp. 30–31)).

As we can see though, the use of a different medium that is developmentally, cognitively and culturally appropriate is vital in communication. The use of drawings or play is a valuable tool. Dr Sunderland (see Chapter 1), in her work with abused children, advocates play, art and story-telling as ways for children to communicate trauma and process it.

In this next piece, a practical approach is outlined to communicate with individuals with a learning disability. In Chapter 6 we will explore further language and its influence in the realm of disability.

COMMUNICATION PASSPORTS FOR PEOPLE WITH INTELLECTUAL DISABILITIES

The following is a guide on how best to communicate clearly with service users who have an intellectual disability, and serves as a very practical suggestion for improving and supporting effective communication.

At a service level, communication for all can be supported by:

- using plain language
- preparing easy-to-read summaries of written documents
- using visual and audio formats to aid communication

- listening
- creating a relaxed environment and allowing adequate time for people to process information and formulate their response
- enabling one-to-one communication if preferred.

Communication passports are designed to support those who are unable to communicate in a conventional way, so that their preferences and views are expressed through the communication passport. Every individual with intellectual disability and/or mental health issues should have a personalised communication passport, relating to all aspects of their life. In this regard, communication passports are often linked in with behaviour support plans and individual care and treatment plans. To ensure best practice, the individual, their family and significant others must be consulted when drawing up a communication passport.

The outcome should be:

- ethical
- promote rights and quality of life
- be current and accurate
- be owned by the individual, rather than professionals.

Source: Mental Health Commission (2009, p. 23)

Again we can see *personalisation* at play here with the service user consulted and involved in tailoring a communication approach that works best for them, it is a clear example of person-centred planning and practice.

THINK ABOUT IT!

How can you marry 'personalisation' in with your communication style? Have you worked with clients with a learning disability? If yes, what were your strengths and what were your 'soft spots' (areas you could improve upon)? If you haven't communicated with people with learning disabilities yet, have you any worries or anxiety about doing so? The first time I worked with people with Down syndrome I was very anxious as I hadn't interacted before with someone with a learning disability and wasn't sure what to expect. From a communication perspective I was concerned I might have difficulty understanding the clients or not responding 'appropriately'. I look back now and wonder what I even thought 'responding appropriately' or not entailed, I must admit I cringe. So if you haven't interacted with a particular group of people, think about, and reflect on, what your expectations are, any anxiety you may feel and how you think this might impact on how you might communicate.

Communication interactions can enhance or jeopardise an individual's sense of agency and dignity. The following piece of research illustrates just that, examining dignity and communication with older people within the health, social care and social work arena.

'TU' OR 'VOUS?': A EUROPEAN QUALITATIVE STUDY OF DIGNITY AND COMMUNICATION WITH OLDER PEOPLE IN HEALTH AND SOCIAL CARE SETTINGS

This study gathered qualitative data from six countries through focus groups and interviews. The older people (65 plus) included those in residential care (e.g. nursing homes) and those who were not. Professionals working with older people (including care workers, nurses and psychologists) also participated in discussions on the role of communication.

Woolhead et al. (2006, p. 363) report that different styles of communication between professionals and older people were found to be capable of enhancing or jeopardising dignity. The use of appropriate forms of address, listening, giving people choice, including them, respecting their need for privacy and politeness, and making them feel valued, emerged as significant ways to maintain older people's sense of self-worth and dignity. The authors continue that despite being aware of good communication practices, health and social care professionals often failed to implement them, citing lack of time, staff and/or resource scarcity, regulation and bureaucracy as barriers. A lack of awareness and effort also emerged as factors. In relation to the impact of communication on dignity, four major categories emerged from the analysis, including:

- forms of address
- politeness and privacy
- feeling valued
- inclusion and choice.

FORMS OF ADDRESS

A very clear area of contention was how older people were addressed. Older people found the use of first names and 'pet' names such as 'dear' or 'love' patronising and disrespectful, feeling that only those close to them should use such terms of familiarity. Have you ever addressed an older client by 'dear' or used their first name without asking them first how they prefer to be addressed? I'm sure most of us have, which is what makes this finding so jolting, as it reminds us that things we don't even consider or feel to be disrespectful can be nonetheless viewed that way by the client.

POLITENESS AND PRIVACY

Politeness, kindness and privacy were identified as not just being important but appreciated by older people. It is important in maintaining the dignity of older people that they were involved in decision making, for example, asking their permission to examine them. The following is an example given by an older person living in a nursing home:

> One [caregiver] came in with a list to check who had to go to the toilet. People don't have to go to the toilet by list. They have to go when they need to. Someone asked her to take them. She looked at the list and said, 'It's not your turn'. That's not treating someone with dignity. (p. 368)

Being treated as a 'task' rather than as an individual with needs, as highlighted above, was identified as an issue in the section on 'feeling valued' by the researchers.

FEELING VALUED

The role of person-centred practice became evident from the findings of this study. Participants identified being listened to, acknowledged as a person and given time as supporting their sense of being valued. Barriers that hindered communication between professionals and their clients included lack of staff, financial resources, awareness and increased bureaucracy and these reduced the feeling of value experienced by individual patients.

INCLUSION AND CHOICE

> I went into this particular specialist and he had an assistant. Instead of talking to me, he was writing all the time. I could have been an elephant. He said, 'Take her in there and tell her to strip down,' and I just said, 'Am I invisible?' (p. 369)

The above example given by a participant reflects a fear expressed by many of the older people, of being treated as an 'object'. Not being included in decision making created a sense that the older person was not seen as a person and their opinions and outlook were not respected. This damaged the older person's sense of worth and left them feeling little more than an object. Woolhead et al. (2006, p. 369) state that 'It was further acknowledged that it was easy to put one's own values onto older people. Often professionals were accused of deciding what was best for patients without considering their views'.

This last point is interesting if seen in relation to the previous research on reflective function; applying your own values to another indicates that you have not considered the other person's beliefs and wishes in the decision making. This is an example of a clear failure of reflective function, and highlights the importance of 'personalisation' in social work, which aims to prevent people feeling devalued with little input in decision making.

As you can see, communication does not necessarily involve the obvious, such as the tone we use when we talk or maintaining eye contact. It can extend to how we treat and interact with another; this study highlights the importance of quality communication in supporting the dignity of the older person or indeed any individual. It reminds us of the necessity to remain aware and vigilant to ensure that we do not lapse into forgetfulness or laxity in our daily practice. This study also links up with the research on reflective function as it gives real-life examples of failures of reflective function. Practical suggestions can be gleaned from this study; from knocking on the door before entering a person's room to involving the person in decision making.

Awareness of older people's needs and how our values can influence how we interact with them was a finding of this research. Cultural awareness is essential to ensure effective communication. As we will see, values underpin how we communicate, thus we must have a knowledge base of other cultures and how they influence communication styles. We must also become aware of our value system and how this influences our perception of other cultures and its impact on how we interact and communicate.

Culture-bound values and implications for intercultural communication

An understanding of cultural differences in communication styles is essential to social workers to ensure effective communication. As discussed in Chapter 1, cross-cultural psychology and the 'Black Perspective' challenge the Euro-American domination of psychology along with its values, which tend to mitigate and pathologise values and experiences that don't reflect this 'world view'. Cultural issues can be overlooked when considering the communication process. In this piece we are going to consider culture-bound values and how they impact on intercultural communication.

> communication between people whose cultural perceptions and symbol systems are distinct enough to alter the communication event.

Intercultural communication is defined (as cited in Robinson, 2007, p. 107) as Robinson further alludes that 'interethnic communication' occurs between members of ethnic groups residing within the same nation state. The following culture-bound values will be explored and how they impact on intercultural communication:

- Individualism – collectivism
- Direct versus indirect communication
- Emotional and behavioural expressiveness

INDIVIDUALISM-COLLECTIVISM

Simply put, individualism, as the name suggests, argues that values, rights and duties originate in the individual with traits such as independence, initiative and assertiveness being prized: such societies include American, English and European. Collectivism stresses that all such values, rights and so on originate in the collective (be that a group or larger society). For an individual within a collectivistic grouping, values that promote the greater good of the group, such as conformity, cohesiveness and harmony, are valued. Most societies in the world operate from a collectivist perspective. Ethnic groups, though they may live in an individualistic society (e.g. U.K.), may follow a collectivistic value system of their ethnic group (for example, Asian) or find themselves torn between both perspectives. Understanding of these perspectives is important when communicating, as what is considered an appropriate mode of communication in one perspective may not be in another, as we will see. Robinson (2007) notes that collectivism is an important influence on child rearing practices, within Asian cultures social order is integral and 'filial piety', where younger members must show respect and obedience to their parents and older members of the family, is imperative. It is not considered acceptable to bring shame or dishonour to the family. How does this influence parent–child interactions? According to Robinson (ibid., p. 116)

In Euro-American families, verbal assertiveness is valued. Children have the right to challenge the directives and decisions of adults. In cultures where individualism is highly valued, people are expected to take the initiative in advancing their personal interests and well-being and to be direct and assertive in interacting with others.

THINK ABOUT IT!

Consider what perspective you were raised in and how that has affected your value system. Reflect on when you have dealt with members from another perspective; were you judgemental towards the value system they were operating within? I have 'caught' myself (through reflective function and self-awareness) having feelings of judgement. I was raised within a family system where individualism was highly valued. I have found myself, at times, perplexed, if not judgemental, of more collectivistic values systems as I struggle to make sense of them from my perspective. Did this affect my interaction and communication style? I'd like to think not as I believe I 'caught' it but I am aware it's there. This applies equally if coming from a collectivistic approach and interacting with someone from an individualistic value system. Reflect on this and note it in your journal.

Robinson (ibid.) relays that when these two perspectives interact it can cause communication problems, for instance, in Japanese society where 'values and norms forcefully promote self-control and avoidance of direct personal confrontation' this emphasis on harmony can clash with assertiveness, which is prized within individualistic cultures.

Direct and indirect communication reflects such perspectives. Collectivistic communication styles tend to be more ambiguous and indirect to maintain harmony, the more direct communication approach favoured by individualistic systems would be considered 'crude and inelegant' within some Asian cultures.

We see again how values influence communication. In the domain of ***emotional and behavioural expressiveness*** we see cultural difference in communication styles. Emotional expressiveness relates to the communication of feelings and thoughts. According to Robinson (2007, p. 120):

> Africans and African Caribbeans tend to be emotionally expressive while whites have a more emotionally self-restrained and often attempt to understate, avoid, ignore, diffuse intense or unpleasant situations. One of the dominant stereotypes of African Caribbeans in British society is that of hostile, angry, prone-to-violence black males. It is not unusual for white social workers to describe their black clients as being 'hostile and angry' ... in contexts where Eurocentric norms prevail, young black people find their more intense expressive behaviour and the more animated communication style criticized and pathologized.

Of course, it is important to remember that these are generalisations; groups and individuals within them are not homogenous: diversity and difference occur. Nonetheless, awareness of the role of culture in interactions and the values that underpin them are essential to good social work practice and effective communication.

In this final section we are going to consider Person-Centred Practice (PCP) and its implications, We came across Carl Rogers earlier and here we meet him again, for PCP has its roots in the Humanist movement.

IMPLICATIONS FOR PRACTICE – PERSON-CENTRED PRACTICE

- Person-centred practice
  - Definition,
  - Person-centred planning and
  - Person-centred thinking skills

What is person-centred practice?

Traditionally, little consideration was paid to the client themselves. Instead the focus was placed on the difficulties they were experiencing, their illness or disability. This reflected a **medical model** approach which viewed the difficulties faced by a person to be the result of their individual issues, impairment or circumstances. The **social model**, also social constructionism, challenges this view, advocating that it is society and its structures that impact on and possibly limit the person. This shift reflects the growing importance of Person-Centred Practice, a movement which began with Carl Rogers, who, along with Abraham Maslow (see Chapter 4), formed the Humanistic movement, which placed emphasis upon the person and their innate dignity. Rogers, in his work as a psychotherapist, introduced the concept of 'person-centred' and also recognition that the quality of the relationship between therapist and client is a crucial factor in the outcome of therapy. The concept of person-centred approach or practice has been embraced by those in the caring profession from nursing to education (child-centred) to community work and social work.

Person-centred planning

Person-centred planning and practice arguably has its roots in the work of Carl Rogers (see Chapter 4). At its core is a focus on how a person wishes to live their life and what needs to happen to make that possible. Fundamentally, it is an approach that places the person as the primary focus and strives to support, not disempower, the individual.

A relationally (relationship) based approach to person-centred planning developed by Talerico (2003) suggests:

- Knowing the person as an individual and being responsive to individual and family characteristics
- Providing care that is meaningful to the person in ways that respect the individual's values, preferences and needs
- Viewing care recipients as biopsychosocial human beings
- Fostering development of consistent and trusting caregiving relationships
- Emphasising freedom of choice

- Promoting physical and emotional comfort
- Appropriately involving the person's family, friends and social network. (p. 14)

The person-centred approach offers a framework, in keeping with Rogers's work, that places the individual at the centre of practice, representing not a simplistic individualised care concept, but instead a fundamental shift of philosophy in the social work arena. The experiences people have when they interact with professionals are what matter most to the people who use services. The quality of this interaction can create a positive sense of well-being and a desire to take increasing control of their life. Conversely, a poor-quality interaction can cause a person to feel anxious, less confident and consequently less independent. Communication forms an essential element in supporting people using a person-centred approach. The following piece suggests how to do just that.

USING PERSON-CENTRED THINKING TO LISTEN AND RESPOND TO PEOPLE

To enable people to have real choice and control over their lives and services, it is suggested that practitioners need to know the answers to the questions set out in Table 3.1. Providers need to know this information and consistently act on it in order to meet the needs of the people being supported. It is not just what staff members do, but the way in which they do it. The quality of the relationship and the interaction between the staff member and the person being supported is essential in ensuring quality services overall. The experiences people have when they interact with professionals are what matter most to the people who use services. The quality of this interaction can create a positive sense of well-being and a desire to take increasing control of their life. Conversely, a poor-quality interaction can cause a person to feel anxious, less confident and consequently less independent.

Table 3.1 Person-centred thinking skills

What do providers need to know about each individual they support?	Person-centred thinking skills that can help
What is important to the person, so that services can be built around what matters to them as an individual.	What is important to the person?
How, when and where the person wants support or services delivered.	How can we best support the person?
What people want today, tomorrow and in the future and how to move towards this.	What is important in the future?
How the person communicates the way in which they want their services personalised.	Communication charts. Decision making agreements.
How to enable people to be part of their communities as contributing citizens.	Presence to contribution. Planning how to move from being present to contributing.
How well are services being delivered, and are they being delivered in the way people want. What do individuals think of the services they receive and how can services be improved.	What is working? What is not working? These questions can be part of a person-centred review.

Source: www.puttingpeoplefirst.org.uk

This framework, reflecting a Rogerian approach, places the individual at the centre of practice, enabling people to have real choice and control over their lives and services; it is not just **what** professional members do, but the **way** in which they do it.

THINK ABOUT IT!

Think of examples from your work practice or experience and the clients you have supported and worked with. Using this table, apply each point to your own experience. Can you transform those previous experiences into a more 'person-centred' approach? Also consider what obstacles might prevent you from doing this and implementing a more person-centred practice. Are there structural ones? Is the organisation you work within person-centred in its ethos and implementation or can you see examples where the organisation itself has made a PCP approach difficult? Reflect upon yourself, are there obstacles within you that make it more difficult to truly adopt a 'person-centred' approach. For example, have you prejudices that might, even unwittingly, make it difficult for you to treat the client as an equal and with complete dignity? For example, if you have had experiences of, or been affected by, crime this might impact on your ability to fully and non-judgementally relate to a client with a criminal record. This highlights the importance of reflective function in ensuring person-centred practice can be fully achieved. Sometimes we are unaware that we are not treating the client with the full level of respect and dignity they require.

The following framework is a really useful taxonomy (or scheme of classification), which allows us to think about different aspects of communication when we're honing our approach as we work with others.

Consider Table 3.2 (Lefevre et al., 2008) and see how you apply it to your daily interactions (perhaps in your reflective diary). While the piece relates to working with children, the skills outlined are transferable to other groups. If it helps, replace the word child(ren) with individual.

Table 3.2 Taxonomy of core condition and skills

Domains	Categories	Dimensions
Knowing	Underpinning propositional knowledge and understanding The impact of communication of any of the child's inherited traits, capabilities or impairments How (adverse) experiences affect children The purpose of communication in context How the social work role and task may affect two-way communication Appropriate models, approaches, methods and skills in work with children	Child Development
Being (1)	Value base – an ethical commitment to • Treating children as competent with a right to participate • Providing information and explanations • Eliciting and taking into account children's views Being able to attend to both children's needs and rights Being child-centred An anti-oppressive approach Core social work values (e.g. being respectful, reliable, providing uninterrupted time, attending to confidentiality)	Inclusive practice

Being (2)	Emotional and personal capacity/capability to ... Work with depth processes in the work not just surface ones • Recognise and use one's own feelings (and what some may refer to as counter-transference) in the work • Feel comfortable to work with children's strong feelings (and what some term transference) Develop relationships with children at a real person-to-person level (e.g. show own humanity, enthusiasm, warmth, friendliness, humour, playfulness, care and/or concern) Use person-centred qualities (e.g. empathy, congruence, sincerity, genuineness, transparency, honesty, openness) Enable children to feel safe and trusting	
Doing	Micro-skills and performative techniques in ... • Establishing trust • Going at the child's pace • Using play, symbolic, creative, non-verbal and expressive techniques Listening Indirect communications Interviewing Using a variety of tools (e.g. ecomaps)	Providing the necessary facilitating environmental conditions

Source: Taken from Lefevre et al. (2008, p. 168).

Choose a client you have worked with, and use the taxonomy to go through each category and its 'dimensions'. How would you apply it to your client? If your client is a young child and you are applying the 'doing' domain, what skills and techniques would you utilise to establish trust to ensure you are proceeding at the child's pace? If you client has a disability, how would you ensure the 'value base' category was being met, and what skills and values would you use to ensure 'inclusive practice'?

THE USE OF SELF AWARENESS IN SOCIAL WORK

This last activity is designed to develop the use of self in social work. This skill relates to the ability to recognise our own thoughts, emotions, values, biases, strengths and weaknesses that drive our behavior. Another aspect of this skill includes our ability to recognise our reactions to cues in our environment and how our emotions impact on how we respond to others. As we have seen, it is imperative that social workers can communicate and forge positive relationships with all people, including those with different value systems, perspectives or life experiences. Where we meet 'differences' the ability to be aware and attend to these 'differences' is vital in affecting the quality of the relationship. Self-awareness is a crucial tool in facilitating this self- knowledge, allowing us to develop and improve how we communicate. So how can we use self-awareness effectively? Using a reflective journal consider the following points:

- Compile a 'self-awareness' inventory or list of your experience in relationship to a particular client. Some of the headings might be:
  - — Emotions
  - — Thoughts

- — Beliefs in terms of differences and similarities including
  - Culture
  - Ethnicity or Race
  - Gender
  - Religion
  - Age
  - Personal history (e.g. abuse, history of violence, mental illness, addiction)
- Explore how your behavior, and particularly your communication approach, is affected by these internal experiences (for example, were any difficult or disturbing to you? Which positively or negatively affected the relationship?)
- What interventions can you use or develop to improve your response to a negative feeling or thought regarding a client to enhance and create a more positive interaction?
- What values are important to you and how do they influence your interaction with the client?
- What do you consider your personal strengths in terms of relationship building and communicating and how do they affect your interactions with the client?
- What do you consider your personal weaknesses in terms of relationship building and communicating and how do they affect your interactions with the client?
- Finally, how can you develop further and implement self- awareness as a skill in your social work practice?

The activity above is a detailed but valuable tool. There has been an emphasis on reflective function and self-awareness in this chapter, but that should hopefully reflect how fundamental knowledge and skills of self-awareness are to effective communication in social work practice. Let's end this chapter with a brief guide from Diggins (2004, pp. 13–14) of social workers who are good at communication; see if you can recognise yourself in the list!

Guide to social workers who are good at communication

- are courteous
- turn up on time
- speak directly to service users, not carers or personal assistants
- don't use jargon
- 'open their ears' and 'think before they talk'
- listen and 'really hear' and accept what carers are saying
- explain what is happening and why
- do what they say they are going to do and don't over-promise
- say honestly when they can't help
- are patient and make enough time to communicate with disabled service users
- recognise the loss of dignity people experience when approaching social services for the first time – the 'cost' in this – and respond sensitively

- don't assume anything about a user's abilities simply because of a disability
- understand the importance of privacy, peace and quiet and users' and carers' choice of meeting place
- know that closed questions can be easier for service users with communication difficulties to answer
- check out that they've been understood
- find a mode of communication that works
- remember that young people may prefer to talk while doing something else
- build trust, empathy and warmth
- work in organisations that help them to do all these things.

SUMMARY

As we have seen, communication skills are a core aspect of social work practice. Communication spans from intrapersonal and the use of reflective function to interpersonal skills from the theoretical to the very practical. Cultural aspects of communication need to be recognised to ensure effective communication can occur; this is also true when working with groups with differing needs and developmental capabilities. The role of interpersonal skills and communication in the social work arena is complex and can be challenging. It is essential to commit yourself to the process of 'reflective function', thus enabling you to assess how well you support clients. Be more aware of how you engage with service-users and pay particular attention to the qualities that form the person-centred practice model; are you empathetic and non-judgemental? A core aspect of social care work is the ability to relate to and support your clients. Hopefully, this chapter has given you food for thought.

chapter

4 APPROACHES TO PSYCHOLOGY

CHAPTER OUTLINE

- What are developmental theories?
- Some key developmental issues
- Social and emotional theories
- Cognitive theorists
- Behaviourism and learning
- Humanism
- Ecological theory
- Case study demonstrating ecological understanding and interplay of factors

In Chapter 1, we briefly examined some of the major approaches within psychology. In this chapter we are going to explore them in greater depth. As always this book cannot be exhaustive and the choice of theories reflects those traditionally studied and considered influential in psychology. The major theoretical traditions are outlined here; however, throughout the book other theoretical frameworks will be considered. All the theories discussed have relevance to social work, but some appear more obvious than others, such as the ecological approach, which attempts to place the individual in his or her context and extrapolate all the various interacting influences that shape a person's life. Within the developmental theories, some can struggle with cognitive theories particularly; the language can be off-putting and the direct relevance unclear, but it is essential to, as practitioners, understand the 'typical' and expected development of a person in order to support that development, and theories offer us a window to do so. Yet it is also important to be able to recognise when development becomes 'atypical' or is not in line with the expected developmental trajectories. As we saw in the preceding chapter, a child's level of development impacts directly on the communication process and knowledge of cognitive theories (which focus on the development of thinking and language) is of critical importance in determining a child's comprehension level and ability to articulate feelings and events. So the study of developmental theories is of central importance to social work. In the next chapter we will incorporate theories into 'human growth and development' across the life span; however, the focus here is on the major theoretical domains and theorists associated with them. It is more useful for the reader to have a footing in the major theoretical approaches so as to better understand the developmental patterns of the life span in the subsequent chapters.

All the following theories will be overviewed with their strengths and weaknesses outlined. Practice examples and some case studies will be used to offer a greater understanding of the theory, and examples of their potential links to social work are offered. An overview of more critical psychology approaches will be addressed; we briefly touched on cross cultural and feminist psychology in Chapter 1, and here they will be discussed in greater depth. The post-psychiatry approach is included in Chapter 7.

WHAT ARE DEVELOPMENTAL THEORIES?

Developmental theories hold a fundamental place not just in the arena of psychology but also in social work. A developmental theory is one which, according to Miller (2002, p. 8), 'focuses on change over time'. When we consider an individual across their life span the one constant is change. At different times in the life span, such as in adolescence, this change may be more urgent than at other times. Many theories have been proposed, some newer than others, that try to explain human development or aspects of it. These theories are generally constructed in an attempt to explain and predict behaviour. Some relate to specific areas, such as cognitive development (Piaget), while others are influenced by a particular approach in psychology, such as the psychoanalytic movement (Freud, Erikson). More modern theories, such as Bronfenbrenner's 'ecological' or 'person in environment' and Elder's 'life course' theory, attempt to gain a broader perspective of an individual's development, the myriad of factors influencing such development and how these shape development across the life span. Before we begin to overview the different domains of theories, we will consider some of the key issues in developmental psychology, such as the nature versus nurture debate. Here, key developmental issues are explained, including the nature versus nurture and 'critical versus sensitive period' debates. The role of nature versus nurture will be discussed, because not only is this a key concept within psychology but it also has clear relevancy to social work in furthering understanding of the mechanisms at play in an individual's development and informing interventions and supports. An '*In focus*' section on extreme deprivation is explored in relation to the 'critical versus sensitive period' debate to contextualise this topic, and the findings of the 'English and Romanian adoptees' (ERA) research project is discussed to concretise this theoretical debate into a real world issue.

SOME KEY DEVELOPMENTAL ISSUES

Nature versus nurture

The nature–nurture debate is one of the key issues in psychology and, more particularly, in understanding human development. Its origins can be traced to the early philosophers, who discussed the nature of humans: are we 'blank slates' as Locke believed, shaped by those around us and the society we live in? Or in keeping with the doctrine of 'original sin', are we born the way we are? These positions reflect the nature versus nurture argument. Nature refers to biological processes, genes and our brain as determinants of our behaviour. Nurture relates to the influence of our environment in our development. The culture we are born into influences how we see ourselves and others and also influences our behaviour. Other environmental influences are child-rearing practices, education and so on.

In the early twentieth century the nature position dominated and this fuelled a belief in racial superiority and differences. By the 1960s this position had changed to a nurture stance, which postulated the importance of environment on a person's development, and can be best seen in the explosion of literature on child-rearing practices.

Nowadays a more reasonable position is generally maintained, recognising the influence of both nature and nurture in human development. Debates continue regarding the degree to which either is involved, their role and the interaction between the two elements. Urie Bronfenbrenner's revised 'bioecological' theory (later in this chapter) best captures this new position, as he demonstrates the many influences that interact to shape development. We still do not understand the complexity of the interaction between nature and nurture and it remains an issue of great interest and importance.

Critical versus sensitive periods of development

We will look at examples of extreme deprivation in the early years to explore the issue of critical versus sensitive periods of development. Does a *critical* period exist in development, meaning that if development does not occur during this stage then the opportunity is lost? Or does a *sensitive* period exist where it is preferable for development to occur, but if it does not, development can occur at a later date? In Chapter 2 Dr Sunderland makes clear her view that early experiences have a fundamental role in shaping a child's brain development, yet some people show greater resilience to adverse events than others, who are badly affected by them. The following discussion illustrates the complexity of human behaviour and that there are no easy answers to be had.

In focus: critical versus sensitive period debate – extreme deprivation

Development in infancy encompasses social, emotional, cognitive and physical growth. What is the difference between critical and sensitive periods? Let's take the example of language. If you believe in a 'critical period' for the acquisition of language, then you would believe that if language is not acquired during a particular period, it would not be possible to acquire language at a later date.

If you believe in a 'sensitive period' of development, then you might believe that if you do not acquire language in the early years, it is possible to do so at a later time. In the debate between critical versus sensitive periods of development, infancy is often examined, as it is a time of huge growth in many areas. The critical versus sensitive period debate is one of the most active in psychology, and cases of extreme deprivation are often examined in an effort to illuminate this debate. Recent examples of children who have suffered extreme deprivation include Romanian orphans whose images shocked us in the early 1990s. Extreme deprivation in infancy offers us an insight as to whether children can recover from adverse experiences in their early years and develop normally with caring and appropriate interventions or whether there is in fact a 'critical period', which cannot be recovered from, leaving the individual permanently and irreversibly affected.

Clarke and Clarke (1976) support the idea of a sensitive period, after which experienced adversity and resulting deficits can be compensated for – an 'initial step in an ongoing life path'. On the other hand, Freud, and later Bowlby, argued that early experience determines later development. Bowlby's work with children in institutional care led him to believe that negative early experiences cannot be reversed in later years, especially in the area of attachment (Bowlby, 1951).

However, in more recent decades this position has been questioned. Cases of extreme deprivation have had quite different outcomes, suggesting that the debate surrounding critical versus sensitive periods isn't quite as clear cut as earlier presumed. Rutter (1989, p. 24) argues that 'even markedly adverse experiences in infancy carry few risks for later development if the subsequent rearing environment is a good one'. Let's consider how true this is by examining some cases of extreme deprivation and their subsequent outcomes.

Skuse (1984) explored case studies of children who spent their early years in conditions of extreme adversity and deprivation, hoping to explore specific questions.

- Are some psychological qualities more sensitive to deprivation than others?
- At what pace does recovery take place and what course does it follow?
- What interventions are necessary to optimise recovery?

Anna was discovered in 1938 at nearly 6 years of age, having spent her life in a storage room tied to a chair with her arms above her head. Severely malnourished, she was skeletal, expressionless, lacking speech with severe motor retardation. While Anna showed some improvement, she never integrated successfully into her peer group even though she was now living with a foster family. Anna received no specialist intervention and, while she made some improvement, she remained severely retarded until her death at the age of 10 (Clarke and Clarke, p. 28).

Isabelle was discovered at 6 years locked in a dark room with her 'deaf-mute' mother. Isabelle was suffering from severe malnourishment, her behaviour was either infantile or like that of a wild animal and she did not seem to possess speech. Experts decided she was 'feeble-minded' (Clarke and Clarke, p. 42). Within 6 years of intensive speech and educational therapy she had achieved a normal level of speech and cognitive function.

LANGUAGE DEVELOPMENT

Let's examine a specific area of development, that of language, to see if we can come closer to a conclusion in this debate of critical versus sensitive periods.

Skuse concludes that the development of language appears to be the most vulnerable to deprivation, but much debate surrounds the question of whether there is a critical period for language exposure and/or acquisition. Hall (1985) replied to Skuse with the suggestion that 'some exposure to language and communication is essential at a very early stage, even if only for a very brief period' (p. 825), while Lenneberg's 'critical age hypothesis' (cited in Curtiss, 1977, p. 208) states that the critical period runs from 2 years to puberty.

Genie was confined in total isolation from 20 months until her discovery at 13 years of age; although intensive language therapy suggested initial promising acquisition, her capacity remained severely limited and she was capable of 'few normal or appropriate acts of communication at 18 years' (Skuse, 1984, p. 562), although Isabelle, confined with a 'deaf-mute' mother, developed normal language skills.

Or we could consider the case of the Koluchova twins, grossly deprived and confined from 18 months to nearly 7 years, who went on to develop normally with respect to language (as well as in every other facet of life) (Skuse, 1984). Was this due to their early normal language exposure before they were confined? Was it because they had each other for company and developed ways of communicating? Or was it due to their later intensive care within a foster family?

English and Romanian adoptees (ERA)

We will turn to the work of the English and Romanian adoptees (ERA) study team and their ongoing research comparing UK adoptees with those adopted into the UK from Romania. The fall of the Ceaușescu regime in Romania created a unique research opportunity through the humanitarian endeavour of removing infants and children from orphanages in which they had suffered severe deprivation.

STUDY

The research (Rutter et al., 1998) studied 324 children who were adopted into the UK. The conditions in which the children had lived in Romania varied from 'poor to appalling' (Rutter et al., 1998, p. 467). They were confined to cots, had few, if any, playthings and barely any stimulation through talk or play, were poorly nourished and often endured harsh physical conditions. Nearly half had been reared entirely in institutions; 18 had had family rearing with only 2 weeks' institutional care; the rest had spent about half their lives in institutions. Half were severely malnourished and suffering from chronic infections.

FINDINGS

- The catch-up with respect to these norms was nearly complete at age four (Rutter et al., 1998).

- Age on adoption was a strong predictor of more positive outcomes with no measurable deficit in those adopted before 6 months. Those adopted after 6 months were more likely to show evidence of deficits.
- Children who had received better individualised care in institutions tended to have higher cognitive scores at age six.

Rutter et al. conclude that 'children who had experienced prolonged privation in poor-quality institutions tended to show a less complete cognitive recovery, although even with prolonged institutional care, cognitive catch-up was very substantial indeed'. Our understanding has certainly extended far beyond early simplistic suggestions that early experience determines all future development. Here we clearly see individual variation at play, which no doubt illustrates the complexity and interaction of multiple factors in influencing outcomes. What can cause these differences in outcomes? This question is one that will arise repeatedly throughout this book.

THINK ABOUT IT!

What can cause the variety of different outcomes? Identify what factors might be at play and how this could influence outcomes. To get you started consider factors under the following headings:

- Within the child (including biological, personality)
- Immediate environment (parents/family, housing, S.E.S. peer interactions, community, stimulating environment)
- Wider environment (culture, government policies including welfare, economic, discrimination)

In Chapter 2 we saw arguments made that the early years of life are crucial to a child's development, and impacts on life outcomes. While the cases presented here mark more extreme experiences, what do you think, based on this research, might be the potential impact on a child's areas of development of an environment that is not nurturing, with poor or little stimulation and parental engagement? Would your conclusions have consequences in terms of your practice or interventions you may utilise or advocate?

With these issues in mind and their potential role in developmental outcomes let us now divert our attention to theories proposed to explain the many different areas or domain of development. We will first consider theories regarding social and emotional development, and in particular those of Sigmund Freud, Erik Erikson and John Bowlby's work on attachment.

SOCIAL AND EMOTIONAL THEORIES

Social and emotional theories relate to the development of our emotions and our personality. Social development refers not just to our relationships with others and how we construe them; it also involves how we see ourselves in the eyes of others. Let's look at an example of social comparison (where we compare ourselves to another). Have you ever looked at a magazine with an image of an impossibly thin model and felt the urge to start a diet? That would be an example of social comparison! So as you can see, social development has two aspects. The two theorists that we will examine both come from the psychoanalytic tradition, yet they have quite different explanations of this aspect of human development.

Sigmund Freud (1856–1939)

Sigmund Freud is considered the founder of the psychoanalytic movement, but what is psychoanalysis and how does it relate to human development? Freud believed that much of human behaviour, emotions and feelings emanated from the unconscious mind. Our behaviour was merely the tip or surface that one could see of the unconscious mind. In order to understand behaviour, Freud believed that the unconscious mind would need to be accessed through techniques such as word association and dream analysis. We are not aware of this part of our mind, yet Freud believed that it held powerful urges that had to be satisfied. This created the impetus for our behaviour. There are three levels of the mind: unconscious, preconscious and conscious.

This interest in the unconscious drives that exist within an individual and their role in conscious behaviour is reflected in Freud's conceptualisation of personality. According to Freud, personality consists of three components: the id, the ego and the superego.

COMPONENTS OF PERSONALITY

- id
- ego
- superego.

The **id** is the only structure present at birth and exists solely in the unconscious mind. Freud (1964, p. 106) describes the id as 'a chaos, a cauldron of seething excitations' and further that 'it is filled with energy reaching it from the instincts, but it has no organisation, produces no collective will, but only a striving to bring about the satisfaction of the instinctual pleasure principle'. The *pleasure principle* is solely concerned with instant gratification regardless of any other consideration. In order to control the impulses of the id another aspect of personality develops – the ego.

The **ego** operates primarily at a conscious level and is driven by the *reality principle*, which acts as a check on the id. The ego examines whether it is safe for the id to discharge its impulses and satisfy its instinctual needs.

Finally, the last component comes to fruition: the **superego**, which in its barest form is the moral voice of the personality and endeavours to control the id, particularly with regard to sexual and aggressive needs. The superego grows out of a child's internalisation of their parents' views of morality and is influenced by the cultural norms of the society of which the individual is a member or to which the individual belongs. The ego stands in the middle between the id and the superego.

THINK OF IT ANOTHER WAY!

As we get older we are taught by parents, school and our culture that expectations of us exist and that our needs cannot always be satisfied. For example, stealing is prohibited and frowned upon in many cultures. I'm hungry and go into a shop to buy some food when I realise I've forgotten my purse. An id response would be to take and eat the food as the id is only interested in satisfying the hunger. However, I've been brought up to believe that stealing is wrong, so I put the food back – this is a superego response. The superego develops as we get older and learn more and more of what is acceptable and the rules we must obey (legal and moral).

From a cultural perspective, the superego offers an interpretation of how children are socialised within their group's or society's belief system and how this may impact on their emotional development and personality formation. For example, I grew up in a society that was still dominated by a strict religious belief system that moderated behaviour. Sex, as part of this belief system, was regulated in society; sex outside marriage was condemned, and within marriage it was only for procreation purposes, not for pleasure. Reflecting back now I can see a lot of adults in the society I grew up in were never allowed to express their sexual instincts (id). Here we can see where the superego (religious belief) dominated the id (sexual instincts). Can it be healthy for a personality that one structure should so control and eradicate another? Common sense dictates not, and Freud would have suggested that such imbalances would affect personality development. We will consider these difficulties later.

THINK ABOUT IT!

Can you think of other instances where such a disparity between id and superego exist? Perhaps parenting practices which are either too lax or too strict? What are the consequences, in your opinion, of these disparities?

Of course, both represent extremes, and that's where the ego comes in. Like the superego, it develops as we get older and acts as a kind of mediator between the id and the superego, trying to find an outcome that will satisfy both. Back in the shop, after I've discovered I've forgotten my money, the ego solution could be for me to ask my friend to lend me the money so I can buy the food. That way my hunger will be satisfied, keeping the id happy, and I won't have stolen anything, keeping my superego happy, and also my mother!

Possibly not the most elegant analogy as the id is not of itself 'bad', but an analogy that makes me smile nonetheless is the clip from *The Simpsons* where Homer has a choice to make: on either shoulder is devil Homer and angel Homer trying to persuade Homer to their way of thinking. The devil is kind of like the id, only interested in having its needs met regardless of consequence, whereas the angel is the superego, chiding Homer to do the right thing even if it costs him his desires. Homer is in the middle, like the ego, listening back and forth to both sides and becoming increasingly overwhelmed in trying to make a decision. When was the last time you experienced that?!

The ego stands in the middle between the id and the superego. As can be imagined, conflict occurs between the competing demands of the id for satisfaction at any cost and the superego attempting to constrain the id. Anxiety occurs when the ego confronts impulses, threatening to get out of control, or external danger.

> Anxiety is a painful emotional experience resulting from internal or external stimulation.

This definition of anxiety by Hall, 1962 (as cited in Passer and Smith, 2001), acknowledges that anxiety can occur from internal or external forces.

THINK ABOUT IT!

What forces external to you cause you discomfort or anxiety, perhaps dealing with members of your family, clients or colleagues? These forces can be varied from personal to work to study. Now think of incidents or issues that cause you anxiety or discomfort and are internal; a major one for me can be perfectionism. I strive to do everything to a certain standard and feel anxiety when I struggle to achieve the standards I've set. Of course, often these standards are too high, increasing feelings of failure. We all have our bug bears; what are yours? This is an important exercise to reflect on as it allows you to catch it and to challenge them, and record them in your reflective journal. Look to your clients as well; what internal and external forces cause them anxiety?

When the ego is unable to produce realistic coping mechanisms in times of anxiety it resorts to what Freud terms 'defence mechanisms' to relieve the anxiety in a safe manner by denying, distorting or falsifying reality.

DEFENCE MECHANISMS

Freud outlined several defence mechanisms that are utilised by the ego when it cannot produce realistic coping mechanisms powerful enough to cope with the anxiety being experienced by an individual. A number of defence mechanisms exist, including:

- repression
- denial
- projection
- displacement.

Before considering the individual mechanisms, a further discussion of their general characteristics is called for. As mentioned above, the defence mechanisms operate by distorting or denying reality in order to reduce anxiety; however, in doing so they impede psychological development by using up psychological energy that would otherwise serve the developing maturational process of the personality. The purpose of the defence mechanisms is a developmental one and, as such, they exist early on and are used by the infantile ego to cope with demands and as a protective measure. Freud claimed that defence mechanisms continue after the infantile stage if the ego has not developed sufficiently and has remained dependent on the mechanisms. Further, the individual's environment can contribute towards the maintenance and dominance of the defence mechanisms. Should a child's experiences be overwhelming in relation to their capacity to cope, the ego can become overly reliant upon defence mechanisms, which in turn leads to the dominance of defence mechanisms over the ego.

Repression is one of the most widely known of the defence mechanisms and was of primary interest to Freud. In the beginning Freud coined the term 'repression' to describe unacceptable or painful mental content that was excluded from awareness. Freud contended that bringing these repressed memories to consciousness would cure the hysteria he was witnessing. Defence mechanisms act to repress painful memories from entering consciousness. These drives and memories trapped in the unconscious strive for release and will occasionally be released in the form of a slip of the tongue: a 'Freudian slip'

An example of repression would be where an individual abused as a child may develop amnesia of the event. **Sublimation** is a component of repression, consisting of a repressed impulse released through a desirable form. An individual with hostile impulses channels those impulses by becoming a prosecuting lawyer; this would be an example of sublimation. Freud is never clear as to whether repression is a fully unconscious act or if there is some degree of awareness on the part of the person.

Denial is another well-known defence mechanism. It involves the denial of an event or emotions associated with an event that is painful and generating high levels of anxiety. Whereas with repression the individual is rendered unaware of an event or of an internal or external stimulation, denial differs in that the person is aware but refuses to acknowledge the reality, and in fact denies it in an attempt to avoid acknowledging the extent of the threat. An alcoholic, when challenged that they have a drinking problem will deny that to be the case. Freud and his supporters contend that denial through a refusal to acknowledge the reality of a situation is necessarily a bad thing as it impedes good mental health, and purport 'reality orientation' as essential to mental health. However, this viewpoint has been criticised and one has to question the validity of this in certain circumstances. Steiner (1966) reported that some Jews held in the Treblinka concentration camp, witnessing death on an unimaginable scale, adopted a belief that death did not exist despite the obvious evidence to the contrary. Could these people really have coped with the reality of the situation they were in and the reality that they could be next? That is the purpose of the defence mechanism: to protect and enable the individual to cope. Is denial, even in circumstances less dramatic than the Treblinka example, truly a survival mechanism, and should 'reality orientation' perhaps be attempted only with great care, for fear of doing more damage? Is the 'reality' of some situations always conducive to mental health?

Projection is considered another primitive defence mechanism and occurs when an unacceptable impulse is repressed and turned or 'projected' outwards and attributed externally. Thus an individual with internal hostile impulses represses these and instead views others around them, external, as hostile. Projection is an inability to recognise hostility in oneself, instead attributing the characteristic to others. An old saying that 'a liar never believes anyone else' captures the essence of projection; an individual with a propensity to lie projects this onto others, thereby believing themself to be honest and those around them to be liars.

Displacement is the shifting of actions or emotions to a substitute individual instead of the intended target due to that target's unavailability or because it is unsafe or unwise to do so. For instance, an individual who is angry with her boss may feel unable to express that anger so instead 'displaces' it onto her spouse, or a child may direct rage towards a peer rather than at the actual target, an alcoholic parent, as it is unsafe to do so.

Many interesting points have been raised in relation to Freud's defence mechanisms, mainly the question of whether these mechanisms are adaptive or maladaptive and of benefit to an individual's mental health. Freud believed that if the repressed thoughts and memories were brought to awareness, this would cure the mental illness afflicting the patient. This has not been supported (Brewin & Andrews, 2000, p. 615); rather this process is seen as a step to recovery rather than a cure-all. As one can see from Freud's theories, an emphasis is placed on explaining 'maladaptive behaviours'.

In the following section on psychosexual theory we explore the concept of 'fixation', where an individual does not pass through the stage but instead becomes fixated or 'stuck' at that point. Freud's psychosexual theory is arguably the most controversial of his theories; people tend to feel uncomfortable around the idea of children and sexuality, and indeed Erik Erikson distanced himself from this part of Freud's conceptualisation. It is important to remember that Freud is describing unconscious motivation here, not conscious.

FREUD'S PSYCHOSEXUAL THEORY

Freud proposed a stage theory of development, suggesting that an individual must pass through one stage to reach the next stage of development. As we will see, Freud believed each stage could have a negative outcome and the individual could become 'fixated' or stuck at that stage.

Importantly, Freud, it could be argued, was one of the first life span developmental theorists as he believed that early experiences could be responsible for behaviour or personality traits in later life. Freud stressed the importance of early experiences in determining the outcomes in later life for an individual.

THE STAGES OF PSYCHOSEXUAL DEVELOPMENT

Freud described five stages we all pass through:

- oral (0–2 years)
- anal (2–3 years)

- phallic (3–6 years)
- latent (6–11 years)
- genital (11+ years).

Benson (2003, pp. 53–5) takes us through the first three stages:

ORAL STAGE

The mouth is the prime source of pleasure, for survival: the baby instinctively sucks. Through oral satisfaction, the baby develops trust and an optimistic personality. Being stuck at this stage is described as 'oral fixation', for example, if weaned too early, the personality may become pessimistic, aggressive and distrusting.

ANAL STAGE

The focus of pleasure shifts to the anus, helping the child become aware of its bowels and how to control them. By deciding itself, the child takes an important step of independence, developing confidence and a sense of when to 'give things up'. However, over-strictness about forcing a child to go to the toilet or about timing or cleanliness can cause personality problems.

Anal fixation – forcing a child to go may cause reluctance about giving away *anything*. The person may become a hoarder or miser. Conversely, over–concern about 'going regularly' may cause obsessive time-keeping or always being late.

PHALLIC STAGE

Children become aware of their genitals and sexual differences. Consequently, development is different for boys and girls.

The Oedipus complex

Each boy unconsciously goes through a sequence of stages beginning with the development of a strong desire for his mother, noticing the bond between his parents (i.e. sleeping together), becoming jealous of his father and hating him, then becoming afraid of his father lest he discover his son's true feelings, which results in the final substage of fear of punishment – castration.

Latency stage During this stage sexual urges remain repressed and children interact and play mostly with same-sex peers.

Genital stage The final stage of psychosexual development begins at the start of puberty, when sexual urges are once again awakened. Adolescents direct their sexual urges onto opposite-sex peers, with the primary focus of pleasure in the genitals.

Aspects of Freud's theories remain controversial; as mentioned many of his followers, including Erikson, rejected his psychosexual theory, and in modern times feminist psychology has labelled concepts such as 'penis envy' as misogynist and patriarchal. Viewed from our modern perspective such accusations are fair; however, one needs to remember the times in which Freud wrote and the attitudes towards women that existed; we must be vigilant against anachronisms. One could view his theory from a more symbolic perspective: 'penis envy' could symbolise 'power', thus it could be argued that maybe women desired the 'power' men held as they themselves were disempowered; the choice is yours.

STRENGTHS OF FREUD'S THEORY

Regardless of the perspective chosen, Freud remains significant. It would be wrong to dismiss him out of hand. Many of us today are comfortable with the role of an unconscious in our conscious behaviour and motivations, and terms such as 'in denial' are in common usage. Internal and external forces were acknowledged, and this is relevant to social work. Aspects of Freud's work have influenced the development of counselling and the therapeutic relationship, as we shall see in Chapter 7. One of Freud's greatest contributions is the recognition that early experiences affect later development and life. Freud's psychoanalytic ideas have influenced the work of many, including Erikson and Bowlby, and led to the evolution of the psychodynamic approach, which recognises that human functioning derives from the interaction of drives and forces within the individual, especially unconscious ones, and between the structures of the personality (id, ego and superego). As we will see, the psychodynamic approach has informed interventions well known to social work.

CRITICISMS OF FREUD'S THEORIES

As we've discussed, Freud's ideas have been criticised by feminist psychology as sexist. One of the strongest criticisms of Freud in current positivistic culture centres on difficulties in testing his theories, as Freud's theory is not observable due to its emphasis on the unconscious; further, as a whole his theory is difficult to measure and results from the few tests carried out have not been favourable. Leading social learning theorist Albert Bandura (2001, p. 19) suggests that psychoanalytic theory 'lacked predictive power and did not fare well in therapeutic effectiveness'. Freud's psychoanalysis is often seen as the preserve of a wealthy middle class and exclusionary of others; it fails to recognise social and cultural elements as we might construe them in the modern day. Finally, Freud's observations were of adults; research of children was not conducted in developing his theory of psychosexual development.

What is the psychodynamic approach?

Confusion is commonplace regarding the difference between psychoanalysis and the psychodynamic approach. The former refers to Freud and his original work, including his therapeutic approach. Freud's focus was on what is sometimes known as 'id' psychology. Those who have followed or been inspired by Freud's ideas fall under the umbrella of the psychodynamic approach, which is an umbrella or catch-all term relating to the evolution of Freud's ideas. As we will see, Erikson (psychosocial) and Bowlby (attachment) were influenced by aspects of Freud's ideas in developing their own theories. Interventions and therapeutic approaches that are psychodynamic, as mentioned, look to the interaction of drives and forces of individuals in order to make sense of their relationships, experiences and how they perceive the world. The psychodynamic approach recognises the role of early experiences in later development and that difficulties faced by individuals have their roots in early childhood, conscious or otherwise.

FREUD'S RELEVANCE TO SOCIAL WORK

The range of influence that the psychodynamic approach has had on social work is broad. Early social work was heavily influenced by the psychoanalytic thinking rooted in a medical model tradition demonstrating little concern with issues of social justice. This was challenged by the 'functional' school of social work in America influenced by the work of Otto Rank. Rank was a follower of Freud. A bitter split between the pair occurred as Rank developed concepts that were deemed to stray too far from traditional Freudian thought. Rank's subsequent work moved away from the more deterministic elements of Freud's beliefs, in turn influencing the evolution of the 'functional' school of social work. In line with Rank's psychodynamic perspective, 'functionalists' challenged the pessimism of Freud, instead seeing human beings as inherently good, with the potential to modify themselves and their environment throughout their life span. In terms of its relevance to social work, a tenet of this school of thought holds the individual as the 'central, active figure'. Within this is the understanding that an individual may resist change even as they reach for growth. This is in line with Rank's assertion of the importance of 'will'. It is recognised that people cannot change others; it is the will of the individual to change. What does this mean for social workers?

CASE STUDY

Maria is a young woman in her early 20s and living with an abusive boyfriend. You have become involved after Maria was hospitalised with broken ribs, which she initially claimed was due to a fall but subsequently admitted was caused by her boyfriend Dave. Your initial dealings with Maria are positive as she confides that she wants to leave Dave and asks for your help. Very quickly Maria changes her mind and insists it was a misunderstanding on your part and that 'Dave loves her' and wouldn't hurt her on purpose. You feel angry with Maria but contain it, and later that evening you row with your partner at home.

1. From this case study identify the beliefs of Rank and the 'functionalist' school of social work as evidenced in Maria's actions.
2. From a Freudian perspective, which of the defence mechanisms have the social worker and Maria deployed?

The psychodynamic approach can also be seen within social work in the psychosocial approach, which inspires interventions and therapies including:

- crisis intervention
- attachment theory
- Erikson's conceptualisation of the 'eight stages of man'
- transactional analysis
- psychoanalytic perspectives developed in relation to systems theory.

In Chapter 7 Freud's contribution to counselling, including an overview of his techniques, will be examined. Staying within the realm of socioemotional development and also the psychodynamic is Erik Erikson's psychosocial theory.

Erik Erikson (1902–1994)

Erik Erikson was born in Germany and became interested in psychology when he met Anna Freud, Sigmund Freud's daughter, who persuaded him to study child psychoanalysis in Vienna. While Erikson was influenced by Freud and accepted some of what he said, Erikson believed that Freud was incorrect in his proposition of psychosexual stages. Instead, Erikson proposed that individuals developed through *psychosocial* stages. Erikson moved to America and joined Harvard Medical School before moving on to Yale. Erikson's first book, *Childhood and Society,* reflected his interest in the role of society and culture on the development of the child. Erikson suggested that personality developed through the resolution of a series of eight major psychosocial stages occurring throughout an individual's life. Each stage involved a different 'crisis' or conflict between the 'self' (individual) and others, including the outside world, which could result in either a positive or a negative outcome. For example, in his first stage of 'Trust vs. Mistrust', if the infant is well cared for and its needs are met, it will develop trust (a positive outcome of this stage). However, if the infant is mistreated or abused, a negative outcome of 'mistrust' will result. Erikson was more positive than Freud, as he believed that negative outcomes in a stage could be resolved at a later date. Further differences existed between the two; core to Erikson's theory was the recognition that societal institutions influence an individual's outcomes. For example, a lack of support from societal institutions would adversely affect the individual's personality development. Equally such institutions could have a positive effect. Freud saw societal institutions as a socialisation agent curtailing a person's instinctual drives. Finally, Freud believed personality development was complete in early adulthood, and Erikson introduced the concept of life span approach to such development.

Erikson was one of the first theorists to see development in a life span context. His eight psychosocial stages are called 'The Eight Ages of Man' and cover the entire life span of the individual.

TRUST VERSUS MISTRUST (0–1 YEAR)

In the first year of life the infant is completely dependent on its caregivers. How well the infant's needs are met and how sensitive the parenting is will influence whether the infant develops trust or mistrust of the world.

AUTONOMY VERSUS SHAME AND DOUBT (1–2 YEARS)

Children begin to walk and assert their independence. As the term 'autonomy' suggests, children can come to believe in themselves and their abilities through the encouragement and support of their caregivers. If the child's efforts are ridiculed or belittled, the child will develop a feeling of shame and doubt in their abilities. Toilet training is seen as a key event which can influence the outcome of this stage.

INITIATIVE VERSUS GUILT (3–5 YEARS)

As the child becomes older they exhibit increasing curiosity and interest, and they initiate play and question more. If this initiative is discouraged or they are held back, they will not develop self-initiative and instead will in turn hold back in later life.

INDUSTRY VERSUS INFERIORITY (6–12 YEARS)

During this time the child begins to attend school and interacts more with peers. If praised in their efforts, they develop a sense of industry and feel good about what they have achieved, which encourages the feeling that they can fulfil their goals. If they repeatedly fail or are not praised when they try, a sense of inferiority will develop.

IDENTITY VERSUS ROLE CONFUSION (12–20 YEARS)

This relates to the adolescent period of life when people are trying to establish their identity, their sense of who they are and their role in life. They are becoming more independent and their peers are increasingly important to them. If they can reconcile these issues, they will develop a feeling of identity; if not, role confusion will result.

INTIMACY VERSUS ISOLATION (20–40 YEARS)

This period is marked by the desire to establish relationships with others. Successful completion leads to a sense of security and intimacy. Avoidance of intimacy or an inability to establish a secure relationship leads to feelings of isolation.

GENERATIVITY VERSUS STAGNATION (40–65 YEARS)

During this period many people have settled down in a relationship and have had children. People also establish their careers. A sense of community and being part of a bigger picture become important. If a person does not achieve these objectives, the resulting feeling is one of stagnation.

INTEGRITY VERSUS DESPAIR (65 YEARS ONWARDS)

In older age, people slow down and begin to reflect on their lives. If the individual feels they have had a successful life, a sense of integrity prevails. If the person believes their life to have been unproductive, a feeling of despair occurs.

STRENGTHS OF ERIKSON'S PSYCHOSOCIAL THEORY

A major strength of Erikson's theory is the introduction of a life span approach to understanding human development, acknowledging that development does not cease or is completed at a given time but is continuous. Erikson identified the importance of society and culture in shaping a child's development, which was quite a divergence from the prescribed thinking at that time. Erikson argues that social forces influence development which occurs with social spheres and is affected by social interactions. Culture as an influence was argued and Erikson's theory holds interest to those from a cross-cultural perspective. Erikson believed that every culture has its own approach and solutions to each life stage an individual passes through; further, Erikson proposed that psychoanalytic theory needed to acknowledge cultural factors as influencing personality development. Erikson's theory, one could argue, sowed the early seeds of the ecological or 'person in environment' approach, as he theorised that people pass through a cog-like system of cycles across their life span contained within a community of lifecycles.

CRITICISMS OF ERIKSON'S PSYCHOSOCIAL THEORY

According to Miller (2002, p. 160), several criticisms of Erikson's psychosocial theory have been voiced, a lack of systematicity being one, which suggests that Erikson's theory is a loose connection of observations, empirical generalisations and abstract theoretical claims. Consequently, it is difficult to state his claims in a way that can be tested or relate his empirical findings to the more abstract levels of the theory. A further criticism is the lack of specific mechanisms of development, Erikson did not explain in any detail how an individual moves from stage to stage or even how he resolves the crisis within a stage. He states what influences the movement (for example, physical maturation, parents, cultural beliefs or the extent to which earlier crises were resolved) but not specifically how the movement comes about. By what mechanisms does an infant learn to trust and when to mistrust? Identity formation in adolescence has been singled out for criticism, as Erikson does not fully resolve in his writings the issue of gender identity development. He suggested that gender identity formation was based on biological-reproductive potential, a position challenged by Gilligan, as we will see in Chapter 5.

ERIKSON'S RELEVANCE TO SOCIAL WORK

Erikson believed that others held a pivotal role in supporting personality development, including teachers, therapists and so on. Though the acquisition of trust is the key task of the first stage, Erikson recognised that as we pass through the life span people would continue to grapple with issues of wariness and uncertainty; thus 'others', including social workers, can offer individuals new opportunities to enable and support individuals to resolve trust issues. Social workers, when taking an individual's history, can use Erikson's framework as a guide; for example, Erikson theorised that those who had not successfully traversed the first stage of 'trust vs mistrust' were likely to exhibit depression and social withdrawal later in life. In using Erikson's stages one might uncover issues of 'mistrust' from the early years in an adult experiencing depression and social withdrawal; further, Erikson argued that such stages can be resolved at a later time with support.

THINK ABOUT IT!

How does the role of social worker fit within Erikson's theory? Consider the influence social workers can have directly on an individual and on a wider level on societal and cultural structures and beliefs.

The final theory we are going to examine under the rubric of socioemotional development theories is attachment, first conceptualised by John Bowlby and developed further by Mary Ainsworth. Again it is another psychodynamic theory and Bowlby was influenced by the work of Freud, as we will see. I would argue that knowledge of attachment is fundamental; it continues to hold a central place within our understanding of socioemotional development.

Attachment theory

Attachment is a 'long-enduring, emotionally meaningful tie to a particular individual' (Schaffer, 1996). It is recognised as one of the most important concepts within psychology and as such has been heavily researched. Our ability to form secure and meaningful relationships not just to our parents or caregivers but also to others later in life is considered a touchstone for healthy and happy functioning. Difficulties in this realm can have immediate and long-term consequences for the individual.

DEVELOPMENT OF ATTACHMENT THEORY

We will look at the following topics in relation to attachment theory:

1. Influences on attachment theory
    - ethology
    - psychoanalysis
2. John Bowlby and maternal deprivation
3. Mary Ainsworth and attachment classifications.

Ethology Ethology is the study of animal behaviour. Psychologists look to this area to gain insight into human behaviours.

Imprinting was coined by Konrad Lorenz to describe behaviour he observed in geese. When hatched they automatically 'attach' to the first moving object they encounter. Lorenz found that newly hatched geese attached to him even though he was not one of their species. Thus Lorenz believed that 'imprinting' was instinctual and could not be reversed. Another researcher who tested how animals develop bonds and attachment was Harry Harlow.

Harry Harlow studied the effects of maternal deprivation in rhesus monkeys. This research involved removing newborn monkeys from their mothers and raising them in isolation without contact from others. The baby monkeys had access to two 'mothers' in their cage: one was made of wire mesh and had a bottle attached so the monkey could feed from it. The other was a 'cloth' figure covered in soft, tactile material but offered no opportunity for the monkey to feed. Harlow noted that when the baby monkeys were given the choice between a wire mesh figure with a feeding bottle or figure covered in soft material, the monkeys chose to cling to the soft material rather than the other figure. Previously, it was believed that the motivation for mammals to attach to a parent was for the purpose of feeding. However, Harlow's study indicated that monkeys sought 'comfort contact' and that social factors were as, if not more, important than feeding. Interestingly, when the monkeys were re-introduced to the troupe they were frightened, exhibited anxious behaviours and had difficulty socialising with other monkeys. This suggested that their early experiences created difficulties for them later in their social relationships with others.

Psychoanalysis *Mother–child relationship*: Freud stressed the importance of the mother–child relationship. Further, many others working in psychoanalysis believed that early experiences could affect a person in later life.

Object relations: A famous psychoanalyst, Melanie Klein, developed the 'object relations' approach, which suggested that the 'loss' of an object could have a potentially negative effect (for example, to an infant an 'object' could be their mother; the loss of the mother perhaps through death or separation could in turn lead to negative outcomes for the child in later life).

2. John Bowlby and maternal deprivation

John Bowlby (1907–1990) originally devised the basic tenets of the theory of maternal deprivation. Bowlby was working in a home for children with behavioural problems. These children had disruptive relationships with their families and it struck Bowlby that these difficulties might hold the key to their emotional and behavioural disturbances. His time there prompted him to train as a child psychiatrist, and he received training at the British Psychoanalytical Society (BPS). While there, Bowlby was supervised by a prominent psychoanalyst, Melanie Klein. Bowlby agreed with Klein's view that early experiences shaped an individual in later life. He also supported Klein's 'object relations' approach and the potentially negative effect of the loss of an 'object'. However, unlike Klein, Bowlby believed that *actual* family experiences were important and possibly the cause of emotional problems experienced by the children. Bowlby also came to believe that relationship problems between parent and child continued to be passed down through the generations; thus, in order to help the child, a practitioner should look at and help the parent.

Bowlby was heavily influenced by the work of ethologists such as Konrad Lorenz and Harry Harlow (see above); this led Bowlby to believe that there was an instinctual aspect to the development of a bond between mother and child, and that there was a 'critical' period for its development. Further, Harlow's research suggested that feeding alone, or the satisfaction of hunger, was not necessarily the primary motivation for bonding, and that more social needs were at play. You will see how these beliefs came to shape Bowlby's attachment theory.

Bowlby's theory of maternal deprivation Bowlby came to believe that if a child experienced a disruption in their relationship with their mother (through separation or death), this had a negative impact on the child. Bowlby believed that there was one fundamental attachment relationship and that was between mother and child; this is termed *monotropism*. Further, he believed that a critical period existed between 6 months and 3 years where attachment must be maintained. In Chapter 5, the concept of maternal deprivation is examined in greater depth.

Mary Ainsworth Mary Ainsworth joined Bowlby's research team; whereas Bowlby formulated ideas surrounding the nature of the attachment relationship, Ainsworth developed a way of actually testing attachment. Ainsworth conducted a huge number of 'naturalistic' observations in Uganda and in America observing the behaviour of mothers and their infants. From these observations she developed a way of testing the quality of the attachment relationship through the 'strange situation'. In the 'strange situation' a mother and her child are placed in a room where their behaviour can be observed. The child should use the mother as a secure 'base' from which to explore. During the experiment a 'stranger' will enter the room twice; once when the mother is present and a second time when the child has been left alone. The baby's reaction to the return of the mother is used to gauge what attachment pattern exists.

The reactions of the infants in this research formed the basis for the classification of attachment styles.

ATTACHMENT CLASSIFICATIONS

Type A – insecure/avoidant

Babies exhibited an avoidance of interactions with the mother on her return. The baby either completely ignores the mother or else displays avoidance behaviours such as turning away or avoiding eye contact. During separation the baby does not display distress or else the distress seems to be related to being left alone rather than the mother's absence.

Type B – secure

Babies classified as securely attached actively seek interaction and contact with the mother, especially during the reunion episode. If the baby shows distress during the separation episode, this is judged to be solely related to the absence of the mother.

Type C – ambivalent/resistant

These babies were extremely upset when the mother left. On reunion with the mother the baby seemed to want to be near her yet 'resisted' her efforts to comfort them. If the mother picked them up, they displayed a great deal of angry behaviours and tried to struggle free.

A fourth classification was added later:

Type D – disorganised

This category relates to babies who displayed 'disorganised' or disoriented patterns of behaviour that could not be classified under the other categories.

Of all the four types of attachment patterns, disorganised attachment appears to be predictive of psychopathology in later life which we will explore in the next chapter.

Internal working model Bowlby believed that the child represents its relationship with its mother internally. It is thought that this model serves as a sort of template for future relationships. According to Smith et al. (2003, p. 98), internal working models are 'described as cognitive structures embodying the memories of day-to-day interactions with the attachment figure. They may be 'schemas' or 'event scripts' that guide the child's interactions and the expectations and affective experiences associated with them'.

Cross-cultural perspective on attachment

'Research using the Strange Situation paradigm in various countries seems to show marked differences in distributions of attachment classifications across cultures... in Germany...Japan...and in Israeli kibbutzim...were seen to deviate strongly from the American distribution...' Van Ijzendoorn and Kroonenberg (1988) continue that a high percentage of Type A (avoidant) classifications were found in Germany, while in Israel and Japan there was a large percentage of Type C (resistant/ambivalent). What could account for these deviations from what was considered the standard or norm? Cultural parenting practices. In an Israeli kibbutz, for example, it is typical for young children to be cared for in a communal setting. In Japan, where the concept of amae (indulgent dependency) exists within family relationships, particularly in the mother–child dyad, young children were extremely upset by the Strange Situation as they were unused to being without their mother. These examples raise the question of the appropriateness of the Strange Situation as a determinant of attachment.

THINK ABOUT IT!

From your personal and professional perspective consider types of parenting practices and cultural concepts that may not fit within 'typical' Eurocentric perspectives. What cultural parenting practices may impact on your practice?

WHY IS ATTACHMENT SO IMPORTANT? RAMIFICATIONS OF DISORGANISED ATTACHMENT

We will consider attachment in childhood and adulthood in the next chapter; however, it is opportune to highlight why attachment is a concern to psychologists and social workers. Attachment as we have seen, involves the formation of our first and central relationship with another (our caregiver). Difficulties in the formation and maintenance of this relationship not only affect the parent–child interaction in the short term but have consequences for the formation of relationships and relationship patterns in later life, from romantic to parenting relationships. Disorganised attachment (DA) was added later in response to children who did not fit the existing three categories developed by Ainsworth. In Chapter 9 on abuse and trauma, disorganised attachment is discussed in greater detail along with its use as a tool for assessing child maltreatment. Here we are going to outline some effects (Wilkins, 2012, p. 19) associated with disorganised attachment to highlight not just its centrality in developing health relationship and sense of self, but also its association to adverse outcomes as we will see; 'Although even the recent edition of the London Child Protection Procedures makes reference to the need for carers to ensure children are able to develop and maintain secure attachments, it would perhaps be more accurate (and realistic) to say that children need to be able to develop organised attachments (secure or insecure). This is because although the secure pattern is quite clearly associated with more positive outcomes for children, neither of the insecure patterns should be considered pathological. In contrast, DA is associated with higher levels (or an increased risk) of dissociative behaviour, controlling, externalising or aggressive behaviour, conduct and attention disorders and borderline personality disorder. DA in children is also a good predictor of hostile behaviour in school settings and children with DA are more likely to present with somatic symptoms of ill-health, social phobia and school phobia.'

Traditionally, attachment followed the binary of positive attachment (secure) or negative forms. Wilkins highlights that there is a greater complexity behind attachment behaviours than this simplistic dichotomy by introducing the importance of consistency. Regardless, attachment is central to outcomes and the following behaviours can help promote attachment.

BEHAVIOURS THAT PROMOTE ATTACHMENT

Bowlby believed 'parental sensitivity' was important for the development of attachment. Ainsworth et al. (1978, p. 152) found that four scales were strongly linked to secure attachment:

- sensitivity
- acceptance
- cooperation
- accessibility.

Just as certain behaviours can promote attachment, others can damage it or are more likely to elicit an insecure attachment pattern. Radke-Yarrow et al. (1985) examined patterns of attachment in 2 and 3 year old children of depressed and 'normal' mothers. They found that the children of mothers with major depression were more likely to have an insecure attachment pattern (type A and C). So how would you observe such interactions and what behaviour indicates attachment?

So how would we observe attachment behaviours?

Herbert (2006, p. 69) suggests we consider if the parent does the following:

- Initiates positive interactions with the infant?
- Responds to the infant's vocalisations?
- Changes voice tone when talking to the infant?
- Shows interest in face-to-face contact with the infant?
- Shows the ability to console or comfort the infant?
- Enjoys close physical contact with the infant?
- Responds to the infant's indications of distress?
- Responds promptly to the infant's needs?
- Responds consistently?
- Interacts smoothly and sensitively with the infant?

Daniel et al. (2010, p. 34) suggest the following activity:

Observe the interaction between a parent or significant carer and a child of any age.

1. Describe the child's initiatives towards the adult and the child's responses to the adult's initiatives.
2. Describe the adult's initiatives towards the child and the adult's responses to the child's signals.
3. What might this tell you about the degree to which the child has learned to rely on the attachment figure?

In the next chapter, attachment is further discussed using the biopsychosocial model as a guide, and assessment of sibling interactions is outlined.

STRENGTHS OF ATTACHMENT THEORY

One clear example of the strength of attachment theory is its longevity; while aspects of it have been reevaluated or discredited, as we will see, it remains dominant in theorising the development of early relationships. Further, it contributes to our understanding of the impact of early experiences later in life; early attachment patterns have been linked to the choices we make in partners in adult life and the attachment patterns we transit through our parenting to the next generation. As attachment theory has evolved, a greater understanding has been gained into the role others (e.g. siblings and grandparents) can play in a child's attachment acquisition. While some theories do not have a clear practice implication, attachment theory continues to be influential as a practice theory.

CRITICISMS OF ATTACHMENT THEORY

Clearly attachment can be critiqued from a cross-cultural perspective, as mentioned earlier. Aspects of the early theory focussed on the mother–child relationship, known as monotropism. However, research indicates that infants form several important attachment relationships with figures other than their mother (such as father, grandparents and siblings). Feminist psychologists have attacked Bowlby's insistence that the mother must remain at home with the child to prevent the child's suffering in her absence. There have been suggestions that Bowlby's research coincided with the return home of male soldiers after World War II and the desire of the government to encourage women to give up their jobs to the returning soldiers. By suggesting that children were being damaged by their mother's absence, it was envisaged that women would not wish to work outside the home. Finally, in terms of the relationship between insecure attachment patterns and negative outcomes, Bowlby emphasised that if a child experienced difficulties in their attachment relationship, this could have disastrous outcomes in later life. Michael Rutter has rejected this bleak view. Rutter has pointed out that all children experience separation at some point (for example, going to school) and that we need to differentiate between different situations.

Recommended viewing – Child of Rage

The following is a link to a documentary, *'Child of Rage'*, which examined a severe form of attachment difficulty in a young girl who had been abused by her father. While it makes for disturbing viewing it is nonetheless recommended to give an insight into attachment disorders. www.youtube.com/watch?v=g2-Re_Fl_L4

So we leave the socioemotional theorists and now explore another domain of development, cognitive.

COGNITIVE THEORISTS

Cognitive development refers to the changes that occur in thinking, memory, problem solving and other cognitive mental abilities, including language. It is important to understand that children 'think' differently to adults and as practitioners we need to have a knowledge base of these differences to ensure we can support children effectively. One of the most famous and important theorists in the field of cognitive development is Jean Piaget, and his work is still influential in areas of psychology and child development.

Jean Piaget (1896–1980)

Jean Piaget developed a four-stage theory to explain how young children acquire knowledge, based on a mass of empirical work, including the study of his own children. Piaget recognised that children's thinking was qualitatively different to adults and at different ages they were likely to make the same 'errors', he concluded that children must successfully negotiate one stage before proceeding to the next. So let's take a look at his theory, starting with his early life.

EARLY YEARS

Jean Piaget was born in Switzerland in 1896. After completing his Ph.D. he developed an interest in psychoanalysis and travelled to France to work in a boys' institution, which had been founded by Alfred Binet. Binet is best known for his work in developing intelligence tests, and Piaget worked on standardising these tests. It was through this work that Piaget came to the conclusion that young children think differently to adults. He noticed that many of the children were giving the same 'wrong' answer. Piaget began to understand that the children handle information differently to adults; as the child became older, their thinking continued to develop and change.

This work and these observations prompted him to develop a theory of cognitive development. Piaget's theory is a 'stage theory', meaning that the individual must pass through one stage before they can progress to the next. Piaget suggested that children pass through four stages of cognitive development spanning the period from infancy to adolescence. Interestingly, Piaget was a forerunner of 'naturalistic observation'. This approach to collecting data relies on observing individuals in their natural environment, rather than in a laboratory. Piaget and his wife, Valentine, observed their three children from infancy and kept detailed journals noting their intellectual development.

Piaget can be daunting to understand, especially his terminology, but don't let that discourage you. Piaget tries to outline how he believes children organise the information that they receive in their daily lives. It is helpful to understand how Piaget believed learning occurs. He used the term 'schemas' to describe 'internal frameworks' that the mind builds as it comes in contact with more and more information.

> A schema is an internal framework that organises incoming information, thought and action.

The mind builds these structures to hold and make sense of incoming information. As the infant gathers more and more information, the schemas become more sophisticated. Piaget believed that in order for learning to occur, a child must experience a sense of 'disequilibration'. This is when an experience occurs that does not fit their existing thinking: the child becomes dissatisfied with their original thinking and must adapt in order to process the new piece of information. This adaptation can be done in two ways: through assimilation or accommodation.

Assimilation is when the child fits incoming information or experience into an existing schema. For example, a young child who sees a fox for the first time might call it a 'doggie'. Here the child is trying to make sense of this new experience by applying an existing 'doggie' schema to the fox, which has four legs and a tail. This makes sense, as a dog also has four legs and a tail. Yet as we get older we come to understand that a fox and a dog are not the same and this might cause us to change our schema. This process is called **accommodation**. Accommodation is when an existing schema changes to incorporate new experiences.

SENSORIMOTOR STAGE (0–2 YEARS)

The baby acquires knowledge about the world through movement and sensory information. The baby:

- learns to differentiate itself from its environment
- develops first schemas
- achieves object permanence
- experiences the emergence of symbolic thought
- develops the capacity to form internal mental representations.

'Sensori' represents the senses or sensation, such as taste, touch, smell, vision and hearing. 'Motor' is another term for movement. Thus the title gives us a clue as to how learning is accumulated during this period: through the senses and movement. During the sensorimotor period the child begins to know about the world they live in by acting directly upon it, through actions and sensory information. Have you ever noticed how young babies are forever putting things in their mouth? This is because they are using their senses to explore the new world they inhabit. Also, as infants begin to crawl, they usually head straight for the kitchen presses, much to the consternation of parents; again this reflects the child's attempts to use their new-found motor ability to explore their environment. The infant is hungry for new experiences and information that will form the basis of their developing schemas. By the end of this stage, infants will have acquired **'object permanence'**. This is a very important concept and represents the understanding that objects continue to exist even when we can no longer see them. A simple test for object permanence is to allow the child to see a toy and then throw a blanket over it. If the child seeks the toy out it is an indication that they understand that the toy continues to exist even when they cannot see it. This ability comes towards the end of this stage. However, as you will see below, recent research has been critical of Piaget's assertion of the stage at which object permanence and, more particularly, mental representation occur. It is now claimed that these are acquired at an earlier age than Piaget suggested. During the sensorimotor stage infants begin to differentiate themselves from the environment.

We are going to overview and critique one of Piaget's fundamental concepts within his theory of cognitive development, mental representation.

Mental representation

Mental representations are cognitive representations of the world and include images, concepts and ideas. They form the basis for problem solving and thinking. Piaget believed that infants did not acquire mental representation until the end of the first stage of development, the sensori-motor period, which occurred between 12 and 18 months.

Piaget proposed that evidence of object permanence, trial and error performance and deferred imitation confirmed that mental representation had been achieved. Object permanence relates to younger children's inability to recognise that an object still exists even when they can no longer see it. Piaget saw this as evidence that children did not have mental representation of the object. He conducted research where he would hide an object under a cloth: if the child had formed an internal representation of the object, then the child would recover the object. Piaget asserted that it was not until the final substage, when the infant recognised that the object still existed, though out of sight, and recovered it, that mental representation had been achieved, as the infant must have retained a memory and concept of the object.

Recent research has been critical of Piaget's account of mental representation, in particular the timing of it. Piaget posits that mental representation does not occur until the end of the sensori-motor stage, but recent research seems to suggest that Piaget underestimated the ability, and thus the age, that infants can acquire mental representation. His theory suggests that the infant goes from not having mental representation to acquiring it in a step-to-step process which does not occur in earlier substages. A stronger hypothesis is that the acquisition of mental representation is a gradual and consistent acquisition from birth. Research suggests that younger infants have demonstrated representation; researchers have proposed that babies of 6 weeks old have limited mental representation (Meltzoff and Moore, 1988). This adds strength to a theory that views the acquisition of mental representation as a gradual and cumulative process resulting in total achievement. Piaget observed the infant's reaching for an object in his empirical work as evidence of mental representation, but this reaching involved motor skills, which may have been absent or immature in the younger infants, possibly explaining the apparent absence of mental representation. For example, an experiment used to test if a child had acquired mental representation involves hiding a teddy bear under a blanket once the child has seen it. The idea is that if a child has achieved mental representation it will know that the teddy bear continues to exist (under the blanket) even though they cannot see it. If the child retrieves the teddy from under the blanket this is taken to demonstrate that the child has mental representation. However, there is one difficulty with this experiment and very young children; perhaps they do know the teddy bear is under the blanket but have not yet got the physical or motor ability to move and remove the blanket to retrieve the teddy bear. This is a good example of why when we read findings or theories we need to look at them with a critical eye.

PREOPERATIONAL STAGE (2–7 YEARS)

Symbolic thinking emerges as the child uses symbols/images to represent objects and solve problems. The child:

- begins to understand classification of objects
- is egocentric
- focuses on just one aspect of a task

- believes inanimate objects have consciousness (animism)
- engages in pretend play.

One of the most notable features of this stage is that the child is egocentric. Breaking the word up gives a clue as to its meaning: 'ego' can mean 'self' and 'centric' refers to the centre of things. So 'egocentric' seems to mean self-centred. However, when used in this context, we are referring to the fact that the child thinks that everyone else sees the world through the child's eyes and does not understand that other people might see or think about things differently, and this is reflected in the child's thinking.

Symbolic thinking develops as the child begins to acquire language (which is, of course, made up of symbols). The child can use this newly developed ability to enhance their thinking. The child can now use words and images (symbols) to represent objects; for example, when a toddler sees a dog they might exclaim 'woof woof'. The child uses that sound to represent a dog. Pretend play is also enabled by symbolic thinking; for example, a stick is transformed into a sword. An interesting aspect of this stage is animism. For example, a parent may admonish a 'bold' table that a young child has just painfully collided with: children at this age ascribe consciousness to inanimate objects.

Implications for practice

In terms of reasoning and planning, children under the age of seven work from direct experiences of what they have actually experienced and through their senses; they remain tied to 'concrete experiences (as you will see, Piaget's next stage 'concrete operation' from 7 to 11 years suggests the same but it is not as rigid as with younger children and research has demonstrated that children have more sophisticated abilities at an earlier age than Piaget theorised). According to Daniel et al. (2010, p. 180),

> if children's thought processes seem bizarre or unusual it may be helpful to try and see the world from their own viewpoint and work out what their logic is. If we apply this to for example, concepts of family relationships, many of the young people encountered in practice are part of reconstituted families and may have half and step-siblings. Understanding these relationships may be even harder for children if they are not living at home. To help children understand where they fit in a family network it could be helpful to draw simple family diagrams or use dolls. They could also be encouraged to play with the concepts by making up other families and working out the relationships.

CASE STUDY

Charlie is 6 years old and has to go into hospital for an operation. His foster mum has asked you to discuss this impending event with Charlie, who has been displaying anxiety regarding it. Keeping in mind what you have learned from Piaget's theory, how would you approach this and what would you need to bear in mind about Charlie's ability to understand?

Consider

Perhaps consider that if Charlie has had no direct experience of hospital, then it is hard for him to make sense of it: the same for an operation. Charlie might be relating an action on his part (being bold) to a belief about why people go to hospital or have operations (as a punishment).

In supporting Charlie you need to make the ideas as 'real' as possible; if you can't take him to the hospital beforehand to have a look around, then a book with pictures would be helpful. Use play for Charlie to work through this new experience or help him to create a storybook around this topic. Ask Charlie about his beliefs about hospital and operations, and why he is having one, to gauge his thinking and see the world from his perspective.

What other aspects might a child struggle with? The death of a loved one, being removed from their parent or moving from foster care to adoption. Think about the implications of Piaget's thinking and how you would support a young child through these scenarios.

CONCRETE OPERATIONAL STAGE (7–11 YEARS)

This is the third stage described in Piaget's theory of cognitive development. The main features of this stage are:

- conservation: the understanding that quantity, volume and length remain the same
- the child becomes less egocentric, taking more easily the perspectives of others (decentring)
- reversibility: the understanding that numbers or objects can be altered and then returned to their original state
- the child can classify and order, as well as organise objects into series
- the child is still tied to the immediate experience but within these limitations can perform logical mental operations.

Children learn through their interaction with concrete or 'real' objects. Further, a child can apply the learning strategies they have developed to real and immediate situations. However, the process of **'decentring'**, where the child becomes less egocentric, enables them to become more flexible in their thinking, as they are now able to factor in other ways of looking or thinking about a situation. Another ability a child develops during this stage is to understand **reversibility**. This concept is best explained with an example: you have a ball of dough and you roll it into a long, cylindrical, snake-like object. Can you return it to its original state, and would it still be the same? Of course it would; we know this because we have embraced the concept of reversibility, which is the understanding that we can alter an object and then reverse the process, returning the object to its original state. Reversibility is necessary for the acquisition of the next concept, **conservation**. Have you ever had to deal with warring children complaining that one is getting more juice than another? You try to explain to them that even though the juice is in differently shaped glasses they still have the exact same amount of liquid in each, although it might not look like it. If they don't believe you, it is probably because they have not yet understood the concept of conservation. As adults we can factor in the shape and size of the glass and understand that the amount of liquid is the same in both glasses. During the concrete operational stage children begin to acquire this ability and apply it to number and weight as well as volume, as shown below. Piaget believed that the acquisition of conservation was an important developmental milestone.

PIAGET'S CONSERVATION STUDIES

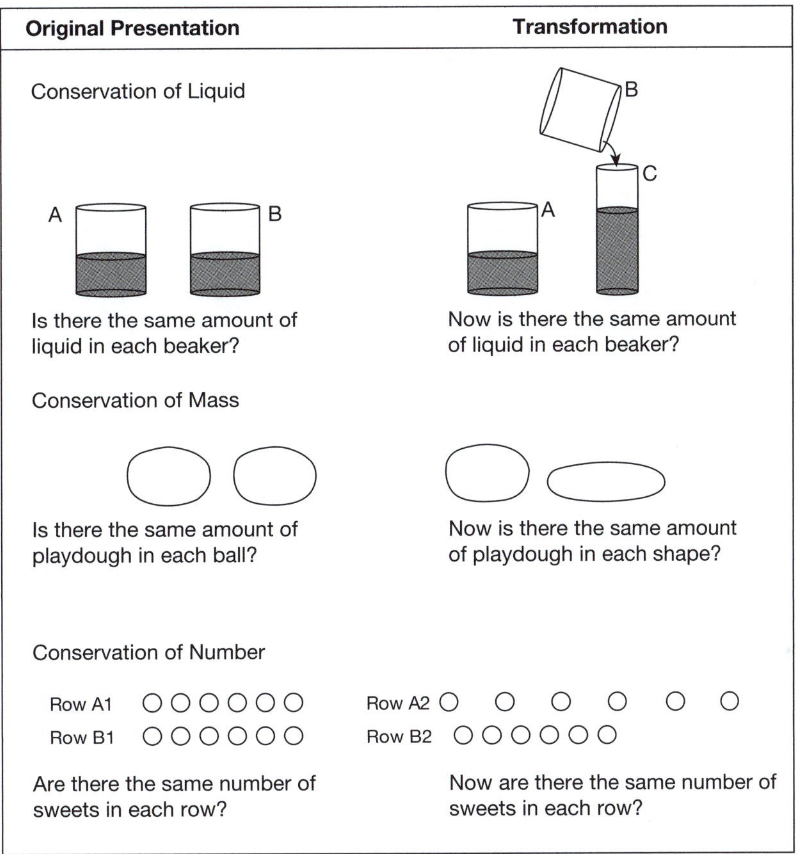

Figure 4.1 Piaget's conservation studies
Source: Hayes (2010)

According to Smith et al. (2003), conservation is achieved at the following ages:

- Conservation of number: about 5–6 years of age
- Conservation of weight: 7 or 8 years of age
- Conservation of volume: between 10 and 11 years of age.

An important aspect of this stage is that children become less **egocentric;** egocentrism is the belief that everyone else sees the world through their eyes, children do not understand that other people might see or think about things differently, and this is reflected in their thinking. Piaget suggested that egocentric thinking is based upon the child's view that the world is 'centred' on her. An example of this is where a child, when asked how the moon moves, believe it 'follows' them. Children who are egocentric struggle to decentre, as can be seen in the following dialogue (Smith et al, 2003, p. 399):

Adult: Have you any brothers or sister?
John: Yes, a brother
Adult: What is his name?
John: Sammy
Adult: Does Sammy have a brother?
John: No

THINK ABOUT IT!

In becoming less egocentric children are better able to consider other viewpoints. What implications might this have for social work practice?

FORMAL OPERATIONAL (12 YEARS ONWARDS)

The main characteristics of this stage:

- Abstract thinking marks this period as the individual is now able to manipulate ideas in their head.
- Inductive and deductive reasoning emerges, enabling the formulation and testing of hypotheses.

This final stage is marked by the acquisition of abstract thinking, as the individual is now able to manipulate ideas in their head. Piaget argues that up to this stage the child can only think about things that are 'real' or concrete. According to Piaget, they are unable to reason about make-believe problems or situations. They can now begin to think more logically and can consider hypotheses or explanations. Inductive and deductive reasoning emerge during this stage, enabling further formulation and testing of hypotheses. **Inductive reasoning** takes a direct experience and moves to develop a more general principle, Lindon (2001) offers some examples:

- A bad experience with a neighbour's dog leads a child to be very wary of any other dogs. She has generalised from direct experience to a wider principle that dogs jump up, bark and are not safe
- Experience of familiar people – family and teachers – leads to general theories of how a given person, or kind of person is likely to react

Deductive reasoning is seen from age 12 onwards and is the reverse of inductive. It takes a general principle and uses it to predict or apply it to a particular event. It's an 'if…then' scenario, and examples (ibid) include:

- If school rules are absolute and apply to everyone, then everyone, including teachers, should follow the rules
- If this is the way in which people react to stress, then I would predict that certain results would follow if these individuals are in a frightening situation.

Of course, there are difficulties with both types of reasoning: the latter can be too rigid, applied to human behaviour that can be unpredictable. Inductive reasoning can also be problematic if one experience is taken and then generalised out.

THINK ABOUT IT!

From a practice perspective, how might using inductive reasoning affect a child's thinking and behaviour in the following scenario:

> Ava is 11, and it has been recently discovered that she has been sexually abused by her teacher for the last 6 months. As a result of a police investigation the teacher has been jailed; however, Ava is refusing to return to school, including a transfer to a new school.

The formal operational stage completes cognitive development according to Piaget; those who have developed his ideas (neo-Piagetians) have included 'post-formal' thought, acknowledging that thinking continues to evolve after adolescence rather than remains static as posited by Piaget. On reaching the formal operational stage adolescents are freed from the binds of the 'concrete' world and are now able to engage in 'abstract thinking'; concepts such as 'justice', which is abstract on many levels, can now be discussed. This stage corresponds to the young person entering secondary school, where algebra, which is entirely 'abstract', is introduced to them. In history, for example, rather than knowledge based on the recollection of dates and events, teens are now asked to analyse and critique these events. These are all higher reasoning activities and are not possible without the more sophisticated logic and problem-solving seen in adolescence.

From a practice perspective this allows a greater engagement with the teen, who can now perspective-take and problem solve. This jump in thinking ability mirrors a growth spurt in the brain, which completes with the frontal lobes in late teens/early twenties, the frontal lobes being the seat of higher reasoning, as we saw in an earlier chapter.

Piaget also did not devote much attention to the role of social learning or that an infant's acquisition of knowledge and abilities could be enhanced by external factors. Piaget's biological background is reflected in his findings and the rigid developmental stages he proposed. Neither did he have the more sophisticated tools of analysis and testing that we have now, such as the ability to track eye movements and physiological changes to unravel the mysteries of knowledge acquisition. Nonetheless, Piaget's theory endures, as it does present a strong overall base and view of the development of children's thinking, although as with all theories it is subject to modification in light of new findings.

STRENGTHS OF PIAGET'S COGNITIVE THEORY

Piaget offered the most comprehensive framework for understanding the development of children's thinking. He identified that children think differently than adults and that, qualitatively, this thinking shifts and changes. While we have already encountered some of the criticisms levelled at his theory and will in a moment consider others, this should not give the impression that Piaget's theory is redundant. His theory is used across many disciplines including education and social work. Perhaps its core strength lies in drawing our attention to the fact that children's thinking is different and we must ensure we factor this is into our practice.

CRITICISMS OF PIAGET'S COGNITIVE THEORY

In addition to criticism of Piaget's underestimation of children's abilities, Miller (2002, p. 77) reflects that further criticism of his theory includes that there is inadequate support for the stage notion. The strongest attacks on Piaget's theory concern his notion of stages which lies at the heart of his theory. Are there, in fact, broad stretches during development whose characteristics apply to all the psychological events during the period? Or does the notion of stages simply confuse and mislead by oversimplifying development and claiming more coherence among concepts than there actually is? A basic issue here is how stages are related to the child's actual intellectual functioning. Another criticism levelled is the 'slighting of social and emotional aspects of development'. Piaget paid relatively little attention to the social and emotional realms in his theoretical or research activities. Moreover, he underestimated the role of sociohistorical influences. It has been said that the child in Piaget's conceptualisation has no social class, sex, nationality, culture or personality.

Lev Vygotsky's (1896–1934) socio-cultural theory

> 'Through others we become ourselves' (Vygotsky, 1978).

This quote captures the essence of Vygotsky's conceptualisation of human development. Miller (2002, p. 368) adds, 'in the Vygotskian-socio-cultural view, humans are embedded in a socio-cultural matrix and human behaviour cannot be understood independently of this ever present matrix'. This approach emphasises the importance of the role of culture in the cognitive development of children.

SOCIO-CULTURAL THEORY

Vygotsky was born in Russia in the same year as Piaget, yet it is only in recent years that his writings have come to the attention of the West. Vygotsky died at a young age and in the years preceding his death he had been under pressure from the government to modify his beliefs and teaching in line with the current orthodoxy. After his death his theories and ideas were repudiated by the Russian government and it is only because his students kept his work alive that we, in the West, have come to know his work. Vygotsky was a cognitive theorist, yet he is sometimes described as a socio-cultural theorist. This is because Vygotsky emphasised the role of others in the development of learning; specifically he acknowledged the influence that social interactions and language, embedded within a cultural context, have on cognitive development. Unlike Piaget, Vygotsky believed that social interactions were particularly influential on cognitive development, as was their wider society, and it is this emphasis that has led to his being described as a socio-cultural theorist.

According to Fox and Riconscente (2008, p. 383):

> Vygotsky views human psychological development as historically situated and culturally determined. As human beings we are born already immersed in an evolved society that uses conventional tools and signs. Development proceeds through the internalization of social interactions, with the fundamental social interaction being interaction through language...The activity of language use is for Vygotsky essentially what it means for thought to be conscious, capable of self-direction, and capable of knowing itself in a systematic way.

MAIN POINTS OF VYGOTSKY'S THEORY

- children learn from others (including other children)
- play is important in the development of learning
- language plays a central role in mental development
- language and development build on each other
- development cannot be separated from its social context.

IMPORTANCE OF PLAY

Like Piaget, Vygotsky emphasised the importance of play. Piaget emphasised the child as a solitary learner, in that when children play they discover new ideas for themselves. Vygotsky, on the other hand, believed that children learn through their interactions with others, who introduce them to new concepts and ideas.

ZONE OF PROXIMAL DEVELOPMENT

The zone of proximal development (ZPD) is '... the distance between the actual developmental level as determined by independent problem solving and the level of potential development as determined through problem solving under adult guidance or in collaboration with more capable peers' (Vygotsky, 1978, p. 86).

The zone of proximal development represents the distance between what the child can actually achieve on their own and what they could achieve with the intervention or help of another. Vygotsky was interested in the role others could play as a 'scaffold', building a bridge to help the child reach their full potential development. For example, as an adult I started going to Irish classes as I was not as fluent in Irish as I wished to be. My tutor ('other') observed the level of Irish I did have and recognised what I could achieve with her help and so she devised a learning plan to enable me to reach my potential. The trick for the tutor was to make sure that it was challenging enough while ensuring it was not so far out of my ability that I could not do it, even with her help. As we've seen, Vygotsky felt that it was through interaction with others that children learn. This applies to an adult trying to brush up on their Irish as much as to a young child learning to tie their shoelaces.

THINK ABOUT IT!

From a practice perspective, how does the role of the social worker fit within Vygotsky's Zone of Proximal Development? Reflect on your role in supporting a child. How does this support manifest itself? Note the different activities and occasions where you have acted as 'other' within a child ZPD and note it in your reflective journal. What other professionals can also be involved in supporting a child's ZPD. Can these be positive and/or negative influences?

RELATIONSHIP BETWEEN LANGUAGE AND THOUGHT

Vygotsky believed that language represents an opportunity for social interaction and learning. Further, this shared experience that language brings is necessary for the development of cognitive ability. When children begin to talk, it opens a window into their minds and we can begin to understand their thought processes.

CULTURAL CONTEXT

It is through the child's interaction with others that they learn the culture they are part of, including language and belief systems. Vygotsky's rejection of Freud is described because of the latter's continued embrace of physiological and universal explanations of behaviour instead of the cultural one that Vygotsky believed to be the best way of explaining behaviour. He also rejected the Piagetian approach that assumed social relations to be secondary to the child's biological nature. Vygotsky, on the other hand, viewed speech to be initially social, with egocentric speech developing after social speech. The strength of Vygotsky's conceptualisations lies in his emphasis on the socio-cultural context of development. Miller highlights the uniqueness, from a developmental perspective, of Vygotsky's weaving together insights from history, linguistics, art and literature into psychology.

CRITICAL PSYCHOLOGY – A VYGOTSKIAN PERSPECTIVE

Holzman's (2011, p. 6) overview of mainstream psychology critique includes

> ...a group of psychologists critical of the epistemology (study of knowledge) of mainstream psychology are those within the socio-cultural and cultural-historical traditions, who draw their inspiration from...the writings of Vygotsky... Mainstream psychology relates to human beings not only as isolated from each other, but as isolated from culture and human history. But, those within the socio-cultural and cultural-historical traditions insist, what it means to develop, learn and live is to engage in human activity so as to become a member of a culture. Like for the social constructionists, human life is understood as a social-cultural historical phenomenon, with language playing a key role in how human beings come to understand and act upon the world.

Here, Vygotsky's theory is clearly aligned within the socio-cultural tradition, recognising the central role of culture in development.

THINK ABOUT IT!

Consider the many aspects of development affected by culture. For example, parenting practices, as we saw in attachment, are clearly influenced by cultural nuances. Identify and consider different ethnic approaches and how they may impact on language acquisition and development.

STRENGTHS OF VYGOTSKY'S THEORY

Vygotsky's approach marked a departure from the mainstream approach to developmental psychology, challenging its focus on individuals. Vygotsky placed an emphasis on the role of culture in shaping cognitive development, arguing the ZPD and the social interaction contained within it allowed for the transmission and sharing of society's cognitive goals and cultural artefacts. The ZPD offers a theoretical lens to view how a child is supported in his cognitive development with the support of a more learned other.

CRITICISMS OF VYGOTSKY'S THEORY

While the ZPD is a valuable theoretical framework, its vagueness is a criticism nonetheless. While ways of measuring Piagetian concepts, such as conservation, exist, the same does not exist for the ZPD. Knowing the width of children's zones does not provide an accurate picture of their learning ability, learning style or current level of development compared to other children of the same age, and degree of motivation. While Vygotsky emphasised the socio-cultural element in development, how this transmission actually works is unclear and needs to be developed further.

This brings us to the end of the section on developmental theorists. Hopefully, you have recognised the range and depth of knowledge that these theorists have attempted to explain. The common thread of these theorists is their emphasis on describing change over time. In the next section we explore behaviourism and learning. Unlike the developmental theorists, behaviourists focus on behaviour and the underlying mechanisms for it.

BEHAVIOURISM AND LEARNING

WHAT IS LEARNING?

Passeer (2001) said that 'Learning is a process by which experience produces a relatively enduring change in an organism's behaviour or capabilities'

Behaviourism is sometimes seen as the counter–point to the psychoanalytic or Freudian approach. As the name suggests, behaviourism is interested in the science of behaviour, while Freud and his followers believed that human behaviour was the result of unconscious urges and drives of the unconscious. Behaviourists rejected this viewpoint, taking instead a far more pragmatic stance, arguing that behaviour was observable and therefore measureable.

Further, the motivation behind these behaviours could be explained and shaped without delving into the 'unconscious'. The definition reflects an underlying precept of learning: the *concept of adaptation*. Ethologists when studying animal behaviour consider not only how the behaviour increases the chance of survival but also how the environment shapes and influences behaviour.

Changes in our behaviour, feeling or emotions allow us to:

- use past experience to predict the future
- adapt to a rapidly changing environment.

As can be seen in the earlier section on 'attachment', this idea that the environment influences an individual's learning and behaviour holds critical importance to the area of social work. It is argued that if we can understand how an individual learns behaviours, both positive and maladaptive, then potentially we have an opportunity to mould and support more 'adaptive' or 'positive' behaviours and also to eradicate or lessen maladaptive ones.

FOUNDERS OF BEHAVIOURISM

John B. Watson

Watson (1878–1958) is considered one of the founders of the behaviourist movement and is best known for his work on the acquisition of fear. Watson challenged the Freudian position that mental illness and phobias are the result of unconscious forces at work within the individual. Historically, psychology had been tied to the discipline of philosophy. Part of this approach included the use of 'introspection', of which Watson was critical, as emotions, feelings and the unconscious are not observable and therefore not measurable in any way. Watson favoured a more scientific approach to gain insight into the human condition. Initially he conducted experiments with animals, but he soon began working with humans. One of his best known experiments was his demonstration that conditioned emotional responses could be created.

'Little Albert' experiment

The experiment conducted by John B. Watson and Rosalie Raynor (1920) was based on the idea that they could instil a fear (conditioned emotional response) of a stimulus in an organism (Little Albert). In the experiment, Albert, who was about 9 months old, was first introduced to various items, including a white rat. Albert showed no fear of these items. At a later stage the researchers emitted a loud noise. Albert reacted by crying and was distressed. The researchers introduced the white rat to Albert who previously had shown no ill reaction to it, and as the child reached for the white rat the experimenters emitted the loud noise that had previously caused Albert to startle and cry. Albert reacted similarly again to the noise. This is the essence of the experiment; the twinning of the loud noise with a neutral stimulus (the white rat). Albert produced a fear response when the white rat was introduced to him, confirming that an emotional response can be conditioned. Further, when similar items to the white rat, such as a rabbit and a white furry mask were introduced to Albert, these items also provoked a fear response. This suggested that the fear response had been transferred or generalised to other stimuli that were similar to the initial stimulus that had conditioned the fear response. Watson and Raynor (1920, p. 14), rejecting the Freudian explanation for phobic behaviour, suggest that,

> It is probable that many of the phobias in psychopathology are true conditioned emotional reactions either of the direct or the transferred type. ... Emotional disturbances in adults cannot be traced back to sex alone. They must be retraced along at least three collateral lines – to conditioned and transferred responses set up in infancy and early youth.

EDWARD THORNDIKE

Thorndike was another important and influential figure in the behaviourist movement. Thorndike's work with animal behaviour and the learning process led him to believe that behavioural responses to particular stimuli are established through a process of 'trial and error' rather than insight. As the animals did not 'learn' quickly but took many attempts, that is, by 'trial and error', Thorndike did not believe their actions to reflect 'insight' but rather a learned behaviour. Of course, this suggestion was not just a challenge to the Freudian perspective but also to a more cognitive explanation for actions and behaviour. In his experiments, the animal eliminated responses that had failed to open a door and increasingly became more likely to perform actions that worked. This process is known as *instrumental learning*, as the behaviour of the organism is 'instrumental' in causing particular outcomes. Thorndike's *law of effect* states 'that in a given situation, a response followed by a satisfying consequence will become more likely to occur and a response followed by an annoying consequence will become less likely to occur' (Passer & Smith 2001, pp. 202–3). Fundamentally, Thorndike's work suggests that behaviour is a function of its consequences. The 'law of effect' was to prove influential in the development of Skinner's theory of operant conditioning.

Ivan Pavlov and classical conditioning

Pavlov's discovery of the principle of classical conditioning was, as is often the case in psychology, accidental. Pavlov was studying digestion in dogs when he noticed that the dogs began to salivate upon hearing the footsteps of the researcher bringing their food. This observation set Pavlov on a new path of exploration. Pavlov was to demonstrate learning by association, which has come to be popularly known as classical or 'Pavlovian' conditioning. Further, this learning process contains an important adaptive function; it alerts the organism to stimuli that signal the impending arrival of an important event (Passer and Smith, 2001).

BEFORE, DURING AND AFTER CONDITIONING

In Pavlov's experiment, before conditioning, a neutral stimulus (the sound of the bell) provokes no response from the dog. During conditioning, the neutral stimulus is twinned with a stimulus (food) that naturally causes a response, referred to as an 'unconditioned stimulus' (UCS). In response to the presence of the UCS (food, in this case), the animal salivates, which is a natural response to the food; this response is called an 'unconditioned response' (UCR). However, the aim of the experiment is for the dog to learn to associate the neutral stimulus (bell) with that of the food (UCS). If the experiment is successful, the dog, on hearing the now conditioned stimulus [CS] of the sound of the bell, will respond by salivating (CR) even though there is no food (UCS) present. This research demonstrated that response could be conditioned, even to neutral stimuli. The process of learning this response is referred to as 'acquisition'. Generally speaking there needs to be a repeated pairing of CS–UCS in order to elicit a strong response.

However, Passer and Smith (2001, p. 196) comment that 'when an UCS is intense and/or traumatic, event conditioning may only require one CS–UCS pairing'. Examples of a possible traumatic event can range from witnessing a car accident to being involved in one. Often people who are involved in serious car accidents find it difficult to be near cars; this is a conditioned response (CR) based on the pairing of the car (CS) with the accident (UCS). It took my mother, after a serious car accident, nearly a year before she was able to overcome her fear and sit in the driver's seat again. This shows that once a conditioned response is initiated it can continue to persist for quite a period. This helps to explain the development of phobic behaviour.

THINK ABOUT IT!

Can you think of other examples where an incident could condition a strong reaction? As mentioned, it would usually need to be traumatic; rape or an assault could elicit such a response. In Chapter 7 we will examine post-traumatic stress disorder (PTSD). Consider how Pavlov's theory might explain such a phenomenon.

The examples just used relate to one incident being powerful enough to condition a response. In general terms, though, it usually takes repeated pairing of CS-UCS to condition a learning or 'acquisition'. As we saw earlier in the 'Little Albert' experiment, Albert's fear response 'generalised' to other stimulus that were similar to the initial stimuli of the white mouse. This shows us that items or events that are similar in some fashion to the initial stimulus can also provoke a response.

GENERALISATION AND DISCRIMINATION: STIMULUS CONTROL STUDIES

When the conditioned response (CR) transfers spontaneously from the initial conditioned stimuli (CS) to one which is similar yet different from it, this is referred to as *generalisation*. Using an earlier example, if my mother after her accident involving a car (CS) had also developed a fear (CR) of buses or motorbikes, this would have represented a transfer from the original stimuli of the car to stimuli (buses and motorbikes) similar yet different from the CS. *Discrimination* is the opposite of generalisation and happens when a conditioned response does not occur when there is a difference between the presented stimulus and the original conditioned stimulus. Using the example of Pavlov's dogs, if the dog heard a bell with a different tone and did not receive the unconditioned stimulus (food), the dog would eventually learn not to salivate to the second tone.

In his article, Windholz (1990) discusses how Pavlov believed he had found the root of neuroses during his experiments with animals. Pavlov was aware of Freud's well-documented case of Anna O., a woman suffering from neuroses. Pavlov believed that neurotic behaviour could be generated in laboratory settings and was not dependent on the unconscious machinations proposed by Freud and his followers. While experimenting with dogs, it was noted that the animals' behaviour became disorganised when discrimination became difficult. This became known as 'experimental neurosis'. Pavlov drew an analogy between the neurotic behaviour of the dogs and that of Anna O., concluding that he had demonstrated elements of neurosis in animals and humans alike within a laboratory setting. Here we can see the essence of behaviourism, that behaviour including mental illness was learned and did not involve unconscious forces or object relations; it was a complete rejection of the psychodynamic theory of Freud and his followers. Of course, if Pavlov believed that neurotic behaviour could be conditioned, did he suggest how to alleviate or extinguish such behaviour? Yes he did. Just as a response can be learned, so too can it be unlearned, according to Pavlovian theory. A conditioned response eventually disappears if the conditioned stimulus is repeated without reinforcement; the decline of the response during repeated stimulation was referred to as *extinction* by Pavlov.

STRENGTHS OF CLASSICAL CONDITIONING

Classical conditioning is a theory that is scientific and thus observable and testable. Pavlov demonstrated through a series of experiments that he could reproduce results, and this lends to a theory's validity. It has implications for education, healthcare and social work in offering a lens through which behaviour can be viewed but also modified. Behaviour modification whose roots lie within behaviourist and learning theories are used in many guises as we will discuss later in this chapter.

WEAKNESSES OF CLASSICAL CONDITIONING

Criticisms of behaviourism abound. It is a reductionist model in that it reduces complex behaviour to smaller parts, and this can lead to difficulties in validity due to its incompleteness. Ethically, behaviourism and 'conditioning' individuals' behaviour may appear manipulative and calls into question who decides what is 'desirable' behaviour and in fact what is 'desirable' behaviour. Classical conditioning is based on observations of dogs salivating. Can such a theory be truly applicable to human behaviour?

THINK ABOUT IT — CASE STUDY

You have been assigned to work with a young mother, Lila, who has addiction issues and her son Trey who is 8 years old. Social services have been involved with the family since Trey was 2 years old. Upon your initial meeting with Lila and Trey, when you introduce yourself Trey reacts aggressively towards you.

From a Pavlovian or classical conditioning approach, one explanation possible for Trey's behaviour is:

> Initially, when Trey was young the social worker was a neutral stimuli. As social workers began to work with Trey a decision was made to place him in foster care, as Lila sought treatment for her addiction issues. Trey reacted badly to being separated from his mother and did not adjust well to foster care. So, for Trey foster care was a negative experience; he associated this negative experience with social workers. Trey now feels fear and anxiety when social workers visit with him and his mum (Basic stimulus-response [S-R] formulation, stimulus is the social worker, response is fear). Assess Trey's behaviour using the following theory we are going to examine: operant conditioning.

While classical conditioning considers the stimulus important in conditioning responses, Skinner's Operant Conditioning theory focuses on the *consequence* of the behaviour as the 'reinforcer', so let's take a look.

Skinner and operant conditioning

> Operant conditioning is a type of learning in which behaviour is influenced by the consequences that follow it.
>
> (Skinner, 1938, p. 14)

Skinner's theory of operant conditioning as touched on in the above quote was strongly influenced by Thorndike's law of effect, which states that behaviour is a function of its consequences. Operant behaviour means that an organism literally 'operates' on its environment in some way; it emits responses that produce certain consequences. Skinner believed that behaviour is shaped by its consequences and that those consequences can be positive or negative. A behaviour followed by a rewarding or favourable response is more likely to be repeated. Conversely, an unfavourable or punishing response to a behaviour decreases the odds that the behaviour will be replicated. This process is a type of 'natural selection', facilitating an organism's personal adaptation. In experiments, the rate at which the rat pressed the lever depended not on any preceding (what went before it) stimuli (as with Watson and Pavlov) but on the consequence following the pressing of the lever.

THE SKINNER BOX

In operant conditioning, behaviour is affected by its consequences but the process is not trial-and-error learning. It can best be explained with an example: a hungry rat is placed in a box. For several days pieces of food are occasionally delivered into a tray by an automatic dispenser. The rat soon goes to the tray immediately upon hearing the sound of the dispenser. A small horizontal section of a lever protruding from the wall has been resting in its lowest position, but it is now raised slightly so that when the rat touches it, it moves downward.

In doing so it closes an electric circuit and operates the food dispenser. Immediately after eating the delivered food the rat begins to press the lever fairly rapidly. The behaviour has been strengthened or reinforced by a single consequence. The rat was not 'trying' to do anything when it first touched the lever and it did not learn from 'errors'.

POSITIVE AND NEGATIVE REINFORCEMENT

As stated, reinforcers strengthen behaviour and can be positive or negative. A positive reinforcer strengthens behaviour, and this is called *Positive Reinforcement.* For example, when a child completes an action or a desired behaviour you would praise (positive reinforcement) them for doing so. The praise strengthens the likelihood of that behaviour being repeated.

Negative reinforcement also strengthens a behaviour but by removing an unpleasant or adverse stimulus. It is NOT the same as punishment, as we will see. Let's look at an example. When learning dance as a child a stick was placed across my back to encourage correct posture, as soon as I had corrected my posture the stick was removed. Funnily enough I didn't like the stick across my back (unpleasant or adverse) but its function was to **strengthen** the desired behaviour (correct posture), and as soon as I complied this unpleasant stimulus (stick) was removed. So, as you can see, negative reinforcement works to **strengthen** behaviour, not lessen or eradicate it – that's the job of punishment!

Punishment is used to suppress or reduce behaviour. It consists of either removing a positive reinforcer or presenting a negative one; for instance, if you continue to be cheeky I'll switch your TV programme off (removal of positive); presenting a negative reinforcer might be the threat of having to do household chores. The punished person henceforth acts in ways which reduce the threat of punishment.

In using Operant Conditioning to understand behaviour, the ABC method is a useful framework:

The ABCs of operant conditioning

Antecedents (the stimulus conditions, such as the lever, the click of the food dispenser, a light that may go on when the lever is pressed)
Behaviours (or operants, such as pressing the lever)
Consequences (what happens as a result of the operant behaviour – reinforcement or punishment).
Source: Gross (2009, p. 176)

THINK ABOUT IT!

Think about how the ABC model might apply to addiction:

A – the antecedent is the condition that comes before the actual behaviour; in the case of addiction the individual might be experiencing feelings of unhappiness or withdrawal
B – the behaviour would be the consuming or taking of a substance (alcohol, drugs…)
C – as a result of the behaviour (taking drugs) the consequence is the mechanism that reinforces this learned behaviour. So in taking alcohol or drugs the consequence is the easing of feelings of unhappiness or feelings of elation.

Can you think of any other scenarios or situations where the ABC approach is applicable? Challenging behaviour, compliance with medication or a programme?

Of course this is a simplistic explanation and as with all theories it offers just one possible explanation. As we will see later in this section, behaviourism, particularly operant conditioning, is utilised in social work.

STRENGTHS OF OPERANT CONDITIONING

Operant conditioning's focus on the consequences of a behaviour as the reinforcer offers a compelling explanation for the learning of behaviour, especially in the young. The application of Operant Conditioning principles throughout many fields and across diverse groups and situations speaks to its strength. One could argue it is a successful counterbalance to more nature-orientated perspectives. As with Pavlov, it is grounded in a scientific approach and relies on measurable and testable phenomenon. However, it has its criticism, including some we saw of Pavlov.

WEAKNESSES OF OPERANT CONDITIONING

As alluded to already, the question of what is 'desirable' behaviour and who decides so arises. Operant conditioning, and behaviourism in general, ignores the role of social constructs and cultural norms in determining what and whose behaviours are not acceptable. Another criticism levelled at operant conditioning lies in the use of rewards or other consequences to shape behaviour. It is argued that the individual is only motivated to change through external motivators, such as rewards, which encourages a shallow and materialistic approach. The most compelling criticism argues that while you may change a behaviour, if the individual returns to the same environment which has not been the subject of modification then it is more likely for the individual's changed behaviour to deteriorate over time. Thus, if you change a child's challenging behaviour but they return to their family, where the same patterns and environment exist as before, it will be difficult for that child to maintain the changed behaviour. This can also be applied to the example of addiction. Should the individual change their behaviour yet return to an environment where drugs are readily available and circumstances of poverty and unemployment remain it is likely for the changed behaviour to deteriorate and the initial behaviour to reassert itself.

Regardless of these criticisms, Skinner believed that behaviourism could be used across many fields for the improvement of the human condition, as he outlines,

THE APPLICATION OF BEHAVIOURISM TO IMPROVE THE HUMAN CONDITION

Skinner desired for his experimental work with animal behaviour to be translated into and applied to human affairs. Buskist and Miller (1982) report that throughout his career and writings Skinner emphasised the importance and need for 'a thorough-going functional analysis of human behaviour and human culture'. According to Skinner (as cited ibid, p. 137): 'By turning from man qua man to external conditions of which man's behaviour is a function, it has been possible to design better practices in the care of psychotics and retardates, in child care, in education (in both contingency management in the classroom and the design of instructional material), in incentive systems in industry, and in penal institutions'. Buskist points to the development of applied behaviour analysis (ABA) as evidence of the call to arms and the successful application of behavioural technology to the analysis and modification of human behaviour. Pavlov also suggested that his principles revealed the cause of neuroses, not in the depths of the conscious but as a learned behavioural response which could be unlearned. So what relevance does behaviourism hold for social work?

Behaviourism – its relevance for social work

Pavlov believed that if something like salivation could be conditioned, then it might also be possible to apply the process to bodily processes that affect illness and mental disorders. As fear is learnt, classical conditioning principles are applied in the treatment of phobias and in aversion therapies. Skinner's 'operant conditioning' theory has been more widely applied in the fields of education, social work including addiction and healthcare. Skinner has offered an explanation as to how individuals, especially the young, acquired difficult or 'challenging' behaviour and a method to modify these behaviours. Operant conditioning is based on the concept of consequences as the reinforcer for the behaviour; the use of praise and star charts encourage behaviour through positive reinforcement, which is always more effective than punishment. Social workers can teach parents these methods to promote or extinguish behaviours. Such techniques are commonly used, not just in the home and educational settings but in residential and respite homes and with groups including those with learning disabilities.

I once worked with a young teen who was disruptive. In addition to not forming a 'judgement' about him I used positive reinforcement techniques (though admittedly I had to wait a considerable amount of time for him to display a behaviour or any action that I could praise!). This teen was so used to receiving negative attention that he was startled by the praise I offered; it encouraged him to continue to try to behave well with me, although unfortunately this did not translate to other staff members, arguably as they continued to interact with him with judgement and negativity. This approach can work particularly well with those who are so used to negative attention, although of course, as mentioned, it can require patience to find opportunities to use positive reinforcement in dealing with those who are disruptive. Further, we cannot solely focus on changing a person's behaviour and ignore the role environment can play; environmental, societal and cultural aspects must be considered too.

Behaviourism marked a very clear departure from psychodynamic theories rooted in the internal machinations of the mind. Pavlov and Skinner through their experiments with animals exposed behaviour and learning from the dark recess of the mind to observable and measurable reactions grounded not in nature but in the nurture perspective. Nonetheless, a major criticism of their work (1st wave behaviourism) is that it is rooted in animal behaviour and experiments. Albert Bandura attempted to progress behaviourist principles within a more social context.

BANDURA'S SOCIAL LEARNING THEORY

Bandura's theory represents the bridge between radical behaviourism and an attempt to ground it within a social context. Bandura (2006, p. 55) felt it too narrow and prescriptive to ignore the role of social modelling. He states,

> I found this behaviouristic theorizing discordant with the obvious social reality that much of what we learn is through the power of social modelling. I could not imagine a culture in which its language; mores; familial customs and practices; occupational competencies; and educational, religious, and political practices were gradually shaped in each new member by rewarding and punishing consequences of their trial-and-error performances.

Social learning rejected traditional behaviourism's emphasis on environment alone (environmental determinism) as the sole influence in learning and behaviour. Instead, the concept of reciprocal determinism (see picture below) emphasised the interactional aspect; individuals learn from their environment but they also affect the way in which the environment works through their behaviour and attitudes. Bandura's theory posits that individuals are influenced by their own thoughts, beliefs and ideas, and this may explain why his theory is sometimes referred to as 'social-cognitive'.

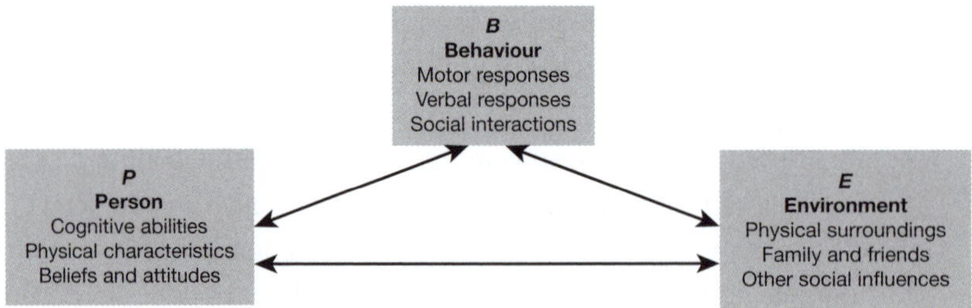

Figure 4.2 Bandura's model of reciprocal determinism

What's going on cognitively?

When the person observes the model (i.e., the person modelling the behavior), (s)he has ideas, personality and thoughts about the symbol.

What behavior is reinforced?

Will there be rewards or benefits through imitation? Punishment?

Social or personal needs met?

Who are the social models?

Who is the child watching, believing, noticing: parents, peers, media?

This belief in the power of social learning was supported in his study of hyper-aggressive boys living in advantaged areas not usually considered conducive to anti-social conduct. Bandura and his colleagues found that parental modelling of aggressive behaviours played a significant role in the familial transmission of aggression. This study led Bandura to attempt to study modelling through learning and social influence experimentally. Bandura was particularly interested in the role of violence on television in social learning of aggression, and to this end he devised the 'Bobo doll' experiment.

THE BOBO DOLL EXPERIMENT

To test his hypothesis that modelling by others plays a central role in learning and the acquisition of behaviour, Bandura devised 'The Bobo doll' laboratory experiment, to clarify the processes governing observational learning (see Chapter 10 where an account of this experiment and an in-depth discussion of this experiment and children's aggression is given). The gist of the Bobo doll experiment consisted of a researcher hitting a doll-like figure. This act was recorded, and the children then watched this recording on television. Afterwards they had access to an actual 'Bobo' doll and the bats used by the researcher. The children re-enacted the violence they had observed in the taping, thus supporting Bandura's assertion that children learn through social modelling, observation and imitation.

Drewes (2008, p. 55) relates that Bandura considered aggressive behaviour, like other forms of social behaviour, to be under stimulus, reinforcement and cognitive control and that children learn what behaviours are appropriate and rewarding. Should they learn that aggressive behaviours are rewarding, they are then more likely to choose aggressive actions in response to conflict situations. The acquisition of aggression is considered in greater detail in Chapter 10.

It is argued that Bandura's theory offers a bridge between behaviourism and cognitive-based theories. More significantly for social work practice, Bandura recognised that cultural and societal artefacts are transmitted through others, and this is how children learn not just behaviour but also language, emotion and attitudes. Bandura's theory has not been without its detractors but first let's consider the strengths of his theory.

THINK ABOUT IT!

Clearly we can see the relationship between modelling of behaviour in the home and the transmission of behaviours and attitudes. We can recognise the influence of siblings and peers, and, increasingly, the media in modelling behaviours and attitudes. However, modelling and social learning can be seen within social work practice, for example through 'shadowing'. Reflect on experiences of shadowing another. What were you observing and trying to learn? When training, shadowing is often used, whether it's part of a placement or more informal, as you try to observe what others are doing so you can 'fit' in. Can there be negatives to the experience of 'shadowing'? Picking up bad habits, beliefs and behaviours? What has been your experience?

STRENGTHS OF SOCIAL LEARNING THEORY

Bandura devised his theory and developed an experimental method to test its validity; this is considered a strength within mainstream psychology. Bandura's acknowledgement of social forces in learning and behaviour, particularly the role of others, gives his theory an added advantage over traditional behaviourism. The interactional nature of learning is contained within his theory; further, it acts as a bridge between behaviourism and cognition, which is an additional benefit as it encases the complexity of the learning process. Finally, social learning can be used to explain a wide range of behaviours across different environments and diverse groups.

CRITICISMS OF SOCIAL LEARNING THEORY

While Bandura acknowledged the influence of others and the interactional nature of learning between the environment and the individual, he never made clear how this worked in more naturalistic settings as his experiments were laboratory based. This leads to the next criticism of the lack of cultural research regarding social learning theory. Further, Bandura used white middle-class children in his sample and thus his experiments lack diversity. Finally, Bandura's social learning theory does not reveal why parental and media influences can differ so much.

Behaviourism as a movement continues to endure. Its significance is felt in disciplines including education, childcare, healthcare and social work, and it informs interventions and therapies. Applied Behaviour Analysis (ABA) is the application of behavioural principles to behaviours of social significance and is used as an approach in behaviour modification within health and social science arenas, particularly with autism. While behaviourism and its rigid and narrow approach to understanding learning and behaviour is less popular within modern psychology, as it ignores the complexity of the human condition, it remains a practically orientated theory with much to offer.

Having examined behaviourism and learning, we will now look at the theories of humanism, which stand quite diametrically opposed to the theories of Freud and behaviourism.

HUMANISM

The view that science is the only reliable path to knowledge is a naïve philosophical assumption which often goes unexamined. The makers of 'normal science' are not the great discoverers who dared to take chances, but the majority of 'normal scientists' who overstress caution and the art of not making mistakes. Science need not confine itself to a reductionist, atomistic view of the world in which man is

> dehumanized. Many non-scientists fear science for they see it as belittling the things they consider beautiful and valuable.
>
> (Maslow, 1965, p. 219)

Maslow's quote is an apt introduction to the field of humanism that developed within psychology. While behaviourism rejected introspection and the untestable nature of the psychoanalytic Freudian tradition, humanism rejected what it saw as the reductionist approach to the understanding of human nature; an approach that humanism felt inherently debased the goodness and innate potential of the individual. Whereas both behaviourism and the psychoanalytic approach were deterministic, humanism proposed the idea of free will and an individual's choice in their actions.

Abraham Maslow and Carl Rogers were to epitomise this viewpoint and are influential figures in the field of humanistic psychology. Both men were interested in the concept of self-actualisation, which, put at its most fundamental, equates with supreme self-expression. Though both are humanistic in their perspective, the direction and application of their work are seen in different fields: Maslow is often found in the field of motivation and Rogers is best known for his work within psychotherapy and its development.

WHAT IS HUMANISM?

Maslow's quote captures the essence of the humanistic perspective on the development and nature of humans. Humanism took a more positive viewpoint of human nature, grounded somewhat in the Renaissance tradition, which celebrated the greatness and beauty of humankind. From the perspective of the history of Western thought, Davidson (2000, p. 1) places humanism as a philosophy 'based on the belief that the human is irreducible to other forms of life, whether material or Divine. To the extent that humanistic psychology has its roots in the humanist tradition, it shares this conviction that the human cannot be understood except in its own terms'.

Humanism proposed that an individual's ultimate goal was towards growth and potential, that this in fact was humankind's instinct and that obstacles (personal and structural) blocked individuals from reaching their true potential. Maslow referred to this potential of 'self-actualisation' and produced a 'hierarchy of needs' to capture the journey towards that end goal. Rogers formulated human goodness, personal growth and potential in terms of psychotherapeutic approaches, such as empathy and genuineness.

According to Diaz-Laplante (2007, pp. 59–60), 'Rogers held that human beings are inherently good and that movement away from goodness is a result of cultural or societal influences.'

THINK ABOUT IT!

What kind of cultural or societal influences do you believe could cause an individual to move 'away from goodness'? Do you think cultural and societal influences are responsible for preventing an individual from achieving their full potential or being 'inherently good'?

SELF-ACTUALISATION

Is self-actualisation a state of being or rather a developmental process? LeClerc et al. (1998, p. 73) are clear that it is a developmental process, commenting, 'this aspect is clearly emphasized by Maslow in his definition of self-actualization as the "full use and exploitation of talents, capacities and potentialities"'. This sets forth the idea of a continuous development of the individual's potential as a central aspect of self-actualisation. The same idea of a developmental process is present in Rogers's definition of self-actualisation as 'the inherent tendency of the organism to develop all its capacities in ways that serve to maintain or enhance the organism' (ibid).

Bugental, a leading figure in the Humanist movement (1964, p. 564), states in his seminal article 'Humanism psychology: A new perspective', 'I propose that the defining concept of man basic to the new humanistic movement in psychology is that man is the process that supersedes the sum of his part functions.' Bugental (as cited in Greening 2007) outlined the major tenets of humanistic psychology or, as it was also known, the 'third force' in psychology, as follows:

Major tenets of humanistic psychology

1. Human beings, as human, supersede the sum of their parts. They cannot be reduced to components.
2. Human beings have their existence in a uniquely human context, as well as in a cosmic ecology.
3. Human beings are aware and aware of being aware – that is, they are conscious.
4. Human consciousness always includes an awareness of oneself in the context of other people.
5. Human beings have some choice and, with that, responsibility.
6. Human beings are intentional, aim at goals, are aware that they cause future events, and seek meaning, value, and creativity.

So, as we can see, central to Humanism is the belief that man is striving to reach his potential; that is his true goal and desire, but how does this belief translate to theory and practice. We are going to first look at the work of Maslow and then see how his ideas have been applied to addiction planning, thus offering a practical application of this theory. Rogers's core theory will then be overviewed. His relevance to psychotherapy is discussed in greater depth in Chapter 7.

Maslow and Rogers: an introduction

ABRAHAM MASLOW

According to Pearson and Podeschi (1999), central to Maslow's work are four intertwining concepts:

- the idea of self
- that we are capable of growth

- that we are responsible for what we become and
- that we are capable of influencing social progress.

The authors continue (1999, p. 43):

> There is an inner core of the self-determining individual in which human freedom for Maslow is a combination of uncovering one's real self and deciding what one will become. This capacity for self-knowledge and willed self-renewal leads to growth (the self-actualizing process), moving the self from one state of consciousness to a more advanced state (e.g., basic needs of safety and belongingness to meta needs of wholeness and justice). For Maslow, knowledge of oneself is not only a path to better individual value choices, but self-actualization also leads to knowledge of universal human nature, for example, awareness of the synthesis of altruism and self-interest.

This fundamental belief framework forms the 'hierarchy of needs', a model for classifying human motives, which is arguably Maslow's most identifiable and well-known work. Maslow published his hierarchy of needs in a paper entitled 'A theory of human motivation' (1943). The hierarchy ascends from basic physiological needs (food, drink, etc.) through to more complex psychological needs, such as security and esteem.

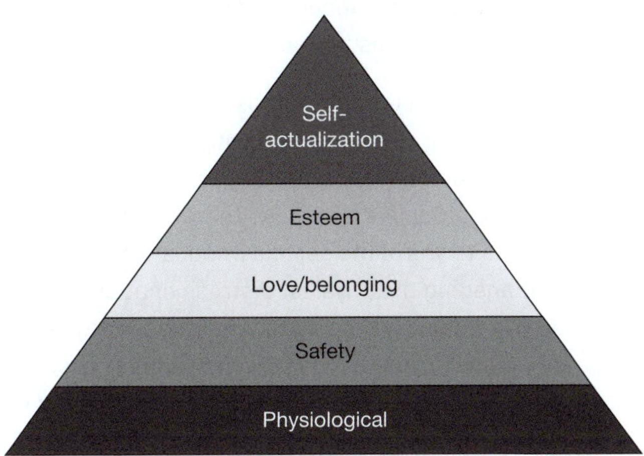

Figure 4.3 Maslow's Hierarchy of Needs
Source: A. Maslow (1943)

The needs at one level must be at least partially satisfied before those at the next level become important determiners of action. When food or safety become difficult to obtain, higher needs are less relevant to the individual, whose attention is geared towards meeting the more basic needs they are lacking.

IN PRACTICE: THE HIERARCHY OF NEEDS AND CARE PLANNING IN ADDICTION SERVICES

Best et al. (2008) suggest that Maslow's hierarchical model of needs be considered as an exemplar in understanding the treatment and service provision of drug addiction.

The authors quote Maslow (p. 306) in terms of the most basic need of his hierarchy – physiological:

> If all other needs are unsatisfied, and the organism is then dominated by the physiological needs, all other needs may become simply non-existent or be pushed into the background. It is then fair to characterise the whole organism by saying simply that it is hungry, for consciousness is almost completely pre-empted by hunger.

Best et al. (2008, p. 306) argue that the parallels between what Maslow is suggesting and drug-seeking

> are obvious with the basic physiological problems associated with drug deprivation, withdrawals, craving and anhedonia. At initial treatment presentation, it is therefore likely that other key issues are masked, and that only where equally pressing deprivations, most likely those caused by homelessness or significant mental or physical morbidities, are met will these arise as presenting needs.'

For the authors there are two major implications of the hierarchy of needs model for the delivery of treatment:

1. That lower-level interventions must precede higher–order ones.
2. That higher–order needs are unlikely to emerge in the initial contact stages.

Best et al. (2008) continue that this has fundamental implications in the area of care planning and review as part of the treatment process. Only as clients and workers manage the physiological needs (through prescribing, detoxification, etc.), 'can treatment start to look at issues of safety, then belonging, esteem and addressing more spiritual needs'. In terms of the second implication of the model, what treatment workers do whilst managing the physical distress of addiction is paramount.

The hierarchy of needs would suggest that any further gains in treatment are predicated on a care planning approach that is not 'addiction-specific' but is trans-disciplinary and grounded on the client's emerging pattern of needs. It would suggest that for many clients what is needed initially is case support rather than 'psychological change', and clients will be sceptical about the benefits of counselling if their needs are not compatible with the middle and higher-order levels of the pyramid. For many clients, the key tasks will be around benefits and housing, access to psychiatric services and general practitioners [GPs], and with little need for targeting lasting change in drug use until these issues have been addressed.

Thus, the central thrust of this article on using the hierarchy of needs as a model for addiction treatment and care provision is that the basic physiological need must be fully resolved before any other 'higher' need is dealt with, and that the introduction of treatments to deal with more 'psychological' issues is likely to be unsuccessful unless physical needs have been fully met. Here the direct relevance and relationship that exists between the discipline of psychology and social care practice is clear.

THINK ABOUT IT!

Can you think of areas other than addiction that the hierarchy of needs can be applied to? How would you integrate this approach within your practice? There are strong arguments to be made that issues such as poverty, poor housing and lack of good nutrition need to be addressed before we can deal effectively with higher order needs.

STRENGTHS OF MASLOW'S THEORY

Maslow's theory integrates biological and social needs within one framework, which was quite a revolutionary step at that time. Maslow's work is influential in the arena of motivation, as he recognised that we have needs and the fulfilment of these needs is a powerful motivating force. Maslow, along with Rogers, introduced 'the third force' in psychology, which emphasised man's inherent goodness, rejecting Freud's more deterministic and pessimistic perspective and behaviourism's reductionism.

CRITICISMS OF MASLOW'S THEORY

The concept of a neat hierarchy moving from one level to the next has come under scrutiny; critics suggest that our needs do not operate in such a uniform, stage by stage approach. Another difficulty lies in its more individualistic orientation, as we saw in an earlier chapter a major criticism of psychology is that it is ethnocentric. Most societies are collectivistic, thus the idea of self-actualisation is one more associated with individualism. In addition, Maslow's running order of 'needs' is unlikely to be homogenous. I may actually place 'love' need as more important than 'esteem' needs, for instance.

CARL ROGERS

Rogers can be placed within the phenomenological approach to personality, which places emphasis on the individual's subjective or private experience of the world. A focus on the 'here and now' and the individual's view of it is a fundamental tenet of this approach, differentiating it from the psychoanalytic approach, which delves into unconscious impulses.

The 'self ' is a fundamentally important aspect of Rogers's theory of personality. The self is the 'I' or 'me' and includes awareness of 'what I am'; ideas, perceptions and values all form the structure of self. This perceived self is the referent (reference point) for the individual's perception of the world and behaviour. Self-concept and self-esteem are related constructs that are informed by the individual's sense of self. Individuals with a strong, positive self-concept will view the world differently to a person with a weak or negative self-concept. Rogers contends that self-concept does not always reflect reality; a highly successful person may privately view themselves as a failure, for example. People use self-concept to evaluate experiences. Further, an individual's tendency is to behave in line with their self-image. Any feelings or experiences that are not consistent with this self-image are threatening and denied admittance to consciousness. This bears a resemblance to Freud's concept of repression.

Anxiety develops, according to Rogers's theory, where the gap between self-image and feelings and experiences that are threatening to the self-image grows; in simple terms, a gulf exists between reality and self-concept. Atkinson (1983, p. 400) contends that, 'an individual whose image is incongruent with personal feelings and experiences must defend himself or herself against the truth because truth will result in anxiety. If the incongruence becomes too great, the defenses may break down, resulting in severe anxiety or other forms of emotional disturbance.' In contrast, the self-concept of a well-adjusted person is flexible and can change to integrate new experiences and ideas. The other 'self ' that exists is the 'ideal self ', which represents that person we wish to be. Should a significant gap exist between our 'ideal' self and 'real' self, this can result in an unhappy individual.

In Rogers's view the sense of self is the critical referent for self-evaluation. The contingencies for approval laid down by others – parents, teachers and other authority figures – inevitably play a significant role in self-esteem. Psychological dysfunction is often a result of having distorted or suppressed inner needs in an effort to satisfy the perceived standards of such dependency figures. From Rogers's perspective, continuing awareness of authentic inner desires is essential to healthy development and 'self-actualisation'.

Gross (2009, p. 745) compares Maslow and Rogers in their shared positive evaluation of personal growth (self-actualisation), further commenting,

> While Maslow's theory is commonly referred to as a "psychology of being" (self- actualization is an end in itself and lies at the peak of his hierarchy of needs), Rogers's is a "psychology of becoming" (it's the process of becoming a "fully functioning person" that's of major importance and interest).

HUMANISM: STILL A FORCE TO BE RECKONED WITH?

Elkins (2009, p. 268) claims that the humanistic psychology of Maslow and Rogers has faded and that 'deterministic, mechanistic, and pathologizing models once again dominate clinical psychology – despite the fact that psychotherapy research clearly supports humanistic values and perspectives'.

Elkins (2009) identifies a lack of acknowledgment as a significant factor in the non-advancement of humanistic psychology. He claims that this has led to an erosion and undermining of the 'third force' perspective, especially in modern-day psychology. Elkins provides such an example in Seligman's positive psychology, which Elkins suggests is a reframing of humanistic psychology's long-standing emphasis upon the strengths and potentials of human beings. Elkins (p. 281) comments,

> Yet, when Seligman and Csikszentmihalyi (2000) edited the special issue of the American Psychologist ... in which hundreds of references associated with this 'new' approach were cited, only Viktor Frankl and Abraham Maslow made the list. Carl Rogers, the first psychologist to reject the pathology model and to develop a scientifically supported theory of psychotherapy that focused on the positive potentials of clients, did not appear in any of the reference lists!

Elkins provides a list of contributions which he feels humanistic psychology has made:

- The humanistic movement was primarily responsible for changing society's perception of psychotherapy from a 'medical treatment for mental illness' into a vehicle for personal growth and a source of support and guidance during difficult times
- Humanistic scholars did groundbreaking work in the area of philosophy of research, writing about the limitations of the natural science model when applied to psychological phenomena and demonstrating the importance of phenomenological and other qualitative approaches in understanding human experience
- The humanistic movement was largely responsible for turning America into a 'therapeutic culture' and helping enlarge the field of psychology from a small guild of about 7000 in 1950 into a profession of more than 90,000 today
- Rogers's Person-Centred Approach (PCA) has been the focus of hundreds of research studies that overwhelmingly have confirmed the effectiveness of his 'necessary and sufficient' conditions of therapy – empathy, congruence and unconditional positive regard
- By emphasising the importance of the alliance, the relationship, the personality of the therapist, and so on in psychotherapy, humanistic psychologists anticipated contemporary meta-analytic studies that have convincingly demonstrated that therapeutic effectiveness is due primarily to contextual factors and not to modalities and techniques
- Humanistic psychology has had a significant impact on other fields, such as education, nursing, social work, organisational development and so on (pp. 282–4).

STRENGTHS OF ROGERS'S THEORY

Rogers and the humanistic approach placed the person in their environment and acknowledged a person's feelings and beliefs as important. In Chapter 7, Rogers's emphasis on these tenets can be seen in his espousal of the importance of the therapist–client relationship. Rogers's work has been influential in fields such as psychotherapy and social work; the roots of person-centred practice (Chapter 7) can be traced to his work.

CRITICISMS OF ROGERS'S THEORY

Major aspects of humanism and Rogers's work are located within the subjective experience of individuals, and this is difficult to assess or test. Concepts central to humanism can be vague, again leading to difficulties of validity. Many aspects of Rogers's theory and humanism in general feel intuitive, almost common sense. While some have argued this a strength those of a more scientific persuasion identify this as another weakness.

WHAT IS THE ROLE OF HUMANISTIC PSYCHOLOGY TODAY?

Clearly, as we will see in Chapter 7 on counselling, the work of Rogers has been, and continues to be, hugely influential in psychotherapy and psychotherapeutic approaches to supporting individuals.

Diaz-Laplante (2007, p. 58) outlines her belief that humanistic psychology offers the best model for intervention in modern-day society: 'Humanistic psychology provides a theoretical framework that invites us to develop models of intervention that engage individuals at all levels – intellectually, spiritually, physically, within the context of their community and intimate relationships, and across all dimensions of the life span.' However, to demonstrate the application of humanistic psychology from another perspective, we can look at the link between positive psychology and humanistic psychology, and the role of positive psychology in the arena of social care work.

POSITIVE PSYCHOLOGY

Positive psychology can be defined as 'a science of positive subjective experience, positive individual traits, and positive institutions which promises to improve quality of life and prevent the pathologies that arise when life is barren and meaningless' (Seligman and Csikszentmihalyi, 2000, p. 5).

The authors outline the field of positive psychology across the following levels:

> At the *subjective* level it is about valued subjective experiences: well-being, contentment, and satisfaction (in the past); hope and optimism (for the future); and flow and happiness (in the present).
> At the *individual* level, it is about positive individual traits: the capacity for love and vocation, courage, interpersonal skill, aesthetic sensibility, perseverance, forgiveness, originality, future mindedness, spirituality, high talent and wisdom.
> At the *group* level, it is about the civic virtues and the institutions that move individuals toward better citizenship: responsibility, nurturance, altruism, civility, moderation, tolerance and work ethic (ibid.).

In studying those whose lives encapsulate positive and adaptive living, it is hoped to develop supports and promote those same traits, characteristics and behaviours in others towards the betterment of all. As already mentioned, positive psychology has its roots in the humanistic tradition (Seligman and Csikszentmihalyi, 2000; Robbins, 2008). Robbins (2008, p. 98) directly links positive psychology to humanistic psychology, commenting that it was, in fact, Maslow who coined the phrase 'positive psychology' more than four decades prior to Seligman's use of the term for his own work and that of others. Not surprisingly, then, Peterson and Seligman (2004) credit Maslow as a pioneer in the study of character strengths and virtues, and they used Maslow's descriptions of the self-actualised individual as a means to identify and validate their taxonomy of character strengths and virtues.

IN PRACTICE: POSITIVE PSYCHOLOGY AND YOUTH WORK

In Chapter 7 we will examine the construct of resilience, which is part of the positive psychology paradigm; here we look at the role of positive psychology suggested by Larson (2000) in the development of youth activities to support and engender positive characteristics, such as initiative and agency within adolescents. Larson (2000,

p. 170) suggests that high rates of boredom, alienation and disconnection from meaningful challenge are not signs of psychopathology, at least not in most cases, but rather signs of a deficiency in positive development. The same might be said for many cases of problem behaviour, such as drug use, premature sexual involvement and minor delinquency; that they are more parsimoniously described, not as responses to family stress, emotional disturbance or maladaptive cognitions, but rather to the absence of engagement in a positive life trajectory.

Youth work is a central part of social care work. In developing his ideas Larson hopes to provide a framework for the development of youth activities that encourage and support the development of positive traits in adolescents. Larson (2000, p. 178) suggests that during more structured youth activities, 'adolescents experience a unique combination of intrinsic motivation and concentration that is rarely present during their daily experiences in schoolwork and unstructured leisure. These two components of experience, I proposed, represent two critical elements of initiative, and when they occur in activities involving a temporal arc of action toward a goal, as is the case with many youth activities, all three elements for the experience and learning of initiative are in play.' Larson relates that these more structured activities towards a goal result in greater positive outcomes, including:

- diminished delinquency
- greater achievement
- increased self-control and self-efficacy.

Through their participation in the youth activities, the adolescents develop a greater sense of initiative and agency. He believes his research 'suggests processes of personal integration that may work in tandem with the sociological processes of social integration' (ibid.).

As we have seen, humanism was and, arguably, remains a powerful force, particularly within social work through its emphasis on the 'person in environment' approach and on an individual's feelings. Humanism ties in with principles of social justice in its recognition that individuals are inherently good but societal and structural elements can negatively impact in their lives. We will come across Rogers's work again in Chapter 7, where he remains an influential figure in psychotherapy and person-centred practice.

We are now going to move on to newer theories, including Bronfenbrenner's ecological theory, which places the person within a series of nested circles which intertwine, influencing that individual's development. I must admit to having a particular fondness for this theory, so powerful and inclusive is it in its theoretical and also practical application and you will find Bronfenbrenner's ecological approach peppered throughout the book, reflecting its importance in considering the person in their environment approach. We will also consider the work of sociologist Glen H. Elder, who applied a sociological approach to understand development.

ECOLOGICAL THEORY

Urie Bronfenbrenner (1917–2005)

This theory looks at a person's development within the context of the system of relationships that form his or her environment. This approach is therefore also aligned to Systems theories, which emphasise reciprocal relationships between the elements that constitute a whole. Relationships among individuals, groups, organisations, or communities and mutually influencing factors in the environment are emphasised. You can see from his theoretical model that there are several systems that impact on the individual's development. This theory is also labelled as 'person in environment' and 'ecological', the latter label capturing its recognition of the influence of environment on development. The really clever aspect of this approach is that it encompasses the immediate environment of the child (parents, siblings) to more distant influences at the outer circle (social welfare policy, for example).

In essence three themes are contained within Bronfenbrenner's ecological approach:

1. the processes and pathways of development
2. the role of context and
3. the interaction of these two.

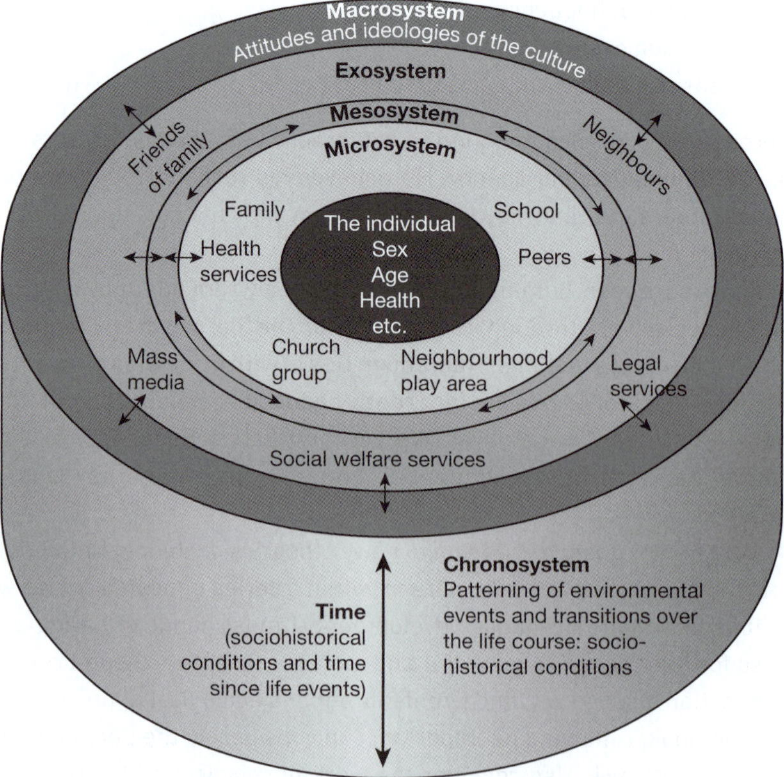

Figure 4.4 Levels of ecosystems
Source: U. Bronfenbrenner (1979)

MICROSYSTEM

This circle takes in the immediate environment of the child and includes family, school/teacher, peers and neighbourhood. Thus, anything that the child interacts with directly or has a relationship with can be included in this circle. Not only do these influences impact on the child, the child also impacts on its immediate environment; relationships at this level impact in two ways. Bronfenbrenner would call this a *bi-directional* influence. For example, a child with challenging behaviour is impacted on by their environment (parenting styles, poverty...), the child also impacts on its environment (affecting the parent(s) with their behaviour).

MESOSYSTEM

This can be a little trickier to understand. Basically, it refers to connections or relationships between different microsystems (for example, linkages between home and school). If a child has a difficult relationship with their parents, this can influence their interactions with peers (linkage between two microsystems, in this case parents and peers).

EXOSYSTEM

While the child does not have an active role or is not in immediate contact with it, this system can nonetheless affect what the child experiences in its immediate context. For example, work problems can affect the relationship between parents and also the child. If the father is promoted in work, this might mean he spends less time at home, leading to arguments with his wife and less time spent with his child. So the child is inadvertently impacted upon by the workplace of his father. The educational system, government agencies and mass media are influences that are seen in the exosystem.

MACROSYSTEM

This system refers to the culture and belief patterns of the people/society in which the child lives.

CHRONOSYSTEM

This relates to changing socio-historical circumstances. Put simply, each generation may have different experiences as time passes. In the 1950s in Ireland, a woman who married had to leave her job if she was employed in the civil service. In the 2000s, women can marry and continue to work. This reflects the changes that have occurred with the passage of time.

Bi-directionality

Bronfenbrenner included *bi-directionality* within his theory; this means that just as an environment can impact on an individual, the individual can also impact on the environment. A simple example is cuts in funding to schools that support children with additional needs. That child may lose a support assistant, and in turn the child now impacts on the school environment as they become frustrated due to the loss of the teaching assistant. Can you think of other examples of bi-directionality?

PRACTICE IMPLICATIONS – ETHNICALLY SENSITIVE PRACTICE

Daniel et al. (2010, p. 39) note that all the layers of influence contained within Bronfenbrenner's ecological theory help shape, directly and indirectly, a child's development. 'Ethnically sensitive practice consistent with an ecological approach that strives to improve the extent to which the material and social environment meets a person's individual needs'. The authors further cite a code of practice which considers issues of race and child protection, 'ethnicity is a concept which belongs to everyone. All practice should be seen in the context of class, race and gender, which in combination will show the uniqueness of all experience. Ethnically sensitive practice is not a "sideline" or an addendum – it needs to permeate practice at all times and at all levels.' Thus, the ecological has strong practice elements allowing us to view development through the lens of a global perspective rather than the more narrow confines favoured by earlier psychologists.

Initially, Bronfenbrenner's theory was a strongly ecological one, emphasising the effects of nurture or environmental influences. He later modified his theory to include the biological aspect of the person, reflecting the current view that both a child's biology and environment interact in the development of the child. This modified theory is referred to as Bronfenbrenner's 'bioecological' theory. On the model in the diagram above you will see that aspects such as the child's sex, age and health are included in influencing development. So, given that nature continues on a given path, how does the world that surrounds the child help or hinder continued development? This is an important question for you to reflect on.

At the end of this chapter a case study is used to demonstrate Bronfenbrenner's approach and dissect the layers of influence that might be at play. The ecological approach is also applied in Chapter 6, with an analysis of the mistreatment of children with disabilities, and again in Chapter 9, on abuse and trauma, to conceptualise factors in child abuse. Before ending with the case study, let's look at the work of Glen H. Elder who applied a sociological approach to developmental psychology.

Glen H. Elder Jr. (1934–)

Elder's theory was introduced to me many moons ago by a Professor of Disability Studies, Elder's theory represents the joining of a sociological approach to developmental psychology and demonstrates how such a twinning can prove fruitful and insightful in better conceptualising patterns of human development across the life span. Arguably, of all the efforts to combine sociology with child development within a theoretical framework, Elder's has been the most successful.

LIFE-COURSE THEORY

Elder's theory represents another approach to conceptualising and understanding human development across the life course. Elder stresses the influence of social forces in shaping the life course and its developmental consequences. According to Elder, life-course theory represents a general change in how we think about and study human lives and development. Where Bronfenbrenner's ecological theory now encompasses the biological influence of the individual, Elder's life-course theory has evolved into an effective way to investigate the impact of social change on the developmental course of human lives. Instead of concentrating on individual case studies, Elder's attention focuses on multiple and interlocking pathways. Let's take a closer look at how Elder has constructed his theory.

Four themes are distinctive of life-course theory:

1. human lives in historical time and place
2. human agency and social constraints
3. the timing of lives
4. linked lives.

HUMAN LIVES IN HISTORICAL TIME AND PLACE

Elder conducted research looking at the lives of boys who grew up during the Great Depression in America and those who grew up in Manchester, showing that they had very different life chances following their involvement in World War II. 'The California boys managed to escape the limitations of their deprived households by joining the armed forces and, after the war, using the benefits of the GI Bill for higher education' (2001, p. 37). Here we can see how historical influences and place can affect the lives of individuals in different ways.

HUMAN AGENCY AND SOCIAL CONSTRAINT

'Within the constraints of their world, people often plan and choose from options that become the building blocks of their evolving lives ... People of the same age do not march in concert across the major events of their life course; rather, they vary in pace and sequencing, and this variation has real consequences for people and society' (p. 38). Having children, starting work or getting married (if at all) occur at different ages under differing circumstances that reflect the individual's personal life experiences and their interpretation of a given situation. For example, I had my son when I was a student in my early twenties, and my friends of the same age who chose to have children did not do so until their mid-30s. This difference in 'building blocks' meant that in some aspects we remained on the same path but in others my life took a different direction in having my child at a younger age than my peers.

THINK ABOUT IT!

This is a very basic example but think of ways your life path has differed from those of your peers. Can you think of other examples from personal and professional experience where an 'event' changed the pathway of the individual, and in what ways?

THE TIMING OF LIVES

Elder (2001, p. 38) explains,

> social timing refers to the initiation of and departure from social roles, and to relevant age expectations and beliefs. The social meanings of age give structure to the life course through age norms and sanctions, social timetables for the occurrence and order of events, generalized age grades (such as childhood and adolescence), and age hierarchies in organizational settings (i.e., the age structure of firms).

LINKED LIVES

Most people's lives are intertwined with others, from their immediate family to more distantly placed work colleagues. Another interesting slant is the intergenerational aspect to this theme of linked lives. A failed marriage can impact on the children when, as adults, their life experience can be linked to the misfortunes of their parents; that is, they may be at increased risk of marital breakdown themselves. Elder comments 'each generation is bound to fateful decisions and events in the other's life course' (p. 39).

Finally, another component of Elder's life-course theory is that of the **cohort effect,** which refers to 'one of the ways in which lives can be influenced by social change. History is experienced as a cohort effect when social change and culture differentiate the life patterns of successive cohorts' (p. 37). What does this mean? In Chapter 6 on disability the example of a child born with Down syndrome is used to highlight Elder's cohort effect. Would the experience of a child born with Down syndrome nowadays be different than if the child had been born in another era? What cultural, social changes, including health and welfare aspects, might influence such a change? The cohort effect highlights the influence of social change upon successive generations. Finally, a small difference in the children's ages at the time the family experienced financial hardship appeared to have influenced outcomes. Those old enough to help the family out appeared to be less severely affected than younger children unable to understand what was happening or perhaps more vulnerable to parental depression or anger.

THINK ABOUT IT!

What other contexts and situations can Elder's approach be applied to? Imagine families with children of differing ages. Do you believe that the older children adjust better than the younger ones to a change in circumstance? Can this experience affect them across their life span?

CASE STUDY DEMONSTRATING ECOLOGICAL UNDERSTANDING AND INTERPLAY OF FACTORS

CASE STUDY

Lily is 2 years old and lives in a neighbourhood affected by economic and social deprivation, including high unemployment levels, addiction and poverty. Lily lives with her mum and younger brother Darren who is 1. Lily's dad isn't around and she misses him when the other children talk about their fathers. The flat they live in is damp and cold, as Lily's mum Susie struggles to find the money to pay for heating. Lily has had continual chest infections and was recently diagnosed with asthma. Susie cannot work, as Lily is often sick, and also believes that she can't access full-time childcare, as it is too expensive and she would lose her benefits for no financial gain. It is difficult enough for her to feed and clothe the children as it is. Susie can't afford to buy her children many treats, such as toys, and the playground that was built in the area has been vandalised. Lily has started to attend a crèche for 15 hours a week as part of the government initiative for disadvantaged children though she misses a lot due to being sick. Lately, staff have noticed Lily has become quieter and withdrawn. When they mentioned this to Susie she confided that she herself had been diagnosed with depression and was feeling increasing overwhelmed. Susie has few social supports and friends and is feeling isolated.

External influences

Government Policy – this is the most distant factor but one that affects Lily's and her family's well-being outcomes. The introduction of (limited) free childcare has given Lily the opportunity to attend crèche, why is this a protective factor? What other external influences including government policy, welfare resources and economic factors can you identify that are relevant to this case study? How do they interact and what impact do they have on Lily and her family? What are the protective factors and risk factors that may be of influence?

COMMUNITY AND PRESCHOOL

In this case study would you identify 'community' as a **risk** or **protective** factor? It is risk in terms of poverty, high unemployment and low levels of cohesion and these are associated with poorer outcomes. There is a lack of play opportunities in the area, since the playground was vandalised. Poor standard housing is a risk factor and is contributing to Lily's health problems. Can you see anything protective in Lily's community? Well there's a crèche which is high quality, so this is protective if it provides a high quality service. What community characteristics can support or detract from well-being and development, how do they interact and how does this impact the family?

Immediate influences

We can see which circle of influence is closest to Lily and has the most direct impact upon her. Let's look at this from a few different areas:

Relationship with parent: What are the protective influences? Are there any negative aspects?

Physical health and well-being: Lily's physical environment within her home is not conducive to general well-being. Is this a risk factor and contributing to her health problems? Could this aspect of physical development impact on Lily's cognitive development? She is missing learning opportunities because of her chest problems (this is potentially related to poor housing, which could be contributing towards or causing her difficulties).

Social Relationships: Susie doesn't have a strong social network, including family, so Lily is missing out on what can be a protective factor. However, now that she is attending crèche she has the opportunity to develop friendships with other children. However, Susie's depression could be in part fuelled by her isolation and lack of social supports, and Susie's mood, in turn, could be affecting Lily's.

Poverty: Lily lives in an impoverished family and in a community of social and economic deprivation. In her home she sometimes goes cold and doesn't have a lot of toys to play with, as her Mum can't afford much. In her community, the playground that was built has been vandalised, so she has no real outdoor space to play in. Living in poor housing has led to her health problems and means she misses preschool often; this could impact on her learning potential.

Can you see the different layers of factors and influences intertwining with each other and affecting Lily's outcomes? A lack of expenditure at government level has led to poor housing, which in turn has affected Lily's physical health directly. Further, structural and societal obstacles impact on this family from a wider level (housing, welfare, childcare policy), which in turn creates poor housing, not enough childcare provision for Susie and poverty. These influences impact directly on the individuals involved. Bronfenbrenner's ecological theory captures the complexity of influences intertwined in a global picture and affecting development.

Finally, using the same case study consider how race, ethnicity, gender or disability, for example, would change the influences and affect development. If Lily had a learning disability or was of Pakistani background, in what ways would this affect the layers of influences at play?

SUMMARY

So we finish our exploration of the major theoretical approaches popular in psychology. In the next chapter on Human Growth and Development we will revisit some of the theories as we pass through the different age stages. New theories specific to particular age groups (e.g. Elkind's theory of adolescent cognition) will be introduced. What, hopefully, is clearer is that no one theory holds the 'answers', reflecting the complexity of the human experience. However, it is nonetheless important that we engage and know the different theoretical approaches and content, so we better understand individual capacities and life stages and are better equipped to support them.

chapter

5 HUMAN GROWTH AND DEVELOPMENT

CHAPTER OUTLINE

- Developmental psychology
- Conception, prenatal development and the first two years
- Fertilisation and conception
- Prenatal development
- Infancy and the first two years of life
- Childhood (2–11 years)
- Physical development
- Cognitive development
- Socioemotional development
- Baumrind's parenting styles and parent–child interactions
- Adolescence
- Sexual maturation
- Cognitive development
- Socioemotional development
- In focus: Lesbian, Gay, Bisexual and Transgender (LGBT) teens
- Adulthood
- Ageing

This chapter proposes to cover a wide gamut as it examines human development across the life span, beginning with conception and finishing at the end of life. To make it more manageable the entire life span will be divided into five categories – conception, prenatal development and infancy, childhood, adolescence and finally, adulthood and old age. Developmental theories will be alluded to, as well as age- or concept-specific theories (e.g. Elkind's theory of adolescent cognition). In addition, domains of development including physical, cognitive, socioemotional and cultural will be discussed while 'In focus' pieces allow you to consider a topic in more depth. A broad knowledge base is required of social workers, and this chapter will endeavour to take you through the psychology of the life span. While it cannot be exhaustive, as all age stages and domains of development are covered, hopefully, you will begin to recognise that these domains are interrelated and interact to influence developmental outcomes. So let's start where it all begins, not at birth but at the moment of they consider conception.

DEVELOPMENTAL PSYCHOLOGY

A characteristic of modern psychological theories of development is that they are systematic rather than unifactorial, that is, considering many rather than just one aspect, in their conceptions about the influences and factors that affect development. Thus, such newer conceptualisations have shied away from nature/nurture or individual/society dichotomies in an attempt to understand development across the life span

- Early and middle adulthood
- Cognitive development
- Socioemotional development
- Late adulthood
- Physical changes
- Cognitive development
- Socioemotional development
- Death and dying
- Terminology
- Phases of dying
- Personal versus role-specific perspective
- Models of dying
- Children's understanding of death

using a more holistic and inclusive approach. This approach emphasises the causal role of various systems of influence that are based, for example, on historical-cultural differences, social strata and other characteristics of the developmental ecology. Put simply, models such as Bronfenbrenner and Lerner's (Chapter 4) hold a more rounded and modern approach to understanding human development. In this chapter we leave more theoretical discussions alone and focus on the changes that occur throughout and across the life span.

CONCEPTION, PRENATAL DEVELOPMENT AND THE FIRST TWO YEARS

Conception and Prenatal Development

- Chromosomes and genes explained
- Genetic inheritance (recessive and dominant inheritance)
- Chromosomal disorders
- Prenatal development, including critical periods in human development
- Hazards during prenatal development

Infancy and First Two Years

Physical Development – Infancy

- Reflexes,
- Gross/Fine motor skills

Cognitive Development – Infancy

- Piaget's
- Sensorimotor
  - Object Permanence
  - Imitation

Social Development – Infancy

- Temperament
- Development of Self
- Attachment (from a biopsychosocial approach)
  - brain development and attachment
  - Psychodynamic – maternal bonding and object relations theories
  - Cultural considerations in attachment

In Focus: Disorganised attachment and psychopathology

In Practice: Assessing sibling attachment

Often when people think of human development across the life span the starting point is birth. However, many of the foundations for development occur at the moment of conception. It is important to understand these processes and what is typical development, in order not just to support it but also to recognise when development deviates and becomes atypical. We will begin by exploring the processes that occur at conception and the possible impact they can have on a child's development after birth.

FERTILISATION AND CONCEPTION

The menstrual cycle occurs in females of reproductive age. At the beginning of the cycle an egg (ovum) begins to develop in the ovary. This egg is released and travels down the fallopian tube. Fertilisation occurs when a woman's ovum or egg is penetrated or fertilised by a man's sperm. The fertilised egg is called a zygote. A continuous process of cell division then occurs until this mass of cells attaches itself to the mother's uterus approximately 10 to 14 days after fertilisation. The man's sperm and the woman's egg each contain hereditary information in the form of chromosomes.

Chromosomes and genes

A chromosome is a tightly coiled molecule of deoxyribonucleic acid (DNA) that consists of smaller segments called genes. A gene can be thought of as your body's instruction manual and genes affect how you look, your health and how your body works. The zygote contains 23 pairs of chromosomes: 23 single chromosomes from the sperm and 23 chromosomes from the egg (in total, 46 chromosomes: 23 pairs). Thus, in the fertilised egg each pair of chromosomes contains one chromosome from each parent. Out of the 23 pairs of chromosomes, it is the final pair (the 23rd) that determines a person's sex.

- in males the 23rd pair consists of an X and Y chromosome
- in females the 23rd pair consists of two X chromosomes.

There are approximately 25,000 genes contained on the 46 chromosomes in each cell in a human body. This means that one chromosome contains thousands of genes. We inherit our genetic make-up from our biological parents through the transmission of their genes during conception.

- Our **genotype** is the sum total of our genetic make-up: the specific genetic make-up of the individual. Our genotype is present from conception and never changes.
- Our **phenotype** is the set of observable characteristics that are produced by that genetic endowment. Phenotypes can be affected by other genes and by the environment (such as climate, diet and lifestyle).

Many kinds of variation are influenced by both genetic and environmental factors. Though our genes govern what characteristics we inherit, our environment can affect *how* these inherited characteristics develop. For example, an individual may have inherited a tendency to be tall but a poor diet during childhood will cause poor growth.

Genetic conditions

Some genes are dominant and some are recessive. Consider the example of hair colour to understand the difference. Brown hair is regulated by a dominant gene, blonde hair a recessive one. My father has brown hair and my mother has blonde; I have brown hair yet my brother has blonde: how is this so? If an individual has one brown-hair gene and one blonde-hair gene, they will have brown hair, because the brown-hair gene is dominant and 'overpowers' the blonde-hair gene. To have blonde hair you must have two blonde-hair genes. So my mother must have two blonde-hair genes and has passed one blonde-hair gene to my brother. My brown-haired father has one brown-hair gene and one blonde-hair gene, and must have passed a blonde-hair gene to my brother, as my blonde-haired brother must have two blonde-hair genes. I always think of genetic inheritance as similar to the National Lottery; you never know the mix of balls (numbers) you might end up with. So conception is literally a lottery!

Certain conditions and disorders are genetically inherited. Here we see both recessive and dominant genetic inheritance at work.

Recessive inheritance

If two parents are both carriers of a genetic condition with a recessive inheritance pattern, there is a one-in-four chance that each child will be affected. So, on average, one-quarter of their children will be affected. There is also a one-in-two chance that each child will be an unaffected carrier, like the parents. Examples of genetic conditions that show a recessive pattern of inheritance are cystic fibrosis, sickle-cell disease, Tay-Sachs disease and phenylketonuria (PKU).

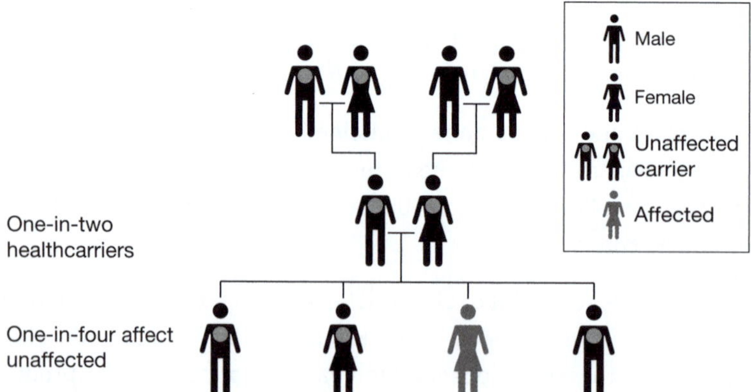

Figure 5.1 Inheritance pattern of cystic fibrosis

Dominant inheritance

If one of two parents is affected by a genetic condition with a dominant inheritance pattern, every child has a one-in-two chance of being affected. So, on average, half their children will be affected, and half their children will not be affected and so will not pass on the condition. However, as chance determines inheritance, it is also possible that all or none of their children will be affected. An example of genetic conditions that show a dominant pattern of inheritance is Huntington's disease.

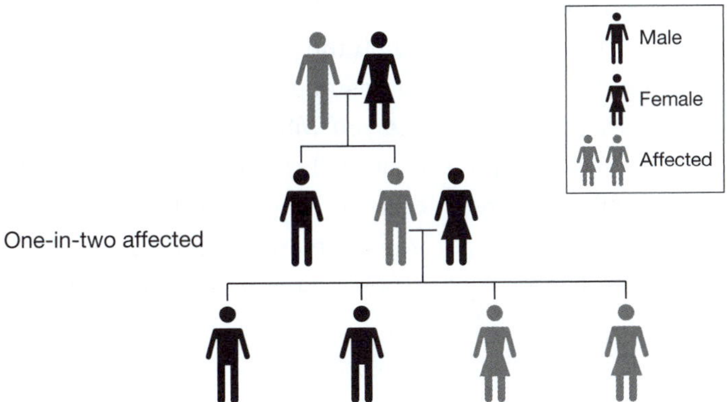

Figure 5.2 Inheritance pattern of Huntington's disease

The major difference between dominant and recessive gene inheritance is as follows:

> **Recessive:** For the child to inherit the condition, it must inherit two variant (affected) chromosomes; one from each parent. Thus a child has a 1:4 chance of inheriting the condition, a 1:2 chance of becoming a healthy carrier and a 1:4 chance of not inheriting the affected chromosome.
>
> **Dominant:** One parent is affected, whereas the other parent can be healthy. At conception, if the variant chromosome of the affected parent is transferred then the child will inherit the condition. It does not matter if the other parent's chromosome is healthy. Thus, with dominant conditions, such as Huntington's disease, the child has a 1:2 chance of inheriting the condition.

Recessive inheritance, ethnicity and cultural practices

Some recessive genetic conditions are more prevalent among certain ethnic groups; for example, Ireland has the highest rate of cystic fibrosis [CF], and Iceland also has high prevalence. Tay-Sachs disease is associated with the Ashkenazi Jews, who tend to practise endogamy, marrying within their own ethnic group. As we saw, both parents need to carry and transmit the gene for a recessive condition to be inherited. We can see how cultural and social practices (such as marrying within a grouping based on ethnicity or class) can increase the likelihood of both parents having it. An explanation suggested for the high rates of CF in Ireland and Iceland relates to both countries being islands; therefore limiting a dilution of the gene pool. While other groups also carry the genes for these conditions, among others, it is noteworthy to see where nature and nurture can collide and how cultural practices pertaining to marriage can impact on the inheritability of some genetic conditions.

Chromosomal disorders

We have seen that gene-linked disorders include cystic fibrosis, PKU and Huntington's disease. These are different to chromosomal abnormalities such as Down syndrome. Both occur at conception but whereas the gene-linked conditions are inherited, chromosomal conditions generally occur through the presence of an extra chromosome. If you recall, each cell has 23 pairs of chromosomes. In Down syndrome an extra copy of chromosome 21 is present. Sometimes you will find Down syndrome referred to as 'trisomy 21', the 'tri-' referring to the three chromosomes present instead of two. Other chromosomal syndromes include Patau syndrome (trisomy 13) and Edwards syndrome (trisomy 18). Sex-linked chromosome abnormalities can also occur, such as Fragile X syndrome. Chapter 6 discusses issues related to disability in greater depth.

Phenylketonuria

Earlier in the section on conception we encountered a genetically inherited condition called phenylketonuria (PKU). This is a condition that, if diagnosed, can be treated and controlled. However, if undetected this condition can lead to severe intellectual disability, as amino acids build up, causing brain damage in the child. It can be treated with a modified diet that excludes the specific amino acid concerned, thus preventing it from accumulating in the child's system. Within the first few days of life a pin prick is made on an infant's heel and blood is extracted and analysed, which allows for a diagnosis to be made.

THINK ABOUT IT! NATURE VERSUS NURTURE

This genetic condition illustrates how nature and nurture can interact and determine the developmental path a child's life will take. While this is a genetic condition (nature) and can't be 'cured', the nature of this condition means that external forces (nurture) can prevent the condition from progressing and disabling the child. If the test is carried out and the condition diagnosed, a modified diet excluding the amino acid responsible results in the child continuing to develop 'normally'. In countries where such tests are not carried and interventions taken (nurture), then this condition which can be treated will lead to eventual catastrophic brain damage, affecting the child's developmental outcomes and life path.

It is interesting to see that even in something so 'biologically' based as genetic inheritance other influences are at play, including marriage practices, health policy and the availability of tests for newborns. Clearly seen is the influence of external factors and influences on prenatal development. Before you read on, identify as many factors as you can that might affect the in-utero development.

PRENATAL DEVELOPMENT

Prenatal development consists of three stages:

1. the germinal stage
2. the embryonic stage
3. the foetal stage.

The germinal stage – approximately the first two weeks of development: when a woman's egg (ovum) is fertilised by a man's sperm, the fertilised egg is called a zygote. Once fertilised, a process of continual cell division begins. Approximately 10 to 14 days after conception the zygote, which now contains a mass of cells, attaches itself to the mother's uterus.

The embryonic stage – end of the second week to the eighth week: the cell mass is now called an embryo. The placenta and umbilical cord begin to develop during this stage and the bodily organs and systems begin to form. By week eight the heart is beating and the brain is forming. Facial features such as eyes become discernible.

The foetal stage – from the ninth week until birth: the embryo is now referred to as a foetus. At 24 weeks the eyes open. At 28 weeks the foetus attains the age of viability, meaning that it is likely to survive outside the womb in the event of premature birth (Hetherington and Parke, 1999).

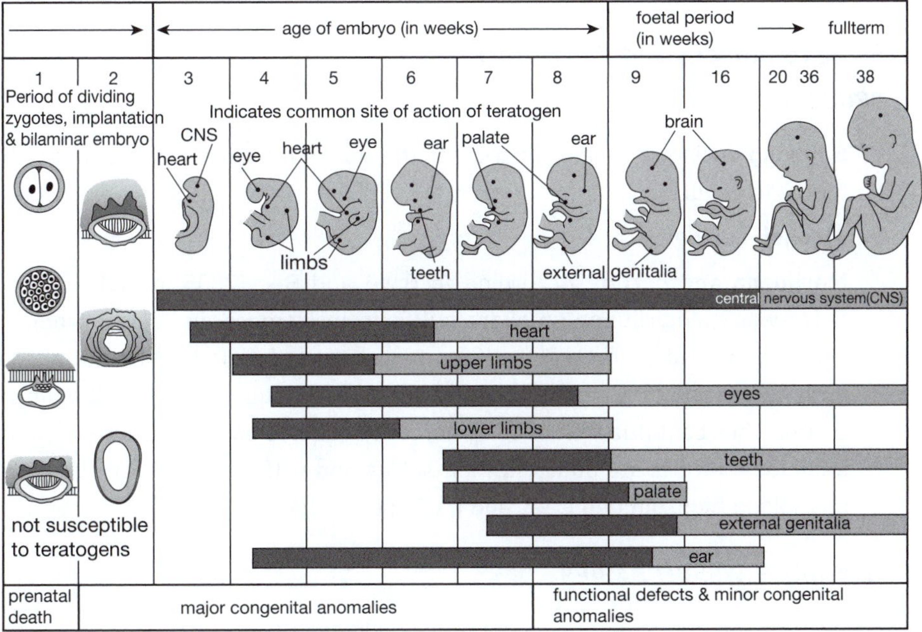

Figure 5.3 Critical periods in human development

Source: Boyd and Bee (2005, p. 65).

Hazards during prenatal development

As we saw earlier, chromosomal and genetic disorders affect the foetus at the moment of conception. Other external factors can affect and influence the foetus's development in the womb. Diet and nutrition can be an influence: If a pregnant mother is not getting the required calories needed, the foetus is more likely to have a low birth weight, compared to pregnant women who gain 26 or more pounds. Factors such as age and emotional stress have been implicated in prenatal development as well as HIV/AIDS and Rubella. Some external influences, known as *teratogens*, can cause birth defects. The timing of exposure and dose of a teratogen can make a difference in outcome. Consider the case of thalidomide, a drug available in chemists for use in easing morning sickness, which was recommended to pregnant women in the late 1950s. As the pregnant women who had taken the drug began to give birth it became apparent that their babies had been affected by the drug. The infants were born with missing or shortened arms and legs. In the table above you will notice periods where different parts of the body are more vulnerable to teratogenic exposure. These women were taking thalidomide for morning sickness, which can occur early in pregnancy; just the time when the limbs of the foetus are vulnerable.

As we examine different teratogens, bear in mind that timing, dose and duration of exposure all interact in determining outcomes. Another influence can be genetic vulnerability, which we will explore below in the section on foetal alcohol syndrome disorder. These multitude of influences illustrate the concept of *individual variation* that runs through developmental psychology.

Some teratogens and their effects

DRUGS

Smoking during pregnancy increases the risk of miscarriage, premature birth and low birth weight.

Alcohol: see below.

Marijuana and heroin: According to Boyd and Bee (2005, p. 67), 'The infants of twice-weekly marijuana smokers suffer from tremors and sleep problems. They seem to have little interest in their surroundings for up to 2 weeks after birth; ... both heroin and methadone ... can cause miscarriage, premature labour, and early death.' They continue that 60 to 80 percent of babies born to heroin- or methadone-addicted mothers are addicted themselves and suffer withdrawal symptoms, such as making high-pitched cries and having convulsions.

LOW-BIRTH-WEIGHT BABIES

- Low birth weight: less than 5½ pounds (2,500 grams) at birth
- Very low weight: less than 3 pounds (1,360 grams) at birth
- Extremely low weight: under 2 pounds (907 grams) at birth.

PRETERM BABIES

- Born before 38 weeks' gestation
- Most preterm babies are low-weight.

SMALL-FOR-DATE INFANTS

- Birth weight is below normal when the length of pregnancy is considered
- Weigh less than 90 percent of the average weight of all babies of the same gestational age.

Cigarette smoking is the leading cause of low birth weight (LBW) in infants (UNICEF, 2004). Adolescents who give birth when their bodies have not fully developed are at risk of having LBW babies. An 'In focus' piece will discuss, in Chapter 8, birth weight and social inequality using Bronfenbrenner's ecological approach and considers how low birth weight can impact across the life span. Low birth weight and preterm are not the only potential consequences of using harmful substances during pregnancy; alcohol in pregnancy has been linked to Foetal Alcohol Syndrome and Foetal Alcohol Effects, conditions which include learning disabilities and behavioural difficulties among their characteristics. Of course, hazards exist for the infant during the birthing process, including anoxia (a lack of oxygen), which can lead to brain damage, and other disabilities including cerebral palsy. The Early Years movement, as we have seen, emphasises the first 2 years especially as critical to developmental outcomes. While we may not wish to be deterministic the early years are important to the developing child: let's take a look. You may wish to revisit Chapter 2 where we examined brain development during this period and saw as the brain becomes more powerful and sophisticated, so does thinking and other capacities including language.

INFANCY AND THE FIRST TWO YEARS OF LIFE

The first two years of life are a time of immense development and growth. This is very obvious in the realm of physical development, where an infant will within a year generally be able to crawl, stand and begin to walk. Within a life span perspective it can be argued that these years are particularly significant for future functioning in later life. Within a nature–nurture context, we will look at the role and impact of 'nurture' (environment) on a child's development. It is important for social workers to have some knowledge of what is considered 'developmentally typical' at different age stages, as deviation away from this can potentially indicate that something's awry. However, as always, temper this with the concept of individual variation; a child who is small for their age may come from a family who are smaller than average. Children with disabilities, particularly learning, will be developmentally delayed in some domains of functioning. With this caveat in place, let us consider how a young child typically develops.

In Chapter 2 we examined the development of the brain across the life span. To recap, the brain at birth weighs 25 percent of its eventual adult weight; by the child's second birthday the brain will have increased to 75 percent of its adult weight. Thus, this period in the child's life represents a period of marked growth. It is therefore imperative that this development is supported and the child suitably stimulated to ensure the best outcomes possible. Brain development and functioning is inextricably tied to cognitive ability, and this has been the impetus behind the 'Early Years Movement'.

As the brain develops, so too do thinking abilities. In Chapter 4 we discussed what is meant by cognitive development and theories related to it. Here we briefly recap Piaget's theory of cognitive development within a specific age period or stage; please see Chapter 4 for a more detailed account of his theory.

Cognitive development

PIAGET'S SENSORIMOTOR STAGE (0–2 YEARS)

Features of this stage include:

- object permanence
- causality
- representational ability
- imitation.

The sensorimotor stage represents the first stage of Piaget's cognitive theory. During this stage we witness the use of the senses and movement by the infant to learn about its world and to construct knowledge of it. As they develop, infants realise that they can make things happen; they bang spoons and throw objects from their high chair. This also highlights that the infant sees itself as separate from its environment and is developing a sense of agency about its actions; in other words, that it is the 'agent' or initiator of its actions. Another aspect to this is causality, when the child begins to recognise a causal relationship that exists; for example, 'If I shake this rattle it will make a noise.'

OBJECT PERMANENCE

Object permanence refers to the understanding that objects continue to exist even when we can no longer see them. Its acquisition towards the end of this stage is considered an important milestone in cognitive development. Related to object permanence is the concept of representational ability. This involves the ability to make a mental representation of an object; that is, to be able to represent it mentally or within your mind. This allows the child to manipulate the object, which can lead to the further acquisition of problem-solving skills. A good way to understand representational ability or mental representation is to imagine you're driving to college or work and you get stuck in a traffic jam. If you know the area you can mentally represent a map of it and start figuring out a new way to get to your destination. You map out your new route in your mind before you commit to it. The ability to map the area in your mind reflects a representational ability. Piaget believed this ability develops between 18 and 24 months of age. Of course, the example used is a sophisticated form of mental representation and involves problem solving, which is something you would see in an older child, nonetheless the basic blocks of mental representation begin at this early stage.

IMITATION

Imitation is the reproduction of an expression or behaviour. Piaget proposed that imitation was achieved at roughly nine months of age and that deferred imitation occurred later, again after the acquisition of mental representation. Meltzoff and Moore (1977) found that babies could, within a few weeks of life, imitate or reproduce a facial expression made by an adult, such as sticking a tongue out. Some have argued that this is merely a reflex; however, Meltzoff and Moore believe it reflects a biologically based capacity to imitate. Meltzoff and Moore (1988) also found evidence of what he believes to be a nine-month-old's capacity for deferred imitation. This means that the infant reproduces a gesture after a certain amount of time has lapsed; for example, the following day. This is noteworthy when we consider that Piaget did not believe that children acquired 'object permanence' until the end of the second year. In order to have object permanence the child must be able to make a mental representation of the object so that they know the object continues to exist even though they can no longer see it. Yet in order to imitate a facial expression these very young infants must already possess these abilities to some degree. Not only does Meltzoff and Moore's research demonstrate that imitation is acquired earlier than Piaget proposed, it would also suggest that infants acquire concepts such as object permanence and mental representation earlier than proposed by Piaget.

THINK ABOUT IT!

Remember Bandura's social learning theory in the last chapter; observation and imitation were core elements of his theory, as they are of Piaget's cognitive theory. Thus we can suggest a link between cognitive theory and social learning, which can lead us to argue that even the very young are capable of learning through observation and imitation – if you choose to accept both theorists' explanations that is! How can this link be useful to social work? If you take an issue such as aggressive behaviour, does this link offer insights into its possible origins? What other areas might also be involved in observation, imitation and cognitive representation; addiction, prosocial behaviour, emotional regulation?

Later on in this chapter we will be exploring the role of parenting; in the section on adolescence we will be considering the role of media in eating disorders. In Chapter 10 an in-depth discussion of aggressive and prosocial behaviour will be outlined. Using Bronfenbrenner's ecological approach, one can see how many layers, beginning within the family and spreading out through peers, community and media, are observed and cognitively stored by the developing child, and what you might see as the potential implications of this for social work practice. Finally we see how even theories from different domains can be interrelated and interact, just like development itself.

Later we are going to look at personality, which falls with the domain of socio-emotional development. Before doing so let's consider temperament. While intrinsic to personality, development is nonetheless a distinct concept with a greater emphasis on biological origins.

TEMPERAMENT

> Temperament is a biologically based propensity for individuals to react emotionally and behaviourally to events in a certain way.

What kind of temperament did you have as a baby?

Were you a happy or easy going baby or did you frequently throw tantrums? Temperament is believed to contribute towards the development of personality. With regard to infancy, theorists have tended to focus on whether an infant's temperament impacts on the parent–child interaction. Another area of interest is whether temperament is stable across a person's life span and if childhood temperament predicts adult outcomes. Thomas and Chess (1977, 1986) asked parents to fill out reports of their babies behaviour and devised a classification of three types of temperament:

Easy babies (40% of sample) – these babies were reported to have regular feeding and sleeping patterns and were not fussy eaters. They were playful and reacted well to new situations.

Difficult babies (10% of sample) – according to parental responses these babies had fussy eating habits, irregular sleeping and eating patterns. They were irritable, threw tantrums when frustrated and cried more.

Slow to warm-up babies (15% of sample) – these babies had mildly negative reactions to new situations. Unlike the difficult babies, whose tantrums might include spitting out food, these babies showed more of a passive resistance; for example, they would let the food drool out rather than spit it out.

CAN YOU SEE ANY DIFFICULTIES WITH THIS STUDY?

Well it's based solely on parental reports of the infant's behaviour and as such might lack objectivity. Yet the idea of infant temperament is an important one, as researchers have continued to develop ways of measuring it. Newer approaches include observing directly the infant's behaviour and asking not just the parents but also other adults to rate the child's behaviour. Buss and Plomin (1984) found that temperament is not that stable in infancy, meaning it can change as the child grows older. Yet others have found stability in some aspects of temperament. Shyness is part of a more general temperament style called **behavioural inhibition** (Passer & Smith, 2001, p. 472). Kagan et al. (1988) examined inhibited behaviours (infants who were quiet, shy and would withdraw from unfamiliar people and objects) and uninhibited behaviours (more sociable, spontaneous and open to new experiences). They found that extremely inhibited or uninhibited temperament was predictive of either childhood shyness or sociability. For example, a highly uninhibited infant became a sociable and talkative 7 year old, while an extremely inhibited infant developed into a shy and quiet child. Kagan's work suggests that there is some evidence of long-term stability in certain aspects of temperament.

Social and emotional development

FREUD'S ORAL STAGE (0–2 YEARS)

As we saw in Chapter 4, Freud considered the mouth as the prime source of pleasure and believed that feeding and, more particularly, the weaning period should be handled with care. He advised against weaning a baby too early or indulging the infant and weaning too late, as either could result in the infant's becoming 'fixated' at the oral stage. This could have negative consequences in later life, including swearing, smoking, biting of nails, overeating and so on. You will notice that all these behaviours are related to the area of the mouth. Freud advised that through oral satisfaction, the baby develops trust and an optimistic personality. If the child experiences oral dissatisfaction, that is, its needs aren't met, then the personality may become pessimistic, aggressive and distrusting.

ERIKSON'S TRUST VERSUS MISTRUST (0–1 YEAR)

In the first year of life the infant is completely dependent on its caregivers. How well the infant's needs are met and how sensitive the parenting is decides whether the infant develops trust or mistrust of the world.

AUTONOMY VERSUS SHAME AND DOUBT (1–2 YEARS)

Children begin to walk and assert their independence. Children can come to believe in themselves and their abilities through the encouragement and support of their caregivers. If the child's efforts are ridiculed, the child will develop a feeling of shame and doubt. Toilet training is seen as one of the key events which can influence the outcome of this stage.

The influence of Freud on Erikson is clear; the latter speaks of toilet training as an important event as did Freud, although from a different perspective. Yet nowadays, toilet training is considered a significant developmental milestone that indicates the child is developing typically (Appendix I outlines in greater detail developmental milestones from 0 to 5 years).

THE DEVELOPMENT OF SELF

The development of a sense of self is a quality that marks us as unique individually, and possibly even as a species. In terms of the development of self-awareness, it is believed that by:

- 18 months old – children learn to recognise themselves
- 2 years old – children begin to express their emotional states.

It is then that they must make the distinction between self and other. Rochat (2001) charts the development of self-knowledge in infants from implicit self-knowledge towards explicit self-knowledge.

Implicit self-knowledge

There are two types of implicit self-knowledge. The first is perceptual in origin and relates to the development of knowledge about our own body through self-exploration and action on objects. The second is social and refers to the development of specific knowledge through our interactions and reciprocation with others. The development of a sense of self can be witnessed through our use of language. Rochat (2001) contends that the use of 'me' refers to the early stage of implicit self-knowledge, while the use of 'I' is accomplished at the explicit stage of self-knowledge, or when self-concept is formed. Regardless of how one conceptualises the development of a sense of self, it is an integral part of the development of an individual.

The concept of the 'other' as being central to our development of a sense of self, in addition to the role of language, can also be seen in the work of psychologist and sociologist George Herbert Mead (1863–1931), who was instrumental in the development of the **symbolic interactionist perspective**. This approach emphasises the importance of language and social interaction for the development of the self. Mead maintained that the child acquires a sense of who they are through play. Role-play and pretence were of particular importance towards this goal. Mead suggested that children did not develop a mature sense of self until they learned to take on the role of the other. Sense of self is tied into how we are socialised, the messages we receive and how we internalise them; it is also linked to identity and personality, which is examined in depth in the section on childhood.

Attachment

Before looking at maternal bonding and object-relation theories, it is useful to ground these theories against attachment, which was outlined in Chapter 4. This early relationship we form with another, acts as a template for our later relationships in life. Thus it is of critical importance that attachment is supported and nurtured, especially at the early stages. The importance of this early relationship can be seen in intervention programmes, where parenting is a significant element, reflecting the recognition that secure attachment is generally associated with better outcomes later in life. Later in the section on adulthood, adult attachment styles and their implications are examined.

We are going to use a biopsychosocial approach in discussing aspects of attachment in this section. From a biological perspective the relationship between the brain and attachment is overviewed. Maternal bonding theory and object relations theory will highlight the psychological component, and cultural aspects of attachment will then be offered, highlighting the myriad of parenting approaches that exist.

BIOLOGICAL – THE BRAIN AND ATTACHMENT

Drs Perry and Szalavitz (2008, p. 85) describe how attachment 'templates' develop through parenting and brain development,

> If you are one of the majority of infants born to a loving home, a consistent, nurturing caregiver—say a mother or father – will be present and repeatedly meet your needs. Time and again, one or both parents will come when you cry and soothe you when you are hungry, cold or scared. As your brain develops these loving caregivers provide the template that you use for human relationships. Attachment, then, is a

> memory template for human-to- human bonds. This template serves as your primary 'world view' on human relationships. It is profoundly influenced by whether you experience kind, attuned parenting or whether you receive inconsistent, frequently disrupted, abusive or neglected 'care'.

Dr Perry links the brain to how attachment develops, so let's take a look at recent developments tracking the relationship of brain development to attachment.

According to Shaver and Mikulincer (2010, p. 167), there is no one brain system solely responsible for the 'attachment behavioural system'. Rather '... brain circuitry used for a range of purposes, such as social perception and memory, emotion, and emotion regulation, underlies attachment-related emotions and behavior as well'. Shaver continues that Coan's Social Baseline Theory (SBT) contends that the human brain was constructed through evolution to rely on relationships with other people's brains. 'That is, the default state of the brain depends on social regulation and self-other co-regulation. When a person is forced to survive without adequate co-regulation, the brain functions and develops in a non-optimal way, in line with what researchers have been showing indirectly all along while focusing on behavior.' What does that mean? We need the interaction and positive support of others to reach our optimum potential in terms of attachment and related behaviours; when we don't receive such interaction and support (secure attachment) we are negatively affected in terms of our developmental outcomes and in our behaviour. This approach ties in with affective neuroscience, as discussed, in the work of Dr Margot Sunderland in Chapter 2. If one accepts the biological explanation alone, the brain is shaped positively or negatively by our relationships in childhood, particularly with our immediate caregivers, this can affect our brain structures or chemistry, which in turn impact on how we relate to others later in life. The psychodynamic perspective would argue that the roots of our relationships lie in our minds, not purely in the brain. The following are two psychologically based theories on the development of our relationships early in life.

PSYCHOLOGICAL – ATTACHMENT

Maternal bonding theory

Herbert (2006, p. 54) comments that the 1970s were a stark 'critical period' for bonding, where it was proposed that during the first hours after birth the mother should engage in bonding with her baby through tactile, visual and olfactory stimulation. It was suggested that interruption of this bonding (for example, where the baby is removed to intensive care) could have negative long-term effects on the mother–child relationship. Thankfully, this stark belief is no longer popular, but maternal bonding still holds interest in many quarters. Studies have found no evidence that disruption of 'close contact' between mother and baby has any impact on their relationship or mothering effectiveness.

Object relations – Melanie Klein

Another conceptualisation of loss is that of object relations, as developed by Melanie Klein. Klein was a famous psychoanalyst, and in developing object relations theory she suggested that the 'loss' of an object could have a potentially negative effect (for example, to an infant an 'object' could be their mother; the loss of the mother through perhaps death or separation could lead to negative outcomes for the child in later life). The focus of object relations theory, unlike Freud, is not the forces of libido and aggression, nor on the adaptive functions of the ego; instead, it is on the complex relationship of self to other. Object relations theory explores the process whereby people come to experience themselves as separate and independent from others, while at the same time needing profound attachment to others. Klein (1952) summarised the core tenet of this theory: 'there is no instinctual urge, no anxiety situation, no mental process which does not involve objects, external or internal; in other words, object relations are at the centre of emotional life' (p. 53). It is interesting that Klein emphasises the notion of the individual experiencing themselves as other and separate from others. The development of a sense of self has also been considered from perspectives other than the psychoanalytic perspective, as we will see later in the chapter.

ATTACHMENT – CULTURAL ASPECTS

In the preceding chapter, the role of culture was briefly mentioned, arguing against an ethnocentric approach to understanding and assessing attachment patterns. Research that compared attachment patterns between countries found that differences in attachment classifications had less to do with 'poor' attachment but result from cultural differences; for instance, the concept of 'amae' in Japan and the collectivistic approach of an Israeli kibbutz. In cultures where children sleep with their parents, often into middle childhood, the Western practice of leaving a baby to sleep by itself or in another room may be viewed with disdain. We have seen attachment from a biological perspective. Music (2011, p. 67) cautions,

> it is argued that attachment theory is a universal biological system, and yet like all theories it developed in a particular time and within a specific cultural framework. It is important to ask whether attachment theory can usefully be applied to other cultures, or whether there is a bias in the research towards parenting styles valued in the West.

Music cites the work of Rothbaum and colleagues, who argue that this bias is inherent in that actual theory of attachment itself, where concepts such as 'autonomy' and independence are valued, reflecting the individualistic values of Western cultures. Nonetheless, research does suggest that across diverse cultures a consistency exists, where attachment security is linked to maternal sensitivity. Attachment appears to be universal in spite of the nuances of cultural practices.

THINK ABOUT IT!

Conduct your own research of parenting practices in different cultures. Are some practices more likely to be assessed as atypical from an attachment theory perspective? From your own experiences, consider the development of relationships within different cultural and ethnic groups. How are they similar and how do they differ. What, if any, cultural parenting approach would you respond to positively or negatively, and why? Note your observations in your reflective journal, as the attitudes we hold can affect our interactions with others.

Attachment is an important theory within psychology and it is a theory that has real practice implications for social work. In the preceding chapter an overview of attachment classifications was outlined. Type B is the only 'secure' type; the remaining three classifications relate to insecure attachment patterns. As mentioned, Type D was a later addition, classifying children as 'disorganised' who did not 'fit' the existing insecure classifications. Attachment can affect later development; in adolescence, insecurely attached teens are more likely to be unpopular. In adulthood, we will see that attachment patterns can still be assessed, and transmission of insecure attachment patterns can occur between parent and child. The following piece outlines the relationship between disorganised attachment and psychopathology (mental disorders or difficulties).

IN FOCUS: THE IMPLICATIONS OF DISORGANISED ATTACHMENT ON PSYCHOPATHOLOGY

While a secure attachment pattern is associated with healthy parenting and positive outcomes for the child, research has considered the long-term impact of insecure attachment and found that disorganised attachment pattern is highly predictive of difficulties later in life. As mentioned, the category of disorganised attachment was added later for children who didn't fit into the original three classifications developed by Ainsworth. According to Music (2011, p. 62),

> These were children who had been subjected to unpredictable and traumatising parenting, and had failed to develop a coherent and consistent strategy to deal with these frightening experiences. They might, for example, wander up to a parent, then move aside, bang their heads on a wall, freeze or indulge in some bizarre behaviours. The parent, who should provide solace or comfort when distressed, was for these children often the person causing the distress, such as by being violent, and so these children could not find a way of getting their attachment needs met ... Not all insecurely attached children have a bad prognosis, but at a year disorganized attachment, that most worrying kind, is a good predictor of psychopathology at 17 years old. Disorganized attachment often occurs alongside other risk factors, such as poverty, single parenthood, violence, drug and alcohol use, and poor neighbourhoods. The disorganized child is likely to suffer from high stress levels, a hyperalert way of being, shows 'helpless' and/or 'hostile' behaviours, and the care they receive is

often inconsistent, confusing, frightening and leaves them feeling dysregulated. Such children fail to find a strategy to cope ... many traumatized children displaying such behaviours ... can seem hyperactive. They can be out of control but also become increasingly controlling as they grow older ... These children end up with deficits in cognitive capacities, in the ability to manage relationships, in the capacity to regulate their own emotions, and in developing consistent interpersonal strategies. Many fail at school, and advance along worrying trajectories, such as into the criminal justice system, psychiatric, or other services.

Smith et al. (2003, p. 105) contend that, 'given the prior links to parental maltreatment and abuse, it may be that the disorganized attachment pattern will be found to be the most relevant aspect of attachment in understanding severely maladaptive or antisocial behaviour in later life'.

THINK ABOUT IT! NATURE AND NURTURE DEBATE

As we talked about the nature/nurture dichotomy in an earlier chapter, could you argue the role of both in the development of attachment?

Clearly, we have a biological and neurological impetus to relate and develop attachment to others. This is the nature element. Yet what is clear is the importance of nurture, the paramouncy of sensitive parenting and how other environmental factors, such as poverty, drug and alcohol use, and neighbourhood, can influence the development of attachment. It is the intricate and interwoven dance between nature and nurture that we will continue to witness throughout this book and across an expanse of topics. One can also recognise the importance of early intervention programmes that support parents, helping them improve their parenting skills.

IN PRACTICE: ASSESSING SIBLING ATTACHMENT

Daniel et al. (2010, p. 35) advocate for the assessment of sibling attachment as a particularly important consideration of care planning. In moving away from Bowlby's concept of monotropism, it is recognised that siblings can have strong bonds and attachments. The authors suggest the Sibling Relationship Checklist as being a valuable tool as it encourages '... close observations and analysis of many dimensions of the sibling relationship, denoting one sibling as child A and the other as child B. First, the worker or carer is encouraged to consider the initiatives and responses of child A towards child B (and then *vice versa*) in relation to key attachment behaviours. These behaviours include:

- Expressions of warmth and affection
- Empathic behaviour towards the sibling
- Shared rituals/routines of play
- Signs of attunement (being in sync and responsive to another)
- Aggression or competition
- Many other aspects of the relationship.

This is a well-tested framework which can act as a lens through which the initiatives and responses of each child towards the other can be analysed.' The authors continue that in observing the interactions, which is a fruitful endeavour in and of itself, it gives opportunity to witness examples of behaviour, including ones which are rivalrous, domineering or even abusive. While it is considered, in principle, preferable to keep siblings together, cases where abusive patterns occur need to be considered in formulating a safe and supportive care-giving plan. For more information on attachment behaviours refer back to Chapter 4.

Attachment has dominated this section, reflecting its importance within psychology but also its implications for social workers. The quality of the relationships we form early in life is fundamental to our development, our personality and informs the relationships we continue to form throughout our lives. We will now move on to childhood, which for the purposes of this section ranges between 2 and 11 years of age.

CHILDHOOD (2–11 YEARS)

SECTION OUTLINE:

Physical Development – an overview

Cognitive Development

- Piaget pre-operational and concrete operational stage
- Theory of mind examined and Sally Ann doll test

Socio-emotional development

- Freud and Oedipus complex
- Erikson's psychosocial
- Socialisation
- gender identity and role of culture
- Personality (temperament, Cattell's 16 personality factors, 5 factor model)

In focus – The role of parenting in development

In focus – attachment and social work

PHYSICAL DEVELOPMENT

Childhood is a period of synchronous growth; that is, slow, steady and consistent development, contrasting with the rapid and uneven growth witnessed in the first 2 years of life and in adolescence. 'Baby fat' declines,while muscle mass and strength improve. Physical development during this time is thought by some as the calm before the storm of puberty, with the dramatic physical changes that come in its wake. The increasing myelination of the Central Nervous System (brain and spinal cord) contributes to improved motor skill and coordination. Generally speaking, there is a tendency for girls to be better coordinated in their movements, while boys have greater speed and strength. Increasing brain size and development (see Chapter 2) are accompanied by growing cognitive abilities.

COGNITIVE DEVELOPMENT

Piaget's pre-operational stage (2–7 years)

One of the most notable features of this stage is that the child is *egocentric*; a belief that everyone else sees the world through their eyes. They do not understand that other people might see or think about things differently, and this is reflected in their thinking. *Symbolic thinking* develops as the child begins to acquire language, which they use to enhance their thinking. The child can now use words and images (symbols) to represent objects. By the end of this stage, features such as animism (where the child ascribes consciousness to an inanimate object) begin to fade.

Piaget discussed pretend play as another feature of this stage, where, for example, a stick is transformed into a sword. Piaget believed that play and imitation were important activities in the developing child. While he saw play's primary function for children as one of enjoyment, he felt that imitation reflected the child's attempt to master or copy some new movement or action from another. Piaget proposed that while play involved a process of assimilation by the child, imitation was a product of accommodation in their construction of knowledge. We see imitation in the young when they copy their parents' actions: mummy hovering, for example.

THINK ABOUT IT!

From either personal or professional experience, recollect children's behaviour where they have imitated another. Can young children's use of imitation have potentially less desirable outcomes? For example, copying a parent smoking, or worse. Could this be a possible factor in the development of adverse behaviours? Can a child 'imitate' from wider circles of influence; siblings, peers, community and the media? What are the practice implications of Piaget's concept of imitation, in your opinion?

We will consider the role of media in eating disorders later in this chapter, can you think of any other behaviours you might also link to media influences? Aggression perhaps? See Chapter 10 for a discussion on the role of media in aggression. From a theoretical perspective we arguably can see the link between cognitive and behaviourist approaches here too; the child copies the behaviour but then internalises it within its cognitive schema or framework.

PIAGET AND STAGES OF PLAY

Piaget conceived that the development of play was broken into three parts; the second stage, termed 'play stage', was witnessed during the pre-operational period between the ages of 3 and 6 years old. This stage is dominated by the child's egocentrism and, as such, the child engages in mainly solitary play as they are generally too egocentric to play cooperatively with others, although parallel play does occur. In the pre-operational stage, symbolic thinking is emerging and this is reflected through the symbolic use of objects and actions during pretend play. Thus, a cardboard box becomes a boat, for example. Play is the work of childhood, suggested Piaget, recognising its centrality to all aspects of development, and he was not alone in emphasising the importance of play. We saw Mead, through *Symbolic Interactionism*, tie play to the developing sense of self. *Vygotsky* too championed play as an opportunity for the child to interact with other children, which in turn increased the potential for learning to occur. Another aspect of play according to Vygotsky is that language is used in the interaction between peers, through negotiation of rules for games and discussions around role playing. Vygotsky emphasised that language and development build upon each other.

Piaget's concrete operational stage (7–11 years)

Children learn through concrete or 'real' objects. Piaget believed that the acquisition of conservation was an important developmental milestone (see the illustration in Chapter 4). There are several types of conservation (length, volume, mass and weight). An example is the understanding that two differently shaped glasses contain the same amount of juice. Reversibility – the ability to mentally undo an action – is reached towards the end of this phase and is needed to enable the child to grasp conservation. Decentring is achieved when the child becomes less egocentric in their thinking and able to take the perspective of others.

THINK ABOUT IT!

Decentring means that children can now take on board the perspective of another person: see things through their eyes so to speak. What practice implications might this have? Imagine explaining to a child of 10 that their Mum is unwell and needs help to get better, meaning the child needs to go and stay with a family member. Will the child be better able to process that information and understand why their Mum needs support if decentring has occurred?

Theory of mind

'Theory of mind' refers to our understanding of people as mental beings, each with his or her own mental states – such as thoughts, wants, motives and feelings. This ability is vital in the arena of social relationships; it enables us to predict the behaviour of others and have insight into their actions. Piaget suggested that children do not develop this ability until the age of six or seven; however, subsequent research has demonstrated that children typically acquire theory of mind earlier than this. The 'Sally Ann doll test' can be used to assess if theory of mind is present.

Imagine a young child watching a puppet show with two dolls named Sally and Ann. Sally decides to go for a walk but before she leaves she places her marble in her basket. After Sally leaves, Ann removes the marble from the basket and places it in her box. When Sally returns where will she look for her marble? If the child replies that Sally will look for the marble in Ann's box (where Ann hid it) then the child does not yet possess theory of mind. To demonstrate theory of mind the child has to be able to appreciate that Sally has her own beliefs about the world which can differ from the child's own. A deficit in theory of mind has been implicated in autism (see Chapter 6). As you can see, theory of mind is important in the social sphere of our lives, where the ability to understand other people's state of mind is essential. The social sphere is considered a key element in healthy functioning through the life span. Our social relationships are linked to our emotional development and well-being, so let's continue on and explore this domain in childhood.

SOCIOEMOTIONAL DEVELOPMENT

Freud's psychosexual stages

ANAL STAGE (2–3 YEARS)

The focus of pleasure shifts to the anus as the child become aware of its bowels and how to control them. In choosing to control bowel movements the child takes an important step of independence, developing confidence and a sense of when to 'give things up'. However, over-strictness can cause personality problems such as *anal fixation* – a child forced 'to go' may develop a reluctance about giving away *anything* and may become a hoarder or miser. Conversely, over-concern about 'going regularly' may cause obsessive timekeeping or always being late.

PHALLIC STAGE (3–6 YEARS)

Children become aware of their genitals and sexual differences. This stage is where the paths of males and females begin to diverge as the realisation of their differences becomes apparent to them. In *The Oedipus Complex*, each boy unconsciously goes through a sequence of stages beginning with the development of a strong desire for his mother. Noticing the bond between his parents, he becomes jealous of his father then becomes afraid lest his father discover his son's true feelings, resulting in fear of punishment – castration.

LATENCY STAGE (6–11 YEARS)

It's during this stage that sexual urges remain repressed and there are no significant developmental events. Freud believed that the most significant thing about children's social behaviour during this period was their preference to play and interact with same-sex peers.

Erikson's psychosocial stages

INITIATIVE VERSUS GUILT (3–5 YEARS)

As the child becomes older they exhibit increasing curiosity and interest, they initiate play and question more. The main aim of this stage is to acquire a sense of purpose. If this is discouraged or they are held back, they will not develop self-initiative instead choosing to hold back in later life.

ERIKSON INDUSTRY VERSUS INFERIORITY (6–12)

This stage is very much influenced by the child's experiences in school. During this time the child begins to attend school and they interact more with their peers. If praised in their efforts they develop a sense of industry and feel good about what they have achieved, which encourages the feeling that they can fulfil their goals. If they repeatedly fail or are not praised when they try a sense of inferiority may develop.

As we have seen, some theories of development focus on one aspect of functioning; for instance with Erikson it's psychosocial or with Piaget it's cognitive. Another area of functioning theory is that of moral development, beginning with Piaget but best known in the work of Kohlberg and Gilligan's subsequent critique. Before we look at these theories, as socialisation is mentioned within them, now is an opportune time to first examine that concept.

Socialisation

Bennett (2005) says that 'Socialisation is the process by which children acquire the values, standards, practices and knowledge of the society into which they are born. It is through this process that children typically come to share many of the aspects of the behaviour, cognition, and emotion of members of their society.'

Socialisation can be studied in a more general sense or in a domain-specific way, looking at specific topics such as gender or the socialisation of morality. Traditionally, children were viewed as 'vessels' or blank slates to be 'filled' with knowledge by their elders. We have moved away from this, recognising the 'active child' (constructivism) who is not a passive agent but an active participant shaping and influencing their environments and also their own socialisation. Bennett (ibid.) offers the following example of *child effects,* the innately given individual differences children have, which can impact on their parent's treatment of them, '... children's gender, physical attractiveness, and most importantly temperament, have all been found to have marked influences on parental behaviour. Thus from birth, parents treat girls and boys in systematically different ways, both wittingly and unwittingly.' A *systems theory of socialisation* was developed by Sameroff (1983, as cited in Bennett, p. 384),

> Key to this approach is that the child is conceived as embedded in a variety of mutually influencing relationships and social structures.

Thus, it is not just the immediate family that socialises the child, that same family is part of a wider system incorporating school, peers, parental employment and so on. Arguably, an important force in the socialisation process is media; television, internet and computer games all play a central role in our lives and thus a central part of the socialisation process. The concept of media as a socialising agent will be explored later in this chapter in relation to eating disorders and then to aggressive behaviours in Chapter 10. Gender identity is another construct powerfully shaped by socialisation in developing our sense of what a boy or girl 'is'. The following piece is an outline of the development of gender identity.

Development of gender (sex-role) identity

SEX DIFFERENCES

Toy Choice: From 2 years of age onwards children appear to show sex differences in relation to their choice of toys. Boys tend to choose trucks, cars and blocks. They also engage more in play involving gross motor activity such as kicking and throwing a ball. Girls, on the other hand, tend to show a preference for dolls, dressing up and domestic play. In school, both opt for same-sex partners when playing, with boys preferring outdoor play or sport-related activities, whereas girls opt for indoor, sedentary activities.

Kuhn et al. (1978) found that by two and a half years of age children had beliefs about sex role stereotypes (a belief that certain activities are suitable for girls and vice versa). The young children reported that girls liked to play with dolls and to help their mother, whereas boys liked helping their father.

DEVELOPMENT OF GENDER IDENTITY

Are you a boy or a girl?

This question will stump or confuse most 2 year olds, if you show them a stereotypical picture of a girl and boy; however, 76 percent will correctly identify the gender.

By 30 months this rises to 83 percent and,

By 36 months the proportion who answer correctly had risen to 90 percent. So we see that as the child becomes older they are more likely to correctly identify gender, and in younger children that they can visually, rather than verbally, identify their gender more easily.

GENDER IDENTITY

By 3 years old most can correctly label their own and others sex or gender. This marks the acquisition of 'gender identity'.

GENDER STABILITY

According to Smith et al. (2003), at approximately 4 years old, most children understand that the gender of a person remains the same or stable. If asked, a girl will answer that she'll be a mummy when she grows up.

GENDER CONSTANCY

By 7 years of age, awareness that being male or female (the biological sex of a person) does not change; for example, if a boy grows his hair long, he is still a boy.

As gender identity develops, children also acquire **sex-role stereotypes,** which are the beliefs regarding what are considered appropriate characteristics and behaviour for boys and girls; this process of learning is called **'sex-typing'**. As might be apparent, sex-typing is learned through a process of **socialisation** where children acquire the beliefs, behaviours and values of their group (society, culture).

THINK ABOUT IT!

Compare and contrast: The cultural or social expectations regarding appropriate behaviour for a girl today compared to a girl born 50 years ago. Do you think attitudes and expectations have changed? What do you think? Do you think the expectations of what is considered appropriate behaviour and sex roles in general are the same for females in the West compared to females in other parts of the world or for females growing up in the UK from different cultural and ethnic backgrounds?

In the following section on adolescence we will explore the development of identity in greater detail given its central association with that age stage. Marcia's theory of identity formation will be examined, as will ethnic identity. As identity is fundamental to adolescence as a developmental milestone, the development of behaviour towards others (prosocial or aggressive) is developmentally characteristic of childhood. In Chapter 10 the development of both types of behaviour from a biopsychosocial perspective are explored to capture the complexity of potential influences involved.

Within the myriad of factors influencing the aggressive and prosocial behaviour, the development of a sense of 'right and wrong' is fundamental. Moral development has been studied by Piaget, who, as we will see, saw it as a reflection of the growing cognitive capabilities of the child. However, it is Kohlberg who is best associated with this area. He is also noteworthy from a critical psychology perspective as will be apparent in Gilligan's critique.

Moral development

Schaffer (1996, p. 290) states,

> the end product of socialization is an individual who can distinguish right from wrong and is prepared to act accordingly. Such an individual can be said to have acquired a sense of morality, that is he or she will behave in ways that uphold the social order and will do so through inner conviction and not because of a fear of punishment.

Moral development can be seen as the understanding of 'right' and 'wrong'. The first thing that should be apparent to us is that different cultures/societies, even families, can have very different ideas about what 'right' and 'wrong' is. **Socialisation** is the process by which a person acquires the beliefs and values of the culture or society they live in. Sociologists would contend that our moral development is socialised and we learn it from our parents (primary agents of socialisation) and then from school, church and our society in general (secondary agents). Freud believed that children developed a moral conscience from their parents in the form of a superego. If you recall your childhood no doubt you have memories of a parent or caregiver admonishing you for being bold or praising you for doing the 'right' thing.

PIAGET'S THEORY OF MORAL DEVELOPMENT

Piaget suggested that peer interaction in childhood occurred around rule-based games. He developed a two-stage theory of moral development through his observations of young children playing and their use of rules when doing so. Piaget noticed that younger children had less of a grasp of the rules than older children. Piaget questioned children of different ages about the rules of the games and formulated the following theory.

Pre-Moral: before the age of five, children do not consider what is right or wrong.

Moral Realism: is witnessed in middle childhood, children's understanding of rules is governed by the influence of authority figures. They believe that rules can't be changed, that they are inflexible.

Moral Relativism: is the second stage of Piaget's theory of moral development and is present from roughly 8 years onwards. It reflects the developing child's growing sophistication in thinking. Children now understand that the rules can be modified through agreements with others.

Rather than fixating on the rules being followed to the letter, children can modify the rules to meet their particular needs. They understand that this doesn't change the nature of the game. The important aspect is that all those participating are in agreement and following the same rules. According to Piaget, moral development was completed in children at approximately 12–13 years of age. Piaget argues that children had made the transition from moral reasoning and development-based rules imposed by adults or authority rules (constraint-based morality) to one based on 'mutual respect', where rules are negotiated from within rather than imposed from outside (Smith et al., p. 273). Older children understand that rules are not absolute but are devices used by humans to get along cooperatively and therefore can be modified with the agreement of others.

Example

When, for example, the young child hears about one boy who broke 15 cups trying to help his mother and another boy who broke only one cup trying to steal cookies, the young child thinks that the first boy did worse. The child primarily considers the amount of damage – the consequences – whereas the older child is more likely to judge wrongness in terms of the motives underlying the act (Piaget, 1932, p. 137 cited in Crain, 1985, p. 118).

Cognitive linked to moral development

We have encountered Piaget as a cognitive theorist, someone interested in how children think and learn to think. Yet reasoning is a cognitive skill and so it's not such a jump to see why Piaget was interested in how they reason on a moral level. Cognitive concepts, such as **decentring,** the ability to see things from another point of view, are central to the development of moral reasoning. Piaget contended that this ability is acquired by the age of ten and it possibly provides an insight into why Piaget used this age to mark the transition into his second stage of higher moral reasoning.

Criticism of Piaget's theory of moral development

One criticism of Piaget's conceptualisation of moral development is the idea that we complete this development at 12 or 13 years of age. It is recognised nowadays that development can constantly change across the life span and moral development is no exception. As we age and gain new life experiences or interactions with others our attitudes change to reflect this. Thus one might anticipate our ideas of 'right' and 'wrong' to change. Another criticism is culturally based. *Westernised* society tends to be far more individualistic than other cultures, which are more 'collectivist' and traditional in their views. In these societies great value is placed on traditions handed down and children are encouraged to embrace the traditions of their forefathers. Thus, as children in these societies develop they become more 'constraint-based' in their moral reasoning, that is, they look to and have greater respect for authority. In the West, we are more individualistic, valuing the rights of the individual. In more collectivist societies the individual is seen as part of a group and that group has a higher value than the needs of one particular individual.

THINK ABOUT IT!

Would you agree that a 13-year-old's ability to reason at a moral level is the same as an adult? If not, consider the points you might raise to support your assertion. From personal or professional experience have you witnessed different ways of understanding or approaches to morality, how 'right' or 'wrong' is conceived of? Are there differences within age groups or ethnic groups, for example?

KOHLBERG'S THEORY OF MORAL DEVELOPMENT

Lawrence Kohlberg was heavily influenced by Piaget's work. As seen, Piaget proposed a two stage approach to moral development. Before 10 years of age a child believes rules are fixed, handed down by a higher authority (such as a parent or adult) and not subject to change. After 10 years of age, the child realises that rules are flexible and can be modified with the agreement of others. Kohlberg went further than this and devised a six-stage approach. Kohlberg's theory is based on interviews he conducted with children and adolescents regarding moral reasoning; Kohlberg devised 'moral dilemmas', the answers to which were used to categorise moral development of which 'Heinz's dilemma' is the best known.

Heinz's moral dilemma

A woman was near death from a special kind of cancer. There was one drug that her doctor thought might save her. The pharmacist in her town had recently discovered this drug and was charging ten times what the drug cost him to make. He paid $400 for the radium and charged $4000 for a small dose of the drug. The sick woman's husband, Heinz, went to everyone he knew to borrow the money and tried every legal means, but he could only get together about $2000, which is half of what it cost. He explained to the pharmacist that his wife was dying, and asked him to sell it cheaper or let him pay later. But the pharmacist said, 'No, I discovered the drug and I'm going to make money from it.' So, Heinz gets desperate and breaks into the man's store to steal the drug for his wife. Should he have done it?

THINK ABOUT IT!

What would your response be and why? If you put this question to children and adolescents are varying ages and backgrounds would you expect differences in their responses, and if so why?

From this dilemma, Kohlberg posed questions including whether it was right or wrong to steal the drug. The responses to these dilemmas form his theory of moral development. Kohlberg isn't particularly interested in the 'yes' or 'no' answer but in the reasoning behind the answer.

Level 1: preconvential morality

Kohlberg (1976, p. 33) thinks of this level as the one '... most children under 9, some adolescents, and many adolescent and adult criminal offenders' occupy.

Stage 1: Obedience and Punishment

Whether something is 'right' or 'wrong' is determined by reward and punishment. There is no 'internalisation' of values; decisions regarding right or wrong are based on whether the result is rewarded or punished. For example, a child at this stage, if given the Heinz's dilemma, would typically respond that Heinz was wrong to steal the drug because it's against the law. They see morality as something external to themselves, something decided upon by adults.

Stage 2: Individualism, Instrumental Purpose and Exchange

At this stage children recognise that there isn't just one correct viewpoint handed down by adults or the authorities. Each person has the own point of view. 'Heinz', they might point out, 'might think it's right to take the drug, the pharmacist would not'. Individual interests are an important aspect of this stage. One boy responded that Heinz might steal the drug if he wanted his wife to live, but that he doesn't have to if he wants to marry someone younger and better-looking (Kohlberg, 1976, p. 24), reflecting the notion of self-interest. They understand that there are no absolutes, that everything is relative. The concept of exchange is also seen during this stage: the idea of quid pro quo or I'll do something for you if you do something for me.

Level 2: conventional morality

This is the level acquired most in our society, the main feature of this level is an understanding that norms and conventions are necessary to uphold society.

Stage 3: Mutual Interpersonal Expectations and Conformity

Living up to what is considered of you by others is considered important. Individuals value trust and loyalty as the basis for moral reasoning and judgements.

Stage 4: Social System Morality

Moral judgements are based on upholding the social values of the society you live in. Right is seen as contributing to society, group and so on. In this stage the individual sees themselves as a member of society and this influences their moral reasoning.

Level 3: postconventional morality

Kohlberg suggested that relatively few achieve these higher stages of moral reasoning where the individual, while valuing societal values and conventions, would go against them if a principle was at stake.

Stage 5: Social Contract

In this stage there is an understanding that differences can exist between a moral right and a legal right. For example, in the case of euthanasia if an individual helped a relative who was suffering to end their life, it would not be legally right, yet perhaps some would feel it was morally acceptable. This example highlights that differences can exist between legal and moral right should a moral principle come into conflict with a societal value. An individual at this level would be willing to judge on the moral principle.

Stage 6: Universal ethical principles

Relatively few attain this stage of moral judgement where a person will follow their individual principles of conscience.

The following research suggests that Kohlberg's moral stages appeared somewhat later than he initially suggested. Further, the higher stages, in particular stage 6, were very elusive.

COLBY, KOHLBERG ET AL. (1983) RESEARCH

Colby et al. undertook a 20 year longitudinal study of moral judgement. Their findings included:

- The use of stages 1 and 2 decreased over time.
- Stage 4, which did not appear at all in the moral reasoning of 10 year olds, was reflected in 62 percent of 36 year olds.
- Stage 5 did not appear until age 20–22 – and never characterised more than 10 percent of the individuals.

GILLIGAN'S CRITIQUE OF KOHLBERG'S THEORY OF MORAL DEVELOPMENT

A former student of Kohlberg, Carol Gilligan, has been a major critic of his work. Gilligan claims that Kohlberg's theory is flawed as his research was based on male responses, and as such it represents a male perspective of moral development and reasoning. Gilligan through her work with women proposes that women apply an ethic of care in their judgements rather than an ethic of justice, which she claims is a male approach to moral judgements. An ethic of care means that the person considers other people and their welfare in their judgement-making process. Gilligan states that Kohlberg's work excludes and devalues how women approach moral reasoning. Yet it is interesting that Gilligan falls foul of the precise accusation she levels at Kohlberg. Gilligan's research has been with females only, thus excluding and marginalising the male perspective.

This section on childhood will end with a piece on parenting, reflecting its centrality to the developing child. While parenting contains many elements, here we will limit our remit to Baumrind's styles of parenting and an In focus piece on child–parent play and its implications. In Chapter 8 forces such as poverty and its impact on parenting are examined. In Chapter 9 parental factors and abuse are discussed and in Chapter 10 the relationship between parenting and prosocial and aggressive behaviour is expanded upon.

BAUMRIND'S PARENTING STYLES AND PARENT–CHILD INTERACTIONS

The role of parenting is perhaps considered one of the most crucial influences in development not just in childhood but also for later life. The emphasis on and plethora of parenting research, support and interventions reflects the primacy attached to this activity. In this piece we will take a more global approach to parenting beginning with Diane Baumrind's parenting styles, and then focussing on parent–child play and its implications.

Diana Baumrind's parenting styles

Attachment is an important aspect in the study of the relationship between parent and child. Research has also been carried out into parenting styles and the differences that appear to exist (some parents adopt a strict approach, while others do not). Diana Baumrind (1966), in her paper 'Effects of authoritative parental control on child behaviour', suggests the following three styles of parenting:

PERMISSIVE

- Parents tend to be relaxed about discipline, avoid exercise of control.
- Parents make few demands upon the child regarding household chores or orderly behaviour.
- Parents see themselves not as active agents shaping the child but as a resource for the child to use.
- Parents do not encourage the child to obey externally defined standards.

AUTHORITARIAN

- Parents value obedience, child in its place.
- When disagreement exists between parents and child, parents favour a punitive approach.
- Parents believe the child should accept the word of the parents, do not believe in verbal give and take or discussions.

AUTHORITATIVE

- Parents encourage verbal give and take.
- Parents willing to share reasoning behind their decision making with the child and are open to adapting.
- Parents set standards for future behaviour.
- Parents praise and affirm the child's qualities.

Implicit in this and other research on parenting styles is that different parenting styles can lead to different outcomes for the child. Dekovic and Janssens (1992) found that children of authoritative parents tended to be more popular, while children of authoritarian parents were less so, illustrating just one outcome affected by parenting approach.

THINK ABOUT IT!

What other different outcomes can you identify where parenting would impact on a child's development? From your personal and professional experience, what behaviours and interactions might reflect the different parenting styles outlined by Baumrind? How would a parent's style impact on interactions with a social worker who is advocating for change within a family? Would an authoritarian parent be less open to taking on board the opinion of another, particularly relating to parenting approach? Would a permissive parent reject an external force being applied to their child's behaviour?

The relationship between parent and child can be key to understanding the developing child. Earlier we saw that attachment is classified through the Strange Situation, which measures the quality of the relationship between the primary caregiver (usually a parent) and the child. Parenting styles also impact on children's development both positively and negatively. Further, play is fundamental to all aspects of a child's development, it is a lens that mirrors how well the child is progressing and can allow insight into their internal world. In the following piece, parent–child interactions are used to assess children's development of social competency.

In focus: parent–child play and its implications

In their study, Valentino et al. (2011) sought to examine how an abusive or 'maltreating' family environment impacts on children's progression of play and development of social competencies in the first 2 years of life. To this end they used longitudinal research of mother–child play interaction, comparing children from non-maltreating and maltreating family homes. The authors outline that child maltreatment represents 'an extreme failure of the early care giving environment'. This affords researchers the opportunity to evaluate the contribution of early care giving to young children's developing play and social skills and the impact of differing environments on cognitive and social development. Previous research has found that (ibid., p. 1281),

> ... studies of maltreated children's social play with peers reveal that by ages 4 and 5, maltreated children engage in less overall play and lower-level cognitive play compared to their non-maltreated peers. Also, differences emerge in maltreated preschool-aged children's pretend play, such that their play is more imitative of everyday routines and less fantasy-based than that of non-maltreated children. Socially, maltreated children have been found to be more aggressive and less competent with their peers and demonstrate poorer skill in initiating peer interactions and maintaining self-control. Overall, these finding suggest that by the preschool years, maltreated children already demonstrate delays in cognitive play maturity and social competence.

These findings demonstrate the importance of play in children's early development, especially in terms of social and cognitive development. Play is more than just children having fun; it provides fundamental building blocks of development, which sow the foundation for their future ability to form successful relationships. These findings also illustrate the deficits that can occur when family environments and parent–child interactions are less than optimal. The authors of this study draw particular emphasis on the ability of a child to initiate actions and especially social interactions. This is an important developmental milestone as

> ... infant behaviour shifts from reacting to the environment to initiating actions. The latter of these behaviours is more cognitively and socially complex as it requires infants to formulate social goals and signal their requests without structure from their interactive partner. Children's increased capacity for initiating or directing social exchanges and their ability to respond to parental requests are two critical aspects of social competence during the second year.'

THE ROLE OF PARENTS

Parents have a critical role in influencing children's play and developing social and communicative behaviours. It is important that parents make themselves available for play and be 'active play-partners' with their children. Valentino et al. (2011, p. 1282) describe how research has established that

> ... mother–child interactions among abusing and neglecting families tend to include less verbal interaction, limited playful exchanges, and less harmony compared to non-maltreating families. Physically abusive parents demonstrate fewer physical and positive behaviours during mother–child interactions, such as handing objects

to the child or praising the child. These maladaptive parent–child interactional patterns are likely to have adverse effects on maltreated children's play and social development.

FINDINGS

Toddlers from abusing families demonstrated significantly less child-initiated behaviour during play than did toddlers from neglecting and non-maltreating families, '... this deficit in social play behaviour among children from abusing families reflects research demonstrating that although maltreatment does not appear to impede the development of basic cognitive processes, maltreatment does adversely affect early social and emotional development' (ibid., p. 1290).

The significant difference in outcome was found in the group of children from the abusive background who had poorer outcomes than those from neglectful homes or homes where there was no maltreatment. It may appear odd at first that the children from neglectful homes were not as adversely affected as those from abusive homes. The authors offer some explanation for this; in terms of an abusive home, the children may have learnt early on not to initiate interactions with a parent who is volatile, unpredictable and potentially violent. Thus, avoidance of interaction would be adaptive in this scenario and thus '... reduced child-initiated play may be experience-dependent and observed among young children from abusing families as an attempt to avoid further abuse experiences'. Neglect, in the long term can be as damaging as physical or sexual abuse, as we will see in Chapter 9, but in the early environment it does not appear to affect the child negatively, in terms of initiated play, as a young child from an abusive home. 'The lack of differences in child-initiated play between children from neglecting and non-maltreating families is consistent with this experience dependent interpretation, where children from neglecting families, although lacking sufficient caregiving, have not experienced the commission of abuse, with the likely accompanying fear.' What is certain is that reduced social initiation hampers a child's ability to form successful relationships with peers and increases the likelihood of problem behaviours in the future.

THINK ABOUT IT!

How would you use this research on child–parent interactions and play? Does it reinforce the importance of observation as a tool when assessing child and parent relationships and outcomes? Consider a checklist which might alert you to difficulties in the parent–child relationship. What behaviours might be included? In terms of play, how could you use play to assess a child's developmental outcomes?

This brings us to the end of childhood. As we have seen, certain elements are key to this stage, including the importance of play, the development of behaviours, prosocial and aggressive, and the parent–child relationship. Interventions from birth through childhood reflect these central concerns through the use of play therapy, behavioural interventions and parenting support programmes, reinforcing how central these areas are to this age stage. Childhood and issues related to it will continue to be discussed throughout the remaining chapters in one guise or another. However, we are now going to move on to adolescence. While all cultures recognise childhood as a distinct age period, the acknowledgement of adolescence as a standalone age stage with its own unique developmental characteristics has its origin in Western societies. In other cultures adolescence as a distinct period is not, or is less likely to be, recognised. Adolescence as a construct has continued to evolve while ethnic and cultural influences impact on how adolescence is construed too. It is clear that this age stage is not homogenous and individual variation is particularly marked as the teen evolves their own identity, an activity considered a core developmental characteristic. In this section we will overview the immense physical changes that accompany adolescence, a cognitive theory specific to teens, the development of identity including ethnicity and the lives of LGBT teens. So let's get started!

ADOLESCENCE

SECTION OUTLINE:

Physical Development

- Overview including brain, patterns of development
- Differences in timing of puberty (and its effects)
- In focus: Eating disorders

Cognitive development

- Piaget formal operational
- Elkind's theory of adolescent egocentrism

Social and Emotional Development

- Erikson and Freud's Stages
- Kohlberg's theory of Moral Development and Gilligan's critique
- Identity development Marcia including ethnic identity self-esteem

In focus: LGBT lives

Adolescence, which comes from the Latin *adolescere* meaning 'to grow up', is seen as a unique transitionary period between childhood and adulthood encompassing not just physical but also social, emotional and cognitive changes. Puberty refers to the commencement and maturation of biological, physical and sexual characteristics and is generally considered in most cultures to signify the change or transition from childhood to adulthood. Adolescence encompasses the behavioural, social and emotional aspects of this transition and is influenced by physical, social and cultural factors.

The World Health Organization (WHO) defines adolescence as the second decade of life, from 10 to 20 years of age. Yet adolescence is not merely chronological age; it is also socially constructed, which means that some societies have different ideas about what 'adolescence' means. In some cultures puberty marks the child's coming of age and ability to take on 'adult' roles. Girls may marry or begin childbearing far earlier than we would be accustomed to in the West.

There is a difference in the age that males and females start their growth spurt:

- Girls: approximately 10 years of age
- Boys: approximately 12 years of age.

So, as we can see, girls begin their development approximately 2 years earlier than boys. It is worth noting that these ages indicate just the beginning of biological changes and not necessarily the associated secondary sexual characteristics associated with adolescence.

SEXUAL MATURATION

One of the most obvious characteristics associated with adolescence is the changing appearance of the teenager. Pubertal timing refers to the commencement of puberty and its associated physical and sexual changes. More noticeable changes in girls are the development of breasts and in boys the appearance of facial hair, for instance. Differentiation is made between primary and secondary sexual characteristics.

Primary sexual characteristics

These are the changes and development that directly involve the sex organs.

Girls – menarche: this refers to the start of menstruation (periods) in girls. The average age of puberty for girls in the UK (menarche) is 12.7 years, within a range of 10.9–16.1 years of age (Malina et al., 2004, p. 314).

Boys – spermarche: this term was coined to mark the sexual maturation of boys, when males become capable of reproduction. 'Spermarche' refers to the first time a boy ejaculates. As this is a private event it is difficult to determine an age for this event or to conduct useful research.

Differences in timing of puberty

While puberty encompasses changes in males and females, we will examine the onset of menarche to examine influences on the timing of puberty. Factors involved include hereditary factors and nutrition. There is a trend for increasingly younger timing of menarche; 100 years ago the average age was between 16 and 17 years of age, now an average age of 12 is usual. Societal influences have been implicated; however, the following is a really interesting piece of research which uses evolutionary psychology in an attempt to explain its findings. If nothing else it highlights the complexity of human development and individual variation.

Early pubertal timing in girls and absent fathers

Research in the field of pubertal timing has found that a number of different factors affect the start of puberty. Physical influences include weight, nutrition and exercise. For example, high levels of exercise in female dancers have been found to delay pubertal maturation. While physical factors may make intuitive sense to us, some other factors might appear more puzzling. Ellis and Garber (2000) relate perhaps one of the most fascinating pieces of research to emerge regarding pubertal timing: that a relationship exists between early puberty in girls and the absence of fathers in their lives. Ellis [2000] cites Belsky et al. (1991), who found that a family environment with an absent biological father and maternal depression related to early pubertal timing in girls. I stress biological father because they found that girls who had stepfathers present in their lives were also more likely to begin puberty early.

Belsky, Steinberg and Draper have proposed an 'evolutionary' explanation for early pubertal timing. Evolutionary psychology attempts to explain human behaviours by claiming that the motivation for these behaviours is found in how we have evolved or adapted to our environment. The main focus of evolution is the reproduction of the organism, so the aim of all human behaviour is seen in terms of survival and reproduction. With this in mind, the evolutionary explanation of early pubertal timing rests on the notion that a girl whose biological father is absent is more 'vulnerable', has fewer resources and less protection, and, as such, it makes evolutionary sense for such a girl to be able to reproduce earlier than females whose biological fathers are present and caring for them. Evolutionary psychology is controversial, with feminist psychology particularly critical. Can you see why?

Effect of pubertal timing

We looked at how factors such as father absence have been implicated in the early start of menarche in girls, but what are the effects of early and late pubertal maturation on females and males? This has been a popular source of research and findings suggest a number of outcomes. Brooks-Gunn et al. (1985) suggested that adolescents who are 'off-time' (early or late maturation) with their peers, experience more stress and as such are more susceptible to adjustment problems in adolescence. A second explanation offered is that early developers, especially females, face more social pressure. If they mature earlier they will face the attention of male sexual interest earlier, as the physical development of their body does not match that of their brain and cognitive development, so they have less-advanced 'thinking' skills with which to handle the increased attention that their early maturation attracts. As such, with teenagers who look older there can be a tendency for them to be viewed as more socially and cognitively developed than they actually are. It is also suggested that in developing earlier these adolescents miss the opportunity to complete the normal development tasks of middle childhood as they fast forward past this stage.

Early maturation

Boys: early maturation appears to be associated with more positive outcomes, particularly in terms of social development; they enjoy prestige.

Girls: in contrast, girls face more problems, including an increased likelihood of negative moods and behaviours. Brooks-Gunn et al. (1985) reported negative body image.

Late maturation

Boys: may demonstrate lower achievement (Dubas et al., 1991), lower self-esteem and happiness (Crockett and Petersen, 1987).

Girls: higher achievement in girls was evident in research conducted by Dubas et al. (1991).

Here we see how physical development influences social development where a relationship between risk-taking behaviours and maturational age has been found. This leads us to another area which on the surface is related to physical development yet whose roots lie in a complex web of factors, including internal ones, such as personality traits, to societal factors, such as the media. Eating disorders are among the most stigmatised (Crisp 2005) and have the highest mortality rate of all mental health disorders. Reflecting the increasing numbers of those affected by eating disorders, including more children and boys than previously witnessed, eating disorders as a mental health issue will continue to be a pressing concern and one you are increasingly likely to meet in your practice.

In focus: eating disorders

Eating disorders, while they manifest themselves in the physical domain (weight loss and disturbed eating patterns), are seen as a psychological disorder. Examining them offers us a bridge between the physical and psychological domains of functioning. So what exactly is an eating disorder?

ANOREXIA NERVOSA

Anorexia nervosa, a Greek term meaning loss of appetite, is an eating disorder that inflicts self-starvation on millions of predominantly females but also males each year. It has been theorised that this disorder allows adolescents to gain control by limiting food intake. Anorexics often obsess about thinness, need attention, lack individuality, and deny sexuality. It affects females fifteen times more than it affects males. It usually begins during adolescence or in early adulthood, but hardly ever occurs in women past the age of 25. The disorder affects one teenager in every two hundred among adolescents aged between sixteen and eighteen.

The **criteria for anorexia nervosa** given by the most recent diagnostic system includes: intense fear of becoming obese, which does not diminish with the progression of weight loss; disturbance of body image, feeling 'fat' even when emaciated; refusal to maintain body weight over a minimal weight for age and height; weight loss of 25 percent of original body weight or 25 percent below the expected weight based on standard growth charts; and no known physical illness that would account for the weight loss (Field and Domangue, 1987, p. 31).

BULIMIA

Bulimia is a Greek word meaning 'ox' and 'hunger', reflecting the binge eating pattern that characterises this disorder during which an individual can consume between 10,000 and 20,000 calories. These binge eating episodes are usually followed by episodes of purging. Purging is accomplished by either of the following methods: vomiting, laxatives, diuretics, enemas, compulsive exercising, weight-reducing drugs and intermittent periods of strict dieting.

Bulimia can be associated with anorexia nervosa. In the past it was actually considered to be a part of the disorder. Most anorexics develop bulimia in the course of their illness. Unlike anorexia, bulimia affects three to 7 percent of women aged between 15 and 35. Bulimia is defined as a syndrome in which gorging on food alternates with purging by forced vomiting, fasting or laxatives (Field and Domangue, 1987, p. 32). The effects on people who suffer from doing this include guilt, depression and disgust with oneself. Bulimics know that their eating habits are unhealthy but fear not being able to stop eating voluntarily.

WHAT ARE THE SIMILARITIES BETWEEN BULIMIA AND ANOREXIA?

Both disorders carry an obsession with weight and body image, and both are traditionally found in white, middle-upper class females. These females usually have the characteristics of being perfectionists, high achievers, often academically or vocationally successful, and have a great need to please others. The mortality rate for eating disorders is higher than for any other psychiatric disorder and studies suggest that the rate has been increasing over the last 20 years.

MENTAL ATTRIBUTES ASSOCIATED WITH TEENAGERS WHO SUFFER FROM BULIMIA AND ANOREXIA NERVOSA

It is important for people to understand that adolescents suffering from eating disorders, both male and female, may not appear to be underweight. Weight is only a physical sign of an eating disorder, when in fact the adolescent is likely suffering from a deeper emotional conflict that needs to be resolved. Eating disorders are addictions to a behaviour and the obsession with food is only a symptom of deeper problems such as low self-esteem, depression, poor self-image and self-hate. Hilde Bruch, a preeminent psychiatrist, describes the relentless pursuit of thinness as an effort to mask underlying problems (Bruch et al., 1988.) The following are some of the mental characteristics of adolescent males and females suffering from eating disorders.

Perfectionism: Many adolescents suffering from eating disorders are perfectionists and high achievers. They strive to reach perfection in every aspect of their lives.

They are eager to please and in the process lose their true selves. When they feel they have failed to reach perfection they often unrealistically blame themselves for their failure and attempt to punish themselves. Punishment often occurs in the form of starvation for anorexics and purging for bulimics.

Low self-esteem: Feelings of inadequacy are common among teens suffering from eating disorders. They have a poor self-image and perception of themselves. They irrationally believe they are fat regardless of how thin they become. They experience a sense of inner emptiness, uncertainty and helplessness, and a lack of self-confidence and self-trust (Bruch et al., 1988.) Often they are afraid of being judged by others or thought of as being stupid. They feel confident if they are losing weight but suffer from feelings of worthlessness and guilt if they are not (Pipher, 1994). It is also common for them to believe they do not deserve good things or to be happy.

Depression: Mood swings, feelings of hopelessness, anxiety, isolation and loneliness are feelings common to sufferers of eating disorders. Bulimics experience a loss of control that leads to depression, whereas anorexics experience depression as a result of gaining weight (Schlundt and Johnson, 1990).

Obsession: These adolescents deal with an intense obsession and preoccupation with food, calories, fat grams and weight. Weight becomes their most important and self-defining attribute. Eating disorders are considered addictions in which starvation, bingeing and purging are the addictive behaviours and food is the narcotic (Pipher, 1994).

Guilt: Adolescents with eating disorders often feel guilty because they do not think they have met the expectations of others. They are striving for the perfect body and for a sense of control, but in this process they start to feel guilty about their habit (Pipher, 1994). Lying becomes essential.

Are we right to concentrate on just the individual or 'intrapsychic' factors that influence the disorder? The role of the media has increasingly become a contentious one, especially in light of the glorification of 'size zero'. The following piece of research focuses on the influence of media in eating disorders.

EATING DISORDERS AND THE ROLE OF THE MEDIA

Recent research (McNicholas et al., 2009) investigated media influences on eating attitudes in adolescents. The authors note that previous research indicates that a relationship appears to exist between the portrayal of thinness in the media and disordered eating.

Media portrayal of weight and shape

Adolescents were asked to consider if media (TV, magazines, newspapers) portrayal of ideal body weight and shape was:

a) Far too thin
b) A little too thin

c) Just right
d) A little too fat
e) Far too fat

The authors report that the majority of teens (68.3%) felt the media portrayal was either 'far too thin' or 'a little too thin'. Interestingly, the majority of female respondents felt negatively affected by this portrayal; this compares to 19.9 percent of males. Almost all parents surveyed felt that the media portrayal of weight and shape was too thin (94.7%); half did not feel adversely affected by this (49.2%), but the majority believed their children to be adversely influenced (71.9%).

Relationship between media portrayal and disordered eating

A significant relationship was found by the authors between the effects of media portrayal of weight and shape and eating psychopathology (disordered thinking and eating). Teens who responded that they felt affected 'a lot' were more likely to have increased levels of body dissatisfaction. The research found that adolescents who were in the 'at risk' group for anorexia nervosa, based on their scoring on the questionnaires used, were most likely to view the media portrayal of weight and shape as 'just right'. The authors note this as a worrying finding considering the increasing representation of 'size zero' as ideal in the media. Further (ibid., p. 212), 'The fashion industry has also reinforced this unrealistic thin body ideal: 25 years ago the average model was 8 percent thinner than the average woman – now models are on average 23 percent thinner.' In conclusion, the research suggests,

> ... that while the media is not always the cause of pathological eating it can interact with other factors in certain cases. It is not known whether 'media influence' induces an ED, or whether the particular psychopathology associated with an ED leads a young person to be supersensitive to body weight and shape and to selectively attend to media reinforced idealized images of beauty.

Finally, the authors direct attention to influential research conducted by Becker et al. (2002) which evaluated the impact of the advent of television in the island of Fiji. Until its arrival, a more 'rounded' body shape was perceived as the ideal, but with the arrival of westernised media, eating disorders, hitherto rare, showed a sharp increase. These findings were replicated in research conducted in Tanzania. These findings flag the issue of media and its influence on our attitudes towards not just eating but also a spectrum of topics. While this research does not purport to say that the media is directly responsible for eating disorders, the role of media in eating disorders cannot be ignored. Increasingly, in terms of our 'socialisation', we are shaped by the power of media and the messages it delivers. Within an ecological framework, one can see how media, though a more distal, external influence, can be a powerful one nonetheless. In Chapter 10, the stigmatisation of anorexia nervosa is discussed in detail.

A lot of attention has been given over to the physical domain within this section on adolescence. This reflects the significant changes that occur in this area of development. It is important to recognise these changes to the body, brain (see Chapter 2) and hormones to realise their role in other areas of development, such as socioemotional development, and to cognitive development, which the growth spurts of the brain herald. We will give a quick overview of Piaget's final stage and then examine Elkind's cognitive development, which deals with adolescent thinking specifically.

COGNITIVE DEVELOPMENT

With the increasing activity seen in the brain, one would expect an increase in the cognitive abilities of the adolescent. This growth spurt brings many changes in the way young adults think, such as a better ability to handle more information and an improved ability to devise mental strategies to help them remember and organise information. The growth of the frontal lobe results in greater ability in higher reasoning and thinking. According to Kolb, the growth in the frontal lobe corresponds with Piaget's formal operational stage of thinking, the main features of which are abstract, inductive and deductive thinking.

Piaget's formal operational stage (age 12 onwards)

The main characteristic of this stage is the growing ability to think in abstract terms and the use of deductive logic. Up to this stage the child can only think about things that are 'real' or concrete. According to Piaget they are unable to reason about make-believe problems or situations. Concepts such as justice, ethics or love are abstract terms; you can't touch them or see them. As the adolescent develops abstract thinking they also begin to think more logically; they are able to consider hypotheses (educated guesses or explanations) and test them. Think of algebra and theorems in school. Shaffer (1999) reports that 12-year-old children, when asked where they'd put a 'third eye' provide more creative answers than younger children at the concrete level. One answer at this higher level was from a child who would put a third eye on their hand so they could use it to see around corners. Reflective of their growing cognitive abilities is the ability to think about their own thoughts. The ability to think abstractly gives us great freedom in our thinking as we are no longer confined to the world of 'real' objects, concepts or ideas.

Is Piaget's abstract thinking related to other areas?

Neurological – there is increased growth in the prefrontal cortex, which is responsible for higher reasoning and thought.

Moral – Kohlberg and Piaget believed that the ability to reason morally at higher and more complex levels came in the early teens.

Self – teenagers can now think about who they are, their different selves and their possible and future selves, which involves the use of abstract thinking.

THINK ABOUT IT!

Ask children and teenagers of varying ages where they would put a third eye and why Note their answers and justifications and see if age differences exist.

David Elkind's theory of 'adolescent egocentrism'

In her teens, my younger sister routinely refused to leave the house because her make-up wasn't right or because she had a spot. I took great pleasure in pointing out that she wasn't that important and who would be looking at her to notice her face anyway! Sound familiar? If it doesn't, count your blessings, but if it rings true, David Elkind has an explanation for this behaviour: the 'imaginary audience', the belief that others are as concerned about the teenager's thoughts and behaviour and that others are as interested in them as they are themselves. It is quite literally the idea that they have an audience watching them. Now in adulthood I care far less what others think of me than I did when I was younger. Yet adolescents do care, very much so, and this is why a pimple on the nose turns into a major crisis as the teenager believes everyone will notice, everyone will be looking at them. This increased self-consciousness in adolescents is referred to as 'adolescent egocentrism' by Elkind. Indeed, it's hard not to feel sorry for the hapless adolescent going about their daily business in the belief that everyone is watching them.

While the imaginary audience forms one part of the social thinking that characterises 'adolescent egocentrism', another aspect of it is called the 'personal fable'. The 'personal fable' refers to the adolescent's belief that their experiences are unique; further, it feeds into a belief that they are not subject to the rules that govern the rest of the world, which contributes to a sense of invincibility. This belief has been implicated in some of the risk-taking behaviours seen in adolescence. Thus, a teenager might take drugs with the belief that they won't become addicted, that it won't happen to *them*. While the belief in the 'imaginary audience' is strongest in early teenage years, it declines as the individual moves into later adolescence. The 'personal fable', on the other hand, can persist into early adulthood.

Cognitive changes and improved capabilities influence social and emotional development as the individual is now better equipped to cognitively process material and information relating to the social world and their emotional state. This increased sophistication is clearly witnessed in the complexity of identity formation in adolescence, which we will examine later.

SOCIOEMOTIONAL DEVELOPMENT

David Elkind describes how adolescent behaviours can be explained by their unique style of thinking. Elkind proposes that the 'personal fable' is responsible for the teenager's belief in their own invincibility and this leads to risk-taking behaviours. Erikson suggests a different explanation from a psychosocial perspective. If you recall from Chapter 4, each of Erikson's stages can have either a negative or a positive outcome. The negative outcome, according to Erikson, is 'role confusion', and it is this that is responsible for risky behaviours. Let's take a closer look.

Erikson's fifth stage: identity versus role confusion

As teenagers make the transition from childhood to adulthood, they face questions of 'who' they are and their future role in life. Erikson's fifth stage reflects this. The major developmental 'crisis' to be resolved is that of 'identity'. Adolescence, at least in the West, is synonymous with angst about 'Who am I?' and 'What is my role in life?', and those who successfully navigate this period develop their identity. Erikson referred to a 'psychological moratorium', meaning the gap between childhood and adulthood, where the teenager explores different roles. By the end of the stage the adolescent will have successfully emerged with a sense of who they are. However, some will be unable to resolve the challenge of emerging identity. According to Erikson, they suffer from 'role confusion', resulting in either isolation or a willingness to take on the identity of others.

Identity is influenced by how the adolescent sees themselves and is also based on their relationships with others and how they perceive others to see them. The concept of identity and self-concept is examined in more depth below. For Erikson, the development of self and identity is a major developmental milestone for the teenager to accomplish. Those who do not resolve this stage face 'role confusion', which leaves the person unsure of who they are and where their lives are going. Role confusion has been linked to risk-taking behaviours. As noted by Erikson, identity is the major developmental 'crisis' to be resolved in the transition from childhood to adulthood. Other theories have been put forward to explain how identity emerges; we will examine identity and also the related concepts of self-concept and self-esteem. Let's look at another approach to understanding how adolescents characterise self-concept.

Definition of identity

Identity is the stable, consistent and reliable sense of who one is and what one stands for in the world. It integrates one's meaning to oneself and one's meaning to others; it provides a match between what one regards as central to oneself and how one is viewed by significant others in one's life.

Identity is not a unitary concept; it can have many aspects:

- religious identity
- sexual identity
- career identity
- cultural or ethnic identity.

THINK ABOUT IT!

Who I am in my work setting can be quite different to who I am at home with my son or out with friends; I am Irish, a woman, mother, psychologist, teacher and friend. How do you see yourself? List some of your roles and identities.

James Marcia: identity statuses and development

Building on the work of Erikson, Marcia suggested that identity involves the adoption of ideals and values, sexual orientation and work possibilities. Having considered the possibilities, the young person at the end of adolescence must make commitments about what to become and what to believe. Marcia used an interview technique to assess identity status. Unlike Erikson, whose theory is a stage-based one, Marcia formulated the idea of status, which allowed for a more fluid conception of identity formation.

Identity statuses

- moratorium (in crisis, no commitment)
- achievement (have had crisis and commitment)
- foreclosure (no crisis and commitment)
- diffusion (might have had crisis, no commitment).

Moratorium

This is marked by intense crisis as the teenager searches out the possibilities, considering different roles in their search for identity. No commitment has been made yet.

Identity diffusion

The main characteristic of this stage is that the teenager is not in 'crisis', actively considering the possibilities; further, they are avoiding making a commitment. The stereotypical difficult teenager watching television and refusing to talk might be said to be in this state.

Identity foreclosure

This teenager might seem like the perfect adolescent who dutifully doesn't question or rebel. This teenager has made a commitment to an identity without going through the crisis and exploring alternatives. Instead, they have accepted a parental or culturally defined commitment. Erikson would believe that the teenager had not tackled the challenges of this period and instead relied on identification with others rather than carving out their own identity.

Identity achievement

The adolescent has come through the 'crisis' and a commitment has been made to ideological, occupational and other goals. They have established a sense of self, of their identity.

Marcia's theory was not stage like but offers four points along a continuum of identity development. Each point, as can be seen above, is different, encompassing a diffuse individual identity to one that is precisely defined and specific. Marcia believed that crises (situations or events) were catalysts motivating movement along this continuum and the different identity statuses. Every crisis results in internal conflict and emotional upheaval, causing the adolescent to question their values, beliefs and goals. In doing so the possibility of new beliefs, values and different choices emerged. These crises allow the teen to develop increasing commitment to a particular identity via the process of identity exploration prompted by developmental crises. Whereas Erikson's adolescent stage of identity pivots on a positive or negative outcome in a stage-like manner, the strength of Marcia's theory lies in its flexibility to move along a continuum with each crisis, reverting to an earlier identity point if necessary. We are going to consider in depth the development of identity within one group, Lesbian, Gay, Bisexual and Transgender, as a lens to understand how identity can be fraught with challenges for some and how this can potentially impact on their health and well-being. Before doing so, let's take a quick look at two important terms, self-concept and self-esteem.

Self-concept and self-esteem

Another term for identity is self-concept, which can refer to all aspects of the self. How we compare ourselves to others and how we evaluate or judge aspects of ourselves is called self-esteem. Harter (1990) defined self-esteem as 'how much a person likes, accepts, and respects himself [sic] overall as a person' (p. 255). During adolescence, self-esteem can be fragile; if you recall Elkind's imaginary audience you can understand that teenagers have the potential to judge themselves mercilessly. In the section on physical development we examined the changes that occur with puberty and how these changes can alter the teenager's self-conception. Piaget maintained that adolescents are now able to think at far higher levels; this increased ability allows them to appreciate fully just how significant the changes are. They also can imagine themselves in the future or in different roles with the acquisition of abstract thinking. This feeds into a greater self-consciousness. Earlier in the chapter we saw that low self-esteem has been implicated in eating disorders. The area of self-esteem has been extensively researched. A relationship exists between low self-esteem and low life satisfaction, loneliness, anxiety, resentment, irritability and depression (Rosenberg, 1985). High self-esteem was found among teenagers who saw themselves as close to their parents (Blyth and Traeger, 1988).

As we've just seen, identity and self-concept are crucial markers of adolescence. Is achieving identity an easy task for most adolescents? Certainly it's a challenging time; most adults I've asked recoil in horror at the idea of returning to their teen years and reliving them. For some teenagers the journey through adolescence and the acquisition of identity can prove more difficult where stigma and discrimination exists.

IN FOCUS: LESBIAN, GAY, BISEXUAL AND TRANSGENDER (LGBT) TEENS

Increasingly, there is growing recognition that the lives of LGBT people have been overlooked, and especially how LGBT people traverse adolescence in their journey towards identity achievement or integration. There has been a paucity of research conducted to better understand their lives and experiences. Like other marginalised groups, LGBT people can face discrimination, isolation and, in some cases, rejection from their families and community. In the past, being gay was classified as being a mental illness and categorised as such within the Diagnostic and Statistical Manual of Mental Disorders (DSM), used by psychologists to categorise mental illness. Coupled with some religious teachings that deem homosexuality to be immoral, one can see how people belonging to the LGBT community may face increased risk of stigmatisation, bullying and discrimination. Individuals who face such barriers and are ostracised are more vulnerable to depression and, in extreme cases, risk of suicide. *Supporting LGBT lives: a study of the mental health and well-being of LGBT people* (Mayock et al., 2009) is a recent research initiative aimed at better understanding the experiences of LGBT people. Before reviewing this research, let us look at the development of sexual identity of lesbian, gay and bisexual youths and a study by Rosario et al. (2011) examining whether different patterns of LGBT identity formation and integration are associated with indicators of psychological adjustment.

According to Herbert (2006, p. 172), in gay and lesbian adolescents sexual and self-identity undergo the following transitions in development:

- Defining oneself as homosexual (gay) or lesbian following experiencing a sense of being different or alienated from heterosexual peers of the same gender as oneself.
- A later reinforcement of this growing awareness by attraction to and/or intimacy with same-sex peers, followed by the dilemma of whether to deny or accede to homoerotic feelings.
- These feelings and subsequent choices are likely to be influenced by homophobic or tolerant within the family, society and the peer group.
- In the case of the former there may be a denial or suppression of a gay/lesbian identity leading to depression, drug abuse, absconding and even suicide in extreme cases.
- In the latter reaction, one of understanding, the path of accepting a gay identity becomes viable and fulfilling.

Herbert highlights that this transition can resolve positively or negatively for the teen. Rosario et al. (2011) looked at this very issue; how do different patterns of LGBT identity formation and integration relate to psychological adjustment? According to Rosario et al. (2011, p. 4), 'LGBT youths often struggle to accept their sexual identity in the context of ignorance, prejudice, and often violence against same-sex sexuality'. While not all LGBT face difficulties in accepting their sexual identity, the authors conclude that those that do face 'poorer psychological adjustment', including '... high rates of depression, anxiety, suicidality, and other behavioural problems ...' Those with 'stagnated identity development are at particular risk'. Identity formation, as we have seen, is a pivotal task associated with adolescence. In this study, the authors are informed by Erikson's theory of identity and personality formation (see Chapter 4). In adolescence, the teen can either positively complete this stage resulting in developing a sense of who they are or, if this stage isn't successfully traversed, 'role confusion'.

Factors associated with positive identity integration and good psychological outcomes include more positive attitudes toward homosexuality, greater openness and disclosure of one's sexuality, and greater involvement in the LGBT community. Each of these factors has been found to be associated with greater psychological adjustment. Relatedly, LGBT individuals who are further along in integrating their sexual identity have been found to have higher self-esteem. Experiences of gay-related stressful events (e.g., rejection, ridicule, victimisation) have been associated with poor psychological adjustment among LGBT individuals. Supportive friends and family are particularly important for the psychological adjustment of LGBT youths, whereas unsupportive family and friends may be detrimental to their mental health. In addition, the existence of a supportive or stressful social context may promote or inhibit sexual identity development.

Supporting LGBT lives

Mayock et al.'s (2009) findings mirror how different factors impact on burgeoning LGBT identity. The authors reflect:

> The result is a report that clearly highlights the negative effects of stigmatisation, marginalisation and discrimination on the mental health of LGBT people. LGBT people, their families and their friends as well as those working within the LGBT sector are familiar with the impact of negative societal reactions to minority sexual or gender identities. Using the concept of **minority stress**, this research clearly demonstrates that it is social and structural factors that account for elevated mental health risks among the Irish LGBT population. The findings show that experiences such as homophobic bullying and violence, invisibility and alienation from family and friends, are all linked to increased mental health risk and suicidality among Irish LGBT people. While the majority of participants demonstrated mental health resilience despite their experience of hostile social environments, a significant percentage reported a worrying level of psychological distress and suicidality. A picture emerged of the most vulnerable participants – on average they realized they were LGBT at 14 years of age, they commenced self-harming behaviour at 15.5, they attempted suicide for the first time at 17 and did not come out to others until age 21. For these participants the 7 years of concealing their sexual orientation or gender identity coincided with particular mental health vulnerability and psychological distress. This period of vulnerability also coincided with participants' school-going years and their negotiation of early adulthood – a time of critical social and emotion development.

The authors of the report reiterate that '... the vast majority of participants never self-harmed or attempted suicide and that a large number reported positive everyday experiences. It is important to reiterate in this context that a preoccupation with risks – frequently (mis)interpreted as individual deficits – belies the reality of LGBT lives and potentially contributes to a construction of LGBT people as deficient and dysfunctional.'

It is clear that structural and societal attitudes can be very powerful influences on developing LGBT identity; this emphasises further the absolute necessity to tackle prejudicial, bigoted and discriminatory attitudes within society towards LGBT people and others who are marginalised. Within Bronfenbrenner's ecological model, one can see the effect of immediate influences (family support) but also the role of more distal factors such as whether anti-discriminatory legislation exists and is enforced, or religious and cultural mores. Finally, the **minority stress model**, which is a conceptual framework for understanding the negative impact on health and well-being caused by a stigmatising social context, has provided a useful lens through which to better understand not just LGBT peoples' lives but also other minority groups.

THINK ABOUT IT!

Using this model and the wider ecological approach, review how different influences intertwine to affect an individual's mental and physical well-being across their life span. Identify other groups who suffer discrimination and explore influences, both immediate and more distal, that increase or reduce such prejudice.

That concludes the section covering infancy up to adolescence; we are now going to explore the often ignored realm of adulthood. Historically, childhood and adolescence have been heavily researched in an attempt to understand development, and to plan and support positive development. In more recent times the issue of old age has begun to be developed in terms of research, policy and practice, highlighting the growing recognition of the paucity of knowledge that exists regarding older people. However, adulthood has still not received recognition as an important area that deserves consideration; hopefully, that will change in the near future. In the meantime we will take a quick journey through this developmental period.

ADULTHOOD

Compared to childhood and adolescence, the period of adulthood has not received the same degree of attention or study. Different sources will use different parameters for the definition of adulthood, but the following are what I believe to be the most universal. Adulthood is treated as two phases within this section as can be seen below. A third section deals with the final developmental task of the life span: dying and death.

- Early (age 20–40) and middle adulthood (age 40–65)
- Late adulthood: age 65 onwards
- Dying and death

Early and Mid-Adulthood

- Ageing
  - Primary and secondary signs
  - Theories
- Cognitive Development
  - Schaie's Theory
- Social and Emotional Development
  - Erikson's theory
  - Levinson's Seasons of Man
- Attachment in Adulthood

Later Adulthood

- Physical changes
- Cognitive Development
  - Baltes' dual process model of cognitive development
- Ageism and the cohort effect
- Case Study – ethical dilemmas in old age care

Early and middle adulthood are amalgamated for easiness of reference; we will explore theories relevant to this period, including Levinson's season of man and Schaie's cognitive theory. Late adulthood or old age will be dealt with separately, in terms of brain changes; see Chapter 2 for further information. So let's begin with a general introduction to ageing and related concepts.

AGEING

Many theories of ageing exist, but first the distinction needs to be made between primary and secondary ageing:

- *Primary ageing* refers to the gradual age-related changes that we have no control over, reflecting the biological aspects of ageing which affect everyone. Changes include greying hair and deterioration in hearing and vision.
- *Secondary ageing* is more individual in that it is influenced by lifestyle and environmental factors, such as lack of exercise, smoking, alcohol consumption and obesity. Disease is a factor in secondary ageing.

Theories of ageing

Damage-based theories suggest that ageing results from a continuous process of damage, which accumulates throughout the entire life span. This approach argues that ageing is predominantly a result of interactions with the environment. *Programmed theories* of ageing suggest that ageing is not a result of random processes but rather that ageing is predetermined and occurs on a fixed schedule.

Signs of senescence

Senescence is the deterioration of bodily functions that accompanies ageing in a living organism. Some signs of ageing include:

- an overall decrease in energy
- the tendency to become easily tired
- changes to skin, such as wrinkles, brown spots on the skin and loss of skin elasticity
- greying and thinning of hair
- a loss or decrease in vision and hearing
- slower reaction times.

EARLY AND MIDDLE ADULTHOOD

Although this period of adulthood has not been as well researched as other stages, some theories do exist in regard to cognitive and social/emotional development. We will consider cognitive theories first, looking at Schaie's theory and that of postformal thought. As you will note, there is no mention of Piaget as he believed cognitive development was completed by adolescence. Schaie's theory offer a more comprehensive approach across the life span.

COGNITIVE DEVELOPMENT

Schaie's theory of cognitive development

Schaie and Willis (2000) offer a theory of cognitive development across the life span, beginning with 'acquisition' and moving towards the end of life with 'legacy creating'. We will examine each stage of this theory within its age specificity:

EARLY ADULTHOOD

- **Acquisition** (childhood and adolescence): This involves the acquisition of mental structures, information and skills in order to gain understanding of the world.
- **Achieving** (late teens to early twenties): Young adults use their knowledge to pursue a career, choose a lifestyle and solve personal dilemmas.
- **Responsibility** (middle adulthood): Individuals use their abilities to solve problems related to their responsibilities to others; for example, family members.
- **Executive** (middle adulthood): This stage reflects a concern for the welfare of the broader social system. Individuals deal with complex relationships on multiple levels.
- **Reorganisation** (end of middle adulthood to the beginning of late adulthood): This stage is marked by retirement. Cognitive tasks involve the reorganisation of life around new interests and pursuits.
- **Reintegrative** (late adulthood): Older adults look back over their lives, to make sense of life. The older person learns to be selective in using more limited energies.

- **Legacy-creating** (advanced old age): This is the final stage of Schaie's theory and represents attempts by the older person to ensure that some part of them will continue after they are gone: that they leave a legacy. Activities such as making a will or funeral arrangements will be engaged in.

Schaie's theory is a stage-based one, concentrating on developmental changes across the span of adulthood into old age. The strength of this theory is that it is very specific in its delineation across the age range of adulthood in comparison to other theories. A different theoretical approach is a continuation of Piaget's formal operational stage and is sometimes labelled as the 'fifth stage'.

POSTFORMAL THINKING

This postformal stage, developed by neo-Piagetians, emphasises not the acquisition of a new stage but rather that the individual is now better able to apply this new level of thinking to problem-solving and reasoning. 'Postformal thought' incorporates the ability to recognise that the correct answer to a problem requires reflective thinking and may vary from situation to situation. Adolescents tend to think in a dualistic manner, such as right or wrong; adults recognise that shades of grey exist and that each situation or problem is unique. Both theories emphasise qualitative differences in how adults think and process information compared to earlier years. Certainly Piaget's formal operational stage is erroneous if one considers it the final point in the acquisition and development of adult cognitive capabilities.

We are going to move on to socio-emotional development, beginning, as always, with Erikson and a recap of his theory, and then a theory specific to adulthood is considered: Levinson's stages of man, which breaks adulthood into tight parameters reflecting the social changes that occur during adulthood.

SOCIOEMOTIONAL DEVELOPMENT

Erikson's psychosocial stages

ISOLATION VERSUS INTIMACY

In this stage Erikson proposes a positive outcome: intimacy, and a negative one: isolation. Intimacy relates to forming an intimate or love relationship and committing to it. Erikson suggested that isolation reflected an individual's hesitation to form a relationship, possibly due to a fear of losing identity or else self-absorption.

GENERATIVITY VERSUS STAGNATION

Generativity comes from 'to generate' and Erikson envisaged this stage as offering the opportunity to the individual to reach out to others and guide the younger generation. This can be seen particularly in child-rearing but also in more civic-minded activities, such as coaching or community involvement. Here the focus lies beyond the self to others. If this does not occur, the individual is faced with feelings of stagnation, where they place their needs above challenge and sacrifice. They are self-indulgent, displaying little interest in work productivity or involvement with younger people.

Levinson's seasons of man

Daniel Levinson (1986) devised a theory that extends over the entire life span but pays particular attention to the 'nature' of adult development. Central to his theory is the idea of four 'seasonal cycles': pre-adulthood, early adulthood, middle adulthood and late adulthood. According to Levinson (1986, p. 3):

> I conceive of the life cycle as a sequence of eras. Each era has its own biopsychosocial character, and each makes its distinctive contribution to the whole. There are major changes in the nature of our lives from one era to the next, and lesser, though still crucially important, changes within eras. They are partially overlapping: A new era begins as the previous one is approaching its end. A crossera transition, which generally lasts about five years, terminates the outgoing era and initiates the next. The eras and the cross-era transitional periods form the macrostructure of the life cycle, providing an underlying order in the flow of all human lives yet permitting exquisite variations in the individual life course.

The scheme was initially based on interviews with 40 men, but Levinson later interviewed women and found they proceeded through the same eras (life cycles) in a similar manner to men. Levinson did however find that women's lives are more closely linked to the family cycle. Underlying Levinson's theory are several important concepts:

- A **life structure** refers to the underlying pattern of an individual's life at a given time and is shaped by their social and physical environment, primarily family and work, although other factors, such as religion and economic status, are often important.
- A **life cycle** relates to the underlying order spanning adult life, consisting of a sequence of eras. The move from one era to another is not smooth; there are cross-era periods of transition which last for about 5 years.

1. *The* ***Early adult transition*** (17–22) is a developmental bridge between pre-adulthood and early adulthood.
2. The **Entry life structure for early adulthood** (22–28) is the time for building and maintaining an initial mode of adult living.
3. The **Age 30 transition** (28–33) is an opportunity to reappraise and modify the entry structure and to create the basis for the next life structure.
4. The **Culminating life structure for early adulthood** (33–40) is the vehicle for completing this era and realising our youthful ambitions.
5. *The* ***Midlife transition*** (40–45) is another of the great cross-era shifts, serving both to terminate early adulthood and to initiate middle adulthood.
6. The **Entry life structure for middle adulthood** (45–50), like its counterpart above, provides an initial basis for life in a new era.
7. The **Age 50 transition** (50–55) offers a mid-era opportunity for modifying and perhaps improving the entry life structure.

8. The **Culminating life structure for middle adulthood** (55–60) is the framework in which we conclude this era.
9. *The* ***Late adult transition*** (60–65) is a boundary period between middle and late adulthood, separating and linking the two eras.

Starting careers and families mark the beginning of early adulthood. Around age 30 an evaluation occurs and people begin to settle down and also work towards career advancement. Another transition begins at age 40 with the realisation that not all the ambitions and goals that were set will be achieved. I have included Levinson's final stage here for ease, although it falls within the section that deals with late adulthood. Before we move on to later adulthood, let us consider attachment in adulthood.

Attachment in adulthood

As we saw in Chapter 4, attachment is considered one of the most important concepts in psychology. It highlights the importance of early experiences on later development. We have already observed how attachment works in childhood but does it really affect us in later life, colouring our choice in romantic partner? Mary Ainsworth developed a measuring tool (The Strange Situation) to assess attachment styles in young children by removing their primary attachment figure from them and charting their reaction. How do we measure attachment style in an adult? Certainly we can't replicate The Strange Situation! Instead a method called the 'Adult Attachment Interview' (AAI) was developed, which questions adults' recollections of their childhood, rating their responses. From this, adults can be classified as being either securely or insecurely attached. So does the Adult Attachment Interview work?

PATTERN OF ADULT ATTACHMENT BASED ON RESPONSES TO THE AAI

Autonomous – secure

Persons who can recall their own earlier attachment-related experiences objectively and openly, even if these were not favourable. These adults openly expressed their valuing of relationships.

Dismissing – detached

Persons who dismissed attachment relationships as of little concern, value or influence; they gave brief accounts, had few childhood memories and often idealised their childhood without being able to provide any supporting evidence.

Preoccupied – entangled

Persons who seem preoccupied with dependency on their own parents and still actively struggle to please them. They gave inconsistent accounts of their childhood. The conflicts they described were often unresolved and still an ongoing issue with them.

Unresolved – disorganised

Individuals who had experienced traumatic separation from the attachment figure and had not worked through the mourning process, or who had experienced severe neglect or abuse.

Reviewing research on adult attachment styles in adulthood, Crowell and Treboux (1995) discovered the following:

> The avoidant group scored lowest on a scale of love and endorsement of a romantic ideal. Ambivalent subjects were characterized by emotional dependency, preoccupation, having ideas of all-encompassing love, and low scores on friendship. Secure subjects scored highest in self-confidence, avoidant subjects highest on avoidance of intimacy, and ambivalent subjects had the highest scores on neurotic love and lowest scores on circumspect love. Love styles were examined in another study of college students in which secure and ambivalent subjects endorsed romantic ideas and avoidant subjects endorsed logical ideas about love.

WHY ARE RELATIONSHIPS IMPORTANT?

According to Clulow (2007, p. 291), Bowlby believed that relationships allow us to '... discover not only our sense of security as human beings but also the kernel of our personal identity, an identity that is essentially relational'. Does this identity and model of relationships carved out in our early lives impact on our adult years? Clulow (ibid.) views

> ... established adult romantic relationships as potential containers of and for attachment behaviour, and contemporary thinking seeks to understand intimacy in adult life as the interweaving of attachment, care-giving and sexual systems of behaviour activated by specific triggers and assuaged by specific responses. Threats to the couple that might activate attachment behaviour come from both internal and external sources. Predictable changes (like the arrival of children) and unpredictable crises (like an affair or serious illness) are filtered through the lens of each partner's internal working models to constitute meaning and register any challenges to 'felt security'.

Relationships allow for two separate identities (me and you) to create an 'us' which gives a space for partners to test out and develop their dearly held assumptions about themselves and each other in ways that hold real potential for affective and cognitive learning to take place.

In terms of a life span and ecological approach, these relationships are crucial for social and emotional development, affecting our ability to parent which has consequences for the next generation. Further, it has been argued that couple relationships can promote the mental health of communities.

> They also provide a boundary delineating between the couple and their socio-economic and cultural environment. As both 'safe haven' and 'secure base' partnerships provide a refuge from the pressures of the outside world and a platform from which adults can contribute to life beyond the concerns of the immediate family (ibid., p. 292).

So we see how the attachment classification we have in childhood can affect the choices we make in our relationships in adulthood. Hopefully, what is becoming clearer is the relationship between early experiences and later development and a sense of continuity in some form across the life span. Of course, that is not meant to be deterministic; one can form close and healthy relationships in adulthood in spite of difficulties in the parent–child relationship. We will revisit this in Chapter 8, where resilience and adversity is discussed.

LATE ADULTHOOD

Late adulthood, marking the period from 65 years onwards, has historically been a neglected area in psychology. This is beginning to change with more interest and research being given to this area. There can be little doubt that the increasing longevity we are experiencing in the West is forcing us to pay more attention to this period of development. To begin with, let us consider the physical, cognitive and emotional issues connected with older age.

PHYSICAL CHANGES

Some of the following changes are witnessed during old age. Individual variation must be taken into account, as lifestyle and other factors can determine the rate of ageing and the magnitude of its effects.

- Loss of brain weight increases after 60 years of age.
- Neurons (nerve cells) are lost in visual, hearing and motor areas of the brain.
- Vision and hearing become increasingly impaired.
- Heart rate slows, as does blood flow.
- Sleep patterns change, less sleep is needed.
- Appearance of skin continues to change, age spots develop.
- There is a loss of weight and height after 60.
- Muscle strength declines, there is less flexibility.

Changes in the ageing brain and dementia are discussed in Chapter 2 on 'brain and behaviour'. As the brain ages, does that mean changes also occur in the cognitive capabilities in older people? Paul Baltes theorised that the type of intelligence witnessed in older people is influenced by age and is qualitatively different; let's take a look.

COGNITIVE DEVELOPMENT

Paul Baltes' dual-process model

Paul Baltes (1939–2006) was a leading researcher in the field of ageing and has contributed enormously to our understanding of this area. Baltes proposed a dual-process model of cognitive functioning. The dual-process model attempts to measure what aspects of intelligence are likely to improve or deteriorate with age. Papalia et al. (2005, p. 654) relate that in Baltes' model mechanics of intelligence are the brain's neurophysiological 'hardware': information-processing and problem-solving function independently of any particular content. This dimension, like fluid intelligence, often declines with age. Pragmatics of intelligence are culture-based 'software': practical thinking, application of accumulated knowledge and skills, specialised expertise, professional productivity and wisdom. This domain, which may continue to develop until very late adulthood, is similar to, but broader than, crystallised intelligence and includes information and know-how garnered from education, work and life experience.

To put this simply you gain wisdom! Let's take a computer game as an example. A younger person's 'hardware' is in an optimal state, and their response speed is quicker than an older person; however, the older person excels in the 'pragmatics' of intelligence and is able to bring years of experience to problem solving in the game instead. Of course, speaking as someone who is in middle adulthood, wisdom is only of benefit if you have the wisdom to recognise it and use it! Still though, as a driver, while my reaction times might be a split second slower than someone younger, my judgement and driving itself benefit from over 20 years' experience, which, I would argue, makes me a better driver than my younger self – that increasing age seems to bring a sense of my own mortality! Erikson's final stage relates to end of life concerns and a sense of fulfilment.

SOCIOEMOTIONAL DEVELOPMENT

Erikson's integrity versus despair

This is the final stage of Erikson's theory of psychosocial development. It is characterised by the features of integrity and despair. The former represents the positive outcome and is associated with a feeling of satisfaction with one's life and achievements. The individual feels content and at peace, reflecting, according to Erikson, psychosocial maturity on their part. However, if the outcome of this stage is that of despair, then the individual believes that they have made many mistakes in their life and that it is too late to correct them. They are unhappy looking back over their life and experience despair as they feel it is now too late to change things. This despair manifests itself in bitterness and anger. An individual in 'despair' may not be accepting of death.

Ageism and cohort effect

In Chapter 4 we examined the theory of Glen H. Elder Jr, which referred to the 'cohort effect', where lives can be influenced by social change. We compared the lives of people with disabilities born in the 1940s to those born today in order to elaborate on what is meant by a 'cohort effect'. It was clear that the lives of those born with a disability today are better than those from generations ago, although of course there is still some way to go before parity is achieved. If we apply the cohort effect to older people, do you think their lives are better or worse than they were several generations ago? It is certain that today people live longer lives and generally have access to better healthcare services in old age. However, in social terms, is the old custom of respecting your elders in evidence as much as it was many years ago? Many cultures have great respect for their older generation, for their wisdom and life experience. Yet in the West it appears that we have started to devalue older people. The current campaigns against ageism would seem to indicate that negative attitudes exist towards older people.

THINK ABOUT IT!

What do you think? Have attitudes towards older people changed in the last 50 years? If so, how and why? What impact has this on the lives of older people?

With an ageing population and its impact on health and care services comes ethical dilemmas. The following case study asks you to consider what you think is the right thing to do. What would you do if a family member asked you to keep a client in the dark about a diagnosis?

Case study – ethical dilemmas in old age care

Moody (2005, p. 583) presents the following case study to capture the ethical dilemmas faced in old age care:

> Sylvia Senex, aged 80, suffers from disabling arthritis and has been living at home with her daughter for the past six years. During this period the mother's memory problems have gotten worse and her care has become burdensome. Mrs Senex was given tests three years ago suggesting dementia but was never told the results. Her daughter has informed her mother that she has a 'neurological problem' and told her what to expect in the future but she has refused to use the word 'Alzheimer's'. She says that her mother would react badly to that word and her brother, despite doubts, defers to his sister as primary caregiver. Mrs Senex has recently started receiving home care services, but the home care agency is disturbed by the fact that she has been kept in the dark about her diagnosis. What should the agency do?

This case illustrates a series of features that are common in cases of old age care that pose ethical dilemmas:

- Dependency. We are confronted here with a chronic, not acute, health problem: indeed, there is more than one problem, with the result that activities of daily living are limited and freedom of action is diminished.

- Shared responsibility. Caregiving is provided by a family member, but there is some prospect of formal care, with tasks shared between formal and informal sectors, raising questions of accountability.
- Diminished mental capacity. There is some indication of diminished mental capacity, posing questions about the patient's ability to render informed consent concerning major life decisions.
- Trajectory of decline. The condition of the patient, if she does in fact have Alzheimer's, is likely to deteriorate further, raising the prospect of later difficult decisions – such as whether Mrs Senex might belong in a nursing home.

This case study and the accompanying ethical dilemmas identified by Moody clearly illustrate the difficulties faced when making decisions regarding the care of the elderly. Using the case study, consider whether you believe Mrs Senex's daughter is right in withholding the information from her mother. Is the agency correct to have concerns regarding the withholding of information from the mother? What are your concerns and what dilemmas do you feel this case study raises?

Hopefully, you will have gained from this chapter a greater understanding of how seemingly unrelated influences conspire in a holistic manner to shape how we develop. The choices we make in our 20s can shape the lives we have in our 60s. We need to grasp the impact of societal attitudes and change on the lives of people as they age. Ageism is a real problem, with huge consequences for individual lives, yet we have seen that societal attitudes can be challenged and changed for the better. We all have our part to play. We are going to end this chapter with the final developmental task that awaits us also: the end of our life. For some, this knowledge and process can occur over a prolonged period, and for a few it is sudden, although the knowledge of ageing and realisation that your life will come to an end is a known for most of us. Naturally, people's lives can end at any time in the life cycle; however, we will take a more general approach here.

DEATH AND DYING

This can be a difficult topic for most people, as many of us have had experience of personal loss of a loved one. The purpose of this section is to introduce some psychological explanations of how we make sense or cope with dying. The main focus will be from the perspective of the person who is dying rather than those surrounding them. Several approaches will be examined; also explored are children's understanding of death. The chapter ends with Murray Parkes' (1998) discussion of bereavement reactions.

The outline of this section:

- Terminology
- Four Models of Dying
- Phases of Dying
- Children's Understanding
- Bereavement Reactions

TERMINOLOGY

Kastenbaum (2000) remarks that the following terminology has evolved as more direct terms such as death and dying are '... too plain spoken a word for some tastes (p. 200)'.

Life-threatening condition may be used where some possibility for recovery exists.

End of life issues refers to any decisions regarding the end of life from medical directives to funeral arrangements.

PHASES OF DYING

Agonal phase comes from the Greek *agon,* meaning struggle. Muscles may jerk and breathing becomes difficult as the body can no longer support life.

Clinical death is when breathing and heartbeat have ceased, although resuscitation may be possible.

Death occurs when all activity in the brain and brain stem has stopped, resulting in brain death which is irreversible.

PERSONAL VERSUS ROLE-SPECIFIC PERSPECTIVE

The *personal perspective* acknowledges that each of us have our own views on dying and death. This perspective is shaped by our life experiences, family, cultural and religious beliefs and even the mass media. Our personal perspective influences our reactions and perceptions to death.

In the *role-specific perspective*, Kastenbaum (2000, p. 210) remarks that there are '... perspectives on dying that are influenced by education, role, and responsibility ... the clergyperson's personal perspective on dying is expected to function within the established framework of theology and custom'. Others within this perspective include nurses, doctors, social workers and trained counsellors, who have a specific role within the process of death and dying. They are influenced by their role and its responsibilities.

MODELS OF DYING

The following three models or approaches to dying highlight that even as we come to the end of our lives many different perspectives exist in its conceptualisation.

- Awareness and Interaction
- Kübler-Ross Stages of Dying
- Coping with dying as a developmental task

Awareness and Interaction

Discrimination and prejudice can continue right until the end of life, with age, social situation or present ability having the potential to influence hospital staff's perception of patients. Glaser and Strauss (1966, 1968) wrote two pieces based on their observations of interactions in several hospitals. From these observations Glaser and Strass identified that different types of 'awareness and interaction' patterns exist. 'Awareness and interaction' refers to awareness on the part of the patient and the communication (interaction) pattern with another (family or medical professional).

Four basic types were identified:

Closed awareness

The dying person does not realize that he or she is dying and the care provider or the interaction partner is not going to tell them. This is a keeping-the-secret context of the communication (or, rather, non-communication). It is of great psychological interest because the tension involved in trying to interact positively with a dying person while at the same time avoiding a disclosure that one fears would be devastating.

Suspected awareness

The patient surmises that he or she is not being told the truth, all the truth and nothing but the truth. There is an effort to check out one's growing belief that the progress of the disease cannot be reversed or halted. The other interactant may or may not suspect that the patient is suspecting, but in any case is resolved not to let the truth slip out.

Open awareness

Both the patient and others are willing and able to share their knowledge and concerns. This does not necessarily mean that they have extensive discussions of dying and death. Rather, it means that everybody involved feels free to bring up the subject whenever it seems necessary or useful to do so. The open awareness context is almost invariably accompanied by less tension and conflict than either of the first two noted.

Mutual pretense

This is perhaps the most subtle and certainly the most discussed type of interaction context. The patient knows he or she is dying. The visitor knows the patient is dying. Both pretend that they don't know. Furthermore, both may be aware that the other person is pretending, too. The mutual pretense act is difficult to sustain; one or the other person may be caught off guard or under pressure and let the horrifying truth escape (cited in Kastenbaum, 2000, pp. 214–215).

Kübler-Ross' stages of dying

Elisabeth Kubler-Ross' book 'On Death and Dying' first published in 1969 proved to be a seminal one. This area had been ignored and Kubler-Ross shone light on to it based on her work as a doctor in American hospitals. Kubler-Ross noted that differences in how we treat death were noticeable. In her homeland of Switzerland as a child she recounted how she and other neighbours visited a local farmer as he lay dying at home and that dying and death seemed to be far more 'natural' than the medicalised environment and approach that appeared to dominate in American hospitals. She believed that a fear of death was strong in American culture and may be due to the fact that we have made death cold, sterile, impersonal and mechanised. Kubler-Ross noted that the American view of death is abhorrence and avoidance of death, whereas in other cultures it is treated as part of a normal transition. Based on her observations and work with dying patients she devised the following five stages of dying that are passed through:

First stage: denial and Isolation

'No, not me, It cannot be true'

The first response is a temporary state of shock. This stage is characterised by isolation, sometimes dying people withdraw. Others can occasionally withdraw from them.

Second stage: anger

'Life is not fair! Why me?'

When denial can no longer be maintained it is replaced by anger, rage, envy and resentment. The anger may be displaced in all directions; the person may feel a loss of control. Life is a constant reminder of death.

Third stage: bargaining

'If you'll just let me live until my grandchild is born ...'

Seeking the chance that one will be rewarded for good behaviour, but really it represents an attempt to postpone the death.

Fourth stage: depression

'What difference does it make anyway?'

Rage and anger are displaced with a sense of loss at the inevitable; this may represent a preparatory grief as the person prepares for death. Other behaviours that might be seen are reactive depression, loss of self-esteem and guilt.

Fifth stage: acceptance

'I've lived a good life, I'm ready to go'

If the patient has enough time, they will become neither depressed nor angry, happy nor sad but void of feelings ('all felt out'). Dying patients find peace and acceptance, their circle of interests diminish and they prefer fewer visits and distractions.

While stage-like in its approach, Kubler-Ross' model has been criticised, because not all individuals behave in the same manner. Some patients will continue to fight until the end, whereas others give up upon the news. Not all individuals follow the same sequence as outlined by the model. Finally, while Kubler-Ross recognises the differences in approach to death between her homeland and the medicalised approach in America, little more recognition was included of cultural differences. While cultural and ethnic influences on death need to be acknowledged, what is clear is that dying and death is a developmental task.

Coping with dying as a life span developmental task

A life span approach recognises that we meet a series of developmental tasks as we progress through our lives which we must resolve. In this light, according to Charles A. Corr, dying is seen as perhaps the final task that awaits us to reconcile. Four challenges await the dying person; physical, psychological, social and spiritual.

Doka (1993) depicts 'phase-specific' tasks that face the individual from pre-diagnostic to recovery (should that occur).

According to Kastenbaum (2000, p. 220) the Corr/Doka perspective offers several important guidelines:

> Dying people still have a need to accomplish. One does not cease coping and striving; indeed, one calls upon all available resources to accomplish the final set of tasks.
>
> The life span developmental task encourages attention to a very broad range of problems and thereby reduces the temptation to view the dying process within a narrowed and possibly oversimplified perspective.
>
> The idea of having to achieve something when we are ageing and, again, when we are dying seems to resonate well with the product and goal-directed character of our society. People who have become achievement and success oriented throughout their lives may find it logical and meaningful to apply this approach to the very end of life.

CHILDREN'S UNDERSTANDING OF DEATH

Nagy's drawings

Maria Nagy conducted research with children with the aim of understanding how they conceive death. To do this she asked the children (ranging in age from three to ten), to draw pictures representing their ideas of death and to explain their pictures. From this Nagy was able to construct a developmental picture of children's conception of death.

The three phases were:

STAGE ONE: 0–5 YEARS OLD

A child of this age does not recognise that death is final. The child looks upon death as being continuous with life; the dead person has merely gone away. It is the separation element that is most distressing to the child. If you recall the child would be 'egocentric' in term of cognitive thinking, and this is reflected in their understanding of death; the dead are understood with reference to one's own experiences (e.g. they don't get as hungry as I do).

STAGE TWO: 5–9 YEARS OLD

The child begins to understand that death is final. 'Death personifications' begin to dominate during this phase with death represented as a figure or person. Two images featured strongly: 'Death' as a separate person or 'Death' depicted as a dead person. 'Death' was usually male and was depicted as a skeleton, angel or even a clown. A theme that was present was that if you were smart enough or ran fast enough you could avoid the death-man.

STAGE THREE: 9 AND 10 YEARS OLD

These children recognised the finality of death as well as its universality: that it comes to all people eventually. It would appear that the child had attained an adult understanding of death.

Bereavement reactions

Colin Murray Parkes (1998, p. 200) outlines three responses common to those bereaved.

The Trauma Response:

An alarm reaction – anxiety, restlessness, and the physiological accompaniments of fear.

Anger and guilt, including outbursts directed against those who press the bereaved person towards premature acceptance of the loss.

Post-traumatic stress disorder, the specific pathological response and the less specific anxiety states and panic syndromes.

The Grief Response:

An urge to search for and to find the lost person in some form.

Relocating the lost person, including identification phenomena – the adoption of traits, mannerisms, or symptoms of the lost person, with or without a sense of that person's presence within the self.

Pathological variants of grief, that is, the reaction may be excessive and prolonged or uninhibited and inclined to emerge in distorted form.

The Psychosocial Response:

A sense of dislocation between the world that is and the world that should be, often expressed as a sense of mutilation or emptiness which reflects the individual's need to relearn their internal model of the world.

A process of realization, that is, the way in which the bereaved moves from denial or avoidance of recognition of the loss towards acceptance and the adoption of a new model of the world.

> This process may be impaired by the feelings of helplessness and hopelessness which characterise depression.

The approaches outlined demonstrate the varied approach to understanding dying and death, and yet if we compare it to research and literature on the beginnings of life end of life issues within psychology fall short. Perhaps it is a fear of death that makes us less likely to want to engage with this topic as we do others?

SUMMARY

So that marks the end of our journey, tracing our development from conception to death. It is difficult to capture the complexity of the many different aspects of development in such a short space. I'm not sure any amount of space would be able to capture it! In truth, we know relatively little about how we become the person we are; our understanding of such things is in its infancy. I hope what is becoming clear is that there are a myriad of factors that interact nested within circles of influence that shape development in every domain. The purpose of this chapter was to offer a more global view of human growth and development across the life span. The remainder of the book examines different aspects of the human experience, including disability, abuse and resilience, so you will continue to meet different age stages as you continue, but these will be specific to a particular topic.

chapter

6 DISABILITIES

CHAPTER OUTLINE

- The Convention on the Rights of Persons with Disabilities: Article 3
- Definitions of disability
- Models of disability
- What is impairment?
- Causes of disability
- Factors that affect the development of disabled children
- Culture and ethnicity
- Categories of disability
- Sensory disabilities
- Intellectual disabilities
- How do children with disabilities affect their parents, siblings, and families?
- A socio-cultural approach to disability

We are going to begin this chapter with an examination of definitions and models of disability. This is merely an introduction to an area that is vast and hotly debated. Nonetheless, the reader will, hopefully, be encouraged to consider their perception of disability, how it is informed and its implications for practice. The next section overviews the different categories of disabilities and some conditions will be considered in greater detail. The final section allows for engagement with aspects of disability, including ethnicity and disability and its impact on parenting. This chapter is not, cannot be, exhaustive; its intention is to introduce the topic of disability, overview the causes and characteristics of categories of disability and offer insight into some aspects of disability and the life course.

THE CONVENTION ON THE RIGHTS OF PERSONS WITH DISABILITIES: ARTICLE 3

The principles of the present Convention shall be:

a. Respect for inherent dignity, individual autonomy including the freedom to make one's own choices, and independence of persons;
b. Non-discrimination;
c. Full and effective participation and inclusion in society;
d. Respect for difference and acceptance of persons with disabilities as part of human diversity and humanity;
e. Equality of opportunity;
f. Accessibility;
g. Equality between men and women;
h. Respect for the evolving capacities of children with disabilities and respect for the right of children with disabilities to preserve their identities.

This chapter begins with the general principles of the Convention on the Rights of Persons with Disabilities 2006 that represented a salient challenge to prevailing attitudes towards disabilities and the stigma and discrimination it breeds. The chapter ends with an examination of the socio-cultural perspective and how it illuminates the role of belief and situates an individual with disabilities within their context and all that is attendant with that. This chapter cannot be exhaustive but offers the reader an introduction to disability from a psychological perspective. An outline of the different categories, their aetiology (causation) and characteristics is outlined to give a broader understanding, while influences such as culture, ethnicity and child effects on family functioning are explored. Disability is not homogenous; this can be seen in the experiences of the individual with a disability but also in how disability is defined, the models adopted and the language used.

DEFINITIONS OF DISABILITY

Defining disability is contentious, as is the use of language, which plays a pivotal role in people's perception and treatment of others. For example, for many years terms such as 'handicap' and 'retardation' were used in discussing disability, but implicit in the meanings of those words, intentional or otherwise, are negative connotations. 'Retardation' means to 'make slow or late', and one of the meanings of 'handicap' is 'a thing that makes progress or success difficult'. In 2007 the American Association of Mental Retardation changed its name to the 'American Association of Intellectual and Developmental Disabilities' (AAIDD) in recognition of the progression away from terminology that contributes to disabling people. 'This new name is an idea whose time has come', says Doreen Croser, Executive Director of AAIDD. 'Individuals with disabilities and family members do not like the term 'mental retardation' and their advocacy is encouraging political and social change at national, state, and local levels. Our members demanded that we keep up with times and they voted for this name change'.

So how to define disability? There are many definitions of 'disability' and the issue of definition has proven to be one of the most contentious issues facing the delegates of the United Nations committee on a Comprehensive and Integral International Convention on Protection and Promotion of the Rights and Dignity of Persons with Disabilities. In 2006 the following definition was suggested as a 'working proposal':

> Disability results from the interaction between persons with impairments, conditions, or illnesses and the environmental and attitudinal barriers they face. Such impairments, conditions, or illnesses may be permanent, temporary, intermittent, or imputed, and those that are physical, sensory, psychosocial, neurological, medical or intellectual.

The International Classification of Functioning Disability and Health (ICF) provided the following definition of disability:

> Disability is a decrement in functioning at the body, individual or societal level that arises when an individual with a health condition encounters barriers in the environment.

These definitions conceptualise disability as a result of an interaction between features of an individual with a health condition and features of the physical, individual and societal environment. It clearly recognises the three dimensions of disability (body, individual and societal levels) and their role in promoting, or not, inclusiveness. These definitions aim to be applicable to the full range and diversity of disability experience at the same time.

THINK ABOUT IT!

How would you define disability? Is it developmental or can it be acquired? Does it have to be permanent or would you include temporary impairment? These aspects relate to the physiological origins but how about quality of life or social impact of the disability? Would you consider that? Would your definition rest in the ability of the individual to participate in day-to-day activities? For example, my brother and I were born with asthma, which at various stages has affected us badly; I missed quite a bit of primary school when I was younger. From one perspective it could be argued that the impact my health condition had on my schooling and social activities would be classed as a disability as it affected my day to day ability to fully participate in society. This perspective would include illness that affects a person's ability to function fully in society. Would you agree? Or is your concept more rooted in developmental disabilities such as Down Syndrome for example? Use this exercise as a chance to really reflect on your perceptions of disability.

What is clear is that it is not the 'condition or illness' itself that is 'disabling'. Rather, it is society's attitudes and barriers that cause the disability to be seen in prejudicial terms with resulting behaviour (discrimination). What does this mean? The use of the word 'impairment' acknowledges the actual physical or mental impairment; disability, it can be argued, relates to all that occurs due to structural and societal obstacles and barriers, for example being a wheelchair user is not in itself disabling. If all buildings were designed to allow use for all, then a wheelchair user would be able to fully participate in society rather than be excluded. Thus, it is not the physical impairment that is disabling; it is how society responds to the impairment. The Union of the Physically Impaired Against Segregation (UPIAS) was formed in the 1970s to agitate and advocate for the rights of the disabled, and their following definition sowed the seeds of the social model of disability and its dualistic approach to impairment versus disability,

> In our view, it is society which disabled physically impaired people. Disability is something imposed on top of our impairments by the way we are unnecessarily isolated and excluded from full participation in society. Disabled people are therefore an oppressed group in society. To understand this, it is necessary to grasp the distinction between the physical impairment and the social situation, called 'disability', of people with such impairment. Thus we define impairment as lacking part of or all of

> a limb, or having a defective limb, organ or mechanism of the body; and disability as the disadvantage or restriction of activity caused by a contemporary social organisation which takes no or little account of people who have physical impairments and thus excludes them from participation in the mainstream of social activities. Physical disability is therefore a particular form of social oppression. (UPIAS, 1976, pp. 3–4)

As we will see, until the UPIAS and others began to challenge how disabled people were treated and perceived the medical model was the dominant force in conceptualising disability and the treatment of it.

MODELS OF DISABILITY

In terms of support for those with disabilities, according to the British Institute of Learning Disabilities, there has been a move away from the medical model to a social model based on inclusion and integration. Historically, disability has been viewed from a **medical model** approach that views the difficulties faced by a person with disability to be the result of their individual impairment. The **social model**, which is more reflective of *social constructionism,* challenges this view, advocating that it is structural and societal obstacles that limit a person with a disability, not the disability itself. For example, if a building is inaccessible to a wheelchair user because it has no ramp, the medical model would view the inability of the wheelchair user to access the building as the result of their impairment or condition. The social model would instead suggest that it is not the physical impairment of the individual that limits their access to the building, but that the fault lies in a society that builds inaccessible buildings.

For those with a disability, attempting to live within the medical-model paradigm, life can be a constant struggle, and yet this can be a double-edged sword as the diagnosis or 'labelling' of the medical model opens access to services. This binary or dualistic approach, reflected in the medical and social models of disability, has drawn criticism from a new wave within the disability movement, rejecting not just the binary approach encapsulated by the medical and social models. Further, the social model itself has been attacked by some who take issue with the separation between impairment and disability; it is argued that impairments and conditions in and of themselves can limit the individual's ability to fully participate, not just the disabling attitudes and structures imposed by society. The critiques of dualism and the social model can be seen within the critical disability studies approach.

Critical disability studies (CDS)

The medical/social model is a binary approach, an approach rejected by those in belonging to the critical disability tradition. According to Meekosha and Shuttleworth (2009, p. 50):

> ...the social model of disability argued for a conceptual distinction between 'impairment' as a functional limitation and 'disability' as a socially generated system of

discrimination. This binary way of thinking about disability has undergone a number of critiques from feminists, cultural studies scholars and postmodernists, which has led to tensions and splits within the disability studies community, particularly in Britain. Using the term 'CDS' is a move away from the preoccupation with binary understandings – social v medical model, British v American disability studies, disability v impairment.

In Chapter 1 *social constructionism* was outlined. It recognises that our understanding and meanings are socially constructed, not merely mirrored. This highlights the role of language and perception in our viewpoint and our behaviour. So, in line with this perspective, discourse surrounding how disability is understood is important. Discussion surrounding the language used to describe disability is similarly contentious; during my work in disability I always used language and terms which recognised the person first and foremost as an individual rather than defined by their disability. For example, rather than say 'disabled person', I would use 'person with a disability'. This 'people first' approach has been challenged and increasingly social work departments and others are using the term disabled person, reflecting criticisms of the former approach that, it is argued, strips the individual of their identity of which their disability is a core element. The importance of language can be seen in the example in Chapter 2, where the term 'shaken baby syndrome' is no longer advocated. As with definitions and models of disability, consensus regarding the use, or not, of 'people first' language remains elusive.

WHAT DO YOU THINK?

What term or language would you use in describing an individual with a disability? Do you agree that the 'disabled person' is more inclusive of identity, and if so why? Think of other groups in society and the labels you would use; a black person or a person who is black; a schizophrenic or an individual with schizophrenia? Would you use 'people first' language with some conditions or groups but not others, and if so why?

We are now going to move away from the conceptual to the next section, which outlines the causes of and different categories of disability. Before we do that it is useful to outline how impairment is defined and the range it covers.

WHAT IS IMPAIRMENT?

The definition covers physical and mental impairments. These include:

- physical impairments affecting the senses, such as sight and hearing
- mental impairments, including learning disabilities and mental illness (if it is recognised by a respected body of medical opinion).

Substantial

For an effect to be substantial, it must be more than minor. The following are examples that are likely to be considered substantial:

- inability to see moving traffic clearly enough to cross a road safely
- inability to turn taps or knobs
- inability to remember and relay a simple message correctly.

Long-term

Long-term effects are those that

- have lasted at least 12 months, or
- are likely to last at least 12 months, or
- are likely to last for the rest of the life of the person affected.

Long-term effects include those which are likely to recur. For example, an effect is considered long-term if it is likely both to recur, and to do so at least once beyond the 12–month period following the first occurrence.

Day-to-day activities

Day-to-day activities are normal activities carried out by most people on a regular basis, and must involve one of the following broad categories:

- mobility – moving from place to place
- manual dexterity – for example, use of the hands
- physical coordination
- continence
- the ability to lift, carry or move ordinary objects
- speech, hearing or eyesight
- memory, or ability to concentrate, learn or understand
- being able to recognise physical danger.

Source: www.nda.ie

THINK ABOUT IT!

Consider the meaning labels attach, be it the medical or social model. Labels are powerful and affect expectations and assumptions. Can you think of examples from your practice, or personal experience, where the understanding of the person with the impairment or diagnosis of a condition was bypassed and assumptions based on the actual impairment itself? For example, I have seen the person lost in the diagnosis where assumptions about what 'was best' for the individual was not based on them, the person and their lived experiences but rather on the diagnosis itself and attending assumptions. Using person-centred practice is a useful approach to ensure that the individual and their wishes are paramount and heard.

Though we must be careful about labelling and the attendant assumptions and expectations that potentially cloud us from the reality of the individual, it is important to understand the aetiology (cause) and characteristics of disability, as a good knowledge base encourages best practice.

CAUSES OF DISABILITY

Genetic, chromosomal and acquired disabilities

In Chapter 5 we explored the development of a human being from conception, and the genetic, chromosomal and environmental aspects affecting the development of the foetus. So this will be a recap. Both chromosomal and genetic disabilities occur at conception, but whereas the gene-linked conditions are inherited, chromosomal conditions generally occur through the presence of an extra chromosome. Each cell has 23 pairs of chromosomes. In Down syndrome an extra copy of chromosome 21 is present. Sometimes you will find Down syndrome referred to as 'trisomy 21', the 'tri' referring to the three chromosomes present instead of two. Disabilities can also be caused by environmental factors or can be acquired at birth or during the life course of an individual. Lack of oxygen (hypoxia) during pregnancy or at birth can cause disability if the brain is starved of oxygen and becomes damaged. The extent of the disability is dependent on the level of oxygen starvation. Lack of oxygen is one of the causes of cerebral palsy (see below). In Chapter 5 we examined environmental factors *in utero*, which are described as teratogens, such as alcohol or maternal illness. A teratogen is an external influence that can cause birth defects; one such syndrome is Foetal Alcohol Syndrome, which is characterised by a learning disability and certain facial features. Foetal Alcohol Effects is not the full blown syndrome but includes some features, such as learning and behavioural issues. The timing of exposure and dose of a teratogen can make a difference in outcome.

Finally, a disability can be acquired by an individual, who was born without a disability, at any stage throughout their life course through accident or illness. For example, a car accident may leave a person with a physical injury, such as paralysis or an acquired brain injury (see Chapter 2). Those from a medical socio-logical tradition (specifically the sociology of chronic illness and disability, Thomas [2004]) would argue that with increasing age one sees growing rates of disability. According to the most recent statistics for Great Britain (Dept. for Work & Pensions, Office for Disability Issues, 2014), 'The prevalence of disability rises with age. Around 6% of children are disabled, compared to 16% of working age adults and 45% of adults over State Pension age.'

CASE STUDIES

What factors may affect the level of impact an acquired disability has on a person's life? The nature of the injury or impairment, the stage of life is occurs at or socio-economic considerations? Consider the multitude of factors within an ecological framework (Chapter 4) of these two case studies:

Jake is 15, was doing well in school and an avid rugby player. He was paralysed from the neck down from a sports injury. He now needs 24-hour care and the school he was attending does not have the facilities to support his return. Jake is very depressed and feels his 'life is over'; he is increasing articulating his wish to die. His father has given up work to look after Jake as the family were unhappy with the type of care and support being offered. Jake's mum continues to work, and as the family's income has decreased, they cannot afford to continue to support Jake's older sister Olivia who is in university 200 miles away. Miles, Jake's father is struggling to cope with the isolation and guilt as he feels increasing resentment and is directing it towards Jake.

Doris is 52 and identifies herself as British Afro-Caribbean; she has three adult children, with her youngest son Raymond, 22, still living with her. Doris is heavily involved with her church and an active member of her community. She was returning from work one evening when she was mugged, which resulted in her hitting her head. This head injury caused a bleed and has left Doris with damage to the part of the brain responsible for memory. Doris has not been able to return to work due to her head injury and is struggling to cope with day-to-day activities. A fire started in her home last week as she forgot that she had left a chip pan on, Ray managed to get them out but the kitchen is badly damaged. Doris now feels she is a danger and nuisance and is showing increasing signs of distress and anxiety.

In terms of external factors, poverty is a powerful one; its relationship to disability captures the influence of bi-directionality and illustrates the ecological or person-in-environment approach. An individual who lives in poverty is more likely to become disabled during their lifetime and a disabled person is more likely to live in poverty. The next piece from the World Health Organization (WHO, 2012) includes poverty as a factor affecting disabled children's development. Though focussing on disabled children, the factors outlined below have much relevance, and can be applied to adults.

FACTORS THAT AFFECT DISABLED CHILDREN'S DEVELOPMENT

- Poverty
- Stigma and Discrimination
- Child–Parent/Caregiver Interaction
- Violence, abuse, exploitation and abuse
- Limited access to services and programmes

As we have seen earlier and will revisit again in Chapter 8, a multitude of factors, biological and environmental, interact, influencing development and well-being positively or adversely. WHO (2012, p. 8) relay that 'Children who experience disability early in life can be disproportionately exposed to risk factors such as poverty; stigma and discrimination; poor caregiver interaction; institutionalization; violence, abuse and neglect; and limited access to programmes and services, all of which can have a significant effect on their survival and development'. Here we witness that marginalised or minority groups and individuals are more vulnerable to risk factors than others, so let's take a look at the findings of the report

Poverty

Poverty as a factor can increase the likelihood of a disability or can be seen as a consequence of having a disability. One aspect of the relationship between disability and poverty lies in the increased risks experienced by those living in poverty, ranging from poorer nutrition and health to ability to access services to maternal stress and depression. Further, as we saw in the case study in Chapter 2, the ability of families with a disabled relative to work can be curtailed. Additional costs can also be seen with disability as again amplified by the case study in Chapter 2.

Stigma and discrimination

In Chapter 8 on environmental stressors and well-being, the role of stigma and discrimination in the experiences of children with disabilities will be examined.

Child–parent/caregiver interaction

The report notes that studies have shown differences between the parent–child interactions where 'mothers or caregivers of children with disabilities usually dominate interactions more than mothers or caregivers of children without disabilities'. Those with especially disabling conditions that require high levels of support can place substantial stress on caregivers. This level of stress can further be exacerbated by negative beliefs and attitudes held in the community. Finally, a lack of access to supportive services can additionally place stress on parents.

The report cautions

> however, an emphasis on barriers and problems risks overlooking the joy and satisfaction that can come from having a child with disability. Children with disabilities are usually loved and valued by their parents and siblings, and mothers in particular may develop many new skills and capacities through their caring roles. Considering that family settings are generally the first learning and protective environments for children, guidance and orientation are critical for families following the immediate identification of a developmental delay or disability in order to promote positive interactions. In addition to a child's immediate family, his or her neighbourhood, community and societal structures also need to be considered.

This final point highlights the usefulness of Bronfenbrenner's ecological model in understanding the myriad of influences upon a person's development and functioning.

Violence, abuse, exploitation and neglect

Children with disabilities are at increased risk of abuse and exploitation compared to children without disabilities. The report suggests that factors such as social isolation and stigma are responsible, be it in their own homes or care centres. This vulnerability is mirrored by research findings '...that children with disabilities are three to four times more likely to experience violence... Data for 15 countries showed that in seven countries parents of children with disabilities were significantly more likely to report hitting them'. Reasons for this increased risk include '...cultural prejudices and the increased demands that disability may place on their families. Children with disabilities are often perceived to be easy targets: powerlessness and social isolation may make it difficult for them to defend themselves and report abuse'. In addition, such abuse and violence can lead to further difficulties for the child, such as behaviour problems and developmental delays.

Limited access to programmes and services

As mentioned earlier, access to services and programmes has been implicated as a factor in disability. The report notes that,

> Access to mainstream services such as health care and education plays a significant role in determining child health, development and inclusion. Children with disabilities often miss out on essential vaccinations and basic treatment for common childhood illness. Adequate health care, including nutrition, reduces child mortality rates and enables children to refocus their energy on mastering important developmental skills'.

The WHO report captures the many layers of risk factors that exist within a disabled child's sphere of influence from the most direct (their parents/caregiver and families) to more distant systems, such as access to services. If we include the concept of double jeopardy the risk factors and vulnerability of the disabled child increases; for example, the level of vulnerability of a middle class white child who is disabled may differ from a child of Asian ethnicity who is living in poverty. In Chapter 8 the dynamic of protective and risk factors will be further discussed to expand our understanding of its mechanisms and relationship to development. Another factor that is clearly influential is that of culture and its role in shaping the outcomes and experiences of individuals with disabilities and those of their families.

CULTURE AND ETHNICITY

Individuals from minority ethnic groups face greater levels of discrimination. Further, this level of disadvantage is increased in relation to disability and gender. Grant et al. (2005) relay that this experience of disadvantage has been termed *double disadvantage* or *triple jeopardy*. 'Higher levels of poverty are also implicated in the greater incidence of chronic conditions within these communities. Studies of disability have highlighted later diagnosis, poor levels of information to service users and low take-up of service provision alongside systematic discrimination in the allocation of welfare benefits' (ibid., p. 515). Here we witness how different systems interacting can create greater levels of discrimination for disabled individuals from minority groups. Language barriers can be a factor in accessing resources and services, and further discrimination can be experienced in the allocation of welfare benefits. The authors caution that '...the specific nature of this experience must be recognized as comprising more than a number of superimposed layers of discrimination. The interaction of multiple kinds of discrimination produces its own particular effect on individuals and social groups, which is more than the sum of its parts' (ibid., p. 519). Within their own culture and communities discrimination and disadvantage may exist in negative attitudes to disability.

Grant et al. (2005, p. 524) relay that communities where the social model has not been embraced and promoted see greater levels of stigma attached to disability, and this stigma in turn affects the levels of support from family members, friends and community members. Finally, some evidence exists that where such stigma exists within the community, '...people may feel greater shame in respect of a disabled family member and attempts may be made to keep the existence of such members a secret'.

Later in this chapter a socio-cultural approach to families of children with intellectual disability will be explored, but first let us overview the different categories of disability that exist.

CATEGORIES OF DISABILITY

1. physical disability
2. sensory disability
3. intellectual/learning disability
4. pervasive developmental disorder
5. specific learning disability.

Physical disabilities

Definition: Kirk et al. (2000, p. 485), suggest that in defining physical disability two categories can be considered; physical disability and health impairment. A physical disability is defined as 'a condition that interferes with a person's ability to use his or her body'. This highlights that most physical disabilities involve difficulties with skeletal, muscular or nervous systems. A health impairment is defined as 'a condition that requires ongoing medical attention'. The categorisation of health impairment as a disability is interesting, as opinion is sometimes divided as to whether cancer, for example, and its effects on a person's ability to interact fully, is 'disabling' in comparison to someone born with a physical disability. As alluded to earlier, do you think the inclusion of asthma within the definition of physical disability, in terms of its physical impact on the individual and consequent inability to fully participate in one or more of life's activities, a correct one? Regardless, there is recognition that any physical condition that limits or impacts on a person can possibly be considered a disability. Health impairments can include conditions such as cystic fibrosis, heart conditions and cancer. Having one of these conditions is not in itself automatically considered a physical disability; it is their potential impact that elevates them to such a classification.

CAUSES OF PHYSICAL DISABILITIES

- congenital disabilities
- acquired disabilities.

Congenital disabilities means that the disability is present at birth (it may or may not have been present earlier *in utero* but it must be present at birth, although the condition might sometimes show itself soon after birth). Congenital disabilities can span from mild to severe and include cerebral palsy, epilepsy, neural tube disorders (spina bifida) and muscular dystrophy, to name just a few.

Acquired disabilities are physical impairments that develop, usually through an accident or illness, after a period of typical development; see Chapter 2 for more on acquired brain injury. In terms of illness always remember that external influences such as poverty can be a powerful factor in the development of chronic conditions, as can a lack of access to services (for example, diabetes if not properly controlled can have serious repercussions).

In focus: cerebral palsy

Cerebral palsy (CP) is defined as a physical condition affecting the part of the brain which controls movement and posture. Individuals with CP may move jerkily or hold themselves awkwardly, reflecting the difficulty in control of muscles. Cerebral palsy can be caused by a number of things, such as an illness during pregnancy, lack of oxygen as a result of complications during birth or a serious accident or illness after birth. The degree of severity ranges widely; some children are only mildly affected, taking only a little longer than others to sit up and walk, and so on. People with a moderate degree of cerebral palsy may require a wheelchair or walking aid for mobility. Some are affected very severely and can do very little for themselves physically.

Causes of cerebral palsy

Cerebral palsy [CP] is caused by damage to, or failure in the development of, the part of the brain that controls movement. This happens before birth, during birth or during early childhood before the brain's growth has reached a certain level of maturity. SPARCLE (a study of participation of children with cerebral palsy living in Europe) relates that:

- CP is the commonest cause of significant motor impairment, occurring in 1 in 500 births or 10,000 new cases a year in the EU prior to recent enlargement.
- Children with CP often have impairments of learning, hearing, vision, communication and epilepsy in addition to their motor ones and so are representative of the wider population of disabled children.
- Children with CP are a group with relatively stable impairment where Participation and Quality of Life (QoL) will be influenced by social and educational environmental factors as well as by medical interventions.
- Adults with CP are disadvantaged in social relationships and employment ... and children are disadvantaged in education, social relationships and employment prospects.

Physical disabilities are not a 'hidden' disability; the nature of the disability is often salient and apparent to those around them. Sensory disabilities can be a 'hidden disability', particularly hearing impairments, which are not as salient or obvious.

THINK ABOUT IT!

Can you identify other 'hidden disabilities'? Neurological ones for example; chronic migraine is now accepted as a neurological, not psychological, condition that can render a person immobile during a severe migraine. What about dyslexia or other specific learning disabilities, other health conditions or how about psychiatric conditions such as schizophrenia? Would you feel comfortable labelling conditions such as bi-polar or schizophrenia a disability acknowledging the impact such conditions have on the lives of those who have them? How about mild depression or anxiety disorder? Would you include less 'chronic' conditions? Consider the role of your perceptions in how you view disability; many are happy to acknowledge more 'biological' based conditions as disabling than those viewed as 'psychological' in origins.

SENSORY DISABILITIES

Sensory disabilities include any impairment to the senses, the most common being visual or hearing impairment. There are degrees of impairment from mild to complete or profound loss. Sensory disability is often an invisible disability, not immediately obvious to those around them. We are going to examine visual disability and communication guidelines for meeting and greeting. Deafness and culture will then be outlined, in addition to the relationship between deafness and mental health.

Visual disability

Generally most people with sight loss can see something, while a minority of blind people can distinguish light but nothing else; others have reduced central vision, while some have no side vision. Some people see everything as a vague blur; others see a patchwork of blanks. There are a number of different eye conditions that can cause types of sight loss. Some people are born with no vision or significantly reduced vision. Others lose vision due to accidents or ageing. The effect of the sight loss varies widely, depending on the condition, its progress and the person's managing skills.

In Practice: Communication Guidelines for meeting and greeting people with visual impairment:

- Greet a person by saying your name, as he or she may not recognise your voice. Do not ask or expect them to guess who you are, even if they know you.
- Talk directly to the person rather than through a third party. It's easier if you know the person with sight loss by name – say his or her name when you are speaking to them. If you don't know their name, don't be afraid to ask, as well as giving your own name.
- In a group situation, introduce the other people present. Address the person with sight loss by name when directing conversation to them in a group situation.
- If someone joins or leaves the group, tell the person with sight loss that this has happened.

- Before giving assistance, always ask the person first if they would like assistance, and if they do, ask what assistance is needed. Do not assume what assistance the person needs.
- If a person with sight loss says that he or she would like to be guided, offer your elbow. Keep your arm by your side and the person with sight loss can walk a little behind you, holding your arm just above the elbow.
- When assisting, it is helpful to give commentary on what is around the person, for example, 'the chair is to your right'.
- If you've been talking to a person with sight loss, tell him or her when you are leaving, so that they are not left talking to themselves.
- If you have been guiding a blind person and have to leave them, bring them to some reference point that they can feel, like a wall, table or chair. To be left in open space can be disorientating for a person with no vision. (www.ncbi.ie)

The person is the expert on what assistance they require. Always ask the person what kind of assistance they need, if any. Only they will know what works best for them and not everyone who has a visual impairment will require the same adaptations.

Deafness

In response to 'A sign of the times' (Department of Health, 2002), a report 'Mental Health and Deafness: towards equity and access: best practice guidelines' (Department of Health, 2005) was developed in England. The following is an extract that questions whether deafness is a disability:

> Deafness and Culture – Most people think of deafness as a disability. That view is often shared by those who acquire deafness through illness or injury. However, many people who are born Deaf and who communicate mainly through sign language see themselves as part of a distinct community with a common language and cultural heritage. Sign language should not be seen as a degraded form of any spoken language. Rather, it is a fully formed language in its own right – readily capable of drama, comedy, poetry and the most evolved forms of prose. It should be remembered, also, that many users of sign language will view English, including written English, as, at best, a second language. It needs also to be born in mind that the vast majority of Deaf school leavers will only reach a reading age of nine. Written communication of complex issues will, therefore, often be insufficient.

An example of sign language being the primary mode of communication can be seen in the case of Martha's Vineyard in America. Due to a genetic marker for deafness a significant proportion of the population were born deaf. Martha's Vineyard Sign Language developed and was used by both hearing and deaf members of the community. As deafness was widespread in the small community it became viewed as the 'norm' and all used sign language to communicate. This example illustrates that what is considered typical or atypical is contextually situated and mediated by external forces. In this chapter a lot more attention is given over to intellectual disabilities, reflecting it as a central characteristic in many chromosomal and genetic inherited conditions; its origins can also lie within acquired brain injury. We will begin by looking briefly at the history of intelligence; this construct forms the core element in assessing intellectual disabilities, though other areas of assessment are being increasingly used. Regarding terminology, as we saw earlier, 'mental retardation' and 'handicap' are no longer used as a result of their stigmatising implications. Again, as with first person use, consensus can be hard to find. I have always used the term 'intellectual disability' to denote intellectual functioning below 85 (we will look at classifications later in this chapter); however, the term learning disability has become more popular and both terms will be used interchangeably within this chapter. To be clear though, a specific learning disability relates to an individual with a typical or 'normal' IQ but difficulties in a specific area of processing or functioning, for example, dyslexia. A learning disability relates to an individual with a below average IQ that falls within the classification of intellectual or learning disability; in this instance the impairment is global, affecting all areas of cognitive functioning, not specific to just one or two aspects.

INTELLECTUAL DISABILITIES

History and theories of intelligence

Francis Galton, a cousin of Darwin, was the first person to attempt to examine the construct of intelligence and to measure it. Alfred Binet had more success and formulated the first intelligence test, the 'Binet-Simon' test, which tests general knowledge that one would expect a child to know. The test was graded in difficulty according to the child's age. The scoring of the test produced a number referred to as the child's mental age. The test was in French, was translated for use in America and became known as the Stanford-Binet test; it is still in use today. The test has been adapted to use the following formula, which calculates Intelligence Quotient (IQ) as the sum of (Mental Age/Chronological Age) x 100.

No matter what the child's chronological age, if the mental age matches the chronological age, then the IQ will equal 100. An IQ of 100 thus indicates a child of average intellectual development. If the mental age is above the chronological age (a more gifted than average child), then the IQ is above 100. If the mental age is below the chronological age, then the IQ is below 100, indicating a possible intellectual disability.

Wechsler tests are used to assess not only intellectual disabilities but also specific learning disabilities (such as dyslexia). These tests consist of the WISC (Wechsler Intelligence Scale for Children) and the WAIS (Wechsler Adult Intelligence Scale). The Wechsler tests moved away from an emphasis on verbal skills to a more varied construct, looking at many elements of 'intelligence', including numerical, processing speed, working memory and perceptual reasoning.

Criticisms of IQ

Berger (1986, in Herbert, 2006, p. 387) outlines two reasons for the negative connotations surrounding the measurement of IQ:

- First, there is now a well-documented historical and contemporary association between IQ testing and allegations of discrimination: racial, educational, or otherwise.
- Second, philosophers, many psychologists, especially those in the developmental and cognitive fields, as well as others are, to say the least, sceptical if not dismissive of the way IQ tests are paraded as devices that can generate a measure that in turn encompasses something as remarkable, complex and subtle as human intelligence.

The issue of racism and IQ is a long-standing one. Richard J. Herrnstein and Charles Murray's *The Bell Curve* (1994) was effectively an apologia or justification for racist attitudes towards black people as it alleged that white people were intellectually superior. Other findings have claimed the Irish as the least intelligent in Europe and women less so than men. We must always critique such findings, as factors such as discrimination and lack of access to education are powerful influences, and, more importantly, the whole construct of 'intelligence' is one that is culturally situated. What might be considered intelligent in one culture would not necessarily be in another. Finally, there is always the adage 'lies, damn lies and statistics'; we should always be mindful of findings and subject them to critique.

What is an intellectual/learning disability?

As noted, intellectual disabilities receive more attention than other categories of disability in this chapter. This is because a lot of social work and students and practitioners will work with people with intellectual disabilities at some point, so it is important to understand the complexity of intellectual disabilities, which are not a homogenous group. As people with learning disabilities (LD) are not a homogenous group, neither is the definition of LD; different jurisdictions, organisations and domains can have varying descriptions. The following definition is from the British Psychological Society (BPS):

People with learning disabilities do not constitute a homogeneous group. However, in terms of diagnosis and classification there are a number of features of learning disability which have gained widespread acceptance across professional boundaries within the UK and America. Irrespective of the precise terminology, or the wording in the various definitions, there are three core criteria for learning disability:

- Significant impairment of intellectual functioning;
- Significant impairment of adaptive/social functioning;
- Age of onset before adulthood.

All three criteria must be met for a person to be considered to have a learning disability.

The American Association on Intellectual and Developmental Disability defines intellectual disability as; 'a disability characterized by significant limitations both in intellectual functioning and in adaptive behavior, which covers many everyday social and practical skills. This disability originates before the age of 18'.

Both definitions recognise not just intellectual functioning but also adaption and social functioning as important elements to be considered when assessing learning disabilities. The BPS maintains assessment cannot be considered fully complete without reference to social functioning. While social functioning is more intuitive and easier to grasp, what does intellectual functioning and adaptive behaviour actually mean? Intellectual functioning, also referred to as intelligence, refers to general mental capacity, such as learning, reasoning, problem solving, and so on. One criterion to measure intellectual functioning is an IQ test. Generally, an IQ test score of around 70 or as high as 75 indicates a limitation in intellectual functioning. Standardised tests can also determine limitations in adaptive behaviour, which comprises three skill types:

ADAPTIVE BEHAVIOUR

Conceptual Skills language and literacy; money, time, and number concepts; and self-direction

Social Skills interpersonal skills, social responsibility, self-esteem, gullibility, naïveté (i.e., wariness), social problem solving, the ability to follow rules/obey laws and to avoid being victimised

Practical Skills activities of daily living (personal care), occupational skills, healthcare, travel/transportation, schedules/routines, safety, use of money, use of the telephone

Source: www.aamr.org

The assessment and classification of learning disabilities have been based historically upon the assessment of IQ. Though more recent developments have encouraged practitioners to consider additional factors, such as the community environment typical of the individual's peers and culture, the main focus in diagnosing a learning disability remains the evaluation of IQ.

THINK ABOUT IT!

Would you argue for the inclusion of factors such as community environment and culture in assessing learning disabilities? If yes, justify why such factors should be considered when evaluating LD; can some factors (e.g. poverty or access to resources) considered within an ecological framework affect outcomes? What do you think?

Classification of intellectual impairment

As we have seen, the construct of intelligence is not without controversy; however, it remains an integral part of the assessment of intellectual disabilities. Using IQ as a measure, intellectual disabilities are classified as follows:

- 50–70: mild learning disability
- 35–50: moderate learning disability
- 20–35: severe learning disability
- below 20: profound learning disability

Source: British Institute of Learning Disability.

These classifications represent different levels of impairment in cognitive functioning. Of course, you will come across different classifications, especially in terms of 'mild', which can range from less than 90 or 85 in some books and organisations.

CAUSES OF LEARNING DISABILITY

The causes of learning disabilities are mainly classified into environmental factors, genetic factors and chromosomal abnormalities. A number of genetic and chromosomal disabilities were examined in Chapter 5. Environmental factors (teratogens), maternal illness and anoxia (lack of oxygen) at birth can be causes of learning disability, as already mentioned.

The British Institute of Learning Disabilities suggests that for about 50 percent of people who have a mild learning disability no cause has been identified. A number of environmental and genetic factors are thought to be significant, although diagnosed genetic causes have been found in only 5 percent of people in this category. Higher rates in some social classes suggest that factors such as large families, overcrowding and poverty are important. Research increasingly points also to organic causes, such as exposure to alcohol and other toxins, hypoxia and other issues at the time of birth, and some chromosomal abnormalities. In people with severe or profound learning disabilities, chromosomal abnormalities are responsible for about 40 percent of cases. Genetic factors account for 15 percent, prenatal and perinatal problems 10 percent, and postnatal issues a further 10 percent. Cases which are of unknown cause are fewer, but still high at around 25 percent. This highlights the role of environmental factors in the causation and development of learning disabilities. As we will further explore in Chapter 8, factors such as poverty and housing conditions continue to affect life outcomes and development.

CRITIQUE OF IQ AS A MEASUREMENT OF DISABILITY

The British Institute of Learning Disability (BILD) outlines the following difficulties of using IQ as a measurement of an individual's intellectual disability: first, there are problems with using IQ alone. Measurements can vary during a person's growth and development. Second, many of us have individual strengths and abilities which do not show up well in IQ tests. It is important to take these into account, as well as the degree of social functioning and adaptation.

CASE STUDY

This final point is an important one. I worked with an individual with Down syndrome (we'll call her Mary) who had an IQ of 65, she completed school and State exams (with the support of additional tuition paid for by her family). Mary worked part-time in an multinational insurance company; she had a very supportive family and a wide social circle, had participated in the Special Olympics and leads a very full and active life. Another service user John had a higher IQ than Mary; his learning disability appeared to have occurred in utero or at birth due to a lack of oxygen and had been undetected until his late teens. John had struggled through school, dropping out at 16 and worked intermittently on the family's small holding (farm). His family did not agree with the diagnosis, insisting he was just a 'bit slow' as he was lazy. He remained isolated socially and was deeply unhappy. The contrast between both individuals is terms of quality of life (QoL) is clear, yet interesting IQ itself was not the deciding factor here.

THINK ABOUT IT!

Identify the different factors in both case studies and their impact on QoL. What are the implications for practice from these examples?

EFFECTS OF CONGENITAL AND ACQUIRED DISABILITY

A distinction needs to be made at this stage between an intellectual disability existing at birth and one which is acquired. In the case of the former, from a developmental perspective, the individual's life course is affected by the learning disability from day one (possibly even before birth if the parents are aware of it), in terms of their own development and in access to education, societal attitudes, and so on. In the case of an acquired brain injury, the intellectual disability is not present at birth but is 'acquired' at a later date in the person's development. Thus the impact of a learning disability on the life course of an individual is not always the same. A person who was developing typically and acquires a learning disability faces changes socially and economically (if they can no longer work as they did before); their personality maybe affected and for those close to them, they now have to process these changes in addition to the loss of the former person/ personality.

IN FOCUS: DOWN SYNDROME AND ELDER'S LIFE COURSE PERSPECTIVE

Down syndrome is the most common of the chromosomal disorders. In the UK, one baby in 1000 is estimated to be born with Down syndrome. Physical characteristics associated with Down syndrome include a downward sloping skinfold at the inner eye corners, flat appearance of the face, protruding tongue and low muscle tone (which means in babies that their head and neck need extra support).

Down syndrome is accompanied by developmental delay: IQ can range from low to severe learning disability. The 'compare and contrast' exercise demonstrates the importance of considering the individual within a broad ecological context and life span perspective.

COMPARE AND CONTRAST

It has been recognised that the quality of life of people with Down syndrome has improved immensely in the last thirty years with increased life expectancy and more opportunities to participate in society. Of course, this does not alter that the lives of those with learning disabilities is marked by social exclusion and oppression compared to others in society. Using Elder's life course theory (see Chapter 4), what do you think was the experience of a child born with Down syndrome in the 1940s or 1970s? Do you think their experience would be different to a child with Down syndrome today? List in what ways and consider what has caused these changes in experiences?

VULNERABILITIES FACED BY INDIVIDUALS WITH MILD INTELLECTUAL DISABILITIES

People with learning disabilities are recognised as a vulnerable group in part due to social exclusion, discrimination and difficulties accessing services and resources, with cognitive deficits that characterise learning disability increasing such vulnerability. The following outlines issues affecting people with mild intellectual disability (MID), including their increased vulnerability to the following risks:

- Poverty and homelessness
- Physical ill health
- Injury and violence
- Psychological disorders
- Victimisation and maltreatment
- Lowered life satisfaction
- Child removal, foster care
- Judicial system failures
- Women are at even greater physical and mental health risk, and
- Women have lowered life satisfaction.

(Psychological Society of Ireland)

There are two identifiable 'groupings' of people with mild intellectual disability. One group is comprised of individuals who have been formally diagnosed as having a learning disability, perhaps having come from a special school background or having received special support in a mainstream school and/or receiving services from a learning disability service. There is another, much broader group of people who have not been formally diagnosed but who nonetheless have levels of impairment and who present with various personal and social problems. Some of the difficulties experienced by both groups include at least some of the following:

- Vagueness about basic facts;
- Illiteracy;
- Problems managing money;
- Overwhelmed by routine demands;
- Difficulty in new situations;

- Poor independent living skills;
- Difficulty understanding consequences of actions;
- Difficulty sustaining relationships;
- Difficulty recognising own needs;
- Being influenced or led in an exploitative way, and acting out in response to frustration.

These difficulties are long-term and lifelong. The demands of ordinary life (i.e. social, educational, domestic, safety, communication) create ongoing threats to people with mild intellectual disability. A particularly clear example of this can be seen in the over-representation of people with learning disabilities and difficulties in the prison system.

EXPERIENCES OF PRISONERS WITH LEARNING DISABILITIES AND DIFFICULTIES

> I didn't know what was going on and there's no one to explain things to you. They tell you to read things and in court you can't just ask for help. The judge thinks you can read and write just because you can speak English.
>
> (Prisoner with LD, as cited in Talbot, 2008, p. 23)

No One Knows sought to uncover the experiences of those with learning disabilities within the criminal system. Talbot (2008), in her research *Prisoners' voices*, drew on the previous work carried out by *No One Knows* in surveying prisoners with LD. Talbot relays the prevalence of those with LD and learning difficulties in the criminal justice system as follows:

- 20–30 percent of offenders have learning disabilities or difficulties that interfere with their ability to cope
- within the criminal justice system
- 7 percent of prisoners have an IQ of less than 70 and a further 25 percent have an IQ of less than 80
- 23 percent of prisoners under 18 years of age have an IQ of less than 70
- 20 percent of the prison population has a 'hidden disability' that 'will affect and undermine their performance in both education and work settings'.
- dyslexia is three to four times more common among prisoners than among the general population
- there is a small over representation of those with autistic spectrum disorder in the special hospital population; prevalence in the prison population remains unclear

Further, the 20–30 percent of prisoners with learning disabilities or difficulties that interfere with their ability to cope within the criminal justice system are:

- at risk of re-offending because of unidentified needs and consequent lack of support or services
- unlikely to benefit from programmes designed to address offending behaviour
- targeted by other prisoners when in custody.

THINK ABOUT IT!

Why do you think people with learning disabilities and difficulties are over-represented within the prison population? In addition to their learning difficulties, which make understanding the legal process difficult, what factors may leave them particularly vulnerable to becoming involved in criminal acts? Factors often include a lack of identification and assessment of mild learning disabilities, inadequate educational support services when they were younger or a lack of knowledge of learning disabilities among professionals. I would highly recommend you to read Talbot's findings as they illustrate the complexity of experiences for prisoners with learning disabilities and the inadequacy of the criminal justice systems to support them.

MILD INTELLECTUAL DISABILITY: IMPLICATIONS FOR SERVICE PROVIDERS

The needs and issues of adults with MID affect a range of agencies and services, including the police, the judicial system, Adult Mental Health Services, child protection services, vocational training and social welfare. Anecdotal clinical evidence suggests that professionals in mainstream agencies with responsibility to provide services to this population do not have sufficient experience or understanding of the issues and have difficulties and challenges with people with MID. In relation to children with mild intellectual disability who are in statutory care, there are additional implications for when they leave care, that is, post 18. The usual 'aftercare' is a transition phase between 18 and 21 years and this is insufficient and inadequate to assist young people with mild intellectual disability to move toward independent adulthood. Specialised, ongoing, adult support services need to be made available to these young people when they leave care. Child protection and welfare issues are also further complicated when children have parents who have an intellectual disability, which is not an uncommon event.

As you have seen, learning disabilities are diverse in their aetiology (causes), they can be acquired at any stage of the life cycle or present at birth, and comorbidity is common (where you see one condition you are more likely to see another), for example cerebral palsy can be comorbid with a learning disability. A multitude of factors can influence the causation and continuance of a learning disability, which on a positive note highlights how good supports and access to services can have a real influence on outcomes. The next category we are going to consider is autism, which is part of a spectrum of pervasive developmental disorders. Unlike a learning disability, you cannot acquire autism; it is developmental, meaning signs of it must be present at a young age. However, as with learning disabilities, it is not a homogenous group, with levels of severity and adaptation present.

Pervasive developmental disorders

AUTISM

As stated, autism is part of a spectrum of pervasive development disorders. The very basic criteria for autism are qualitative impairment in reciprocal social interactions, verbal and non-verbal communication and imaginative activity. Individuals with autism can have mild to severe symptoms. Autism was first described by Hans Asperger and

Leo Kanner in the 1940s, independently of one another. Kanner and Asperger chose to use the term 'autistic' to reflect one of the main characteristics often witnessed, that is, a withdrawal from others. *Autos* denotes 'self' in Greek, and Frith (1996, p. 7) comments that 'this narrowing could be described as a withdrawal from the fabric of social life into the self '. In the 1950s, when the disorder was first recognised, its causation was believed to be poor parenting; there were no special schools and education was not considered an important element in the treatment of autism. This changed as a result of research findings which shone a new light of understanding and inquiry upon this disorder, influencing attitudes towards its causation and treatment.

Autism may coexist with intellectual disability or other disorders of development and can occur with other physical or psychological disorders. It is estimated that 40–60 percent of those diagnosed with autism spectrum disorder have intellectual disability. It appears to affect males more than females; the male:female ratio for autism is 3 or 4:1. ICD and DSM are the 'manuals' used by psychologists and clinicians to outline and diagnosis mental health conditions. Some of the features present in autism include the following:

- Autism is classified as part of the pervasive developmental disorders.
- It affects males predominantly and individuals with autism display marked abnormalities in their capacity for reciprocal social interaction, in language and communication and in the development of symbolic play.
- With respect to the communicative abilities, a person with autism takes a literal meaning from what is said; so if it was said that Mary had a hard neck, rather than believing Mary to be brazen the individual would believe Mary to literally have a hard neck.
- They also display repetitive behaviours and activities of play (Carr, 2003).
- Individuals with autism also exhibit an apparent inability to empathise with others.

Recent changes in diagnosis

Within DSM-IV (Diagnostic and Statistical Manual-Fourth Edition), a set of pervasive developmental disorders are considered 'autism spectrum disorders (ASDs)' and include Autistic Disorder, Asperger's Disorder and Pervasive Developmental Disorder Not Otherwise Specified (PDD-NOS). Asperger's Syndrome, while sharing features such as abnormalities in reciprocal interactions and restricted, repetitive patterns of activities and interests, differs from classic autism in so far as no delay in language development or intellectual development occurs.

Recently, changes have occurred in how autism is classified. In the latest edition (DSM-V), the separate labels of Autistic disorder, Asperger's disorder, Childhood Disintegrative disorder and PDD-NOS no longer exist, having been replaced with an umbrella term *Autism Spectrum Disorder* (ASD). It is now the severity that will classify the diagnosis into Levels 1, 2 or 3. Areas including challenges with communication, restricted levels of interest, amount of support needed and repetitive behaviours will determine the level of severity diagnosed. It is argued that the four categories in DSM-IV were not being applied consistently and having just one umbrella term should improve clinical assessment of autism. Further, DSM-V argues that

> Under the DSM-5 criteria, individuals with ASD must show symptoms from early childhood, even if those symptoms are not recognized until later. This criteria change encourages earlier diagnosis of ASD but also allows people whose symptoms may not be fully recognized until social demands exceed their capacity to receive the diagnosis. It is an important change from DSM-IV criteria, which was geared toward identifying school-aged children with autism-related disorders, but not as useful in diagnosing younger children.

THINK ABOUT IT!

For those with autism and their families might these changes cause anxiety and worry? With the removal of Asperger's Syndrome what might that mean for an individual who has that diagnosis, and how will it impact on access to services and benefits which are predicated by a formal diagnosis? Could it lead to individuals previously diagnosed to be re-evaluated, and could this be potentially worrying for them and their families?

Such changes might make sense to clinicians but could they be potentially confusing for individuals with autism and their families? Finally, the changes in how a condition is labelled can have repercussions for the expectations, stereotypes and attitudes towards groups of people; we must never forget that such 'manuals' can exert huge influence as we will see in Chapter 7, where the inclusion of homosexuality as a mental illness in DSM will be discussed.

So we have seen that how autism is classified has changed, as too the early belief that it was caused by 'refrigerator mommy' syndrome: in other words, a cold unresponsive mother. Understandings of the aetiology of autism have progressed; let's take a look at some theories.

COGNITIVE THEORY OF MIND IN AUTISM

Research conducted with children of typical development, with autism and with Down syndrome, has found that both groups of children without autism did well on the 'Sally and Ann' exercise (see Chapter 5) that tests the existence of theory of mind; but the children with autism performed poorly. An example of this lack of theory of mind can be seen in an example related by Margaret Dewey (Frith, 1996, p. 182) of an autistic boy who was sent to the kitchen to get himself a drink of milk. His father came in to find the child pouring the carton of milk down the drain. The father started shouting at his son to stop, which the child did and began crying, but made no attempt to explain why he had done it. It later transpired that the child believed the milk to have gone off and was doing what he had witnessed his parents do with bad milk; pour it down the drain. The child did not defend his action when told to stop: exactly what one would expect from a child who does not realise that someone else does not necessarily have the same knowledge as himself. Thus being shouted out was a shocking turn of events that made no sense to him at all.

BIOLOGICAL CAUSES

Biological research suggests a neuro-developmental aspect to autism and holds genetics as instrumental in its origins. Oliver Sacks, in his book *The Man Who Mistook His Wife for a Hat*, describes the autistic artist José, who had developed apparently normally until a childhood illness caused swelling to the brain that caused irreparable damage. José displayed many autistic characteristics and this could suggest that in some cases neurological damage can be held accountable. Recent developments and research in neurology claim to have found that some autistic people have shorter brain stems than individuals with typical development. There also exists the relatively recent association between the MMR vaccine and autism, which remains unproven.

GENETIC FACTOR

Initially, the possibility of a genetic factor in autism was disregarded, as early studies suggested that the likelihood of having more than one autistic child in a family was relatively low at 2 percent. However, more recent studies have increased the incidence rate to 4 per 10,000 base rate in the general population, which is considered quite high. Subsequent twin studies confirm a very strong genetic component, and it is now accepted that the inheritance of autism exceeds 90 percent (Rutter et al., 1997).

TREATMENT

While there is no cure for autism (Cohen and Volkmar, 1997), treatments do exist. These tend to follow a behaviour-modification approach; for example, the Lovaas method is popular, particularly for targeting challenging behaviours. The Treatment and Education of Autistic and Communication-related Handicapped Children (TEACCH) approach emphasises an intensive structured educative programme that aims to make the world intelligible to the autistic child by acknowledging deficits and building on the strengths of the child. The provision of a structured environment seems to be desirable, according to the findings of Rutter and Bartak (1973). Rutter (1998) maintains that both clinical and experimental studies have shown the importance of basic cognitive deficits in the disorder and this has led to a focus on educational and behavioural approaches to treatment, and systematic evaluations show their efficacy. They now constitute the mainstay of treatment and all over the world special schools and classes for autistic children have been developed. People with autism face many obstacles to participating in society, from educational to social. Certainly the lack of educational facilities and funding for such services is well documented.

The final category of disability we are going to examine is specific learning difficulties (SLD), which contains conditions such as dyslexia (words), dyscalculia (numbers) and Attention Deficit Disorder (ADD) and Attention Deficit Hyperactivity Disorder (ADHD). Again, not all would agree with the labelling of the last two conditions as SLD, rather classifying them as behavioural difficulties. Nonetheless, if one recognises SLD as an individual of typical intelligence but with difficulties functioning in specific areas of cognition than it is fair to include. Though it is argued that ADD and ADHD may have a genetic bias, it is a polemical topic with others suggesting it is more representative of external influences such as poor parenting practices and even diet. Dyslexia and Dyscalculia are recognised as occurring due to differences in how the brain processes information; it presents in people with typical IQs but who experience difficulty processing words or numbers as symbols; this should not be confused with literacy problems, which are not a result of processing difficulties. Dyslexia and dyscalculia are developmental conditions that are life-long, whereas literacy issues are the product of environmental factors and can be corrected with the appropriate educational supports.

We are going to focus on ADHD, as it is a condition that causes much debate from questions surrounding its validity, whether it is a cultural construct, and the use of amphetamines such as Ritalin as a treatment.

Specific learning disability – ADHD

The main features of attention deficit hyperactivity disorder (ADHD), according to the American Psychiatric Association, include hyperactivity, impulsiveness and an inability to sustain attention or concentration. These symptoms occur at levels that cause significant distress and impairment and are far more severe than typically found in children of similar ages and developmental levels. More common in boys than in girls, this disorder often develops before age seven, but is usually diagnosed between ages eight and ten. Children with ADHD:

- have difficulty finishing any activity that requires concentration
- don't seem to listen to anything said to them
- are excessively active – running or climbing at inappropriate times, squirming in or jumping out of their seats
- are very easily distracted
- talk incessantly, often blurting out responses before questions are finished
- have serious difficulty waiting their turn in games or groups
- may have specific learning disabilities.

Rutter (1998) relates that ADHD was initially conceived to be the result of some type of 'minimal brain dysfunction', resulting in the hyperactive symptomology that is associated with this condition. However, this more 'medicalised' view was discredited by research findings that established that most children with ADHD did not have apparent brain dysfunction. These findings heralded a new conception of the cause of ADHD, leading to a shift in focus of researchers along the flowing lines:

1. One set of investigative approaches sought to determine whether hyperkinetic (hyperactivity or frenetic activity) disorder differed meaningfully from other syndromes of disruptive behaviour involving oppositional or conduct problems. The

findings showed that it did, although they also suggested that the syndrome was probably not as common as the prevailing diagnostic practice in North America would lead one to believe.

2. A second set of studies concentrated on investigations of cognitive and attentional deficits. The findings have been consistent in showing their presence, but the precise nature of the deficits remains somewhat elusive.
3. A third research approach has concerned evaluation of the efficacy of drug treatment, especially the use of stimulants. The findings have been very consistent in showing major short-term benefits, although there is more uncertainty regarding long-term gains. Also, it has seemed that, in the longer term (a necessary perspective with a chronic disorder), it is advantageous to combine medication with psychological interventions. Initially it had appeared that the drug response was diagnosis-specific, but it is now clear that that is not so.

In more recent times, two other research perspectives have come on the scene:

4. Fourth, there is growing evidence that there is a strong genetic component and that this applies to hyperactivity well beyond the range of the relatively narrow diagnostic concept as used in the UK and much of the rest of Europe.
5. Fifth, epidemiological and longitudinal studies have shown the importance of hyperactivity (dealt with as a behaviour rather than a diagnosis) as a risk factor for conduct disturbance. It remains uncertain, however, whether this antisocial progression requires, in addition to hyperactivity, the presence of psychosocial adversity.

ADHD remains controversial; critics argue against the use of drugs such as Ritalin to medicate the condition, claiming it has led to the over-medicating of children, and point to the increasing influence of pharmaceuticals in child psychiatry. Concerns have been voiced regarding the misdiagnosis of ADHD. ADD and ADHD have been critiqued as a cultural construct, as the studies outlined above reveal no evidence of brain dysfunction has so far been found. So is ADHD a cultural construct?

IS ADHD A CULTURAL CONSTRUCT?

In America, ADHD is now the most frequently diagnosed paediatric neurobehavioural disorder with over 8 percent of children under 18 diagnosed with the condition. If you factor in parent-reported ADHD within a four-year period an increase of 22 percent was recorded. Variance in the assessment of ADHD has led to substantial differences in epidemiological studies ranging from 0.5 percent to 26 percent prevalence. UK prevalence rates are much lower than rates witnessed in the United States, and this has led to questions about the perceptions surrounding child and adolescent behaviour. Timimi and Taylor (2004, p. 8), in debating for and against ADHD as a cultural construct, pose the question, 'Are differences in the rate of ADHD a reflection of changes in its incidence or in society's tolerance for behaviour that does not conform?' Timimi (p. 8), in arguing for this position, reflects that 'despite attempts at standardising criteria, in cross-cultural studies major and significant differences between raters from different countries in the way they rate symptoms of ADHD, as well as major differences in the way children from different cultures are rated for symptoms of ADHD, are apparent...To explain the recent rise, to epidemic proportions, of rates of diagnosis of ADHD, a cultural perspective is necessary. The immaturity of children is a biological fact, but the ways in which this immaturity is understood and made meaningful is a fact of culture. In modern Western culture many factors adversely affect the mental health of children and their families. These include loss of extended family support, mother blame (mothers are usually the ones who shoulder responsibility for their children), pressure on schools, a breakdown in the moral authority of adults, parents being put in a double bind on the question of discipline, family life being busy and "hyperactive", and a market economy value system that emphasises individuality, competitiveness and independence'.

Taylor argues against ADHD as a cultural or social construct; he claims that if social determinants of ADHD existed then one would expect 'it' to make the whole population more hyperactive. Taylor (ibid., p. 9) claims that '...the prevalence of a diagnostic category such as ADHD would have to be increasing over time and be related to social structures'. Finally, Taylor points out that ADHD affects 'all classes' and that 'powerless groups', such as immigrants, do not show markedly increased rates of ADHD. This example highlights several points; the nature–nurture interaction arguments, and cultural and societal attitudes that influence the lens through which behaviour is viewed. The dominance of the medical model approach in ADHD, the influence of profit driven pharmaceuticals and the use of medication are other important aspects to this debate.

What, hopefully, is becoming clearer is the role of social and cultural factors within the study and experience of disability. We will finish this chapter considering how the socio-cultural perspective offers a lens through which to understand disability. Before doing so we are going to look at research on disabled child effects on families, which attempts to illuminate the potential impact of a disabled child on family functioning.

HOW DO CHILDREN WITH DISABILITIES AFFECT THEIR PARENTS, SIBLINGS, AND FAMILIES?

According to Hodapp and Dykens (2009), traditionally the focus of research examining the impact of children with disabilities has been to view them as 'stressors' on the family system. Yet research findings do not support this overtly negative perception, with 'only slightly negative outcomes' present. Mothers with a disabled child tend to be slightly more depressed compared to mothers without a child with a disability. A slight increase in divorce rates of couples raising a child with a disability is witnessed, while for parents of a child with Down syndrome the rate may be lower than average rates. The authors (ibid, p. 102), acknowledging the over emphasis on the negative effects, pose the pertinent question, 'most families do seem affected – either negatively or positively – by raising their child with disabilities, and one might ask what constitutes the active ingredients of the child's effects on others'. Answers to this question are elusive and intricate; the following are considered to play a role as a child influence on parental stress, behaviours and emotions:

- Maladaptive behaviour
- Health problems
- Infant crying and irritability
- Timing and certainty of diagnosis

Maladaptive behaviour – this factor has proven to be a robust predictor of maternal stress and health. Parents experience stress in the face of maladaptive behaviours, and such behaviours are more likely to be present in children with intellectual disabilities and certain genetic conditions. The amount and severity of maladaptive behaviour influences the levels of stress experienced.

Health problems – health conditions can accompany certain conditions; for example, half of infants born with Down syndrome have congenital heart defects and it is common for babies with Down Syndrome to be hospitalised in their first year.

Infant crying and irritability – Hodapp & Dykens relate that some infants with intellectual disabilities show increased irritability and aversive crying, which is a risk factor for child abuse and adversely affecting mother–child interactions

Certainty of diagnoses – Parents where there was no clear diagnosis for the child's intellectual disability fared worse when compared to parents with a confirmed diagnosis.

These findings begin to reveal the complexity of factors interacting to influence outcomes, and of course it also illustrates that no clear answers are readily available. Family systems and dynamics remain unique and intricate. The role of family, its functioning and the systems it contains remains of integral interest to social workers. We are going to end this chapter with a more global perspective, which attempts to situate the disabled individual within a socio-cultural context.

A SOCIO-CULTURAL APPROACH TO DISABILITY

As we have moved through the book, emphasis has been placed on recognising the complexity of influences involved on developmental outcomes. Bronfenbrenner's ecological framework, outlined in Chapter 4, recognises that factors do not exist within the individual alone; instead we are all nested with systems and circles of influence from the most immediate to the most distant. We have discussed ADHD and the question as to whether it is a cultural construct; arguably all constructs are social and cultural. The socio-cultural approach highlights that an individual is '...surrounded by social context, ecology, resources, local meanings and understandings, and the possible life pathways available' Skinner and Weisner, (2007, p. 302); further they argue that culture is more than ethnicity:

> Socio-cultural understandings move from an understanding of culture as something that ethnic groups share to culture as a system of meanings and practices that evolves between families, the medical and service community, and larger political, social, and economic worlds.

So what does this mean for the study of disability and the experiences of individuals with disabilities? Consider the belief systems, shared or contested, regarding the causes of disability, and recall early beliefs that held cold and unresponsive mothering responsible for autism reflective of a time where the mother-child relationship was viewed as supreme (remember 'monotropism' in attachment in Chapter 4?). If we elaborate on this point, it has ramifications for the beliefs concerning the treatment and care of those with disabilities and plays a core role in stigma. Skinner and Weisner (2007, p. 302) reflect: 'Disabilities, in addition to their cognitive or physical manifestations or genetic etiologies, are sociocultural phenomena. How disability is defined and labelled, families respond and adapt, barriers and opportunities are created, differences in abilities are linked to other societal differences, and professional practices and institutions develop are all social and cultural constructions that have evolved over time at multiple levels within particular historical and political contexts'. We are returned to the earlier piece on culture and ethnicity, which revealed that communities who had not embraced a social model approach and understanding to disability were more likely to stigmatise disabilities. The socio-cultural perspective argues that the most important influence on developmental pathways is where that individual is going to, and does, grow up: more than just location but encompassing the community, its resources and ways of life and its shared beliefs (ibid.). This applies to beliefs surrounding disability and applies to all facets and stages of human development and behaviour. As the authors elaborate (ibid., p. 303), '...the crucial areas of sociocultural investigation include examining how constructions of disability are linked to other cultural ideas such as the meaning of personhood, equality, difference, and individual rights; the ways that general community understandings of gender, poverty, class, or race in turn influence understandings of mental retardation and other disabilities; the role of legislation is not disabled; how social roles and self-understandings are organized around and informed by disability; and how concepts of disability and rehabilitation are shaped by special programs and agencies that serve persons with disabilities'. They argue that a socio-cultural approach, with its broad context and focus on the day to day lives of those with disabilities and their families, is well placed to offer a complete picture of disability.

THINK ABOUT IT!

Disability is identified as one area that benefits from a socio-cultural approach. Identify other areas where such a perspective can be employed; for example, gender or different stages of the life course (childhood to old age). Consider your professional and personal experience to understand how a sociocultural perspective is useful to practice.

SUMMARY

Beliefs are powerful, as the socio-cultural perspective highlights, and inform stereotypes and stigma. In Chapter 10 we will examine stereotyping, labelling and discrimination. In Chapter 9 the abuse of people with disabilities is discussed including a piece on the maltreatment of children with disabilities from an ecological approach, which illustrates further the need for a more holistic and global understanding of the influences at play.

In this chapter we have seen the categories of disabilities that exist and the variety of factors and influences involved. It is fundamentally important to remember that it is environmental and social factors that can cause the disadvantage, prejudice and discrimination to those with disabilities. Attitudes can be changed and environmental factors modified to ensure an inclusive society for all.

chapter

7 MENTAL HEALTH

CHAPTER OUTLINE

- Introduction
- What is mental health?
- The medical and psychosocial models
- The anti-psychiatry movement
- Approaches to understanding mental health problems
- Childhood mental health disorders
- Adult mental health disorders
- Counselling theories

INTRODUCTION

Mental health, illness, disorders – again we encounter language and how it is loaded. So too is the concept of mental health, itself polemical and controversial at times. This chapter, as with the book, is written from a psychological narrative and the language and concepts discussed here reflect that perspective. This chapter, though rooted in the psychological tradition, includes concepts and ideas relevant to social work, allowing for not just a broader level of knowledge but engagement with differing perspectives. Reflecting psychology's bias towards psychopathology or the study of thinking, feeling and behaviour considered maladaptive, this chapter will predominantly focus on mental health disorders. We will consider how mental health is defined, and overview models associated with mental health difficulties and the critiques offered. In reaction to the emphasis on maladaptive functioning, positive psychology grew, interested in the study of those who prosper particularly in the face of adversity and in the study of the mechanisms at play, such as 'flow' and 'resilience'. The emphasis of this chapter is narrow and deals with the aetiology (causes) and classification of mental disorders. The following chapter leads on from this one and explores, in greater depth, well-being and environmental stressors, psychosocial resilience and adversity, and the factors, characteristics and interplay that occurs, to include groups vulnerable to mental health problems. While this may give the impression of dichotomy and bias towards the more medicalised approach to mental illness and well-being that arguably exists within psychology, here it is merely a reflection of the enormity and scope of mental health and the influences that act upon it and a belief that dividing it between two chapters may better capture its many aspects.

Mental health is such a vast field; all domains of functioning are involved and many disciplines are interested in its study and practice. How we define and perceive mental health problems reflects cultural and societal beliefs, values and attitudes.

What is considered to 'deviate' from the norm in one culture, community or group can differ vastly from another. Kuhn maintained that paradigms must be challenged in order to initiate change, and this is particularly pertinent to the field of mental health. For example, the Diagnostic and Statistical Manual of Mental Disorders (DSM), used for mental health disorders, classified homosexuality as a mental illness, and this was not removed until 1973 and replaced with a category known as *ego-dystonic homosexuality*, which was included in DSM's third edition in 1980 and was characterised by: (1) a persistent lack of heterosexual arousal, which the patient experienced as interfering with initiation or maintenance of wanted heterosexual relationships, and (2) persistent distress from a sustained pattern of unwanted homosexual arousal. This new diagnostic category was criticised and removed in 1986. For many, the criminalisation and classification of homosexuality as a mental illness is and would be repugnant, yet some 'groups' continue to view homosexuality as 'deviance'. Deviance within the sociological tradition denotes a move away from the centre (to deviate), from the 'norm'. In Ireland, unmarried mothers were considered deviant and treated as such. This concept reminds us that what is considered 'the norm' reflects societal, cultural, community and personal values, but importantly for this chapter begs the question 'who' decides what 'normal' is and what is a 'deviation' from it? This is a key element in discussing mental health challenges and their classification. Feminist critique points to the traditional male bias in making such determinations; historically, disorders of the womb and woman's inferior capacity were held accountable for female 'hysteria' and mental health problems. The dominance of Western attitudes to mental health contained within diagnostic tools and journal articles argues towards ethnocentrism. We will examine critiques of psychiatry and psychology, starting where it began with the anti-psychiatry movement and later the critical and post-psychiatry movement. Given the scope of mental health, this chapter is illustrative but not exhaustive.

Here we will begin that journey with a discussion of how we think of mental health. Mental health disorders associated with childhood and adulthood are outlined in addition to their causes and characteristics. While it is not possible to discuss each disorder in depth, conduct disorders, schizophrenia and depression are given a more in-depth focus. The chapter ends with the major psychological theories associated with counselling and therapeutic interventions.

WHAT IS MENTAL HEALTH?

The WHO has proposed the following definition of mental health:

> a state of well-being in which the individual realizes his or her own abilities, can cope with the normal stresses of life, can work productively and fruitfully, and is able to make a contribution to his or her community.

Further, it has been argued that mental health is more than the absence of mental illness alone. Mental illness as a term is problematic; we saw in the chapter on disabilities that language can label individuals and influence how they are perceived and treated. For the remainder of this chapter, mental health disorder or problems will be used interchangeably, yet how do we define it? In the UK, the *Mental Health Act 2007* defines mental disorder succinctly; 'Mental disorder means any disorder or disability of the mind'. Of course, the 'mind' is not just the biological brain but encompasses all aspects of functioning, our emotions, cognitive patterns and social understandings. When we speak of mental health problems or disorders, while some arguably may have a biological component (genetics, chemical), all will have a psychosocial dimension.

Defining any construct is fraught, particularly one as broad as mental health. Jahoda (1958) elaborated on this by separating mental health into three domains:

1. mental health involves 'self-realisation', meaning that individuals are allowed to fully exploit their potential.
2. mental health includes 'a sense of mastery' by the individual over their environment and
3. positive mental health means 'autonomy' that is; having the ability to identify, confront and solve problems.

It has been suggested that Jahoda's conceptualisation of mental health is heavily influenced by Western cultural ideas of individualism and is therefore not applicable to other cultures, which are more collectivist in orientation. The definition of mental health is therefore clearly influenced by the culture that defines it and has different meanings depending on setting, culture and socioeconomic and political influences (social constructionism). To elucidate further on how mental health problems are conceived and perceived let's examine early models of mental health.

THE MEDICAL AND PSYCHOSOCIAL MODELS

Wyatt and Livson (1994, p. 120) suggest that there are two general models of mental disorder to which most mental health practitioners and theoreticians subscribe; the medical and the psychosocial models. The **medical model** conceptualises a patient's maladaptive psychological, emotional and interpersonal experiences primarily in terms of organic, biochemical or physiological aetiology, leading its adherents to advocate biochemical or physical methods of treatment. Psychotherapy and social therapies are then viewed as adjuncts or additions to medical interventions.

The **psychosocial model**, by contrast, conceptualises emotional disturbances as primarily the consequence of social, psychological, interpersonal, cultural and ethical conflicts. Within this framework, psychotherapy and social interventions are deemed the primary modes for helping clients resolve their conflicts; psychotropic medications may or may not be used as adjuncts to the psychotherapeutic process.

Beecher (2009, p. 10) defines the medical model further, suggesting two approaches to its conceptualisation. The first theme is a causal or *aetiological model* (also known as the biomedical model), which defines mental illness as a disorder of the brain or nervous system and which is amenable to pharmacological or physical treatment. The second theme is referred to as a *practice-oriented* (help or treatment) model, which 'focuses on the identification of a problem through diagnosis and then the prescribing of treatment to ameliorate or eradicate the problem'.

Criticisms of a medical-model approach stem from its limited scope in considering the person's external environment, and claim that it is too problem-focused. A further criticism is that it can result in the individual with a mental illness being seen only as the illness. In other words, practitioners see only the disorder and not the person. McLean (1990, cited in Beecher, 2009, p. 10) concluded that the view of mental illness as a 'disease of the brain' perpetuates this depersonalisation of the individual with mental illness and their family. Inherent within the medical versus social model is the criticism of a binary and dualistic approach that fails to capture the complexity in mental health and mental disorders. This criticism was applied to the arena of disability as witnessed in the preceding chapter and arguably is valid here. A more fundamental critique of which model is more appropriately applied to mental health problems is the question of what is 'madness' and who labels it as such? The anti-psychiatry movement challenged the status quo and threw down the gauntlet on these issues.

THE ANTI-PSYCHIATRY MOVEMENT

R. D. Laing expounded his political views in *The Politics of Experience* (1968). He regarded madness as the product of a struggle between a repressive society and the individual who is seeking to escape its repression. The main purpose of psychiatry is to medicalise defiance and persecute the non-obedient in order to teach its citizens how to conform to society's norms. Thomas Szasz's contribution to the anti-psychiatric movement was made in his famous and controversial book, *The Myth of Mental Illness* (1974), which described mental illness as a metaphorical illness, because 'the mind (whatever that is) is not an organ or part of the body. Hence it cannot be diseased in the same sense as the body can.' Szasz drew attention to psychiatric prejudice and the role of values in psychiatric decision making.

Irving Goffman, a sociologist, articulated the impact of psychiatric labelling on the mentally ill in his influential book, *Asylums: Essays on the Social Situation of Mental Patients and Other Inmates* (1961). Goffman's theory of labelling is examined in more depth in Chapter 10, which focuses on the experiences of women in a domestic violence refuge. An idea allied to Goffman's concept of psychiatric labelling is how language can shape our perception of a given thing, person or construct. This realisation is reflected in the change of language in recent years when discussing aspects of mental health. 'Therapy' has largely replaced 'treatment' and the 'patient' is commonly referred to as a 'client' or 'service-user'. Indeed, one aspect of Laing's political argument was his contempt for psychiatric literature, which he referred to as a vocabulary of denigration. Nasser (1995, p. 746) believes the ultimate success of the anti-psychiatry movement lies 'in the shift of focus from large mental institutions to the provision of care in the community'. In chapter 10, the stereotyping and stigmatisation of mental illness, anorexia nervosa will be explored. Before we leave the anti-psychiatry movement and move to the later movements of post and critical psychiatry, we are going to look at Rosenhan's work *On being sane in insane places*, which fundamentally challenged the classification of mental disorders.

On being sane in insane places

> If sanity and insanity exist, how shall we know them?
>
> (Rosenhan, 1973)

As Rosenhan highlights, ideas of 'normal' and 'abnormal', of what is deviant to one and not to the other, raise questions as to how we classify mental disorder. This concern was at the heart of Rosenhan's study where he and seven others presented to mental hospitals with one symptom, hearing voices. All were diagnosed with paranoid schizophrenia and admitted. Once admitted to the hospital all the 'pseudopatients' acted normally, showing no further symptoms, and requested to be released. Interestingly, other patients recognised that the researchers were pseudopatients and not unwell, yet none of the staff did. Within the hospital environment, normal behaviours such as writing notes or requesting to be released were viewed by staff as signs of mental illness. When they were eventually released, all of the pseudopatients were labelled as 'schizophrenia in remission', not healthy or sane. Rosenhan noted that this diagnosis carried stigma that would make it difficult to engage in daily life. Rosenhan challenged how diagnoses were made, classifications agreed upon and how 'normal' behaviour when viewed through a lens corrupted by a pathological environment (mental hospital) and a label (mental illness) were seen as abnormal or proof of mental illness. Rosenhan's work shares much with Goffman's research on labelling and its de-humanising effects as we will see in chapter 10. Rosenhan's study was (Ross & Kavanagh, 2013, p. 469), '... more than the report of an immensely inventive piece of research ... ; it is a proclamation, a moral outcry, a scream of pain and a demand that the world bear witness to the consequences of wrongful diagnosis, of ungrounded labelling, of institutions whose very design shapes errors of diagnosis'. Rosenhan's quote which opened this piece remains as valid today as it did 40 years ago and demands of us to continue to challenge and be mindful that while mental health problems may be influenced by biology, it is always a socially and culturally bound construct. While the anti-psychiatry movement represented the first wave of critique, others have followed. We're going to briefly consider critical and post-psychiatry movements.

THE CRITICAL AND POST-PSYCHIATRY MOVEMENT

The seeds of the critical psychiatry movement were sown in discussions surrounding the Mental Health Act 2007. This movement builds on the critiques of the anti-psychiatry movement, although proponents do not advocate the overthrow of psychiatry. The dominance of the medical model is questioned as is the concept that the origins of mental health problems necessitate the involvement of the brain, as Duncan Double elaborates, 'I've always said the essential message is that psychiatry can be practiced without taking the step of faith of believing that mental illness is due to brain pathology, such as a chemical imbalance in the brain. This is commonly what patients are told, but the evidence is against it. Don't misunderstand what I'm saying. Of course mental illness must show *through* the brain – but not necessarily *in* the brain. There are implications for both assessment and treatment in practice. Diagnosis is not about finding an entity of some kind, but about providing understanding. We also need to be more sceptical about treatments, such as medication.' Post-psychiatry, while also critical, is best represented in Bracken and Thomas' 2001 (p. 724) paper which charged: 'Post-psychiatry emphasises social and cultural contexts, places ethics before technology, and works to minimise medical control of coercive interventions.' They set out the goals of post-psychiatry (2001, p. 726) as follows:

Goals of post-psychiatry

IMPORTANCE OF CONTEXT

Contexts, that is to say social, political and cultural realities, should be central to our understanding of madness. A context-centred approach acknowledges the importance of empirical knowledge. In the next chapter we will see how the main manual for Diagnostic and Statistical Manual of Mental Disorders (DSM) recently removed psychosocial and environmental stressors, which, in terms of the post-psychiatry movement, must be seen as a retrograde move.

ETHICAL RATHER THAN TECHNOLOGICAL ORIENTATION

> '...clinical effectiveness plays down the importance of values in research and practice. All medical practice involves some negotiation about assumptions and values'.

RETHINKING THE POLITICS OF COERCION

> 'Many service users groups question the medical model and are therefore outraged that this provides the framework for coercive care. This is not to say that society should never remove a person's liberty because of their mental disorder. However by challenging the notion that psychiatric theory is neutral, objective, and disinterested, post psychiatry weakens the case for medical control of the process'.

The emergence of a policy shift could be witnessed with an acknowledgment of the links between poverty, unemployment and mental health leading to a focus on tackling disadvantage and social exclusion, in contrast to the dominance of a biomedical approach to mental health and its provision (as referred to earlier, see Chapter 8 for a discussion of the removal of psychosocial factors from the manual used to classify mental disorders). Rolfe and Cutcliffe critique (2006, p. 621), 'Some psychiatrists have tried to redeem themselves by reviving old ideas like the "biopsychosocial" model, which they hope will counter the reductionism of the "medical model", without altogether abandoning scientific psychiatry. Foremost among these advocates of an alternative psychiatric paradigm are Bracken and Thomas (2001), who first advocated the idea of 'post-psychiatry', wondering what psychiatry would be like if it could accommodate contemporary *philosophical* positions – regarding the self, citizenship, lived experience, community, race, power, and so on. Their work has gone some considerable way to answering such questions – and to realigning at least their own practice. However, by revising psychiatry they avoid addressing the forces that sustain psychiatric medicine. In particular, they avoid asking the most obvious question: what would a world *without* psychiatry be like?

THINK ABOUT IT!

What would a world without psychiatry be like? What would be the alternatives and how would that affect your practice? Where did your understanding of mental 'illness' originate? How has your perception of mental health disorders influenced your practice?

With these caveats in place, we move on to a brief general overview of mental health determinants, followed by more in-depth outlines of mental disorders in childhood and adulthood. Newer approaches to understanding mental health will be examined.

Table 7.1 Mental health determinants (WHO, 2012)

Level	Adverse factors		Protective factors
Individual attributes	Low self-esteem	↔	Self-esteem, confidence
	Cognitive/emotional immaturity	↔	Ability to solve problems and manage stress or adversity
	Difficulties in communicating	↔	Communication skills
	Medical illness, substance use	↔	Physical health, fitness
Social circumstances	Loneliness, bereavement	↔	Social support of family and friends
	Neglect, family conflict	↔	Good parenting/family interaction
	Exposure to violence/abuse	↔	Physical security and safety
	Low income and poverty	↔	Economic security
	Difficulties or failure at school	↔	Scholastic achievement
	Work stress/unemployment	↔	Satisfaction and success at work
Environmental factors	Poor access to basic services	↔	Equality of access to basic services
	Injustice and discrimination	↔	Social justice, tolerance, integration
	Social and gender inequalities	↔	Social and gender equality
	Exposure to war and disaster	↔	Physical security and safety

Table 7.1 captures the different layers or levels of influence upon a person from intrapsychic (within the person) factors to more distal ones. The concept of factors as either risk or protective is commonly understood; however, the mechanisms behind their interactions remain less clear. As we saw in chapter 4, Bronfenbrenner's ecological approach can be a useful framework to illustrate the varied layers and their interactions. In the

next chapter we will delve into the concept of adversity and resilience and how protective and risk factors interact influencing outcomes, further the disproportionately poor outcomes for Black and Minority Ethnic groups in mental health are discussed. In Chapter 9, where abuse and trauma are discussed, the concept of factors involved in forms of abuse will be addressed. Let us return to approaches advocated in the study of mental health, beginning with Rutter's elaboration of the biopsychosocial model.

APPROACHES TO UNDERSTANDING MENTAL HEALTH DISORDER

The biopsychosocial model

The biopsychosocial model allows for the amalgamation of a biological approach to understanding mental disorders, acknowledging the physiological aspect of the person (including genes, brain, cells, etc.); the psychological approach meanwhile focuses on preceding mental states and the social aspect captures influences external to us. This approach recognises different psychological models (psychodynamic and cognitive-behavioural, for example) in the search for understanding. The social approach considers patterns of maladaptive stress and social interactions in the causation and maintenance of mental disorders. Rutter elaborates with an example for each mechanism at play within the biopsychosocial approach.

Rutter biopsychosocial approach (1989)

BIOLOGICAL PATHWAYS

Genetics: for example, a possible genetic component in the link between conduct disorder in childhood and personality disorder in adulthood.

Biology: for instance, the purported link between pregnancy and birth complications and schizophrenia in adult life.

PSYCHOLOGICAL PATHWAYS

Cognition: children raised in high-risk environments are less likely to develop later psychiatric disorders when they have a higher IQ or greater scholastic attainment.

Social skills: the importance of early child-rearing would be emphasised

Self-esteem/self-efficacy: low self-esteem may leave the individual vulnerable to later psychiatric disorders. High self-esteem/self-efficacy may serve as a protection against future problems.

Habits, cognitive sets, coping styles: an inability to cope with stress may result in increased difficulty in coping throughout childhood and adulthood.

ENVIRONMENTAL PATHWAYS

Linked experiences: many life experiences are inter-linked. For example, children who spend their early years in institutional settings are less likely to have access to a supportive extended family when they themselves become parents.

Shaping environments: individuals may shape their adult environments through decisions made in childhood. For example, there is the link between education in childhood and occupation in adulthood.

Rutter demonstrates links between one aspect of development and another, for instance educational attainment reducing the likelihood of psychiatric disorders in later life. It would be wrong to think of this as a linear relationship; if I do well at school in spite of difficulties I may face, educational attainment increases my likelihood of employment or even going to college, which reduces the likelihood of living in poverty. If I am earning a salary, my access to more life choices improves, such as where I live and participation in social activities. We see, from looking at the different pathways and the few examples of factors given, the multiplicity that exists and complexity of interactions that are possible. The next model represents a narrowing of focus on the elements of risk and vulnerability and how they interact. Vulnerability at its most simple relates to internal aspects, while risk relates to external stressors (see Chapter 8 for more discussion).

Vulnerability–stress model

The origins of this model lie in the theories of both Beck and Sameroff. The underlying premise of Beck's diathesis–stress model of depression suggests that an individual is at greater risk of depression when they encounter stress if they have a pre-existing vulnerability or diathesis (Greek for disposition). This concept can be applied to many different aspects of functioning as well, including addiction, and to physical health conditions from cancer to asthma. Sameroff's transactional model of development argues that both nature and nurture are constantly being changed by their interaction with one another. This means developmental outcomes are neither a function of the individual nor the context alone but rather the interaction between them. Thus, this model describes the way in which child, parent and environment affect each other and the child's development.

The vulnerability–stress model suggests that individual mental health problems are triggered and develop in response to underlying vulnerabilities within the person and external stressors. It is the interaction of these two elements (nature–nurture) that creates and maintains individual competencies over time. There has been some criticism of this approach; it has been suggested that the field of stressors has not been given the same attention as that of vulnerabilities. Also, scant regard has been given to the potential for vulnerabilities to generate new stressors in an individual's life, and for stressors to introduce or worsen vulnerabilities.

THINK ABOUT IT!

Some questions to consider in attempting to unravel vulnerabilities and stress include:

1. How do vulnerabilities change with age? It seems unlikely that most would be static or unchanging.
2. Are there sensitive or critical periods for vulnerabilities to be impacted by stressors?
3. Are there matches between specific vulnerabilities and specific stressors that make particular psychopathologies (mental disorders) more likely to develop?
4. How do early caregiver–infant relationships develop into 'internal' vulnerabilities and 'external' stressors later in childhood?
5. What are the roles of resilience and protective factors in the development of well-being?
6. Is the good mental health of children and youth supported by anything other than the absence of vulnerability and stress?
7. Do any of these models pertain to the majority of the world's children and youth, who live outside the generally privileged conditions of most families in North America and Western Europe? Culture provides context and meaning to stress, vulnerability and psychopathology.

While these models remain popular in psychology and psychiatry, the next model has increasingly been adopted within mental health work and by those interested in an approach rooted in the influence of social and external forces.

The recovery model

This model is increasingly adopted as mental health moves from a medicalised model to one acknowledging social and external influences and reflects the change from an institutional approach to one of community care. At its heart is the recognition that recovery is not the end point or goal but rather a journey. Further, the profession-centred debate regarding which model of mental health a team adopts distracts teams from the advantages of embracing a recovery model of mental health. Such a model fits with an affirming, aspirational and solution-focused approach based on integrating models. Rather than asking whether 'a single dominant model or theory of mental distress' or 'a babble of multiple theoretical perspectives' will be effective, this model recognises the need to 'develop a tight bundle of relevant responses congruent' with those of the service user. Moving beyond the one-model-fits-all approach to a service-user-centred approach recognises that this bundle will vary from service user to service user (MHCIRL, p. 18).

Regardless of the model adopted it is evident that mental health is a lifelong journey consisting of developmental milestones along the way, with layers of influence interacting and shaping outcomes and the role of the individual in impacting on, and shaping the environment around them. We are now going to focus on mental health disorders associated with childhood and then adulthood. It is not possible, as mentioned, to be exhaustive here; as such, the following chapter is dedicated to psychosocial resilience and adversity, allowing for a greater discussion on the role of factors such as poverty in mental health and well-being. Before we look at disorders across the life span, let us consider an illustrative diagram of the possible risks to mental health over the lifecycle. An overview of major transitions faced from infancy to adolescence is also outlined.

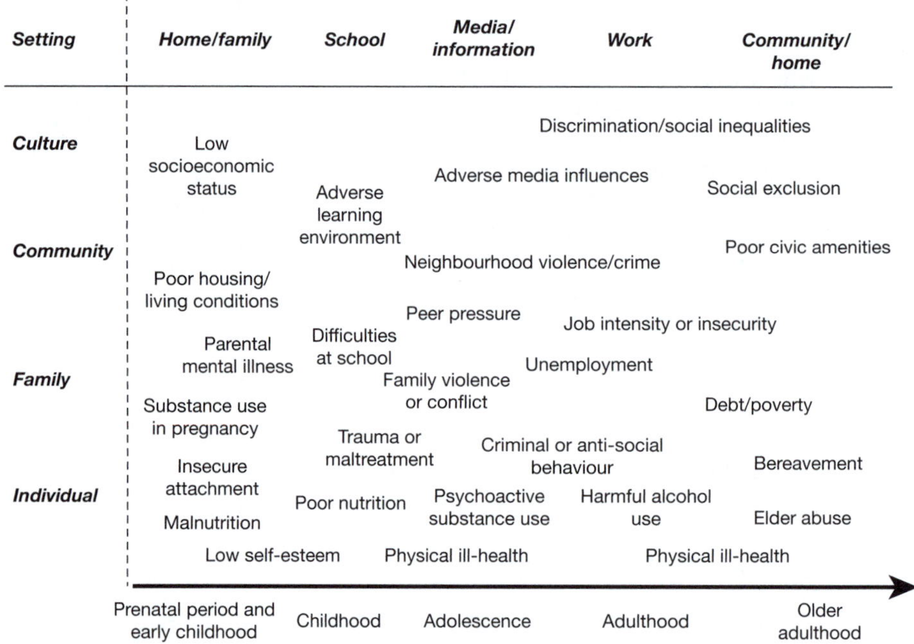

Figure 7.1 Schematic overview of risk to mental health over the life course *(Adapted from: WHO, 2012).*

As Figure 7.1 illustrates, a multiplicity of external factors exist, affecting individual outcomes. Should more risk factors accumulate as the person moves through their lifecycle it is argued that so too does the likelihood of adverse outcomes. Yet this begs the question, do some risk factors create a greater 'risk' than others and do some factors combine to create a greater likelihood of mental health disorders?

THINK ABOUT IT!

Let's consider attachment as an example, an early risk factor would include a poor or chaotic parent–child relationship. Does this create a vulnerability within the child, which as they age increases the likelihood of them engaging as adults in unhealthy relationships? These factors, internal or external, intertwine absolutely but are some factors more potent in combination with others and with greater influence on outcomes? Consider the factors you think are the most powerful in influencing mental health and well-being and why?

Answers don't come easily. Another aspect to be considered when exploring the journey through the lifecycle and mental health is the role of developmental transitions we all make, such as adolescence, although it may have different meanings. Adolescence, as we discussed in Chapter 5, is a period of development that can be tumultuous in and of itself. The following (Carr, 2003) are major life transitions from infancy to adolescence and difficulties commonly associated with each stage.

ADJUSTMENT TO MAJOR LIFE TRANSITIONS

Problems of infancy and early childhood

- Sleep problems
- Toileting problems
- Learning and communication difficulties
- Autism and pervasive developmental disorders

Problems of middle childhood

- Conduct problems
- Attention and overactivity problems
- Fear and anxiety problems
- Repetition problems
- Somatic problems

Problems in adolescence

- Drug abuse
- Mood problems
- Anorexia and bulimia nervosa
- Schizophrenia

Child abuse

- Physical abuse
- Emotional abuse and neglect
- Sexual abuse

Adjustment to major life transitions

- Foster care
- Separation and divorce
- Grief and bereavement

Autism and ADHD were explored in the previous chapter and child abuse will be discussed in Chapter 9. Addiction is covered in depth in the next chapter on stressors and well-being. While we have explored criticisms of psychiatry and the classification of mental health disorders, it is important to maintain a knowledge base of the current understanding of mental health disorders. This section overviews disorders associated with childhood through to adulthood. Greater depth will be given to some of the disorders to give a fuller picture of approaches to them or associated factors.

CHILDHOOD MENTAL HEALTH DISORDERS

Depression (childhood)

We will examine depression in greater detail in adulthood, including theories associated with its emergence. In childhood, as many as 1 in 10 children between the ages of 6 and 12 experience persistent feelings of sadness – the hallmark of depression. Since children may not be able to express or understand many of the core symptoms that would indicate depression in adults, it is important to be aware of some key behaviours – in addition to changes in eating or sleeping patterns – that may signal depression in children.

The Royal College of Psychiatrists lists the following symptoms of depression experienced by children and teenagers:

- Being moody and irritable – easily upset, 'ratty' or tearful.
- Becoming withdrawn – avoiding friends, family and regular activities.
- Feeling guilty or bad, being self-critical and self-blaming – hating yourself.
- Feeling unhappy, miserable and lonely a lot of the time.
- Feeling hopeless and wanting to die.
- Finding it difficult to concentrate.
- Not looking after your personal appearance.
- Changes in sleep pattern: sleeping too little or too much.
- Tiredness and lack of energy.
- Frequent minor health problems, such as headaches or stomach-aches.

Depression is increasingly becoming recognised as an issue that is affecting more and more children. Another issue commonly associated with childhood is Attention Deficit Hyperactivity Disorder (ADHD), discussed in Chapter 6, which can continue into adulthood too. Difficulties that occur in childhood can continue to persist into adulthood or escalate. Conduct disorder and Oppositional Defiance Disorder are two such conditions that can escalate to anti-social personality disorder in adulthood. This is not to say that one causes the other, but merely to acknowledge that a relationship exists between them, arguably reflective of factors merging and accumulating over the years.

Disruptive, impulse-control, and conduct disorders

CHANGES TO CLASSIFICATION IN DSM V

This is a new category in DSM-V amalgamating 'Disorders Usually First Diagnosed in Infancy, Childhood, or Adolescence' (including oppositional defiance disorder and conduct disorder) with 'Impulse-Control Disorders Not Otherwise Specified' (intermittent explosive disorder, pyromania and, kleptomania). This new category *Disruptive, Impulse-control and, Conduct Disorders* is characterised by problems in emotional and behavioural self-control. DSM-V states, 'Because of its close association with conduct disorder, antisocial personality disorder has dual listing in this chapter and in the chapter on personality disorders. Of note, ADHD is frequently comorbid (existing with another condition) with the disorders in this chapter but is listed with the neurodevelopmental disorders.'

Oppositional defiant disorder

According to Hartman (2007),

> Oppositional Defiant Disorder is, in my book, a red flag. It is an indication that there is something else going on. I have never... seen a kid that meets criteria for ODD and did not meet criteria for some other diagnosis. It is as if the oppositional and defiant behaviour is a coping strategy for dealing with other issues or a poorly functional reaction to other issues that are not being dealt with.

A distinction can be made between oppositional defiant disorder (ODD) and conduct disorder, with the former reflecting a less pervasive disturbance than the latter and possibly being a developmental precursor of conduct disorder. In other words, ODD is a less severe form of, and can be a precursor to, conduct disorder. It represents a child or teenager acting in a deliberately hostile fashion. Another possible distinction is that ODD is sometimes directed within the home, whereas the progression to conduct disorders includes a continuation of hostility outside of the home.

CASE STUDY

Harry is a 9-year-old boy who lives with his mum, Kim, and his younger brother, Ben, who is 7. They live in social housing in an area of socio-economic deprivation. Kim began attending a course for early school leavers in a local college a year ago and is feeling very positive about her future. She split up from the boys' father, Jason, 3 years ago due to his continuing drug addiction. After the split Jason got clean and became very involved in the boys' lives, becoming particularly close to Harry. Recently, Jason started using again after the death of his mother. Kim noticed a change in Harry's behaviour. He became increasingly defiant within the home and directed a lot of anger at Kim in the form of verbal aggression and vandalising the house. After only 3 months of using again Jason was found dead from an accidental overdose. Since Jason's death Harry's behaviour has spiralled and Kim is struggling to cope despite the support of her mother. Kim says her 'nerves' are at her again and she has been prescribed anti-depressants and tranquilisers by a local GP. She has started to miss classes on her course and is considering dropping out. Kim's parenting approach swings from cajoling permissiveness to yelling and shouting. Harry has started staying out late and getting into trouble in his area. Kim says she fears he's going down the same path as his father.

What do you believe are some of the triggers for Harry's behaviour? Make two columns, labelled internal and external and list the factors and influences you believe are involved in Harry's behaviour. Which factors are risk or protective, justify your choices.

Conduct disorder

Children with conduct disorder (CD) exhibit behaviour that shows a persistent disregard for the norms and rules of society. CD is one of the most frequently seen mental health disorders in adolescents. Because the symptoms are closely tied to socially unacceptable or violent behaviour, many people confuse this disorder with either juvenile delinquency or the turmoil of the teen years. Children who have demonstrated at least three of the following behaviours over 6 months should be evaluated for possible conduct disorder:

- stealing
- constantly lying
- deliberately setting fires
- skipping school
- breaking into homes, offices or cars
- deliberately destroying others' property
- displaying physical cruelty to animals or humans
- forcing others into sexual activity
- often starting fights
- using weapons in fights.

In addition to the behaviours that characterise CD, DSM-V now includes emotional and interpersonal functioning, such as limited empathy and a lack of concern for the feelings, wishes and well-being of others.

Rutter (1998, p. 807) outlines the four main advances he suggests have been made with respect to conduct disorders:

Developmental continuities and discontinuities

- Greater awareness of the extent to which conduct disorders have their origins in the preschool years.
- Realisation of the high frequency with which there is a progression to personality disorders in adult life.
- Evidence has accumulated on the reality of important changes for the better in adult life if there is a sufficiently major change in the relevant life circumstances.

Sharpening of diagnostic concepts

- Recognition that oppositional defiance disorder in early childhood often leads to conduct disorders in later childhood.
- Importantly, the differentiation between 'life-persistent' and 'adolescence-limited' antisocial problems.

Recognition of the importance of risk factors associated with individual characteristics

- Temperamental features
- Reading and other cognitive difficulties
- Genetic factors.

Advances in approaches to treatment

- Attention has been paid to the cognitive processing of experiences, to social problem-solving, to patterns of family interaction, and to the need to focus on schools as well as families.

Rutter (1998) concedes that conduct disorders remain a challenge and that therapeutic outcomes remain modest rather than hugely significant. He further highlights that a particular difficulty lies in engaging families in treatment.

THINK ABOUT IT!

Using Rutter's overview, consider what interventions you would recommend both in terms of prevention and intervention. For example, Rutter suggests the origin of CD can be witnessed in the preschool years, thus programmes emphasising prosocial behaviour and emotional regulation, such as Sure Start or The Incredible Years, might be one recommendation. Rutter notes difficulties in engaging families in treatment; what would you recommend? These are just two examples. Consider other approaches aimed at prevention and intervention.

While CD is often associated with males, girls too are diagnosed with this disorder. One study focussed on the continuity of CD in girls as they transitioned from adolescence (age 15) into young adulthood (age 21). According to Bardone et al. (1996, p. 821), 'the study sought to identify their outcomes in three domains: mental health and illegal behaviour, human capital, and relationship and family formation...in general...conduct disordered girls developed antisocial personality disorder symptoms by age 21. Conduct disorder exclusively predicted at age 21: antisocial personality disorder, substance dependence, illegal behaviour, dependence on multiple welfare sources, early home leaving, multiple cohabitation partners, and physical partner violence.'

This paints a pessimistic picture. Lahey et al. (2002, p. 334) in examining continuity of CD and predictors of improvement noted that in previous studies only 40 percent of children diagnosed with CD in childhood maintained that diagnosis into adolescence, 'This suggests that slightly more than half of children with CD cease to meet criteria for CD sometime during late childhood or adolescence.' In identifying the predictors of improvement the authors state (ibid., p. 346–7) that 'Boys who meet criteria for CD in childhood are more likely to improve if they have less serious conduct problems and fewer ADHD symptoms at baseline and have the advantages of high verbal intelligence and affluent and well-educated parents who are not antisocial.' The role of social factors in the maintenance of CD is clearly identified: among others, poverty and low educational attainment. In the next chapter we will explore social stressors and their role in adversity and resilience. CD is linked to the development of anti-social personality disorder, which is one of the areas discussed in mental health problems in adulthood.

ADULT MENTAL HEALTH DISORDERS

Anxiety disorders

As we saw in Chapter 4, anxiety is a painful emotional experience resulting from internal or external stimulation. Anxiety disorders are recognised within DSM-V. Anxiety is an emotion characterised by feelings of tension, worried thoughts and physical changes such as increased blood pressure. People with anxiety disorders usually have recurring intrusive thoughts or concerns. They may avoid certain situations out of worry. They may also have physical symptoms such as sweating, trembling, dizziness or a rapid heartbeat. Anxiety disorders differ from normal feelings of nervousness. Untreated anxiety disorders can push people into avoiding situations that trigger or worsen their symptoms. People with anxiety disorders are likely to suffer from depression, and they may also abuse alcohol and other drugs in an effort to gain relief from their symptoms. Job performance, school work and personal relationships can also suffer.

TYPES OF ANXIETY DISORDERS

- panic disorder
- generalised anxiety disorder phobias
- post-traumatic stress disorder
- obsessive-compulsive disorder.

Anxiety disorders are the most common of the 'emotional' disorders. Post-traumatic stress disorder (PTSD) is a disorder that can occur in people who have experienced or witnessed life-threatening events, including serious accidents or violent personal assaults such as rape. People who suffer from PTSD often relive the experience through flashbacks or nightmares, have difficulty sleeping and feel detached or estranged. PTSD is discussed in Chapter 9 on abuse and trauma.

Schizophrenia

Sometimes a picture paints a thousand words. It is difficult for many of us to imagine or to understand an experience, especially one involving hallucinations or delusions, unless we have experienced it ourselves. For instance, it can be difficult to imagine what life might be like for someone with schizophrenia. Louis Wain, an artist famous for his drawings of cats, capture his descent into psychosis in a series of drawings, I'd recommend looking them.

Schizophrenia is a psychotic disorder that involves severe disturbances in speech, thinking, perception, emotion and behaviour. The National Institute of Mental Health (NIMH) states that schizophrenia is 'the most chronic and disabling of the severe mental illnesses' (2009, p. 1). The term 'schizophrenia' was introduced in 1911 by Eugen Bleuler and, in Latin, means 'split mind'. Bleuler was attempting to capture how psychological functions appear to be split or disconnected in schizophrenics compared to typical people, whose functions are quite unified. Whereas depression is considered to be a disorder of mood, schizophrenia is sometimes suggested as a disorder of thought. As you will see, there is variety in the symptoms of schizophrenia which has led to the premise that schizophrenia constitutes a group of disorders, not unlike other chronic illnesses. Symptoms usually first appear in early adulthood. Men often experience symptoms in their early 20s and women typically first show signs of the disorder in their late 20s and early 30s.

FEATURES OF SCHIZOPHRENIA

Carr (2003) amalgamated the following features of schizophrenia based on ICD-10 and DSM-IV (diagnostic manual) descriptions. The following are features of the disorder:

- **Perception:** individuals may experience auditory hallucinations; their ability to focus on important information or stimuli to the exclusion of other stimuli becomes impaired.
- **Thought/cognitive:** the thought process becomes disordered and delusions may occur. Logical trains of thought become difficult to form or follow.
- **Emotion/affect:** anxiety and depression may occur during the prodromal stage and inappropriate and flattened affect may also be present.
- **Behaviour:** during the prodromal period sleep patterns can be affected and behaviour can be impulsive and compulsive. During psychotic episodes negativism, catatonia (impairment of movement) and mutism can occur.

Schizophrenia subtypes – changes to DSM classification

The DSM-IV subtypes of schizophrenia (i.e., paranoid, disorganised, catatonic, undifferentiated, and residual types) have been removed due to their limited diagnostic stability, low reliability, and poor validity. Instead, a dimensional approach to rating severity for the core symptoms of schizophrenia is included in DSM-V.

EARLY WARNING SIGNS OF SCHIZOPHRENIA

Changes in mood such as moodiness, depression, inability to cry, excessive crying, laughing for no particular reason or inability to laugh.

Sensory changes such as hearing voices, unusual sensitivity to noise or light.

Changes in activity such as becoming extremely active or inactive, or sleeping excessively or hardly at all.

Changes in social behaviour such as avoiding social situations, dropping out of activities, refusing to go out, allowing relationships to deteriorate, saying irrational or inappropriate things, using peculiar words or making meaningless statements.

Changes in relations with family such as constantly arguing, never phoning home, phoning home at strange times of the night.

Changes at school or work such as problems in concentrating, declining academic performance.

Changes in behaviour such as strange postures, prolonged staring, extreme religious beliefs, using illegal drugs.

Changes in appearance such as wearing bizarre clothes, poor personal hygiene.

(*Source*: Schizophrenia Ireland, 2005, p. 16)

Clearly, there is significant diversity in the symptoms presented in schizophrenia. This is reflected in the classification system devised for schizophrenia and also in the aetiological factors that are believed to contribute to the disorder. This diversity has implications for the course and treatment of schizophrenia. Many factors have been studied in examining the causes of schizophrenia. It is believed that a number of biological and environmental factors play a role in the onset and course of the disorder. There is a genetic vulnerability for this disorder, but while this can contribute towards schizophrenia, it does not necessarily cause it. Rather, it would appear that many factors interact to cause schizophrenia; family or environmental stress, possibly drug taking, with genetic vulnerability being the strongest predisposing force. Studies have shown that identical twins have a higher concordance rate than fraternal twins and that adopted children whose biological parent is schizophrenic have a higher rate of concordance than if the adopted parent suffers the illness. Thus, although the origin of schizophrenia has not been identified, scientists know that there is some hereditary basis or genetic predisposition for the disease, as it tends to run in families.

Factors in schizophrenia

BIOLOGICAL FACTORS

Dopamine hypothesis

This approach suggests a dysfunction of the mesolymbic dopaminergic system. Pharmacological treatments of schizophrenia have centred on neuroleptic medication, which prohibits dopamine activity in people. It has been suggested that the effect on behaviour does not alleviate immediately even though the drug immediately affects dopamine levels. According to Carr, 25 percent of schizophrenics do not respond to anti-psychotic drugs. If the dopamine hypothesis was the cause of schizophrenia, one would expect all sufferers to benefit immediately from drugs reducing dopamine levels. Finally, an interesting point has been raised as to whether dopamine levels are *caused by* the schizophrenia rather than causing the disorder.

Neurodevelopmental hypothesis

There is growing support for the neurodevelopmental hypothesis that argues that prenatal neurological insults and prenatal intrauterine environment, such as maternal flu virus, may be responsible for schizophrenia (Murray and Lewis, 1987, cited in Carr, 2003). This could tie in with structural abnormalities found in scans of the brains of some with schizophrenia.

COGNITIVE FACTORS

Some cognitive theorists maintain that schizophrenia is due to a defective attentional mechanism, which normally filters out irrelevant stimuli, resulting in an overload of internal and external stimuli, thus explaining the schizophrenic's feeling of being overwhelmed by disconnected thoughts. Other cognitive theories include the cognitive bias theory and the prodromal hypothesis.

FAMILY DYNAMICS

It would appear that schizophrenics from families who exhibit high levels of expressed emotion are more likely to relapse compared to those from families with lower levels.

In videotapes of the behaviour of schizophrenics in the former group, where families were more likely to make negative comments, the schizophrenics engaged in four times as many strange and disruptive behaviours than did the schizophrenics in families with lower expressed levels of emotion.

SOCIO-CULTURAL FACTORS

Evidence suggests that schizophrenia appears to be of higher prevalence in poorer or lower socio-economic populations. However, does poverty contribute to schizophrenia, or vice versa? The **social causation hypothesis** maintains that people who live in poorer urban settings experience more stresses and this leaves them vulnerable to developing schizophrenia. On the opposite side is the **social drift hypothesis,** which argues that people with schizophrenia find it increasingly difficult to maintain professional and personal lives and begin to drift into poorer economic conditions and live in increasingly low-cost urban environments.

The WHO study of schizophrenia has concluded that it is quite culture-free insofar as there is prevalence of the disorder across the globe (Jablensky et al., 1992). What does appear to be culturally relevant is the recovery rate, which is higher in the developing world than in America and Canada. Possible explanations are the stronger community ties and social support demonstrated towards the schizophrenic patient found in these countries. What is certainly not in doubt is that schizophrenia remains a complex disorder for which no one factor has yet conclusively been identified as a cause.

IS SPLIT PERSONALITY (DISSOCIATIVE IDENTITY DISORDER) THE SAME AS SCHIZOPHRENIA?

Confusion can arise from Bleuler's description of a 'split' in schizophrenia; he was referring to the disconnected nature of processes such as thought and language. Multiple personality disorder, or as it is more commonly referred to, dissociative identity disorder (DID), should not be confused with schizophrenia. Many differences exist: epidemiology, treatment and even professional recognition of the disorder itself. Since the film *The Three Faces of Eve* and the book *Sybil* have raised the profile of this disorder, the numbers of those claiming to be affected has increased significantly. Critics also point to high-profile criminals who have attempted to blame their crimes on this disorder. With DID an individual can have other separate and distinct personalities, as well as the 'host' personality, within the one body and with no or limited knowledge of the other personalities.

Theories have been suggested to explain this phenomenon that characterises DID but a diathesis–stress model has been generally accepted (Maldonado et al., 1998). High levels of abuse and trauma in childhood, as the individual's personality is developing and at a fragile point, have been held responsible. As a coping mechanism the child might dissociate themselves from the reality of the trauma they are experiencing. Some create new identities in an attempt to distance themselves from the trauma; this dissociation brings a degree of relief and in doing so reinforces the dissociation. As the child reaches adulthood, rather than the alternate personality being integrated into a unified personality they remain separate, acting as a protection against further suffering. Frank Putnam, in his study of 100 diagnosed DID cases, found that 97 reported high levels of physical and sexual abuse. Treatments for schizophrenia are very different to approaches used in the treatment of DID.

TREATMENT OF SCHIZOPHRENIA

There is no cure for schizophrenia, but treatments are available to reduce the intensity and frequency of the symptoms. Medication and psychosocial treatments can help some people with schizophrenia to lead highly productive and rewarding lives, while for others the disorder continues to cause impairments in function despite treatment and family support. A variety of antipsychotic medications are effective in reducing the psychotic symptoms present in the acute phase of the illness, and they also help reduce the potential for future acute episodes. Before treatment can begin, however, a psychiatrist should conduct a thorough medical examination to rule out substance abuse or other medical illnesses whose symptoms mimic schizophrenia. People with schizophrenia abuse drugs more often than the general population. Substance abuse complicates the diagnosis of schizophrenia and also reduces the effectiveness of treatment. If a patient shows signs of addiction, treatment for substance abuse should be pursued along with other treatments.

RECOVERY AND REHABILITATION

When the symptoms of schizophrenia are controlled, therapy can help people learn social skills, cope with stress, identify early warning signs of relapse and prolong periods of remission. Many people with the disease, following treatment, can reach their full potential by managing the illness. Because schizophrenia typically strikes in early adulthood, individuals with the disorder need rehabilitation to help develop life-management skills, complete vocational or educational training and hold a job. For example, supported employment programmes have been established to help persons with schizophrenia achieve self-sufficiency. These programmes provide people with severe mental disorders with jobs in competitive, real-world settings.

Many people living with schizophrenia receive emotional and material support from their family. Therefore, it is important that families be provided with education and assistance in managing their relative's disorder. Such assistance has been shown to help prevent relapses and improve the overall mental health of the family members as well as the person with schizophrenia. People with schizophrenia may receive rehabilitation services on an individual basis, in the community, or in a hospital or clinic. When living alone or with family is not an option, supportive housing is often available and includes halfway and group houses as well as monitored cooperative apartments (*Source:* www.healthyminds.org).

As we saw in the critiques of the critical and post-psychiatry movement the medicalised approach to understanding and treating mental health disorders is held to be insufficient and flawed, potentially doing more damage to an individual. The following piece illustrates a different approach to supporting those with schizophrenia, which is rooted in autonomy and personhood.

Hearing Voices Network

> The Hearing Voices Network was started by Marius Romme (psychiatrist) and Sandra Escher (journalist) in Holland. Romme had been struggling to treat a woman whose voices had not responded to neuroleptic drugs. She arrived at her own, nonmedical way of understanding the experience and challenged Romme to appear on television to discuss her experiences. After the broadcast, over 500 'voice hearers' phoned in, most of whom had not been in contact with psychiatric services. This led to the formation of Resonance, a self-help group for people who heard voices and who were dissatisfied with medical diagnosis and treatment for the experience. The Hearing Voices Network was established in Britain in 1990 after a visit by Romme and Escher. The network now has over 40 groups across England, Wales and Scotland, and offers voice hearers the opportunity to share their experiences using nonmedical frameworks. The groups are open only to voice hearers, who share ways of coping with the experience and discuss their explanatory frameworks (which do not necessarily exclude medical ones). The network operates nationally and internationally, in alliance with sympathetic professionals. It validates voice hearers' own accounts of their experiences and makes it possible for these experiences to become meaningful.
>
> Taken from Bracken and Thomas (2001, p. 726)

Schizophrenia is potentially a debilitating disorder, which in the West sees many pushed to the margins of society. Depression, especially bi-polar and major depressive episodes, can too debilitate an individual. We are going to look at some of the factors and theories associated with depression.

Depression

Along with anxiety disorders, mood disorders are the most frequently experienced psychological disorders. Depression is a disorder where, clearly, the individual's mood is affected. Those affected by depression often suffer from very low moods and feelings of helplessness. DSM includes bipolar disorder, major depression disorder and some new entries including disruptive mood dysregulation disorder and premenstrual dysphoric disorder. It is important to recognise that there is a difference between having a 'bad day' or having feelings of 'low mood', and depression. Also, there are different forms of depression, the main ones being bipolar depression (referred to in the past as manic depression) and major depression disorder.

Earlier in the chapter issues of classification were discussed. In the previous chapter the diagnosis of children with mental health problems, such as ADHD, illustrates how polemical it is. DSM outlines the inclusion of a new category in its latest edition to counteract and, 'To address concerns about potential overdiagnosis and overtreatment of bipolar disorder in children, a new diagnosis, disruptive mood dysregulation disorder, is included for children up to age 18 years who exhibit persistent irritability and frequent episodes of extreme behavioral dyscontrol.' Here we see an acknowledgment of the growing trend in over-diagnosing or labelling children with mental health disorders. Caution needs to be used in doing so, as labelling can stigmatise and cause discrimination.

THINK ABOUT IT!

Once a child is labelled with a mental health disorder, does this affect other perceptions, behaviour and treatment towards the child? Does it affect how the child thinks and feels about themselves and what they now might perceive is expected of them? The self-fulfilling prophecy suggests that we respond differently to a labelled individual; if I am told a child has severe behavioural problems, even unconsciously my thinking and behaviour shifts and now can create that very behaviour. Can you think of instances where a label was attached to an individual? Reflect on how that may have influenced your perception and behaviour.

DEPRESSION AND SADNESS ARE DIFFERENT

In life most of us will experience sadness through the death or loss of a loved one or some trauma or stressor such as divorce or losing a job. It is normal to experience sadness surrounding such events; however, with time, the sadness should begin to ease. There lies the main difference between depression and sadness; sadness usually has a trigger or event that causes it and it does ease with time. Depression, on the other hand, does not lessen with time, continuing for months, if not years. There is not always a clear trigger or event that has precipitated the onset of depression. Depression is a more severe and intense experience and can have a very disabling effect upon an individual's life, leaving some unable to function in their lives.

Symptoms of depression can include:

- depressed mood; lack of interest in, and pleasure from, almost all activities
- decreased appetite leading to weight loss
- insomnia or hypersomnia, psychomotor agitation or retardation
- lack of energy
- feelings of worthlessness and guilt
- inability to think clearly or concentrate effectively, indecisiveness
- thoughts of death, suicidal thoughts.

Blatt and Zuroff (1992, p. 158) outline that investigators from several different theoretical positions have identified two major types of experience that can result in depression:

- disruptions of gratifying interpersonal relationships
- disruptions of an effective and essentially positive sense of self.

Whereas Beck (1983), for example, describes differences between patients primarily in terms of current cognitive distortions (Beck and CBT are discussed at the end of this chapter), Bowlby (1980) discusses differences in terms of the attachment patterns formed in the patient's childhood.

FACTORS IN MOOD DISORDERS

Biological

- Genetic – studies of twins and adoption studies seem to suggest a genetic basis or predisposition to mood disorders. Bipolar depression appears to have a stronger genetic component.
- Neurochemical – brain chemistry has been examined in an effort to understand the causes of depression, with underactivity of certain neurotransmitters appearing to play a role. Abnormalities in two chemicals in the brain, serotonin and norepinephrine, might contribute to symptoms of depression, including anxiety, irritability and fatigue.

Psychological

1. **Personality-based vulnerability:** this is a theory advocated by psychoanalysts Freud and Abraham, who believed that early losses or rejection created a vulnerability, triggering an underlying rage or grief process that left the individual susceptible to depression in later life. Blatt's attachment and autonomy theory also focuses on early child–parent relationships, which engender vulnerability to developing depression in later life, in response to two distinct stressors:

    - loss of attachment relationships may precipitate depression in those who experienced neglecting or overindulgent parenting
    - loss of autonomy may precipitate depression in those whose parents were punitive or critical.

2. **Humanistic:** Martin Seligman posits that the 'me' generation, which propounds individuality and self-control has contributed to the rapid increase in depression witnessed since the 1960s.
3. **Cognitive:** Aaron Beck has put forward the 'depressive cognitive triad' to explain the negative thinking patterns that appear with depression. The triad consists of negative thoughts about oneself, the world and the future. This approach highlights the depressed individual's focus on their 'failures' and inability to take any credit for their positive actions – 'depressive attributional pattern'. These negative schemas, developed in early life, lead to negative automatic thoughts and cognitive distortions which maintain a depressed mood. Negative schemas have their roots in loss experience in early childhood, including:
    - loss of parents or family members through death, illness or separation
        - loss of positive parental care through parental rejection, criticism, severe punishment, over–protection, neglect or abuse
        - loss of personal health
        - loss or lack of positive peer relationships through bullying or exclusion from peer group.
4. **Family systems:** this approach focuses on the structure and functioning of the family as being involved in the development of depression. It is posited that maladaptive functioning prevents the child from completing age-appropriate developmental

tasks. Further, disruption in the family structure though bereavement, parental discord, divorce and abuse can lead to depression. Finally, in adolescence, family enmeshment and related parent–child conflict over individuation may be associated with depression.

What is noteworthy within the personality and cognitive approaches to understanding depression is the emphasis placed on early experiences in the formulation and precipitation of vulnerability to the development of depression later in life. This emphasis fits within a developmental approach to the understanding of human development.

SELIGMAN'S THEORY OF LEARNED HELPLESSNESS

As with Skinner's experiment (Chapter 4), Seligman was experimenting with dogs and their behaviour, during the course of his experiments he noticed a phenomenon that led him to develop the theory of learned helplessness. Seligman demonstrated that following a series of uncontrollable, stressful events dogs fail to respond on simple tasks. Seligman proposed a learned helplessness hypothesis: that uncontrollable events produce an individual who perceives that response is useless and whose motivation to respond is weakened. The phenomenon of learned helplessness bears much in common with depression in humans. The theory was reformulated (Abramson et al., 1978) in order to take account of explanatory style, that is, the way people explain negative events to themselves. People who have a pessimistic explanatory style explain negative events as stable, global and internal. Such people are believed to be more predisposed to depression than people with an optimistic explanatory style, who explain negative events as unstable, specific and external.

The reformulated learned helplessness model (Abramson et al., 1978) bears a striking similarity to the negative cognitive triad in Beck's cognitive theory of depression (Beck et al., 1979) as seen in Table 7.2.

Table 7.2 Learned helplessness model/cognitive theory of depression

Abramson, Seligman and Teasdale (1978)	Beck, Rush, Shaw and Emery (1979)
Internal attributions	Negative thoughts about the *self*
Global attributions	Negative thoughts about the *world*
Stable attributions	Negative thoughts about the *future*

However one formulates the aetiology and factors involved in depression, it is clear that it has a major impact on people's lives. The following short account of research highlights the prevalence of mental illness in prisons.

PRISON AND MENTAL DISORDERS

Kelly (2007, p. 374) found strong evidence of a high prevalence of mental disorder in prisons: one systematic review of 62 studies from 12 countries found that 3.7 percent of male prisoners and four percent of female prisoners had psychosis, while 10 percent of male prisoners and 12 percent of female prisoners had major depression.

THINK ABOUT IT!

An interesting question to consider is whether those with mental illness are at higher risk of being incarcerated or whether the experience of being imprisoned causes or contributes to mental illness; what do you think?

A relationship between depression and suicide exists, but, needless to say, not everyone who has depression will contemplate suicide. Nonetheless depression is a predictor. Suicide is an issue that is gaining growing recognition as figures increase for those ending their lives. In addition, particular groups appear more vulnerable, such as young males. We are going to look at research into male suicide which considers suicide from a sociological and psychological perspective.

In focus: suicide

DEFINITION

Suicide is defined as the wilful taking of one's own life

- The WHO estimates that 500,000 people worldwide commit suicide annually; about 1.4 every minute.
- In the United States, suicide rates among 15 and 24 year olds have tripled since 1960.
- Women make about three times as many suicide attempts as men, but men are three times more likely to actually kill themselves. These differences may be due to:
  - a higher incidence of depression in women
  - men's choice of more lethal methods, such as shooting themselves or jumping off buildings.
- The rate for both genders is higher among those who have been divorced or widowed.
- Women who commit suicide have a relatively greater tendency to be motivated by failures in love relationships, whereas men have a greater tendency to be motivated by failure in their occupations.
- A history of sexual or physical abuse significantly increases the likelihood of later suicide attempts (Garnefski and Arends, 1998).
- Depression is one of the strongest predictors of suicide; approximately 15 percent of clinically depressed individuals kill themselves.

MOTIVES FOR SUICIDE

There appear to be two fundamental motivations for suicide:

1. the desire to end one's life
2. the desire to manipulate and coerce other people into doing what the suicidal person wants.

In one study, 56 percent of suicide attempts were classified as having been motivated by the desire to die (Beck, 1976). Parasuicide is an attempt that does not end in death; often seen as a cry for help or an attempt to coerce people to meet one's need.

NATIONAL SUICIDE RESEARCH FOUNDATION: YOUNG MEN'S STUDY

From a sociological perspective

A sense of community (social integration) and shared values (social regulation) can influence the behaviour and actions of individuals. In this context, the social changes that have occurred merit investigation in terms of their impact on men's sense of personal worth and belonging in our modern society. Previous research has speculated that socio-cultural changes in Western societies in recent years have adversely affected men more than women and that a gender difference has emerged in terms of how 'the self is seen or construed'. Furthermore, increased individualism may be contributing to a greater sense of isolation for young men, as women tend to remain more socially connected and view the self as interdependent with others, whereas men are more likely to view the self as separate.

Psychologically

The individual's perceived sense of control is also important in determining how problems are dealt with and challenges in life are met. By clarifying young men's existing sense of control, realistic and meaningful health promotion strategies may be identified.

Anomy

Anomy describes the unbalancing of social forces that affect individual action. It is based on the notion that society usually exercises control over individual behaviour and desire through social rules and norms, and when these rules and norms break down, individual behaviour is no longer regulated by society. At an individual level it can be described as a personal feeling of not being part of, or responsible to, society. Without a sense of accepted social values, individual behaviour or desire may not be controlled or regulated and the level of so-called deviant or unacceptable behaviour, including suicide, increases.

At an individual level

Changes in personal circumstances can lead to uncertainty or can upset the normal way of life. Negative events, such as job loss or divorce, can upset the balance or equilibrium that previously governed an individual's way of life. Anomy is also related to the values and expectations in a society and the means to achieve these expectations. When there is a discrepancy between expectations and means to achieve them, then the level of anomy increases. While anomy contributes to our overall understanding of suicide as a social problem, as a symptom of social transition, it may be difficult to apply to the understanding of individual deaths by suicide.

Here we understand that social changes can affect a person's sense of self and their identity: the direct linking of sociological influences on a psychological one (self-esteem, identity).

THINK ABOUT IT!

Glen Elder, in Chapter 4, discusses his life-course theory, which argues that social changes impact on the developmental life-course. If we take young males who are identified as a vulnerable at-risk group for suicide, what social changes have occurred that may be affecting them negatively? Why are females not apparently as affected?

Further, Elder's research of The Great Depression in America looked at the effects of a severe recession on developmental outcomes. In Europe, many countries have been plunged into a major recession, some teetering on bankruptcy. In Ireland, research confirms that a social change such as recession is linked to an increase in suicide rates.

SUICIDE AND ECONOMIC ADVERSITY

Economic adversity, and recession specifically, has been shown to result in an increase in suicide rates. Studies have also shown that factors in the current economic crisis, such as falling stock prices, increased bankruptcies and housing insecurity (including evictions and the anticipated loss of a home), and higher interest rates, are all associated with increased suicide risk. People who are unemployed are two to three times more likely to die by suicide than people in employment. A recent Irish study has shown that during the boom years of the 'Celtic Tiger' in Ireland male and female rates of suicide and undetermined death were stable from1996 to 2006, while suicide among unemployed men increased. Unemployment was associated with a 2–3 fold risk of suicide in men and a 4–6-fold increased risk in women. A recent analysis of European suicide rates and unemployment increases following the economic crisis showed that the steady downward trend in suicide seen in European countries before 2007 'reversed at once in 2008' with a small increase in 2008 and a further increase in suicide rates in 2009. This increase in rates corresponds with 'a swift increase in unemployment rates' in 2009 to a rate that was 35 percent above the 2007 level in Europe. The researchers also note that 'the countries facing the most severe financial reversals of fortune, such as Greece and Ireland, had greater rises in suicides (17 percent and 13 percent, respectively) than did the other countries' By mid-2010, one in ten calls to the Samaritans in Ireland were described as 'recession-related' and in June 2010 some 50,000 calls were received, up from an average of 35,000 in other months. The suicide rate in Ireland increased from 424 in 2008 to 527 in 2009, an increase of 24 percent. This followed a small but continued reduction in the number of suicides over the previous years.

In the next chapter the relationship between poverty, unemployment and mental health will be explored further. It is clear that the effects of social change on mental health are tangible and, in keeping with Elder's research (Chapter 4), affect the next generation and their developmental outcomes as well.

Finally, we will end this section with personality disorders. Earlier we saw how continuity can be seen in the progression that can occur from conduct disorder to antisocial personality disorders. DSM classifies personality disorder within three cluster types. We will briefly overview anti-social personality disorder, given its relationship to conduct disorders.

Personality disorders

There are ten disorders classified within the umbrella term of personality disorders. These are divided into three clusters:

Cluster A: odd or eccentric (paranoid, schizoid, schizotypal)

Cluster B: dramatic, emotional or erratic (histrionic, narcissistic, antisocial, borderline)

Cluster C: anxious and fearful (obsessive-compulsive, avoidant and dependent)

Should you choose to you read through the descriptions of each type, you may well recognise some aspects of your own personality. This doesn't necessarily mean that you have a personality disorder. Some of these characteristics may even be helpful in some areas of your life. However, if you do have a personality disorder, these aspects of your personality will be quite extreme. They may spoil your life, and often the lives of those around you.

HOW COMMONARE PERSONALITY DISORDERS?

- About 40–70 percent of people on a psychiatric ward will have a personality disorder.
- About 30–40 percent of psychiatric patients being treated in the community by a psychiatric service will have a personality disorder.
- Around 10–30 percent of patients who see their general practitioner (GP) will have a personality disorder.

ANTISOCIAL PERSONALITY DISORDER

Antisocial personality disorder is a condition that affects a person's thoughts, emotions and behaviour in a way that is disruptive, and may be harmful to other people. People with this personality disorder exhibit traits of impulsivity, anger and associated behaviours, including irresponsibility, recklessness and deceitfulness. They have often grown up in fractured families in which parental conflict is typical and parenting is harsh and inconsistent. Antisocial personality disorder is not usually diagnosed before the age of 18, but characteristics of the disorder can be recognised in younger people as conduct problems. Early treatment of children (aged 5–11 years) and young people (aged 12–17 years) with conduct problems may help to prevent antisocial personality disorder from developing later.

Guidelines for working with people with antisocial personality disorder

The UK National Institute for Clinical Excellence (NICE) has produced guidelines for those who work with people with antisocial personality disorders. The guidelines aim to outline how healthcare professionals can manage and prevent this particular disorder.

- Staff working with people with antisocial personality disorder should recognise that a positive and rewarding approach is more likely to be successful than a punitive approach in engaging and retaining people in treatment.
- Cognitive problem-solving skills training should be considered for children aged 8 years and older with conduct problems.
- For people with antisocial personality disorder with a history of offending behaviour who are in community and institutional care, consider offering group-based cognitive and behavioural interventions (for example, programmes such as 'reasoning and rehabilitation') focused on reducing offending and other antisocial behaviour.

(*Source*: www.nice.org.uk)

This brings us to the end of our overview of some of the mental health disorders in childhood and adulthood. The final section looks at psychological interventions, including CBT. Three major psychotherapeutic theories will be examined; Freud's psychoanalytic/psychodynamic approach, Rogers's Humanistic/Person-centred perspective and Cognitive Behavioural Therapy, to include the work of Ellis and Beck. Here we see a continuance of the work and influence of Freud and Rogers (see Chapter 4) and how different perspectives, such as cognition and behaviourism, are melded and transformed into a therapeutic intervention.

COUNSELLING THEORIES

Introduction

The aim of this section is to provide a brief introduction to the theories of three of the leading psychotherapeutic approaches: Freudian (psychoanalytic), Rogers (humanist/person-centred therapy) and cognitive behavioural therapy (CBT). Other approaches do exist, such as Gestalt, Reality and Existential therapy, and many therapists will use an amalgam of these approaches in their practice. To be clear, this introduction is not meant to be exhaustive nor does it equip an individual to become a counsellor. Rather, you will learn, through the counselling theories outlined and the skills suggested, how to better support service users. Consult Chapter 3 on communication and relationships in social work, which includes material on practical skills, values, critical reflection and person-centred approach, which originates from Carl Rogers's work. We will explore Rogers's counselling or therapeutic theory as well as Freud's (see Chapter 4 for an overview of other aspects of their work).

Theories used within counselling/therapy

Freud & Psychoanalysis

Overview of theory

Therapeutic relationship & techniques

Strengths and limitations

Freud and psychoanalysis

Before reading this section on Freud, it is preferable to have read the section on Freud in Chapter 4, where his conceptualisation of personality, psychosexual development and defence mechanisms are discussed.

Freud is credited by many as the founder or father of psychotherapy. He certainly developed what one of his clients described as the 'talking cure', or what we in the present day would term psychotherapy or counselling. Freud's approach is referred to as 'psychoanalysis', capturing the analytical nature of the interaction between therapist and client. Freud's theories have fallen from grace, reflecting perhaps an unease with the sexual elements of his theory. His formulations surrounding psychosexual stages, including the Oedipal and Electra complexes, have been rejected by many, including his followers, such as Carl Jung and Erik Erikson. However, to disregard the work and importance of Freud would be a mistake. The idea of an unconscious is widely accepted and key concepts such as defence mechanisms are prominent in psychotherapeutic work. Certainly, his assertion that early experiences affect our later development and the importance of the parental relational bond are cornerstones of psychological discourse. Perhaps the best thing to do is to decide for yourself what you think of his work and its relevance.

Freud's early years were to prove instrumental in his development of psychoanalysis. He was influenced by the work of Janet and Charcot, who demonstrated the use of hypnosis. This suggested to Freud that the emotional distress he was witnessing in his clients had its roots in the unconscious, and in order to alleviate the distress the unconscious must be accessed. He developed techniques to access and interpret the unconscious, including dream interpretation, free association and transference, which we will look at more closely below. His work as a psychiatrist dealing with women suffering from 'hysteria' was pivotal to the development of his ideas. Freud found that the symptoms of hysteria eased once the women had reported unpleasant and frightening sexual experiences. Freud conceptualised that these childhood sexual experiences, which he did not believe had actually occurred in reality, were the result of the individual's own childhood sexual needs (libido or sexual energy). This energy passes through the psychosexual stages: oral, anal, phallic, latent and genital, as discussed in Chapter 4. If the individual does not successfully transition through a stage they become 'fixated', and this leads to psychopathology in later life.

Another potential area for psychopathology was in the development of personality, which involved three structures: the id, the ego and the superego. The id is the only element present at birth and is governed by the 'pleasure principle', the ego as it develops is governed by the 'reality principle' and is the rational part of personality development. Finally, the superego or conscience reflects the input of familial and cultural moral mores, which shape the individual's sense of morality. Healthy personality development, according to Freud, is based on the resolution of psychosexual and psychosocial issues at the appropriate stages. Unsuccessful resolution, such as fixation, or not meeting a critical development task, leads to psychopathology. Anxiety (Hall, 1962, as cited in Passer, 2001) is a painful emotional experience resulting from internal or external stimulation. When the ego is unable to produce realistic coping mechanisms in times of anxiety it resorts to what Freud termed 'defence mechanisms' to relieve the anxiety in a safe manner by denying, distorting or falsifying reality. A number of defence mechanisms exist, including repression, projection, reaction formation, denial, displacement and regression, and these are covered in Chapter 4. The Freudian approach is considered to be deterministic, meaning that a person's development is determined by factors over which they have no control and certainly no free will. As previously outlined, Freud believed that human nature was motivated by irrational forces, unconscious elements and instinctual drives (such as the id). Freud had followers who disagreed with aspects of his theory, especially the psychosexual elements, and broke away. These include Carl Jung (his approach is analytical psychology) and Erik Erikson (psychosocial approach). Those who followed Freud are often described as neo-Freudian and give consideration to social and cultural factors in development. Other important figures include Margaret Mahler, and her theory of 'object relations', and Bowlby, who was a member of the British Psychoanalytical Society until he was expelled by Freud's daughter, Anna. A distinction between Freud and his followers is that Freud's focus was on the 'id', whereas those who followed are often labelled 'ego psychologists' as they are more interested in this element of personality development.

THERAPEUTIC RELATIONSHIP AND TECHNIQUES

As referred to earlier, several techniques were employed by Freud to bring repressed material to the surface in order for the client to gain a better insight into their difficulties and allow for personality reorganisation. The main techniques in psychoanalysis included:

- relationship between therapist and client
- free association

- analysis of resistance and transference
- dream analysis.

RELATIONSHIP BETWEEN THERAPIST AND CLIENT

The relationship between therapist and client offers opportunities for the therapist to understand the roots of the client's difficulties. In traditional psychoanalytic practice the therapist sits with their back to the client who lies on a chaise longue or couch, so that the therapist can remain a blank slate on which the client can 'project' their true feelings, desires and assumptions. It is through this process that the client will increasingly project their feelings of repressed anger or despair towards others (e.g. parents, authority figures) onto the therapist. If the client behaves in a disgruntled way towards the therapist, this could indicate that this is how the client behaves towards others. Transference and counter transference also involve the therapist–client relationship. Transference is when the client redirects their feelings from a significant other onto the therapist. Examples of transference can include erotic feelings towards the client, as happened in one of Freud's earliest cases, or feelings of anger, distrust or dependency. Freud came to realise that analysis of the transference relationship allowed him to explore the meaning behind it, which aided the client's treatment. Counter-transference involves the redirection of a therapist's feelings towards the client; in other words, it is when a therapist becomes emotionally entangled with a client. For example, a client might remind the therapist of an important figure and this can affect how the therapist relates to the client. Or, as happened to Freud, the therapist can develop sexual feelings for the client. In research conducted by Pope and Tabachnik (1993), 87 percent of therapists reported having been sexually attracted to at least one if not more of their clients.

FREE ASSOCIATION

This involves saying whatever comes into the mind; if hesitation occurs in responding, the therapist interprets this as significant as it indicates that the unconscious is attempting to block material from coming into consciousness.

DREAM ANALYSIS

This technique can allow the therapist to gain access to deeper parts of the client's personality through unlocking and interpreting the meaning of their dreams and fantasies. Dreams symbolically represent the client's inner feelings, motivations and desires.

Traditional psychoanalysis is not commonly practised nowadays, as it involves seeing the psychoanalyst every day or at least three times a week. This is not only a time-consuming endeavour for most but a costly one, making it almost prohibitive. Further, the therapist doesn't talk much during the session, only occasionally offering an interpretation if required. From Freud's initial approach of psychoanalysis have come others branches of psychotherapy. An umbrella term that can be used for these branches is psychodynamic psychotherapy, which refers to therapy that uses some of the same theories and principles of psychoanalysis but differs in the techniques and the client–therapist relationship. With this approach, the therapist sits face-to-face with the client; the therapist will talk and the process is far more interactive. Clients will generally see their therapist once a week. While the unconscious is considered, it is not given the same importance as in psychoanalysis. Other issues including social and cultural factors are taken into account in formulating the roots of the client's difficulties.

STRENGTHS AND LIMITATIONS OF THE PSYCHOANALYTIC APPROACH

Aspects of Freud's theory have been adopted by other therapists in their work with clients. The importance of defence mechanisms is recognised, as are the concepts of transference and counter-transference. Essentially, Freud has offered a comprehensive system of personality and cemented the role of the unconscious in behaviour. Most importantly, his theory emphasises the profound effect of childhood development on later development.

Limitations of the psychoanalytic approach include not just the expense but also the long-term nature of this type of counselling, which is particularly unsuited to crisis counselling. Further, in classic psychoanalysis the role of culture and social factors are not considered, making this approach unsuitable for work with culturally diverse client groups or in social work. Freud's formulation was based on his work with neurotic people; he generalised his observations to others. Further, it is very hard to scientifically test many of Freud's central concepts, which by modern standards is considered a weakness. In a review of studies examining the effectiveness of long-term psychoanalytic therapy (including psychodynamic therapies which are rooted in psychoanalytic theory), de Maat et al. (2009) found that this form of therapy was effective for a large range of pathologies, with success rates of up to 71 percent.

As we have seen, Freud can rightly be seen as the father of the talking cure; however, his psychoanalytic formulation of therapy was to fall from favour and was replaced by newer approaches, one of which was developed by Carl Rogers.

Carl Rogers and person-centred therapy

While Freud's approach to psychotherapy was deterministic, Rogers rejected this view of human nature, believing in the inherent goodness of humans and their desire to move towards self-actualisation (see Chapter 4). Rogers's formulation of a more humanistic therapy was a reaction against Freud's psychoanalytic approach. In keeping with the tenets of humanism, Rogers wished to develop a therapy that emphasised the client's own resources for becoming self-aware. Rogers believed that the client had the capacity for self-growth and to resolve obstacles in order to achieve growth. With this form of therapy, the therapist does not 'direct' the client, instead believing the client has the personal 'resources' or capacity to become aware of the obstacles that exist in their life. The role of the therapist is supportive rather than directive. In his seminal book *On Becoming a Person*, Rogers says: 'It is the client who knows what hurts, what directions to go, what problems are crucial, what experiences have been deeply buried.'

One of the most important tenets of Rogers's theory was the quality of the client–therapist relationship. Studies continue to find that the most important variable in therapy outcomes is the client–therapist relationship. Qualities in the therapist that affect this relationship include empathy, congruence (genuineness), unconditional acceptance and respect for the client. Unlike the psychoanalytic approach, Rogerian therapy does not rely on techniques as such; rather, emphasis is placed on the client–therapist relationship and creation of an atmosphere of trust, warmth and security, which will enable the client to explore the difficulties they are experiencing. If techniques do exist, it could be argued that these involve listening skills, reflection of feelings and clarification. Another difference to Freud's approach is the emphasis placed on the 'here and now' rather than exclusively focusing on childhood events and relationships. Rogers's approach in therapy considers the client's sense of self as crucial. As discussed in Chapter 4, the self is the reference point for how an individual perceives the world and behaviour and also for self-evaluation. Divergence can exist between an individual's sense of self and reality; a person who is perceived by others as successful and competent may privately suffer from self-loathing or low self-esteem. Anxiety is created when a gulf exists between reality and self-concept. Self-evaluation plays a key role in Rogers's therapeutic discourse and is tied to self-esteem through the approval we look for from others, such as parents or friends. Thus, psychological difficulties can manifest as a result of having suppressed inner needs in order to try to satisfy the perceived standards of such dependency figures. The goal of therapy from this perspective is the awareness of inner desires in order to 'self-actualise'.

The following terms are instrumental to Rogers's theory and his therapeutic work:

- congruence
- empathy
- unconditional positive regard
- presence.

Rogers considered congruence or genuineness of vital importance. Unlike psychoanalysis, where the therapist remains a blank slate for the client to project onto, the Rogerian therapist allows the client to see the 'real' them as they really are. In other words, the therapist's internal and external experiences are the same; the therapist is authentic.

Empathy is seeing the client's world as they do, of having a subjective understanding of the client. According to Rogers, empathic understanding is:

> If I am truly open to the way life is experienced by another person, ... if I can take his or her world into mine, then I risk seeing life in his or her way ... and of being changed myself, and we all resist change. Since we all resist change, we tend to view the other person's world only in our terms, not in his or hers. Then we analyse and evaluate it. We do not understand their world. But, when the therapist does understand how it truly feels to be in another person's world, without wanting or trying to analyse or judge it, then the therapist and the client can truly blossom and grow in that climate (Rogers, 1961).

Unconditional positive regard is the expression of fundamental respect for the person as a human being. The therapist accepts the individual's right to their feelings.

Presence is the capacity to 'be with' the client fully and in the moment or present. The therapist is engaged and immersed in the relationship with the client.

STRENGTHS AND LIMITATIONS OF PERSON-CENTRED THERAPY

The greatest strength of Rogers's person-centred therapy is the importance he places on the client–therapist relationship. Studies have found that this relationship and the quality of it is one of the most important variables in determining the outcome of therapy. This approach recognises the inner and subjective world of the client and emphasises the importance of the 'person' within the therapeutic dynamic rather than therapeutic techniques or outcomes.

As this approach is so non-directive, the therapist engages in mirroring back content; for example, if a client says she hates men because of a relationship breakdown, a Rogerian therapist will mirror back what she has said: 'So you hate all men'. A potential criticism of this technique is that it brings little of the therapist's own self into the relationship. Also, the past is not considered particularly relevant, with the emphasis on the present, which can be viewed as a shortcoming when dealing with certain clients or contexts.

THINK ABOUT IT!

What factors might interfere with your being genuine with service users?

Chapter 3 discusses the integration of a person-centred approach within your practice in relation to self and relationships with others. In Chapter 2 we saw a person-centred approach advocated for those with dementia, and again in Chapter 6 on disabilities we saw how it could be utilised into practice. This demonstrates the centrality of the person-centred approach in social work, where Rogers's understanding of the importance of the quality of relationship and of empowerment resonates and highlights just how influential his work has been.

In Chapter 4 we saw theories pertaining to cognition and behaviour; within the following piece we see these different perspectives combine to present a therapeutic approach that recognises the relationship of how we 'think' to our behaviour and emotional state. Interestingly, both theorists we're about to review originally trained and practised as psychoanalysts.

Cognitive behavioural therapy

Cognitive behavioural therapy (CBT) is a therapeutic approach that recognises the relationship between thinking patterns or systems (cognitive) and behaviour or action. In Chapter 3 we examined behaviourism, principles of reinforcement and learned behaviour, and saw the application of behaviourism to changing individual behaviour in the form of Applied Behaviour Analysis (ABA). CBT is an umbrella term for therapies that use behavioural and cognitive techniques. To define CBT very simply, how we think about ourselves and situations determines how we feel, act and behave.

Maladaptive or dysfunctional behaviour is the result of cognitive distortions or maladaptive thinking. CBT emphasises the ability of people to make changes in their lives without having to understand why the change occurs. This differs from the psychodynamic approach, which delves into the 'why'. With CBT, clients are given 'homework' to help them change. The popularity of CBT lies in its effectiveness but also in the brevity of treatment, which makes it less costly. Two figures associated with this style of therapy are: Albert Ellis, who was the founder of an early form of this approach known as Rational Emotive Behaviour Therapy (REBT) and, more recently, Aaron Beck, who developed cognitive therapy. First, let's examine the work of Albert Ellis.

ALBERT ELLIS AND RATIONAL EMOTIVE BEHAVIOUR THERAPY

Though Ellis was originally a psychoanalyst, he became convinced that irrational thought processes, not unconscious forces, were responsible for maladaptive behaviour. Ellis believed that in challenging these irrational thoughts one could effect change and restore the person to healthy functioning. He devised an ABCD model in which his theory is reflected:

A Activating event that is the trigger
B Belief that is activated by A
C Consequences that follow the belief (these can be emotional and behavioural)
D Disputing or challenging the belief system to change the maladaptive consequences.

Dryden (1999) outlines that rational and irrational beliefs lie at the heart of REBT. Rational beliefs are associated with healthy psychological functioning. The primary goal of REBT is to enable clients to change their irrational beliefs to rational ones.

Dryden (1999) summarises the four basic types of irrational beliefs:

- demands
- awfulising or catastrophising beliefs
- low-frustration-tolerance (LFT) beliefs
- beliefs where the self, others and/or life conditions are depreciated.

The four contrasting types of rational beliefs are

- preferences
- anti-awfulising beliefs
- high-frustration-tolerance beliefs
- beliefs where the self, others and/or life conditions are accepted.

Irrational beliefs are defined through their inconsistency with reality; that is, they are illogical, which leads to unhealthy results for the individual. The role of the therapist is to challenge the irrational beliefs.

Table 7.3 Irrational ideas that cause disturbance and alternatives that might be offered by a rational-emotive therapist

Irrational belief	Rational alternative
It is a dire necessity that I be loved and approved of by virtually everyone for everything I do.	Although we might prefer approval to disapproval, our self-worth need not depend on the love and approval of others. Self-respect is more important than giving up one's individuality to buy the approval of others.
I must be thoroughly competent and achieving to be worthwhile. To fail is to be a *failure*.	As imperfect and fallible human beings, we are bound to fail from time to time. We can control only effort; we have incomplete control over outcome. We are better off focusing on the process of doing rather than on demands that we do well.
It is terrible, awful and catastrophic when things are not the way I demand that they be.	Stop catastrophising and turning annoyance or irritation into a major crisis. Who are we to demand that things be different from what they are? When we turn our preferences into dire necessities, we set ourselves up for needless distress. We had best learn to change those things we can control and accept those that we can't control (and be wise enough to know the difference).
Human misery is externally caused and forced on us by other people and events.	Human misery is produced not by external factors but rather by what we tell ourselves about those events. We feel as we think, and most of our misery is needlessly self-inflicted by irrational habits of thinking.
Because something deeply affected me in the past, it must continue to do so.	We hold ourselves prisoner to the past because we continue to believe philosophies and ideas learned in the past. If they are still troubling us today, it is because we are still propagandising ourselves with irrational nonsense. We *can* control how we think in the present and thereby liberate ourselves from the 'scars' of the past.

Source: Passer and Smith (2001, p. 581).

AARON BECK AND COGNITIVE THERAPY

Aaron Beck, like Ellis, started his career as a psychoanalyst and also became disillusioned with the psychoanalytic approach. Beck, like Ellis, recognised the cognitive role (thought processes) in his client's continuing difficulties. Beck saw that his clients demonstrated self-critical cognitions and termed this maladaptive thinking 'automatic thoughts'. Beck became convinced that emotional disturbances were the result, not of the actual event, but of the client's interpretation of it. For example, if I wave at a friend as I pass her by in my car and she doesn't reciprocate I would assume it was because she hadn't seen me. However, another person who might be depressed or suffering from low self-esteem might interpret that same situation as evidence that they were being ignored. So it is the interpretation that an individual ascribes to a situation that can cause the feelings and behaviour. Beck concentrated on encouraging his clients to pay attention to their 'internal dialogue' or the voice in their head that guided their behaviour.

COGNITIVE BEHAVIOURAL THERAPY

Cognitive behavioural therapy (CBT) is an umbrella approach encapsulating many of the ideas of Ellis and Beck. MacLeod (2003) relates that historically CBT is the most recent of the major therapy orientations, with new elements being added to it, including strategies for cognitive intervention. The following is an example of how a CBT programme might look:

1. Establishing rapport and creating a working alliance between counsellor and client. Explaining the rationale for treatment.
2. Assessing the problem. Identifying and quantifying the frequency, intensity and appropriateness of problem behaviours and cognitions.
3. Setting goals or targets for change. These should be selected by the client and should be clear, specific and attainable.
4. Application of cognitive and behavioural techniques.
5. Monitoring progress, using ongoing assessment of target behaviours.
6. Termination and planned follow-up to reinforce generalisation of gains.

Source: MacLeod (2003), p. 138

According to the Royal College of Psychiatrists, CBT is used successfully to treat anxiety, phobia and bi-polar disorder, to name just a few. Further, it is considered the most effective psychological treatment for moderate and severe depression. For many types of depression it has been found to be as effective as anti-depressants.

TEN KEY PRINCIPLES OF CBT

Change	→	your thoughts and actions
Homework:	→	practice makes perfect
Action:	→	don't just talk, do!
Need:	→	pinpoint the problem
Goals:	→	move towards them
Evidence:	→	show CBT can work
View:	→	events from another angle
I can do it:	→	self-help approach
Experience:	→	test out your beliefs
Write it down:	→	to remember progress

STRENGTHS AND LIMITATIONS OF CBT

Cognitive behavioural therapy has a wide applicability from phobias to depression. Beck's work in particular has proven very effective in the treatment of mild and moderate depression. This approach is short-term and focuses on challenging present thinking to change behaviour and improve affect. It encourages the client's belief in their own capacity to change and discourages dependence on the therapist.

CBT has been nicknamed by some therapists the 'band-aid' therapy, quick and convenient. This approach does not explore the 'why' of how a person feels or has developed their thought processes; it treats the manifestation rather than the root, it could be argued.

Factors involved in therapeutic outcomes

Rogers's identification of the importance of the relationship between therapist and client has been further elaborated upon by Carr:

> **Client characteristics** associated with therapeutic outcome: personal distress; symptom severity; functional impairment; case complexity; readiness to change; early response to therapy; psychological mindedness; ego-strength; capacity to make and maintain relationships; the availability of social support, and socio-economic status (SES).
> **Therapist characteristics** that have been associated with therapeutic improvement: personal adjustment; therapeutic competence; matching therapeutic style to clients' needs; credibility; problem-solving creativity; capacity to repair alliance ruptures; specific training; flexible use of therapy manuals; and feedback on client recovery (2007, vi).

NICE advises on best practice in ensuring outcomes. It outlines some of the benefits that result from the provision of an effective psychotherapeutic programme at national level:

> The potential benefits of robustly commissioning an effective service providing CBT for the management of common mental health problems include:
>
> - reducing the risk of people proceeding to a more severe form of their condition
> - reducing the suicide risk
> - reducing the number of antidepressant medications prescribed
> - reducing referrals to secondary care services
> - providing access to coping strategies and support as an alternative to taking sick leave from work because of depression
> - retaining employment, even where the individual may suffer from stress, anxiety or depression, and enabling people on benefits to return to work more quickly
> - reducing inequalities and improving access to CBT
> - increasing patient choice, and improving partnership working, patient experience and engagement
> - better value for money, through helping commissioners to manage their commissioning budgets more effectively – this may include opportunities for clinicians to undertake local service redesign to meet local requirements in novel ways.
>
> *Source*: www.nice.org.uk

What is evident from this is the interplay of factors that contribute to an individual's mental health. Within an ecological approach (Bronfenbrenner, 1979) one can see that policy and funding issues at a national level have a direct effect upon the experiences of an individual experiencing mental health problems. The lack of availability and accessibility of psychotherapy causes further family distress, employment difficulties and additional pressure placed on an already overstretched and under-resourced hospital system. It is clear that psychotherapy is an effective treatment for many types of mental health problems.

This completes our introduction to some of the counselling approaches that exist. Each of the three theories presented offers something unique. In the psychoanalytic tradition the notion of defence mechanisms and transference are considered by therapists nowadays to be relevant. Carl Rogers's person-centred approach took the emphasis away from technique and placed it firmly on the client, revealing the essential nature of the therapist–client relationship in therapeutic outcomes. Finally, it can be argued that CBT has revolutionised psychotherapy, introducing an effective yet short treatment for the various difficulties individuals face. The brevity of the treatment and resulting cost- effectiveness of CBT compared with other longer and more costly forms of therapy have made it an attractive alternative for health and social-care services.

SUMMARY

Hopefully, at the end of this chapter, you will appreciate the complexity of psychopathologies that exist, from their aetiology to their characteristics. The anti-psychiatry movement argued against the medicalised approach to mental disorders and demonstrated the social and cultural elements of classifying and determining what is considered a mental disorder. It could perhaps be argued that nowadays there is a tendency to 'pathologise' normal behaviours as problematic; for example, feelings of sadness and grief are surely 'normal' reactions to the loss of a loved one. When do we decide when this reaction is no longer 'normal' and needs an intervention? Regardless, it is clear that people with mental health issues are excluded and isolated from society in varying ways, including attitudes and stigma towards mental disorders. This is an opportunity to reflect on your attitudes and consider whether it creates barriers for those who are affected by it. In the following chapter, mental health and well-being continues to be addressed, although the emphasis will be on adversity and resilience and the psychosocial influences associated with it and vulnerable groups.

chapter

8 WELL-BEING AND ENVIRONMENTAL STRESSORS

CHAPTER OUTLINE

- What is health and well-being?
- Vulnerability and resilience: theoretical approaches and considerations
- Psychosocial factors affecting well-being
- Poverty
- Community
- Culture and ethnicity
- Parenting
- Positive psychology and resilience
- In focus: alcoholism and drug addiction
- Drug abuse and its impact on interpersonal adjustment
- Social and psychological needs of children of drug-using parents

Throughout this book we have considered the role of biological, psychological and social factors in an individual's development. Influences and their relationships to one another exist within an individual's environment, immediate and distant, affecting outcomes. Bronfenbrenner's ecological model illustrates that in order to gain a greater understanding of how we develop and the outcomes that unfold, we must look at the different influences on an individual and how they interact to shape the developmental pathway. Traditionally, focus, particularly within psychology, was aimed at forces 'within' the person: the biological and psychological influences believed to shape development. Now a greater recognition of influences outside the person and their impact on outcomes is increasingly recognised and understood. Factors such as food poverty, low income and other social variations enhance, or erode, well-being and health outcomes and point to diverse social factors involved in well-being. In this chapter we will focus on the role of environmental stressors, such as poverty and community and their relationship to the psychological development and well-being of an individual. Adversity and resilience are terms commonly used in highlighting that some circumstances or factors can be protective and supportive of outcomes or, at the other end of the spectrum, risk-orientated and adverse. We will discuss considerations and issues regarding risk and resilience, then examine environmental stressors associated with poorer outcomes. Resilience and a strengths-based approach act as a counter balance to these discussions: a reaction against psychology's emphasis on pathology, deficit and the medical model, aligning itself to social justice principles. Resilience can be supported and has practical applications, as will be seen in its use with young people in care.

WHAT IS HEALTH AND WELL-BEING?

The World Health Organization's Ottawa Charter of Health Promotion provides the most widely cited definition of health promotion (WHO, 1986, p. 40). It places emphasis on the idea that the promotion of health is a process that requires broad participation:

> Health promotion is the process of enabling people to increase control over, and to improve, their health. To reach a state of complete physical, mental and social well-being, an individual or group must be able to identify and to realize aspirations, to satisfy needs, and to change or cope with the environment. Health is, therefore, seen as a resource for everyday life, not the objective of living. Health is a positive concept emphasizing social and personal resources, as well as physical capacities. Therefore, health promotion is not just the responsibility of the health sector, but goes beyond healthy life-styles to well-being.

This definition covers wide territory indeed, including as it does environmental as well as individual factors in the range of resources that define health and well-being. The obvious implication is that the promotion of health and well-being must focus on both the individual and the environment. This calls for the involvement of a much broader array of interventions and factors than does the traditional medical model approach. Indeed, many of the determinants of health are arguably beyond the control of the health care system.

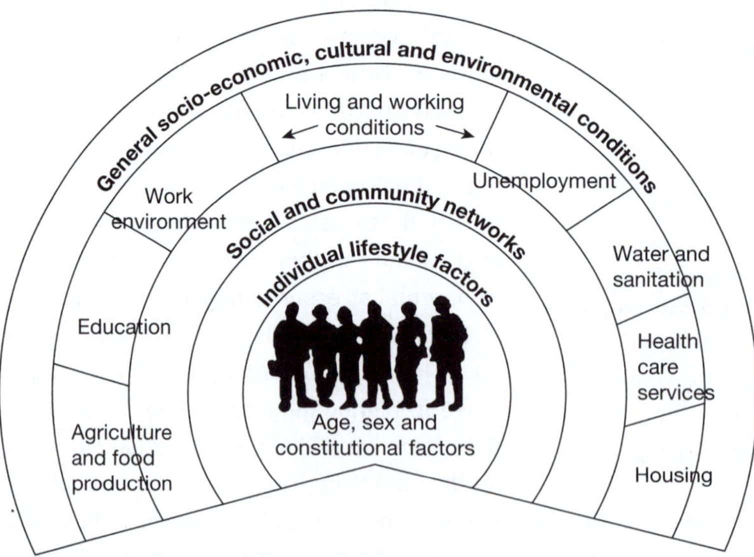

Figure 8.1 Social determinants of health and well-being

Source: WHO

As the diagram illustrates, factors that influence health are varied and involve a multi-layered and complex interplay. Before examining potential psychosocial factors involved in adversity and resilience, let us consider different theoretical approaches conceptualising this interaction and dynamic. The focus of this chapter is on environmental factors and their involvement in outcomes, according to Teater (2010, p. 6):

> At the foundation of current social work theory and practice is psychosocial theory. Modern social work theorists have emphasised the importance of contextualising the human person in relation to their social environment, and the social work profession has viewed the person as interrelated and interdependent with their environment, but individuals are able to influence and changes their environment. Psychosocial theory provides the context in which other theories and methods should be understood by social workers, particularly as it lays the basis for modern social work theories. The Psychosocial Theory which originated from psychoanalytic and psychodynamic casework has had a significant impact on social work.

You can see from the layout of the earlier diagram that it is modelled on a systems approach that is arguably transactional in nature. One such theory that locates the person in relation to their environment, is transactional and reflects a systems-based perspective is Bronfenbrenner's ecological model (Chapter 4). The **systems perspective** sees human behaviour as the outcome of reciprocal interactions of persons operating within linked social systems. Systems theories highlight those concepts that emphasise reciprocal relationships between the elements that constitute a whole. These concepts also emphasise the relationships among individuals, groups, organisations, communities and mutually influencing factors in the environment. Bronfenbrenner's theory locates the individual within a complex nesting of contexts that include psychosocial influences, both immediate and distal. We will explore some of these influences to illustrate their impact on health and well-being, including environmental stressors such as poverty and inequality. Other theoretical approaches used to conceptualise the interaction between protective and risk factors include work by Sameroff, whose **'transactional model'** of development describes the ways in which the child, parent and environment affect each other and the child's development.

VULNERABILITY AND RESILIENCE: THEORETICAL APPROACHES AND CONSIDERATIONS

Reflecting its broad appeal and application, definitions of resilience are wide and diverse, as are the approaches to its theoretical conceptualisation. Masten (2001, p. 228) offers the following definition,

> resilience refers to a class of phenomenon characterized by good outcomes in spite of serious threats to adaptation or development.

Carr (2004) mirrors the emphasis on lack of psychopathology in the definition he proposes: 'the capacity to withstand exceptional stresses and demands without developing stress-related problems' (p. 300). Behind these definitions of resilience, several different approaches have been proposed in understanding the concept.

Luthar and Zigler (1991), in their review of research into resilience, outlined two central aspects associated with this construct:

- stress and
- competence.

Risk, threat or stressors have been used interchangeably to refer to the class of phenomenon considered to increase the likelihood of negative or maladaptive outcomes. Adverse life events have long been considered predictive of poorer outcomes among adults and youth, evidenced by a plethora of empirical research (Tiet et al., 1998).

Beardslee (1989, p. 267) comments that there have been four approaches to the study of resilience:

1. longitudinal studies of children considered at risk due to economic factors, minority status and other variables;
2. epidemiological studies that focus on populations considered disadvantaged;
3. studies that investigate responses to specific stressful circumstances, for example medical illness; and
4. studies that have explored the experiences of being raised in a home with an affectively disordered parent.

Werner (1993, p. 29) succinctly judges that 'the concepts of *resilience* and *protective factors* are the positive counterparts to the constructs of vulnerability (which denotes an individual's susceptibility to a negative outcome) and *risk factors* (which denote biological or psychosocial hazards that increase the likelihood of a negative development outcome)'. Garmezy (1983) outlines three categories of factors that appear to offer protective value:

- personality factors
- family cohesion
- an availability of support systems external to the child or individual.

Rutter (1987) suggests that protective factors can sometimes be seen as mere antonyms to risk factors and counters that this approach is of little value. Rather he proposes the concept of processes or mechanisms in which both risk and protective factors interact in a dynamic, synergistic manner. Waller (2001) contends that very few research studies have attempted to gauge resilience from a more ecological perspective, charting the presence and interaction of variables across many levels between individual and social systems (for example, societies, communities or organisations) and further points out that human development does not occur in a vacuum (p. 290).

Risk, threat or stressors have been used interchangeably to refer to the class of phenomenon considered to increase the likelihood of negative or maladaptive outcomes. Adverse life events have long been considered predictive of poorer outcomes among adults and youth evidenced by a plethora of empirical research (Tiet et al., 1998;

Larson, 1988). Luthar and Zigler (1991, pp. 6–7) report Horowitz's categorisation of five types within risk literature as follows:

1. high-risk infant literature
2. conduct disorder literature (see Chapter 7 for more information)
3. behavioural teratogenesis (see teratogens in Chapter 5)
4. critical or sensitive period research (see Chapter 1)
5. developmental psychopathology (concerned with emotional and social maladjustment and competency)

This interactionist approach underscores the complex nature of outcomes and can be used as a template to gain insight into the diversity and variability that marks outcomes in groups considered at risk. Yet when one examines the early theoretical expositions of resilience the construct was treated as a static, unidimensional state as evidenced in the work of Anthony (1974), who used the metaphor of three dolls to explain vulnerability. The dolls were composed of glass, plastic and steel, representative of degrees of vulnerability. When the hammer of adversity struck the glass doll it shattered, the plastic one was left permanently scarred, whereas the steel doll emitted a momentary chime but remained unblemished. The steel doll was analogous to the 'invincible' child. Of course this analogy is lacking the 'cloth' doll, which is flexible and can be patched!

The idea of 'invincibility' and notion of resilience as a static trait are now recognised to be also lacking. Resilience is seen, according to Wilkes (2002), as a 'multidimensional characteristic' rather than earlier classification as a domain general trait which now encourages us to question how resilience differs '... by context, time, age, gender, and cultural background' (p. 229). Richardson (2002) reflects that interest in resilience and a more strengths-based approach reflects a paradigm shift across academic disciplines from the problem-orientated and reductionist approaches that had previously dominated.

Traditionally, factors, both risk and protective, were thought of in terms of an accumulative effect. The more risk factors the greater the likelihood of adverse or poorer outcomes. A major weakness in this conceptualisation of risk or adversity lies in its lack of recognition of how some factors are more likely to be found in combination with others. The lack of acknowledgement of the relationship and processes at play between risk factors is echoed by Sabates and Dex (2012, p. 6), who comment,

> While there are discussions in the literature about how best to measure some individual risk factors, there are fewer considerations of how to measure multiple risks. The most common method has been to count them up paying no attention to which combinations are present in two, three, four or the higher risk combinations ... Although this aggregate measure has been found to result in better overall prediction when modelling development outcomes, it obscures what may be important distinctions in the nature of the resources or the threats children face. Neither is a simple numerical aggregate measure conducive to understanding the processes that affect children's development.

THINK ABOUT IT!

As has been suggested, some risk factors are more likely to be associated with or accompany other risk factors; the same is true for protective factors. Identify what risk factors you believe are more likely to be linked with others, for example, poverty and addiction or poverty and mental health. Do the same for protective factors. Reflect on the choices you made and your rationale for doing so.

Later in this chapter, positive psychology will be explored with practical applications offered such as the strengths-based perspective as an approach to supporting clients.

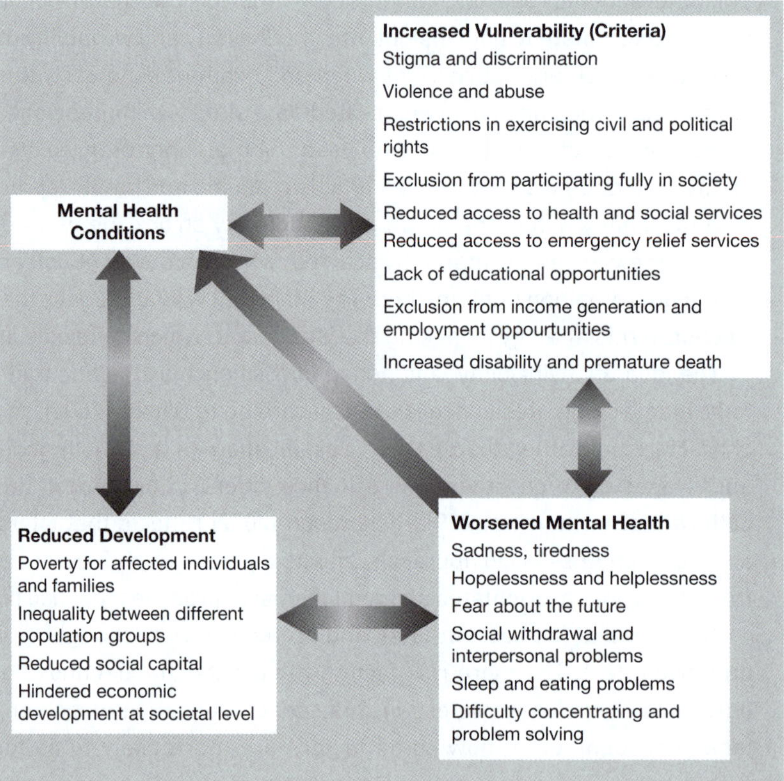

Figure 8.2 Vulnerabilities, mental disorders and adverse development outcomes
Source: WHO (2010).

PSYCHOSOCIAL FACTORS AFFECTING WELL-BEING

The diagram above highlights the relationship between vulnerabilities and adverse developmental outcomes, in this case specifically to mental health. The diagram illustrates the multi-layered and interactional nature of factors to outcomes. The role of psychosocial and environmental issues in the origins, course and treatment of many, if not all, mental health disorders is recognised. The problem is that there has not been any wide agreement as to which aspects of the psychosocial context should be included within the diagnostic system. In DSM-IV, a method for the listing of psychosocial and environmental problems was introduced that may have an impact on prevention, diagnosis and intervention. Examples include death in the family, discrimination, problems at work, inadequate resources and homelessness. Below is a list of the different issues considered by DSM-IV as relevant in the manifestation and management of psychological difficulties:

- Problems with primary support group, for example, death of a family member; health problems in the family; disruption of the family by separation, divorce or estrangement; removal from the home; remarriage of a parent; sexual or physical abuse; parental overprotection; neglect of child; inadequate discipline; discord with siblings; birth of a sibling.
- Problems related to the social environment, for example, death or loss of a friend; inadequate social support; living alone; difficulty with acculturation; discrimination; adjustment to life-cycle transition (such as retirement).
- Educational problems, for example, illiteracy; academic problems; discord with teachers or classmates; inadequate school environment.
- Occupational problems, for example, unemployment; threat of job loss; stressful work schedule; difficult work conditions; job dissatisfaction; job change; discord with boss or co-workers.
- Housing problems, for example, homelessness; inadequate housing; unsafe neighbourhood; discord with neighbours or landlord.
- Economic problems; extreme poverty; inadequate finances; insufficient welfare support.
- Problems with access to health care services, for example, inadequate health care services; transportation to health care facilities unavailable; inadequate health insurance.
- Problems related to interaction with the legal system/crime, for example, arrest, incarceration; litigation; victim of crime.
- Other psychosocial and environmental problems, for example, exposure to disasters; war or other hostilities; discord with nonfamily caregivers, such as counsellors, social workers, or physicians; unavailability of social services.

THINK ABOUT IT!

As you can see, the list of factors is comprehensive. Consider which you think play the greatest role in contributing toward mental well-being, or lack of. It is important to note that many, if not all, of these factors are ones that can be changed.

Interestingly, Axis IV, which classified psychosocial and environment problems in the older DSM-IV version was recently removed, as the newly published DSM-V has decided not to develop its own classification of psychosocial and environmental problems. If we were to look at this from a social model perspective, arguably this can be seen as a retrograde step with external influences on mental health no longer included in psychological classifications of mental disorder.

We are going to explore a handful of environmental stressors and factors, and their impact on outcomes. The first we will consider is Poverty.

POVERTY

In the preceding chapter on mental health, poverty as a factor was touched upon, while Chapter 6 on disabilities clearly outlined the relationship between poverty and disability. Here Sabates and Dex (2012, p. 6) elaborate:

> The measurement of the risk factor of living in poverty has probably been given the most extensive examination in the literature. Poverty, most commonly relative poverty, can be measured by an income definition, or by other measures of whether families have or want, but do not have, various common consumption goods. The term 'material deprivation' is commonly used to describe the absence of one or more consumption good that the majority of people in a society can have if they wanted them.

Types of poverty

TEMPORARY OR TRANSIENT POVERTY

A key contribution of poverty dynamics research (as discussed further below) is that it challenges the traditional view of 'the poor' as a homogenous and essentially static population. In fact it is not the same households who are poor year-on-year – there is a substantial turnover from one year to the next. A positive aspect of this is that for the majority of people who experience poverty, it is not a fixed unchanging status. Approximately half of those who are poor in one year are not poor one year later. The average length of time spent in poverty is between one and two years. This means, however, that over a period of several years, many more people experience poverty than are poor in any single year. (Dept. for Work & Pensions, 2014, pp. 98–99)

PERMANENT POVERTY

The most commonly used definition of persistent poverty is when a household experiences relative income poverty for at least three years out of a four-year window. Whilst this shows that only a small (though not insignificant) fraction of the population suffer long sustained spells of poverty, this represents a relatively large fraction of groups such as lone-parent families. Rather than particular risk factors being associated with either shorter-term or longer-term poverty, evidence suggests that a sliding scale of poverty persistence results from an accumulation and intensity of risk factors. That is, the characteristics that explain belonging either to the temporary or persistent poor are the same, except that the persistently poor tend to suffer a greater number of these characteristics to a more intense degree (ibid.).

As our understanding of definitions of poverty has evolved so too has our understanding of the factors and characteristics associated with, and increased likelihood of, poverty.

Characteristics related to poverty

The following characteristics are among those most frequently cited as having a key relationship with either longer poverty spells or future poverty (ibid., pp. 55–6):

1. Worklessness and Low Earnings
2. Low Parental Qualifications
3. Family Instability
4. Family Size
5. Parental Ill health and Disability
6. Educational Attainment
7. Housing
8. Neighbourhood
9. Debt
10. Drug and Alcohol Dependency
11. Child Ill Health and Disability
12. Non-Cognitive Development
13. Home Learning Environment, Parenting and Aspirations

As mentioned, the relationship between poverty and disability is dealt with in Chapter 6. Here we are going to examine how poverty and SES are involved in the domain of physical health, in this example increasing the likelihood of infants being of low-birth weight. SES is generally defined as the social class or standing of an individual or a group; it is often measured through a combination of income level, education and occupation. This example illustrates how the impact of poverty on a child and their family can affect all areas of development; physical health, learning, social and emotional development.

Low birth weight and social inequality

McAvoy et al. (2006) highlight how social inequalities exist in the incidence of low-birth weight (LBW). In the report the indicator used for low birth-weight babies was a weight less than 2500 grams (5 ½ pounds). 'Certain women are especially vulnerable to poverty and social exclusion and are therefore likely to suffer health inequalities in relation to their pregnancy and their babies. These groups were identified and include teenage mothers, lone parents, disabled women, Travellers, refugees and asylum seekers, other ethnic minority women, women prisoners and homeless women (p. 28).' Further '... it is evident that women in lower socioeconomic groupings are more likely to experience a teenage pregnancy and, as young mothers (aged 19 years or less), they are more likely to deliver a low birth-weight baby. Teenage pregnancies are associated with prematurity and the preterm delivery rate of teenagers far exceeded matched controls of women aged 20 – 24 years in one maternity hospital. Almost 90 percent of attendees at an Adolescent Antenatal Booking Clinic were recorded as being in the lowest socio-economic group and most had poor educational attainment. 87 percent of these mothers had left school. It is also well recognised that pregnant schoolgirls suffered from poor housing, overcrowding and high unemployment rates (p. 23).' Madden (2012, p. 2) examined the relationship between LBW and SES, as children who are LBW have poorer outcomes including '... foetal and infant mortality, as well as with short and long-term morbidity. In addition, there is fairly extensive evidence that LBW is also regarded as a risk factor for a number of health and non-health outcomes in later life.' In Table 8.1, Madden analyses birthweight by social class, with 'no class' signifying that the person has never worked. Intrauterine growth restriction (IUGR – poor growth of the baby while in the womb) was also included along with preterm and LBW.

Table 8.1 Birthweight by social class

	Professional, Managerial	Non-manual, Skilled manual	Semi-skilled Unskilled	No class
LBW (%)	5.18	5.49	6.89	9.35
Preterm (%)	5.72	6.68	8.18	8.71
IUGR (%)	1.87	2.01	2.01	3.94

As you can see from Table 8.1, these conditions are more prevalent in those groups from lower SES. Regarding IUGR, Maddens points out that there is relatively little difference between the first three social class groupings but there is a substantial jump for those who have never worked (no class). Overall, those in the 'lowest' SES are at higher risk of having a baby born with LBW or IUGR.

The above research demonstrates how social factors such as SES, poverty and low educational attainment can impact not just the individual, in this instance the mother, but also her baby before it is even born! This highlights the inter-generational nature of poverty and inequality often seen in studies. So, as we have seen, income, education, areas of poor housing or high unemployment can have a detrimental influence on an individual. Hopefully, it is becoming clearer how a myriad of factors can influence different outcomes and areas of development. It also highlights 'double jeopardy' (see Chapter 1), where one risk factor is witnessed, other risk factors are likely to also co-exist. Dept. of Education (2012) argues '... more focus is now being directed to this theme (poverty and inequality). Policy initiatives and guidance introducing assessment frameworks have sought to highlight the need to see children's well-being in the context of wider socio-economic circumstances and for assessment of children's need to take an holistic approach drawing on ecological theory'.

COMMUNITY

What does 'Community' mean? Community is a broad term and can involve many different aspects from the physical environment itself, the people who inhabit it or more philosophical ideas such as social capital.

Social capital

McPherson et al. (2013, p. 2) outline the following different theoretical approaches in defining social capital:

> Putnam defines social capital as a key characteristic of communities. In Putnam's definition, social capital extends beyond being a resource to include people's sense of belonging to their community, community cohesion, reciprocity and trust, and positive attitudes to community institutions that include participation in community activities or civic engagement.

Social capital is considered a key factor in health and well-being. The WHO in their report *Early Child Development: a powerful equalizer* (Irwin et al., 2007) highlight the importance of family and community relationships and resources in stimulating the physical, emotional and social development of children and young people at key life stages. Irwin et al. (2007, p. 5) comment, 'The environments that are responsible for fostering nurturant conditions for children range from the intimate realm of the family to the broader socioeconomic context shaped by governments, international agencies, and civil society ... These environments and their characteristics are the determinants of ECD (early child development); in turn, ECD is a determinant of health, well-being, and learning skills across the balance of the life course.' Community social capital, such as schools and neighbourhoods, high in quality and cohesion is associated with better health and well-being outcomes according to McPherson et al. (2013).

THINK ABOUT IT!

Identify individuals, groups and resources within a community that build social capital, thinking of your own community or those you work within. Using the 'First Three Years' movement, do you believe that pre-schools and crèches also form part of the fabric of the community and contribute to community social capital? How would you support your answer?

Focusing on child well-being, how do we actually measure or judge it within a community? Costello (1999, p. 37) offers the following indicators:

Indicators of child well-being within the community

- Availability of quality play space and a clean environment
- Level of contact with peers
- Access to preferred leisure/play areas

- Proximity of community resources to the family home
- Level of geographic mobility of child
- Level of social capital within community.

ASK YOURSELF

Using these indicators, how would you rate the community you live and work in? Positively or negatively? Are there any other measures you would use to evaluate how a community influences child health and well-being?

CULTURE AND ETHNICITY

BME Mental Health Marginalisation

People from black and minority ethnic (BME) communities tend to have poorer health, a shorter life expectancy and have more difficulty in accessing health care than the majority of the population with IAPT (2009) commenting, 'cultural and social differences may be a barrier for some BME communities in accessing psychological therapies. The stigma or lack of understanding of mental health problems may be a prohibiting factor for some individuals. For example, there is not a specific word that means "depression" in certain languages, including Punjabi, Urdu and Hindi ... Community isolation may be a barrier for individuals from the "newer" influx of ethnic minorities, i.e. new European Union member states or emergent African communities. These individuals may have little or no understanding of the availability of services provided in this country, and may become isolated from many statutory services, including the wider health services. Issues relating to migration status can exacerbate such problems. In such circumstances, a person's mental health may not be their priority.'

Issues such as political will, stereotypes and the wisdom of applying Western constructs of mental illness to BME populations have consorted in the disproportionately poor outcomes witnessed. According to data from *Count Me In*, a census focused on collecting statistics on mental health services and ethnic minorities, men from BME heritage are three times more likely to be admitted to a psychiatric unit than the general population, and BME women are two times more likely. Other disparities witnessed include the higher rates of black men who are sectioned in Britain and the longer periods they are detained for compared to their white counterparts. In mental health hospitals research has found that staff perceive those of African Caribbean heritage to be more aggressive and dangerous despite no evidence supporting this belief. Another aspect to these inequalities lies in BME groups accessing mental health services. Loewenthal et al. (2012, p. 44) argue, 'The barriers for people from BAME communities have been stated to include practicalities such as languages used for health information through to attitudinal challenges faced by mainly Eurocentric-focused health professionals in understanding the cultural diversity of both the expression and treatment of mental health problems.'

What is clear is that factors such as transcultural psychiatry (see Chapter 1) and the issue of ethnocentrism, stereotype and discrimination, and political will, or the lack of it, can be central to health policy and practice. We are also going to examine how poorer outcomes in physical health are related not just to poverty and poor housing, but also to ethnicity as we overview the health outcomes of the Travelling community. Before leaving mental health, the following diagram represents an approach used in Newham (IAPT, p. 9), which has a 63 percent BME population; the approach is multi-focused to ensure that psychological service provision is effective and responsive to meet the needs of local people.

We have seen the relationship between mental health and ethnicity and race, here we are going to focus on aspects of physical health and well-being. A powerful example can be found in recent research, which examined the health outcomes of an indigenous ethnic group, *Our Geels: The All Ireland Traveller Health* Study (2010). You will see from this study how members of the Traveller community have poorer health outcomes than settled people.

Ethnicity and health outcomes

According to Pavee Point, an advocacy group representing Travellers, 'Travellers require special consideration in health care because they are a distinct cultural group with different perceptions of health, disease and care needs.' The study found that the Traveller community have significantly lower life expectancy figures (Traveller male is 61.7 years and a Traveller female is 70.1 years) and poorer health outcomes. Let's contrast that to the average life expectancy for an Irish man and woman; The WHO regularly monitors life expectancy figures throughout the world. Ireland has seen a continual increase in life expectancy rates:

Table 8.2 Ireland life expectancy rates

	1990	2000	2012
Male	72	74	79
Female	78	79	83

THINK ABOUT IT!

What do you think accounts for such vast differences in life expectancy? What can cause such extreme differences in life expectancy?

As Pavee Point indicated, cultural differences in perceptions surrounding health are factors. Other factors include social exclusion of and discrimination against Travellers in accessing State services, including health, education and employment. Mayock et al. (2009), in a study of another marginalised group, LGBT, proposed the concept of **'minority stress'** as a factor in poorer health outcomes experienced by minority groups, as experiences of prejudice and discrimination result in a deleterious effect on their health and well-being.

Stigma and discrimination – children with disabilities

Those with disabilities are another group where marginalisation, stigma and discrimination can be seen and result in poorer outcomes. According to WHO (2012, p. 8), children with disabilities are among the world's most stigmatised and excluded children. Limited knowledge about disability and related negative attitudes can result in the marginalisation of children with disabilities within their families, schools and communities. In cultures where guilt, shame and fear are associated with the birth of a child with a disability they are frequently hidden from view, ill-treated and excluded from activities that are crucial for their development. As a result of discrimination, children with disabilities may have poor health and education outcomes; they may have low self-esteem and limited interaction with others; and they may be at higher risk for violence, abuse, neglect and exploitation. Some children with disabilities may be more vulnerable to discrimination and social exclusion than others due to multiple disadvantages arising from impairment, age, gender or social status. Other influential factors may include geographic location (living in rural, disperse areas), belonging to a minority language group. For example, girls with disabilities can be particularly at risk of being discriminated against as well as children from poorer households and those from minority ethnic groups.

PARENTING

In the following chapter on abuse and trauma and throughout the book, parenting has been a central element in discussion of well-being and developmental outcomes. We are first going to consider the impact of poverty on parenting; one such impact is that parents, according to Daniel et al. (2010, p. 56) '... are likely to suffer more from physical ill health than the general population and to have a higher risk of suffering depression. Parents with physical and mental health difficulties were found also to be more likely to have a child with challenging behaviour. The *cumulative* stressors of low income, poor housing and a greater likelihood of lone parenthood need to be considered by practitioners when offering support ... the current position tends to coalesce around an interactional model whereby poverty is seen to interact with other psychological, social, emotional and inter-personal problems to drag parenting down.' Another aspect of parenting is that of the parent–child relationship itself; in earlier chapters we considered this interaction in terms of play and disorganised attachment patterns. Here we focus on the features of the parent–child relationship deemed to be of most importance.

What are the key features of the parent–child relationship?

> The nature and quality of family experiences influence not only how a child copes with life growing up, but also help to determine the quality of their relationships, parenting and mental health in adulthood. (Gilligan, 1995)

Each child has a unique relationship with its parents and siblings. Guralnick (1997) highlights three features of the parent–child relationship as important:

- The quality of parent–child interaction.
- The extent to which the family provides the child with diverse and appropriate experiences within the surrounding social and physical environment.
- The way in which the family ensures the child's health and safety.

Taken from (DOHC, 2003, p. 10)

Many theories exist in respect to parenting and also the role of the child, yet Sameroff's transactional model is the basis for many child–parent interventions. Sameroff recognised that the direction of effect between parent to child and vice versa is not one way but is mutual or transactional. This recognition is fundamental to parenting or child interventions, acknowledging that the child is not passive but an active agent, impacting its environment just as the environment impacts the child. The transactional model of parent–child interactions can be witnessed in intervention programmes such as the Parent Plus Programme. Gilligan (1995, p. 71), reflecting on parenting interventions, suggests that 'To be effective, family support must be responsive and accessible: above all, it must connect with the family who need the support when they need it. ... Family support must be offered and available on terms that make sense within the lived reality of its target users. In practice this will mean emphasising a low key, local, non-clinical, unfussy, user friendly approach.'

THINK ABOUT IT!

We have seen in the article on BME and mental illness a questioning of the wisdom of applying Western ideas to ethnic groups. If we apply this to parenting practices, ask yourself the following. Consider cultural diversity in your neighbourhood or among the children you work with, and list the various ethnic and cultural backgrounds. Are there differences in child rearing and parenting practices that you have seen or encountered? Reflect on how such differences may have implications for your practice.

We are going to outline an assessment of needs framework to demonstrate the different aspects that can be considered in determining factors, risk and protective, and outcomes when assessing children and their families.

Assessment of needs: risk protective factors

The Assessment Triangle is included in this chapter as it gives another perspective to understanding the layers of factors and influences involved in child outcomes. It reflects Sameroff's transactional model, which focuses on the interactions between child, parent and environment. Though the emphasis of this chapter is on environmental stressors, such stressors can impact on parenting capacity and ability, which in turn impacts on child outcomes. In the triangle we see parenting capacity identified as core in influencing child well-being across many domains, and this is reflected in several

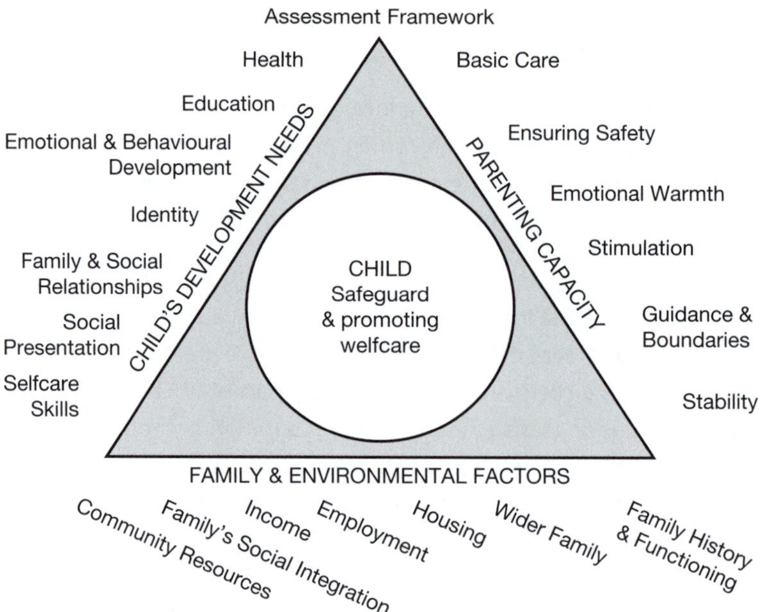

Figure 8.3 The Assessment Triangle

Source: Taken from *Working Together to safeguard children* (2013, p. 20).

chapters in this book that have dealt with the role of parenting. The triangle also recognises the needs of the developing child, which is applicable to any age group, and, finally, family and environmental factors, which we have focussed on in this chapter. Before we leave factors and influences and their role in outcomes, it is timely to outline the principles involved in assessing these many and varied factors that are implicated in well-being, and specifically safeguarding and promoting child welfare.

According to *Working together to Safeguard Children* (2013, p. 20), the following are principles and parameters of a good assessment:

High quality assessments:

- are child-centred. Where there is a conflict of interest, decisions should be made in the child's best interests;
- are rooted in child development and informed by evidence;
- are focused on action and outcomes for children;
- are holistic in approach, addressing the child's needs within their family and wider community;
- ensure equality of opportunity;
- involve children and families;
- build on strengths as well as identifying difficulties;
- are integrated in approach;
- are a continuing process not an event;
- lead to action, including the provision and review of services; and
- are transparent and open to challenge.

In the next chapter we will discuss in greater detail safeguarding children and concepts of abuse.

THINK ABOUT IT!

How would you assess factors affecting parenting capacity and how would you address such factors? In the next chapter, an example of an Attachment Interview is given, which may elucidate some of the critically important aspects of parenting to be aware of.

Traditionally, within psychology a tendency exists to focus on maladaptive conditions and behaviours. We discussed this briefly within Humanistic psychology in Chapter 4. Here we are going to explore further positive psychology, which examines how people thrive.

POSITIVE PSYCHOLOGY AND RESILIENCE

Within the field of psychology there is an emphasis on examining abnormal feelings, emotions and behaviours; in other words, focusing on psychopathology. Positive psychology is a new movement which grew as a reaction against this emphasis on psychological dysfunction within psychology. As the name suggests, its focus is on examining healthy and well-adapted individuals in order to understand the factors that contribute to their good functioning, opening the door to understanding and health promotion (Seligman, 1992). In other words, positive psychology is the scientific pursuit of optimal human functioning and the building of a field focusing on human strength and virtue. In Chapter 4 we examined Humanism, encompassing the work of Maslow and Rogers, whom it has been argued were the forerunners of positive psychology. Within this field lies many new concepts, one of which is resilience.

Definitions of resilience

Resilience may be defined as 'unusually good adaptation in the face of severe stress' (Beardslee, 1989, p. 267) and has been applied to a wide spectrum of domains, from psychology to social work to education (Masten, 2001). Within the domain of psychology, resilience has been explored in issues ranging from psychopathology, child development, elderly populations and individuals with disabilities. Masten (2001) relates that interest in resilience has its roots in work done in the 1970s examining children at risk of psychopathology. It reflected the move towards a strengths-based approach, rather than the traditional deficit model that previously underpinned much theory and applied research. Resilience has an applicatory nature in policy and practice, potentially informing interventions that aim to prevent problem behaviours and psychopathology, and offer opportunities to strengthen those identified as vulnerable (Rutter, 1987).

A strengths-based approach

A theoretical perspective that sits comfortably within the study of resilience is that of *The Strengths Perspective*. This perspective, according to Teater (2010, p. 39), '... shifts social workers away from a focus on clients' problems, deficits and labels towards interactions and interventions that focus on the clients' strengths abilities, resources and accomplishments. The strengths perspective is based on the fundamental belief that focussing on individual strengths versus deficits or limitations is the true avenue for therapeutic progress.' Jacqueline Corcoran (2011) concurs: 'Strengths-based' practice in social work takes on a variety of meanings. It is a philosophy and a way of viewing clients as resourceful and resilient in the face of adversity. It is also considered a method of practice, although there is no strengths-based model of practice per se. Instead, various practice models may be categorised under the rubric of strengths-based practice as long as they hold, as their fundamental assumptions, that the social worker's relationship with the client is one of collaboration and that people are resourceful and are capable of solving their own problems. Prior to the advent of strengths-based perspectives and practices, the dominant ideology involved an 'expert' practitioner diagnosing clients and determining what needed to be done. People were viewed largely in terms of their pathologies, weaknesses, limitations and problems. In strengths-based models, in contrast, the helper, in collaboration with the client system, identifies and amplifies existing client system capacities to resolve problems and improve quality of life. Strengths-based approaches can be viewed as respectful towards and empowering of the oppressed and vulnerable people to which the field of social work traditionally has been committed.

According to Saleebey (2009), six guiding assumptions underpin the Strengths Perspective:

1. Every individual, group, family and community has strengths
2. Trauma, abuse, illness and struggle may be injurious, but they may also be sources of challenge and opportunity
3. Assume that you do not know the upper limits of the capacity to grow and change and take individual, group and community aspirations seriously
4. We best serve clients by collaborating with them
5. Every environment is full of resources
6. Caring, caretaking and context – care is essential to human well-being.

We have seen factors and environmental stressors that contribute to adverse or negative outcomes, but do factors exist that strengthen well-being and resilience? It may be easy to imagine such influences being the mirror opposite of the risk factors; however, other than caring relationships you may be surprised with the other two most commonly identified protective factors.

Three protective factors that increase resilience are

- caring relationships,
- high expectation messages
- opportunities for participation and contribution.

How do we implement these within our practice? As we saw earlier, Gilligan discussed the importance of parenting intervention programmes that aim to support families. In

Chapter 4, we saw that attachment does not lie uniquely with the primary parent as first envisaged by Bowlby; deep attachments and caring relationships can lie outside of the parenting relationship. In the following piece on resilience and young people in care we will see the role of expectation, participation and contribution in bolstering and supporting the development of resilience. In terms of social work with families, Saleebey (2009, p. 15) outlines how strengths-based social work can be implemented:

- Listen to their story
- Acknowledge the pain
- Look for strengths
- Ask questions about survival, support, positive times, interests, dreams, goals and pride
- Point out strengths
- Link strengths to families'/members' goals and dreams
- Link family to resources to achieve goals and dreams
- Find opportunities for family/members to be teachers/paraprofessionals.

THINK ABOUT IT!

In the families you work with, can you see any of the three resilience factors, and as a social worker how can you support and strengthen these factors?

As seen the concept of resilience is not a purely theoretical one; it has a 'practice' element, which can be seen in research by Robbie Gilligan, who examines 'resilience, roles and relationships for children in long term care'.

Resilience and young people in care

Gilligan (2008, p. 46) argues that 'work and recreation settings may be sources of resilience-enhancing experiences for young people in care and young care-leavers. Recreation and work may offer opportunities to develop a precious sense of mastery in certain spheres of activity and to broaden social networks. They may also help to cultivate a set of social roles that may enhance health and well-being for the young person.' This piece of research examines this theme through a specific focus on the needs of young people in long-term care.

Gilligan (pp. 41–2) quotes a number of examples given by social workers and carers that attest to the benefits of participation: Participation in recreational activity may widen and strengthen the range of relationships the young person can access in their social network (McGee et al., 2006;as cited in Gilligan, 2008). It may also increase educational attainment and achievement (Mahoney et al., 2005; as cited in Gilligan, 2008). Among the other advantages that may flow from participation in recreational activities is that they may often serve as a pathway for the young person to work opportunities.

Gilligan emphasises the role carers and social workers can play in strengthening participation and creating opportunities for children to build successful lives. Carers, social workers and other professionals may have important parts to play in helping young people to tap into those resources and particularly into the opportunities for supportive roles and relationships in work and recreation settings.

Carers may be able to assist in:

- cultivating positive expectations in the young person; something that may be very important in relation to issues such as future educational participation and attainment
- serving as a role model or identifying other role models appropriate for the purpose
- supporting initial connections and sustaining ongoing engagement in a recreational or work-related activity.

Social workers may be able to assist by:

- giving due attention to the potential of recreational and work-related experiences in the lives of young people in care
- helping to nurture such interests in young people in care
- providing training and support to carers in that regard
- appreciating the power of positive role models for young people in care and, for example, the specific (and under-recognised) contribution, in this regard, that male foster carers may be able to make
- recognising the value of continuity in care placements and relationships into young adulthood and the need to avoid premature rupturing of viable placements at what may be both a psychologically vulnerable developmental stage and, effectively, an arbitrary administrative cut-off point in a young person's care career.

These guidelines not only highlight the relationship between recreational participation for young people in long-term care and its potential for building resilience and encouraging life-enhancing skills, they also show the pivotal role carers and social workers can play in shaping and supporting the lives of these children. It also emphasises that sometimes it is the 'little' things, such as encouraging a child in a sport or a recreational activity, that can be vital to the overall development of the child or teen. We sometimes think that intervention must involve professionals or therapy and so on, whereas simply encouraging the child in an activity can prove to be highly effective.

We are going to end this chapter on environmental stressors with a detailed *In focus* exploration of addiction, which is arguably one of the most pressing social concerns and is an issue that is prevalent in the work of both psychologists and social workers. Addiction doesn't just impact the individual's life; it has a ripple effect. It touches the lives of many and society at large. This piece begins by looking at addiction from a psychological perspective of definition and classification. However, the real emphasis here is to look at the effects of addiction on interpersonal relationships, concluding with research exploring the social and psychological needs of children of parental addiction.

In doing so it is hoped to illustrate not just the narrow confines of classifications but to move to a more nuanced look at addiction.

IN FOCUS: ALCOHOLISM AND DRUG ADDICTION

What is addiction?

Addiction, or dependence, is defined as 'a cluster of three of more symptoms listed below occurring at any time in the same 12-month period' (American Psychiatric Association [APA], 1994, p. 176).

Those symptoms are:

1. tolerance, or needing more and more of a substance to achieve the same effect
2. withdrawal, which involves unpleasant symptoms when the body is deprived of the substance, resulting in more frequent use to alleviate the negative symptoms
3. taking the substance for a longer period of time or in larger amounts than originally intended
4. unsuccessful desire to minimise use of the substance
5. much time spent to obtain, use or recover from the effects of the substance
6. social, occupational or recreational activities are missed because of substance abuse
7. substance use is continued despite knowledge of causing a problem.

If neither tolerance nor withdrawal are present, then at least three of the remaining symptoms must be present (APA).

Did you know?

- One in fifteen children will become alcoholic in their lifetime because of genetic predisposition (Weber and McCormick, 1992).
- Children from alcoholic families are four to six times more likely to become alcoholic than children raised in non-alcoholic homes (Weber and McCormick, 1992).
- By their mid-20s, nearly 80 percent of young adults have used an illicit drug.

Types of drug abuse

- Habitual and chronic polydrug abuse
- Experimental or recreational drugs abuse.

Carr (2003, p. 590) remarks that seven categories of possible explanation for drug abuse exist:

> **First**, biological theories of drug abuse focus on specific genetic factors; on temperamental attributes that are known to be strongly genetically determined; and on the role of physiological mechanisms in the development of tolerance, dependence and withdrawal.

Second, intrapsychic deficit theories point to the importance of personal psychological vulnerabilities in the development of drug-using behaviour patterns.

Third, cognitive-behavioural theories underlie the significance of certain learning processes in the origin and formation of drug problems.

Fourth, family systems theories emphasise the importance of parental drug-using behaviour, parenting style and family organisation patterns in the aetiology and maintenance of drug abuse.

Fifth, the role of societal factors, such as social disadvantage, neighbourhood norms concerning drug use and abuse, and drug availability, are the central concerns of sociological theories of drug abuse.

Sixth, multiple-risk factor theories highlight the roles of factors at biological, psychological and social levels in the aetiology of drug abuse.

Finally, change-process theories offer explanations for how recovery and relapse occur.

Can addiction be treated?

There are several successful treatments for addiction. It goes without saying that the earlier the addiction is treated, the easier it will be to control. Some of the most effective treatments for addiction are 12-step programmes such as Alcoholics Anonymous (Weber and McCormick, 1992). Other treatments include individual and family therapy, group therapy, educational programmes and self-esteem-building and anger-management workshops.

DRUG ABUSE AND ITS IMPACT ON INTERPERSONAL ADJUSTMENT

Drug use, according to Carr (2003, p. 589), impacts on interpersonal relationships and involves the following possible ramifications:

> Within the family, drug abuse often leads to conflict. Individuals that abuse drugs within a peer-group situation may become deeply involved in a drug-oriented subculture and break ties with peers who do not abuse drugs. Some develop a solitary drug-using pattern and become more and more socially isolated as their drug using progresses. ... Within the wider community, drug- related antisocial behaviour such as aggression, theft and selling drugs may bring youngsters into contact with the juvenile justice system. ... Drug- related health problems and drug dependency may bring them into contact with the health service.

It is clear that addiction affects not just the individual who is addicted but also has ramifications for those around them, especially their families. The following piece of research delved into the experiences of children of drug-using parents to capture the impact on their well-being.

SOCIAL AND PSYCHOLOGICAL NEEDS OF CHILDREN OF DRUG-USING PARENTS

Children in this study (Hogan, 1997) experienced exposure to parental opiate use in different ways. Half had been prenatally exposed to opiates, according to parents. All had experienced the effects indirectly, however, either through changes evident in parental behaviour and/or through separation from and loss of parents. Many had been exposed at an early age to the legal system, having experienced their parent being incarcerated, and in some cases witnessing the arrest and visiting a parent in prison. The majority of the children had experienced separations from parents due to parental incarceration, hospitalisation and/or inability to provide care. Few of the children showed evidence of social-emotional problems relating to parental drug use, with only one child having received treatment for psychological or behavioural problems.

Impact on children's school progress

The majority of children were experiencing difficulties at school. These problems were related to poor attendance, concentration difficulties, poor work completion and low levels of parental involvement with their education.

Key-worker concerns about drug use and parenting

Key workers also had three primary areas of concern about the ability of drug-using parents to provide adequate caregiving to their children; an inability to provide consistent quality caregiving, neglecting the children's physical needs and children having contact or witnessing drug use and paraphernalia. It is important to note that a handful of parents existed where no concerns were raised by the key-workers regarding their parenting and caregiving.

Implications for children's development

The difficulties children experienced included higher levels of separation from and loss of parents and lessened parental involvement in their lives, in some cases raising concerns of neglect. A good deal of tension existed in the home and the children were subject to harsh discipline in some cases. Furthermore, they were exposed, to varying degrees, to the lifestyle associated with opiate dependence, including drug-taking activity and crime.

What are the implications of these findings for children's development?

First, separation from and loss of parents was a particular problem in the lives of the ten children studied. Other research has found that disruption to parental care, especially early disruption of maternal care, is linked to children themselves having long-term difficulties in parenting their own children. It has also been linked with depression, and in the shorter term, with problems with peer relationships.

Low levels of involvement by parents who are present in the home, such as low levels of supervision and monitoring and infrequent communication with children, have been linked to a range of problem behaviours in children, and especially to fighting, non-compliance and delinquency. They have also been linked with depression; in its extreme form, low parental involvement implies neglect of children's basic physical care, which has serious health, as well as psychological, implications.

Low levels of emotional involvement by parents, or a lack of closeness and supportiveness, also appears to have negative implications for children's well-being. It has been identified as a factor in delinquency in adolescents.

In spite of these potentially negative implications for children, it should be noted that the problems listed above were not experienced to the same degree by all families. Furthermore, there was evidence that families coped differently when such problems did arise, depending on a number of circumstances, including the duration and extent of the drug problem, the type of services available to parents, and the degree of social support from the community and from family members. In addition, individual children appeared to cope differently with problems in the home associated with parental drug use, showing different levels of resilience. It would be incorrect, therefore, to assume that all children are at risk for the range of problems described here.

These findings highlight the interesting role of resilience in determining the individual outcomes of the children who participated in this study. Also demonstrated is the complex nature of the developmental outcomes and how difficult it can be to extricate the different factors at play and their impact on individuals. The study did outline policy implications from the findings, showing that research informs policy informs practice. The policy recommendations regarding services and interventions suggested include:

- interventions to counteract the negative social and psychological effects on children
- steps to be taken to prevent children of drug users from becoming drug users themselves.

SUMMARY

Chapter 7 on mental health and this chapter can be read together as the former looks more intently at processes involved 'within' the individual, while this chapter aims to be a counterbalance, shifting attention to external influences at play in health and well-being. It is interesting to note, however, the removal of 'psychosocial and environmental' influences from the latest DSM classification of mental disorders, highlighting the tension that can exist between the world of psychiatry and psychology and those who acknowledge the significant role such influences play in well-being, mental or otherwise. Within this chapter we have discussed how risk and protective factors need to be seen as an interactive and dynamic process and how positive psychology and its espousal of a strengths-based approach attempts to counter the more deterministic and reductionist perspectives traditionally associated within psychology. We see certain themes appear throughout the book, including the role of parenting and poverty on outcomes. In the following chapter on abuse and trauma we will see again the role of parenting but also that of culture, community and society as factors involved in neglect and abuse. This surely highlights the pivotal influence that more distal influences have across all aspects of development and experience.

chapter

9 ABUSE AND TRAUMA

CHAPTER OUTLINE

- Introduction
- In focus: an ecological analysis of mistreatment of children with disabilities
- Defining abuse
- Ecological approach to the conceptualisation of factors associated with abuse and mistreatment
- Types of abuse
- At-risk groups
- Trauma

INTRODUCTION

Safeguarding children and other vulnerable groups is a core element of social work. This chapter will introduce you to the key aspects of abuse and trauma with an emphasis on the psychological aspects rather than legislation, policy or practice pertaining to social work. We begin with a discussion on the question of intentionality and its role in defining abuse. The different categories of abuse, their characteristics and associated factors will be overviewed. Groups vulnerable to abuse will be examined, such as the increased risk of abuse faced by those with mental illness. Further, an 'In focus' piece on the abuse of disabled children will allow for greater elucidation of the mechanisms involved. Societal and cultural influences can be overlooked when attempting to understand the mechanisms involved in abuse and its perpetuation. A case study focussing on the Irish experience is given to illustrate how 'society' can be a factor in abuse; abuse which could be seen from within homes to institutions, reflecting the influence of societal attitudes and values in the perpetuation and denial of abuse. While a snapshot can only be offered, it is a powerful one illustrating how the role of attitudes towards women and children created and allowed for wide scale abuse. Of course, it would be unwise to think of this example as a one off. Values and attitudes, as we will see, play a powerful role in the construction of abuse and its perpetuation. The final section of the chapter gives greater focus to the perspective of those victimised, and the search for meaning and Post Traumatic Stress Disorder [PTSD] are explored.

IN FOCUS: AN ECOLOGICAL ANALYSIS OF MISTREATMENT OF CHILDREN WITH DISABILITIES

DEFINING ABUSE

Before looking at the issue of intentionality and how we define abuse, it is timely to consider the use of language in labelling abuse. We saw in Chapter 2 that the Crown

Prosecution Service advised that the term 'non accidental head injury' replace that of 'shaken baby syndrome', the latter being considered 'emotive', highlighting how language can influence attitudes and perceptions. In the UK, 'safeguarding children' is increasingly replacing the term 'child protection', as evidenced in the recent policy document *Working together to safeguard children* (Dept. of Education, 2013), which defines safeguarding and promoting the welfare of children as:

- protecting children from maltreatment;
- preventing impairment of children's health or development;
- ensuring that children grow up in circumstances consistent with the provision of safe and effective care; and
- taking action to enable all children to have the best outcomes.

THINK ABOUT IT!

Reflect on the different reactions to, and understanding of, the terms child protection and safeguarding children. From a parent's perspective, what do you think their reaction to 'child protection' would be? Fearful or maybe defensive? Is 'protection' suggestive? Do you think 'safeguarding' would elicit the same response? The language we use and how it's perceived can impact on the relationship between service user and social worker.

For the purposes of clarity the term abuse or maltreatment will be used. While safeguarding children encompasses a wider focus, the main emphasis of this chapter is on the characteristics of, and factors involved in, neglect and abuse. So when considering how we define abuse, an immediate issue that should be addressed is that of intentionality.

Neglect and abuse: an issue of intentionality?

It can be controversial to draw a line between abuse and neglect as both can have devastating effects. Intentionality can offer an (albeit simplistic) approach to differentiating between abuse and neglect. Whereas abuse is intentional on the part of the abuser, neglect reflects a passive ignoring of the child's needs, including physical, safety and emotional ones. Typically, parents who neglect their children do not do so intentionally. Rather, neglect arises through parents' lack of awareness of, or capacity to meet, their children's needs. While neglect is not intentional, if you agree with the above definition, it is still a form of abuse and its effects are as significant as other forms of abuse. The question of how to measure neglect will be explored later in the chapter when we examine neglect and other categories of abuse.

Cultural aspects of defining abuse

As we saw in the previous chapter, ideas of child well-being have evolved from the norm of 'spoil the child, spare the rod'. Davies and Ward (2012, pp. 17–18) elaborate on the cultural aspects of defining abuse:

Definitions also vary between cultures. In the UK, for instance, the physical abuse of children was not recognized as a form of maltreatment until the 1880s, and smacking was considered to be acceptable parental behaviour for at least another century. It is still legal in this country, although it has been outlawed in much of the rest of Europe. Witnessing intimate partner violence has only relatively recently been recognized as a cause for concern. The parameters have changed as the impact on children's welfare has become better understood. In some cultures both the physical abuse of children and intimate partner violence are still regarded as normative adult behaviours, with the result that identifying maltreatment and developing an appropriate response becomes a complex issue in a multi-cultural society. Nevertheless, it is possible to make too much of cultural differences: abuse is often defined as a failure to meet the child's developmental needs, and there is a very significant cross-cultural consensus about the basic needs for healthy child development.

What is child abuse?

The World Health Organization defines child abuse as follows:

> Child maltreatment, sometimes referred to as child abuse and neglect, includes all forms of physical and emotional ill-treatment, sexual abuse, neglect, and exploitation that results in actual or potential harm to the child's health, development or dignity. Within this broad definition, five subtypes can be distinguished – physical abuse; sexual abuse; neglect and negligent treatment; emotional abuse; and exploitation.
>
> *Source:* WHO (2010)

This definition is wide and encompasses many forms of maltreatment from neglect to exploitation, which can include trafficking and grooming. Before exploring the different categories of abuse, we are going to overview an ecological approach to conceptualising factors associated with maltreatment. Ecological models of development can offer a theoretical basis for mapping out multiple factors, risk and protective, and from the immediate to more distal. Bronfenbrenner's ecological theory is outlined in Chapter 4, and an 'In focus' piece using ecological analysis to elucidate the maltreatment of children with developmental disabilities can be found in the section on those vulnerable to abuse.

ECOLOGICAL APPROACH TO THE CONCEPTUALISATION OF FACTORS ASSOCIATED WITH ABUSE AND MISTREATMENT

The ecological approach, as mentioned, offers a useful framework to examine factors at play in neglect and abuse, or 'maltreatment' as it tends to be referred in North American literature. Though the following information deals with factors relating to children, it is applicable to other groups vulnerable to abuse.

Before we consider factors contributing to neglect and abuse, it is important to bear in mind that 'contribute to' is not the same as 'cause'; it merely reflects that a relationship exists between two variables. Usually, when we look at most phenomena, causation involves a complex interaction of differing contributing factors.

Thomas et al. (2003) take an ecological approach to conceptualising the factors that can contribute to child abuse and maltreatment, separating the origins of abuse into four strands:

1. the child
2. the family
3. the community
4. the society.

THE CHILD

To be very clear, in no way is it suggested that the child is responsible for the abuse or neglect that they suffer. When we examine factors involved that potentially increase the vulnerability of a child to abuse, what we are doing is looking for any factors that make it more likely for a child to be victimised and abused. Certain factors have been found to be more prevalent in cases of abuse, including:

- disability
- age
- gender
- premature or low birth weight
- developmental delay or frequent illness.

Though children are obviously not responsible for the abuse inflicted upon them, certain child characteristics have been found to increase the risk or potential for maltreatment. Children with disabilities, for example, are significantly more likely to be abused (Crosse et al., 1993; Schilling & Schinke, 1984). Evidence also suggests that age and gender are predictive of maltreatment risk. Younger children are more likely to be neglected, while the risk for sexual abuse increases with age (Mraovick & Wilson, 1999). Female children and adolescents are significantly more likely than males to suffer sexual abuse. Later in this chapter we will examine an ecological approach to the maltreatment of children with disabilities within the section on vulnerable groups.

THINK ABOUT IT!

Why do you think younger children and those with learning disabilities are particularly vulnerable to being abused or neglected? What characteristics might they share? For example, those with learning disabilities will have a developmental age that is lower or younger than their chronological (actual) age. From a cognitive perspective the younger the child, the less developed their capacity for thought and reasoning, making it easier to manipulate them. What are the implications from an emotional point of view or in terms of their dependence on adults to care for them? In terms of bi-directionality from a parent's perspective looking after young children is more intensive and demanding, so too is caring for children with additional needs – this is known as 'child effects', where the child impacts on those around them and their environment. How might this increase a child's vulnerability and why?

THE FAMILY

Thomas et al. (2003) outline the following family characteristics linked to child neglect and abuse:

- substance abuse
- domestic violence
- lack of parenting skills.

Families where substance abuse is an issue have been found to be at higher risk of abuse, with the authors suggesting that substance abuse is present in 40 percent to 80 percent of families in which children are victims of abuse. As we saw in the previous chapter, research indicates that children whose parents are addicts experience difficulties in the parental relationship, which is often marked by absence, lack of engagement or loss. Their children are at higher risk of neglect and the research suggests they often live in homes fraught with tension. Further, they are exposed to parental lifestyles that place them at greater risk of abuse. In general, a lack of parenting or communication skills also increases the risks of maltreatment of children, as does domestic violence within the home. Wilkins (2012, p. 15) relates that caregiver characteristics particularly associated with neglect and abuse, and known as '**the toxic trio**', are;

- drug or alcohol dependency,
- mental health difficulties or
- domestic abuse.

THE COMMUNITY

Factors related to the community and the larger society are linked with child maltreatment. As we saw in the previous chapter, poverty is a risk factor associated with poorer outcomes across a range of different domains and areas. Poverty, for example, has been linked with maltreatment, particularly neglect, in each national incidence study (Sedlak & Broadhurst, 1996), and has been associated with child neglect by Black (2000) and found to be a strong predictor of substantiated child maltreatment by Lee and Goerge (1999). In the previous chapter, we overviewed the relationship between poverty, inequality and poorer outcomes. Bishop and Leadbeater (1999) found that abusive mothers reported fewer friends in their social support networks, less contact with friends and lower ratings of quality support received from friends. Violence and unemployment are other community-level variables that are associated with child maltreatment. Later we will examine a community approach to the prevention of abuse which illustrates how 'community' can influence such outcomes.

THE SOCIETY

Perhaps the least understood and studied factors in child maltreatment are those at a societal level. Ecological theories propose that factors such as narrow legal definitions of child maltreatment, social acceptance of violence (as evidenced by video games, television and films, and music lyrics), and political or religious views that value non-interference in families may be associated with child maltreatment (Tzeng et al., 1991). Society, as a term, is broad and encompasses many aspects: political, social and religious institutions, values and the media to name but a few. The following case study demonstrates how a distal factor such as 'society' can create and perpetuate abuse.

Society as a factor – a case study

Society as a factor in abuse is an important consideration as it is open to change; ways of thinking or prejudice which increase the likelihood of abuse can be challenged. While it might seem irrelevant to discuss Ireland's systemic and ingrained history of abuse, we must never fall into the trap of believing such widespread abuse cannot and will not happen again or in different jurisdictions. The mechanisms, values and influences underpinning such wide-scale abuse are not unique. The case study focuses on one aspect, 'values', to illustrate their influence. This example shows cultural attitudes and values that fostered and enabled abuse within the home and in institutions, and it demonstrates that ethnic groups hold their own beliefs and value systems which can increase or reduce the risk of abuse. Ireland has a shocking history of abuse, including institutional abuse which saw collusion between the State and Church. This surely leads to the question of whether Irish society, and, more specifically, 'Irish culture', is a factor in the levels of abuse documented. Even now, in 'modern' times, vestiges of these values remain, as witnessed in a recent court case in the south of Ireland, where over a dozen men, including a priest, lined up to shake the hand of a man convicted of sexual assault – in front of the victim – demonstrating that while much has improved, changes in attitudes and values do not always happen quickly.

The following extract from 'Ireland and Rape Crises' (McKay, 2007, p. 94) illustrates attitudes that have existed in Ireland and the roles culture and society play in abuse. In her article, Susan McKay offers insights into attitudes in Ireland towards the area of abuse, including domestic violence and rape. She offers the following as an example of Irish cultural values and their role in the perpetuation of such abuse: 'In 1969 the legendary Irish agony aunt, Angela MacNamara, had warned in the *Sunday Press* [Irish newspaper] that it is the nature of a man to be the aggressor – the one who initiates and that if a girl allowed a man to fondle and embrace her ... she cannot blame him if his nature propels him in passion to seek the ultimate closeness of sexual intercourse.' McKay offers another shocking example: Dr Percy Patton who in the 1970s and 1980s carried out most of the medical examinations of women who had alleged rape to the Gardaí [Irish police]. He declared (*Irish Review*, 2007, p. 94), 'the fear of parental rebuke and the fear of pregnancy are the two outstanding reasons why so many willing partners, later on reflection, decide to report their case as one of rape'. Finally, McKay reveals that some medical textbooks suggested to trainee doctors that 10 of 12 rape allegations were false and that the doctor needed to single out 'the chaste from the wanton, ... the shy and bewildered from the brazen and affectedly hurt'. It is clear from these examples alone that Irish culture was hostile to allegations of rape and attitudes that held women responsible for the actions of males. It is arguable that these values were heavily influenced by the Madonna/whore symbolism that can be seen in aspects of Catholicism, although this dichotomy of women is not unique.

THINK ABOUT IT!

While the values may date from the 70s and 80s, can you identify value systems and beliefs which increase the likelihood of abuse and violence, particularly towards women and children? Rape myths continue to exist; what effects do they have on potential victims and how can we combat them in society?

ETHNICITY

Ethnicity is difficult to define, particularly given its subjective nature, although consensus exists that it can encompass common ancestry and elements of culture, identity, religion, language and physical appearance. Ethnicity has been recently implicated in the Rotherham review,

> Several people interviewed expressed the general view that ethnic considerations had influenced the policy response of the Council and the Police, rather than in individual cases. One example was given by the Risky Business project Manager (1997–2012) who reported that she was told not to refer to the ethnic origins of perpetrators when carrying out training. Other staff in children's social care said that when writing reports on CSE cases, they were advised by their managers to be cautious about referring to the ethnicity of the perpetrators.
>
> (Jay, 2014, p. 92)

Fear of accusations of racism and ethnocentrism can influence social workers and others as to how they deal with individuals, groups or situations. Perhaps such fears are partially rooted in Lord Laming's report, which concluded that racism had played a part in the litany of failings that led to the death of Victoria Climbie. However, we must always be cautious in ascribing too much emphasis on ethnicity instead of challenging the mechanisms of power, control and dominance that underpins rape. With respect to the Rotherham case, Nazir Afzal, the Crown Prosecution Service's lead on child sexual abuse and violence against women and girls, has argued against the idea that religion itself, rather than male power, drives such abuse. In terms of ethnicity and religion, Afzal highlights that it is in fact British white males who make up the majority of offenders but elements in the media appear to highlight offenses committed by certain ethnic groups.

THINK ABOUT IT!

This is a good opportunity to reflect on your own attitudes towards different ethnic groups or value systems; recognising stereotypes or fears can be powerful, allowing us awareness and improving our practice. Reflect and makes notes in your journal as to how fears (of accusations of racism, for example) and different beliefs system may affect your practice and what you can do to improve this.

In the previous chapters we have seen factors involved in different aspects of development and outcomes. In the last chapter our focus was on psychosocial factors, risk and protective, involved in adversity and resilience, including how parenting capacity can affect children's outcomes. A summary of factors involved in abuse is outlined below. We have seen the multifactorial nature of abuse presented from an ecological perspective already; later an ecological analysis of the maltreatment of children with disabilities will elaborate further the mechanisms involved in neglect and abuse.

Risk and Protective Factors

A combination of individual, relational, community and societal factors contribute to the risk of child maltreatment. Though children are clearly not responsible for the harm inflicted upon them, certain individual characteristics have been found to increase their risk of being maltreated. Risk factors are contributing factors – not direct causes. While traditionally the focus has been on identifying risk factors, researchers, practitioners and policy-makers are increasingly thinking about protective factors in children and families that can reduce risks, build family capacity and foster resilience. For example, personal characteristics identified with resilience in maltreated children include a child's ability to recognise danger and adapt, distance oneself from intense feelings, create relationships that are crucial for support and project oneself into a time and place in the future in which the perpetrator is no longer present (Mrazek & Mrazek, 1987). Later in this chapter, abuse of vulnerable groups, such as those with disabilities and the elderly, will include associated factors. For now, a general summary of factors involved in abuse is outlined:

EXAMPLES OF RISK FACTORS

- disabilities or mental retardation in children that may increase caregiver burden
- social isolation of families
- parents' lack of understanding of children's needs and child development
- parents' history of domestic abuse
- poverty and other socio-economic disadvantages, such as unemployment
- family disorganisation, dissolution and violence, including intimate-partner violence
- lack of family cohesion
- substance abuse in the family
- young, single, non-biological parents

- poor parent–child relationships and negative interactions
- parental thoughts and emotions supporting maltreatment behaviours
- parental stress and distress, including depression or other mental health conditions
- community violence.

Protective factors are the opposite of risk factors and may lessen the risk of child maltreatment and exist at individual, relational, community and societal levels.

EXAMPLES OF PROTECTIVE FACTORS

- supportive family environment
- nurturing parenting skills
- stable family relationships
- household rules and monitoring of the child
- parental employment
- adequate housing
- access to health care and social services
- caring adults outside the family who can serve as role models or mentors
- communities that support parents and take responsibility for preventing abuse.

(Thomas et al., 2003)

As we saw in the previous chapter, it is important to recognise that factors, both protective and risk, are accumulative, meaning that they gather or grow by gradual increases, potentially over the life span. Some factors can be related to, or are more likely to occur in conjunction with, another; thus where you see poverty you are more likely, or less, to see the presence of other factors. This is illustrated in research as Sabates and Dex (2012, p. 4) reflect, 'In the UK, the consequences of exposure to multiple risks have been investigated for children born in 1958 and in 1970 using the British birth cohort studies. For instance, early exposure to multiple risks in childhood has cumulative effects throughout the life course, influencing both behavioural adjustment during childhood and psychosocial functioning during adulthood.'

We will see factors associated with vulnerable groups later, but first let us consider the different categories of abuse. As the chapter cannot be exhaustive, the main categories of abuse are discussed; however, it is important to remember that many forms of violence and abuse exist and do so within different contexts and groups. From grooming to trafficking, domestic violence, bullying and violence within same sex relationships.

TYPES OF ABUSE

Neglect

'Neglect is the persistent failure to meet a child's basic physical and/or psychological needs, likely to result in the serious impairment of the child's health or development. Neglect may occur during pregnancy as a result of maternal substance abuse. Once a child is born, neglect may involve a parent or carer failing to:

- provide adequate food, clothing and shelter (including exclusion from home or abandonment)
- protect a child from physical and emotional harm or danger; ensure adequate supervision (including the use of inadequate care-givers)
- ensure access to appropriate medical care or treatment.

It may also include neglect of, or unresponsiveness to, a child's basic emotional needs.' (HM Government, 2010, p. 38)

What do we mean by basic needs? While physical and emotional needs are obvious needs, so too are medical and educational ones. Horwath (2007,) offers a breakdown of 'basic needs' into specific ones:

medical neglect	nutritional neglect
emotional neglect	educational neglect
physical neglect	lack of supervision and guidance.

A lack of supervision and guidance is a particularly pertinent one if you consider the figures for children hurt or killed in an accident, both within the home (such as drowning or poisoning) and outside of the home. We will consider a case study relating to a lack of supervision in a moment. First though let us consider nutritional neglect from a more polemical angle.

THINK ABOUT IT!

We are going to address a somewhat more contentious issue in how we define neglect, that of childhood obesity. Within 'medical neglect' is the understanding that certain medical or health conditions must be monitored and controlled. My parents spent a lot of time between doctors, physiotherapists and hospitals trying to control both my, and my brother's, chronic asthma. Even with their vigilance and resources my brother spent time in hospital seriously ill. Imagine neglect of another health condition such as diabetes which can be fatal; if a parent is continually unwilling or unable to meet such a need, then does it become a child protection issue? Where children are born with health conditions it may be easier to label it neglect if medical needs are not met. However, what about cases where the neglect results in a health condition occurring that was not pre-existing? Childhood obesity as a child protection (CP) issue is polemical, and many would argue against it as a CP concern. While parental failure to provide adequate treatment for conditions such as asthma, epilepsy and diabetes is recognised as neglect, what of obesity, which has very clear associations to poorer physical, social and emotional outcomes? For it to be considered a CP concern, would the obesity need to lead to diabetes which saw the child hospitalised because the condition was not managed? Further, does neglect only occur where there is a lack or 'paucity' in meeting a need? What if the need is 'over' met? To use a different example, what of extreme 'helicopter' parenting, where the child is overly supervised and cosseted, or enmeshed parent–child relationships? Are these not stifling and damaging to the child's welfare? Yes, there is an element of playing devil's advocate here but it does go to the heart of how we define neglect and our perception of it.

A CASE STUDY OF NEGLECT – ACCIDENTAL POISONING

Lexi is 22 months old and was admitted to hospital with vomiting and general listlessness. Her mother Michelle said she had some friends over the night before and had put her daughter to bed at 9pm and later fed her at 6am. She later awoke at 1pm to find her daughter vomiting and very red in the face; the child had a glass of brown liquid beside her. Hospital tests revealed the presence of lye in the brown liquid, which had been used by some of the mother's friends to free base cocaine. Urine tests confirmed the presence of cocaine in Lexi's system. Lexi's oesophagus was badly damaged as a result of the poisoning. Michelle is adamant that she did not know that some of her friends were engaging in freebasing and that only drink was meant to be consumed.

We can see from the case study how accidents can feature within neglect due to factors including a lack of supervision, poor environment or drug paraphernalia in the home. Many cases of neglect involve on-going neglect. In Chapter 2 we discussed the impact of stress on the developing brain and how it can disrupt and alter neurological and endocrine functions, and this is echoed by the *Neglected Child Reunification Study* (as cited in Davies and Ward, 2012, p. 31), which suggests that these changes may have longer term effects which:

> '... results in increased vulnerability to a range of psychological, emotional and, probably, physical health problems throughout the life span. Both structural and functional abnormalities are found in maltreated children's brains. Changes are seen in the prefrontal cortex, corpus callosum and hippocampus – all areas concerned with emotional life and its regulation. Physical, behavioural, emotional and attachment systems are dependent on these structures functioning normally. There are therefore potentially highly damaging and long-term effects for those suffering neglect.'

Even in the resilient child who appears better able to adapt to their neglect the consequences of neglect and emotional abuse can include an inability to read and respond appropriately to everyday social situations, and they can struggle to manage emotions such as fear and anger. Encouraging studies are suggesting that early interventions that improve the child's caretaking environment can modify the maltreatment effects (ibid.) Finally, before we leave neglect it is worth noting that the neglect of adolescents has been identified as a major issue that often goes unnoticed. Historically, the focus of literature and practitioners has been on the young, and this emphasis can also be witnessed within this chapter. However, there is growing recognition that abuse can occur at any stage in the lifecycle. Davies and Ward (2012, p. 20) note, 'adolescents can be neglected by services as well as by their families. Better understanding of what constitutes adolescent neglect might lead to prompter identification and service response. It is clear that neglect is age-related, and as children grow older it is defined not only by parental behaviours but also by the way in which young people experience them.'

How to measure neglect – unanswered questions

According to UNICEF's (2014, p. 18) recent report *Hidden in Plain Sight*, examining violence towards children, neglect remains difficult to measure due to under reporting and the social taboo associated with such violence. Cross-cultural considerations, such as cultural norms, make defining and measuring neglect and violence more difficult, the report identifies the following questions as key to the contentious issue of how to measure neglect:

- What are the minimum requirements associated with caring for a child?
- What constitutes failure to provide 'adequate' food, shelter, clothing and protection?
- How can we measure whether caregivers' neglectful action or inaction is truly intentional or rather is attributable to their social or economic status, including poor education and lack of awareness of a child's needs?
- How can we quantify parental support and love towards a child?

As we have seen, a definition for neglect does exist in the UK but nonetheless the questions posed point to the contextual and subjective nature involved in defining neglect. Earlier in the book parenting practices and cultural norms were discussed; some research has suggested that practitioners react differently in how they perceive behaviour if they feel it is reflective of a cultural norm or parenting practice.

THINK ABOUT IT!

You have responded to concerns expressed by a teacher that one of her students has revealed that they are 'slapped' a lot at home for being bold. The teacher is concerned that the boy who is 11 is being physically abused. You conduct a home visit:

Scenario 1: The boy's family are originally from Nigeria and belong to an evangelical Christian church. They explain that within these beliefs it is permissible to chastise your child and to slap them as punishment; further they insist it is also acceptable within their culture. They are adamant that they love their son and are doing what is best for him by instilling respect. They wholly reject that they are in anyway abusive.

Scenario 2: The boy's family are British white, and when asked if they are slapping their son the father says it was how he was raised and it didn't do him any harm. The boy's mother admits losing her temper and hitting him as she finds him to be bold on purpose to 'wind her up'. Both parents wholly reject that they are doing anything 'wrong'.

Would your perception of what's happening differ because one family identifies their culture and religion as the reasoning for their use of slapping as chastisement? Would you be more inclined to judge the second family more critically as they do not promote such beliefs in their use of punishment? Does it make a difference that one family's intent is to instil respect, whereas the mother in the second family is venting frustration at behaviour she believes to be deliberately antagonistic and bold?

Emotional abuse

Historically, emotional, mental or psychological abuse was not recognised or given the same level of focus as sexual and physical maltreatment. Recognition of emotional abuse has grown and now a greater understanding of its effects exists. We will examine its impact on attachment, specifically disorganised attachment pattern and its implications for social work.

Emotional abuse, sometimes known as psychological abuse, is on-going neglect of a child's emotional needs and can include humiliation, ridicule, criticism and punishments for minor misdemeanours.

ATTACHMENT AS A TOOL TO ASSESS CHILD ABUSE

The theory of attachment, including the effects of disorganised attachment (DA), has been outlined and discussed in Chapters 4 and 5. Emotional abuse directly impacts on attachment and its formation. The following piece discusses the use of disorganised attachment as a tool for social workers to assess child maltreatment due to the indicative link between the two. Wilkins (2012, p. 15) argues that social workers '... have at their disposal a powerful tool for discriminating between children who may 'only' be at risk of poor outcomes and those at risk of genuinely significant harm'. More significantly, 'The advantage that the identification of disorganised attachment offers over the identification of various caregiver characteristics (such as drug or alcohol dependency, mental health difficulties or domestic abuse – the 'toxic trio') is that the latter are only associated with child maltreatment, whereas disorganised attachment is not just associated with child maltreatment but is indicative of it.' Wilkins (p. 18) further elaborates that: 'The overlap between maltreatment and DA is so significant that together with certain other 'caregiver characteristics' – namely, unresolved loss, disconnected/ extremely insensitive or dissociative caregiving and low reflective function – DA is the most reliable indicator of child maltreatment currently available.'

Before going further it must be made clear that Wilkins is not advocating for the use of DA as a sole tool in determining if maltreatment exists, but for its use as a powerful one to be used in conjunction with others. As you will recall from Chapter 4, disorganised attachment as a classification was added later for children who did not fit the existing attachment classifications. The assessment of DA was developed by Main and Hesse and is best conceptualised, '... as a (sometimes momentary) breakdown of a child's organised attachment pattern. This breakdown indicates that the child lacks a coherent pattern of coping behaviour – in effect, the child is attempting to resolve a paradox by engaging two opposing behavioural systems at the same time – the attachment system, with the goal of bringing the child closer to their attachment figure and a "flight or fight" system, with the goal of protecting the child by moving away from the source of danger. For children with DA, they cannot resolve this conflict as it is the carer who is both their attachment figure and the source of their fear. In Main's evocative phrase, these children are experiencing "fear without solution". Infants display this conflict through their behaviour – they may approach the carer whilst turning their head away, they may freeze or move in slow motion. Older children can be prompted to display elements of disorganisation by asking them to contemplate attachment-related scenarios (e.g. via the Child Attachment Interview).'

CHILD ATTACHMENT INTERVIEW

The attachment interview Wilkins refers to was developed by Target and colleagues (2003, p. 174) and is suitable for children between 8 and13 years of age. It consists of 14 questions and accompanying probes, the questions are as follows:

1. Who is in your family? (lives with you in your house)
2. Tell me three words that describe yourself (examples)
3. Can you tell me three words that describe what it's like to be with your mum (examples)?
4. What happens when your mum gets upset with you?
5. Can you tell me three words that describe what it's like to be with your dad (examples)?
6. What happens when your dad gets upset with you?
7. Can you tell me about a time when you were upset and wanted help?
8. What happens when you're ill?
9. What happens when you hurt yourself?
10. Has anyone close to you ever died?
11. Is there anyone that you cared about who isn't around anymore?
12. Have you ever been away from your parents for the night or for longer than a day?
13. Do your parents sometimes argue? Can you tell me about a time when that happened?
14. In what ways do you want/not want to be like your mum/dad?

When assessing DA, prevalence rates were found to be higher in children with carers suffering from depression, alcohol dependency and mental health issues, yet Wilkins (2003, p. 17) relays that '... by far the highest prevalence is found in samples of maltreated children with figures of upwards of 80 percent being typical'. Thus lies the rationale for using DA as a tool in assessing child maltreatment; the existence of DA in and of itself points to the existence of abuse. Of course, it must be re-iterated that the existence of DA does not *prove* maltreatment, merely it is a strong indicator of it. Equally, Wilkins (2003, p. 26) cautions; 'social workers should not discount the possibility of maltreatment simply because they have not assessed the child as presenting with disorganised attachment. Munro's arguments (quoted in Wilkins) about the risks of "confirmation bias" in social work assessments also need to be borne in mind. If social workers begin their assessments with a fixed view of a family and seek only to use the theory and practice of disorganised attachment to confirm this view, then their assessment is likely to prove inaccurate.' Finally, even without the existence of maltreatment a child with DA and their parent(s) still need help and support, as attachment is fundamental to the well-being and outcomes of a child. For those interested in the use of DA in child protection work, 'the Assessment of Disorganised Attachment and Maltreatment (ADAM) Project', devised by David Shemmings, has been rolled out to 23 child protection organisations across the UK and Europe.

Physical abuse

Physical abuse, referring to deliberately inflicted injury, can occur in families and can be accompanied by other forms of abuse, such as sexual abuse and emotional abuse. It has been suggested that where physical abuse exists you are more likely to see neglect also. Physical abuse includes hitting, shaking, throwing, poisoning, burning or scalding, drowning, suffocating, or otherwise causing physical harm to a child.

According to NSPCC (2012), of the children physically abused in the UK every year around:

- 379,000 are injured
- 70,000 require medical attention
- 2800 attend an Accident and Emergency department (A&E).

They continue that 7 percent of children in the UK experience serious physical abuse, while 21 percent suffer serious or intermediate physical abuse by the age of 18. Further, the leading cause of death in toddlers and babies is non-accidental violence. As we have seen with neglect and other forms of abuse, high risk factors include alcohol or drug dependency, mental health difficulties and violence. Recent case reviews in England, Wales and Scotland (ibid.) '... show irrefutably that ... physical abuse is concentrated within those families where there are multiple high risk factors'. The NSPCC argues that these findings demonstrate the need to 'break the cycle of abuse' and propose the following approach to that end.

BREAKING THE CYCLE OF ABUSE

There is a clear cycle in maltreatment. Each life stage has moments where effective interventions can take place, but also where things can be made worse. Risk-taking behaviour as a result of early abuse, such as drug taking, can then impact on parenting behaviour and the social environment, which can then lead to further abuse. The cycle is not inevitable. There are many opportunities to break it by reducing risk factors and increasing protective factors ... Features of programmes that have been shown to be effective in minimising the danger to children living in high-risk families include:

Bolstering protective factors

Strong family relationships and a positive social environment can make a real difference to the long-term outcomes for a child who has been physically abused. Work to strengthen families, to encourage clear boundaries with positive, non-physical discipline techniques, promoting mutual support between peers experiencing similar issues, and avoidance of peers involved in antisocial behaviour, criminal or substance-abusing behaviour, can be powerfully protective – even in the face of other adversities.

Strengthening families

Relationships between children and their non-abusive parents can often suffer because of the violence within the family. Encouraging a warm and supportive relationship with the non-abusive parent or carer can make a world of difference in promoting strong attachments, repairing bruised relationships and restoring a child's self-esteem and emotional well-being.

Addressing mental health issues

Focusing on the mental health of every family member has been shown to prevent recurrence of abuse and ensure better outcomes for the child.

Thinking 'family'

When addressing problems such as mental illness, substance misuse and domestic abuse, adult services need to support their clients as parents and provide children with the help they need. Men can have a profound impact on families and need to be central in strategies for intervention. Professionals must consider and engage the key men in a child's life, to assess the risks they pose and the strengths they bring to family life.

Early intervention

> Offering preventative home visiting services to families at risk at the earliest stage – during the antenatal period – is critical to stopping abuse, helping children recover and protecting society from the long-term costly consequences of violence in families. To ensure high-risk families get the support they need, these practices need to be embedded across public services and policy.
>
> (NSPCC, 2012, pp. 8–9)

THINK ABOUT IT!

Using the NSPCC framework, how would you incorporate or implement some of their approaches aimed at reducing the risk of physical abuse within families? Family is clearly identified as of significant importance in reducing the risks of abuse; identify what protective factors you believe most pertinent to strengthening and supporting families, justify you choices and make suggestions as to how to implement them.

On a sombre note, a recent report on cultural and geographical differences in the occurrence of child physical abuse revealed, 'We conclude that child physical abuse is a widespread, global phenomenon affecting the lives of millions of children all over the world, which is in sharp contrast with the United Nation's Convention on the Rights of the Child' (Stoltenborgh et al., 2013, p. 81). This belief is supported with the recent UNICEF (2014) global report *Hidden in Plain Sight*, which reports that six in ten children between the ages of two and 14 experience frequent violence.

Sexual abuse

The same report concluded that approximately 120 million girls under the age of 20 either have been raped or experience some form of sexual assault. It is notoriously difficult to gauge the prevalence of sexual assault and rape as many are not reported for many years after, or not all. Another difficulty can lie in retrospective reporting, where survivors may choose not to discuss their experiences or where the passage of time can affect the recollection of their experience. Sexual abuse covers a wide breadth from touching to penetration, can occur within the family home or at the hands of a stranger and can affect all groups in society, although some are more vulnerable to sexual abuse, such as children, those with mental health difficulties and those with learning disabilities.

Child sexual abuse, according to *Working together to safeguard children* (2010), 'involves forcing or enticing a child or young person to take part in sexual activities, not necessarily involving a high level of violence, whether or not the child is aware of what is happening. The activities may involve physical contact including assault by penetration (for example, rape or oral sex) or non-penetrative acts such as masturbation, kissing, rubbing and touching outside of clothing. They may also include non-contact activities such as children looking at, or in the production of, sexual images, watching sexual activities, encouraging children to behave in sexually inappropriate ways, or grooming a child in preparation for abuse (including via the internet). Sexual abuse is not solely perpetrated by adult males. Women can also commit acts of sexual abuse, as can other children.'

4-Stage model of sexual abuse (offending)

We have discussed the role of factors so far. Here we are going to examine a model which attempts to explain the processes that exist for a sexual offence to occur. A four-stage model of sexual abuse (offending) developed by Finkelhor (1984), which attempts to bridge both sociological and psychological perspectives. The model outlines four stages or pre-conditions of abuse that are passed through in order for the sexual offence to occur.

The Four Pre-Conditions of Abuse

1. Motivation to abuse sexually
2. Overcoming Internal Inhibitions or 'Giving Permission'
3. Overcoming External Inhibitions or 'Creating the Opportunity'
4. Overcoming the Victim's Resistance.

Brown (2011, p. 15) elaborates on each of the stages highlighting the many aspects in operation as a person decides to abuse.

Motivation to abuse sexually

In order for any sexual offence to occur the offender must be motivated to carry out such an act. The motivation is seen as arising from a number of sources, which vary according to the individual's experiences and situation.

Overcoming internal inhibitions

As is evident from studies, there are a number of individuals who find the prospect of sexual activity with children arousing but who do not offend because their own inhibitions prevent them from doing so. The vast majority of sex offenders know that their behaviour is illegal, and hence regarded as wrong, and in order to offend have had to overcome any such inhibitions. They may do this in a number of ways, such as developing distorted cognitions to justify and excuse their behaviour. They may also use alcohol or drugs as disinhibitors and then use cognitive distortions to blame the substances for the offending rather than seeing it as a way of allowing themselves to behave in a way that they already want to. Others may lack these inhibitions altogether.

Overcoming external inhibitions

Once any internal inhibitions against carrying out the offence are overcome, an individual must then establish a situation in which the abuse can occur and overcome any external obstacles that may arise. The grooming process (preparation of the victim and the environment) is part of this stage.

Overcoming the resistance of the child

The final precondition focuses on the methods the offender employs to overcome any resistance by the victim. Grooming of the victim may include developing a friendship with the child, using bribes, affection and gifts, or involve threats or even physical force. Some offenders may target children who are perceived as being vulnerable in some way.

Finkelhor's model is popular as it attempts to describe the stages passed through in order for a sexual assault to occur. It melds sociological and psychological perspectives and is multi-causal and comprehensive. However, its weakness is that it is descriptive; it has not been tested empirically either in terms of its application to treatment or prevention. Nonetheless, it offers an interesting insight into the possible mechanisms at play in the process of offending.

As we saw, some groups are more vulnerable to being abused, such as children, those with mental health issues, those with disabilities and the elderly. We are going to look at two of these groups, those with disabilities and the elderly. An ecological analysis of the maltreatment of children with disabilities will offer another opportunity to examine the multiplicity of factors involved.

AT-RISK GROUPS

Abuse of people with disabilities

People with disabilities may have a higher vulnerability to abuse due to social circumstances linked to their impairment. For example, children or adults with disabilities may be exposed to higher risks within services where there are not appropriate safeguards in place. They may be more isolated from friends and family, which renders them more vulnerable to abuse. People with disabilities may feel disempowered from making complaints, may find it more difficult to communicate, or to be taken seriously if they do complain. So they may be easier for abusers to victimise. Vulnerable groups are those with extensive or complex health care needs; those who cannot advocate for themselves; those with impairments which are expressed through challenging behaviour or other stigmatising conditions; those who are involved in the criminal justice system; those placed in institutions; and those from disadvantaged communities.

FACTORS THAT INCREASE VULNERABILITY TO ABUSE

- There is a lack of awareness among carers, professional and the general public of the vulnerability of disabled children and the indicators of abuse
- People hold beliefs that disabled children are not abused or beliefs that minimise the impact of abuse. These can lead to the denial of, or failure to report, abuse
- Lack of appropriate or poorly coordinated support services can leave disabled children and their families unsupported and physically and socially isolated. Isolation is widely considered to be a risk factor for abuse
- There is a lack of comprehensive and multi-agency assessment and planning in relation to indication of need at an early stage. This leads to both a failure to promote the child's welfare and a failure to identify early indications of possible abuse
- Assumptions are sometimes made about those with disabilities, for example, their mood, injury or behaviour. This can result in indicators of possible abuse being mistakenly attributed to the individual's impairment
- Dependency on an abusing carer can create difficulties in avoiding or communicating about abuse, especially if this is a key person through whom the individual communicates.

(Daniel et al., 2010, p. 83)

As we can see the factors identified increase the risk of abuse and range from the immediate environment, such as dependency on caregivers, to more distal ones, such as poorly coordinated support services. In terms of accessing supports, people with disabilities face particular barriers in doing so;

BARRIERS TO ACCESSING SUPPORTS

The significant barriers to people with disabilities accessing support and redress include:

- Being unable to name and identify abuse due to a lack of experience, awareness and knowledge
- Past experience of care or medical practices that undermined or transgressed personal boundaries and bodily integrity
- Disempowerment and low self-esteem
- Isolation (including physical, communication, social)
- Having one's credibility questioned particularly persons with intellectual and mental health disabilities
- The capacity of staff with whom they are in contact to detect and respond to abuse

- The capacity of the justice system and other redress mechanisms to provides an accessible system to deal with complaints from people with disabilities
- The absence of a system of independent advocacy, particularly in closed environments
- Negative attitudes
- Failure of staff to identify where abuse is occurring within intimate relationships
- Fear of consequences of disclosure, including retaliation, rejection or being moved from home to service environment. These fears are likely to be particularly significant if the person is reliant on the abuser for the activities of daily living.

In order to better understand the complexity involved in the maltreatment of individuals with disabilities we are going to examine research which used Bronfenbrenner's ecological approach to analyse the abuse of children with disabilities from the microsystem through to macro-level influences. As you will recall from Chapter 4, Bronfenbrenner's ecological model offers a comprehensive framework situating immediate influences such as socio-demographic characteristics (age, gender) to macro-level (cultural norms) within systems interacting with one another, influencing the likelihood or not of, in this case, abuse.

In focus: an ecological analysis of mistreatment of children with disabilities

Algood et al. (2013, p. 1143) note 'The individual child is an inseparable part of a social network, which is composed of the micro-, meso-, exo-, and macrosystem. The theory emphasizes the importance of considering cultural, political, economic, and demographic factors in shaping the family dynamics.' In their study Algood et al., use Bronfenbrenner's model to offer insight into the systems at play; let's take a look.

SOCIO-DEMOGRAPHIC CHARACTERISTICS

Age

As mentioned earlier, a child's age is a factor in abuse with younger children particularly vulnerable; further, where abuse is at the hands of a family member it is likely to continue into childhood. Similar results have been found where maltreated children with behavioural problems abused before the age of three are ten times more likely to suffer ongoing episodes of maltreatment.

Gender

Findings tend to show girls at greater risk of sexual abuse and boys of physical abuse. This pattern is not reflected in studies of children with disabilities, where boys are more likely to be abused than girls. Boys are 'significantly more likely to be sexually abused than girls' (ibid), although the authors acknowledge that disabled boys constitute a larger proportion in the general population. Explanations suggested include parents may be more likely to respond negatively to a son than a daughter and that boys with disabilities might be more disruptive.

MICROSYSTEM

At its simplest, this system can be thought of as the child's interpersonal relationship with others in the direct setting where the child is embedded. As this is usually the home, Algood et al. contend that this system is particularly relevant to the abuse of children with disabilities, which can occur at home or within the parent–child relationship.

Parent–child relationship

As we discussed in Chapters 2 and 6, caring for a child with disabilities can place pressure on families, particularly if the child is unwell or has challenging behaviours. The authors confirm this, commenting that children with disabilities require extra care and supervision and are likely to exhibit behaviour problems. Their behaviour problem can negatively affect their bonding with their parents and increase the likelihood of maltreatment in the home.

Domestic violence

While research has consistently supported an overlap between domestic violence and child maltreatment, Algood et al. report that few studies have examined this relationship if the child has a disability. 'Nevertheless, one study reported that domestic violence co-occurs with physical abuse among children with disabilities ... from a sample of 4503 abused children that there were records of domestic violence within the families of 17 percent of children with disabilities and 16 percent of children without disabilities. Although the study reported no significant differences in the rate of domestic violence between disabled and non-disabled children, the 17 percent rate is almost three times higher than the base rate of 6 percent co-occurrence in other community samples.'

MICROSYSTEM – PRACTICE AND POLICY IMPLICATIONS

So what can we learn from these findings? Algood et al. suggest a thorough assessment be made of the child, including the parent–child relationship and a family history, to ascertain any history of violence. The authors deem this important given the heightened level of risk of abuse that exists for children with disabilities. Further, the development of skills in communicating with non-verbal clients is advocated when interviewing; the authors note that knowledge of disabilities and its effects on family dynamics are essential for practitioners.

EXOSYSTEM

According to Algood et al. (2013), 'Bronfenbrenner asserts that exosystems are both formal and informal, such as parents' employment, social network, neighborhood characteristics, relations between school and community. Relevant exosystem level factors are parenting stress, parents' social network, and area of residence.'

Parenting stress

Parents caring for children with disabilities may experience high levels of stress, and this increases the likelihood of maltreatment. In terms of bi-directionality, studies have found that parents of children with disabilities are more vulnerable to economic stress. Within this example we can see how having a disabled child can create economic hardship, which creates further stress.

Parents' social support

The quality of parents' social support network can affect the quality of the parent–child relationship. Having a good social support network has been identified as a protective factor, especially in stressful situations. Parents in lower income families tend to have fewer social contacts and when stressed are less likely to receive social support; this increases the risk of them becoming overwhelmed and possibly abusing.

EXOSYSTEM – PRACTICE AND POLICY IMPLICATIONS

At the exosystem level, there is a need for practitioners to address the issue of stress experienced by parents, their lack of social support and the impact of the area of residence on children and family. The important role of parents in the life of children with disability is a major consideration. As studies have shown, with added financial, physical and emotional demands, parents raising a child with a disability experience increased levels of stress. Interventions need to address the interaction between the child and the parent to ascertain the risk factors which exacerbate parenting stress: respite and community outreach programmes to support parents.

MACROSYSTEM

This system represents the culture, sub culture and its values, beliefs and ideology. Within this broader understanding, influences such as role expectations can impact parental behaviour and developmental outcomes. 'It is critical to examine roles and expectations of parents and children, cultural values that influence parental perceptions of the meaning and cause of a disabilities, and societal responses to persons with disabilities.' This understanding can support practitioner's awareness of factors, risk and protective, for abuse and neglect relevant to racial and ethnic minorities and their families.

MACROSYSTEM – PRACTICE AND POLICY IMPLICATIONS

'At the macrosystem level there is a need for policy-makers to consider culture both as a potential risk or protective factor for potential abuse of children with disabilities ... before policies, programs and intervention are implemented, researchers and policy makers must have a sense of how parents raise and discipline their children, their thoughts on the etiology of illnesses and disabilities, their view on the meaning of disability from a cultural perspective and the different treatment modalities based on culture. For example, the researchers pointed out that policy-makers should recognize the importance that diverse families place on their extended family and other supports to assist in relieving stress and in abuse prevention.' (Algood et al., 2013)

THINK ABOUT IT!

We have seen an ecological perspective applied to the maltreatment of children with disabilities. Consider other groups who are vulnerable to abuse and apply Bronfenbrenner's ecological framework. For example, another vulnerable group for abuse are those with mental health disorders. Using Chapter 7 on mental health and the factors identified, apply your knowledge to the framework to build a more comprehensive picture of the many systems of influence involved.

Elder abuse

Growing awareness of the prevalence and occurrence of elder abuse has led to increased activity in terms of research and policy in this area. This form of abuse is complex and involves issues such as the social construction of old age as a 'problem', the increasing demographic of an ageing population and the policy implications that come with this. It reflects also the changing family patterns that are now seen. In the past, people would have cared for older members of their families; however, with the splintering of families, dislocation and so on, increasingly the care of the elderly is entrusted to the State. It is suggested that generally the abuse is not intentional but is a reflection of carer stress or ignorance, highlighting the important role that agencies can play in supporting carers. Relationships of dependency can increase vulnerability to abuse and neglect. This can be found in familial situations but also in institutional contexts such as nursing homes. Prevalence can be difficult to gauge as older people can feel a sense of shame or unwillingness to reveal that they are being abused. First, how is elder abuse defined?

> a single or repeated act or lack of appropriate action occurring within any relationship where there is an expectation of trust which causes harm or distress to an older person or violates their human and civil rights.

Abuse may be categorised under physical abuse, sexual abuse, financial/material abuse, neglect (by omission or commission) and discriminatory abuse. Elder abuse and neglect are being increasingly identified as international social problems in a growing older population. International studies estimate the prevalence of abuse in the community at between 1 and 5 percent of the population aged 65 years and older; however, these figures are regarded as an underestimate.

RISK FACTORS ASSOCIATED WITH ELDER ABUSE

Daichman (2005, p. 326) relates risk factors identified by the World Health Organization through elders' focus groups:

- being old
- being ill
- living alone
- isolation

- family history of mistreatment
- lack of a social network
- lack of information about available resources
- poor contact with peers
- inter-generational conflict.

What is significant from these findings is the social element, be it isolation or dependency on others; a familial history of mistreatment is also common, which highlights the complexity and inter-generational nature of abuse and violence within families.

PATTERNS AND CONTEXTS OF ELDER ABUSE

Patterns of abuse and abusing vary and reflect different circumstances:

- long-term abuse, in the context of an ongoing family relationship, such as domestic violence or sexual abuse between spouses or generations
- opportunistic abuse, such as theft, occurring
- situational abuse, which arises because pressures have built up and/or because of the difficult or challenging behaviour of the older person
- neglect of a person's needs because those around him or her are not able to be responsible for their care; for example, if the carer has difficulties because of debt, alcohol or mental health problems
- institutional abuse, which may result due to poor care standards, lack of positive responses to complex needs, rigid routines, inadequate staffing and an insufficient knowledge base within the service
- unacceptable 'treatments' or 'programmes', which include sanctions or punishment such as withholding of food and drink, seclusion, the unnecessary and unauthorised use of control and restraint or the over- or under-use of medication
- racist and discriminatory practice by staff, including ageism, racism and other discriminatory practices, which may be attributable to a lack of appropriate guidance
- inability to get access to key services such as health care, dentistry and so on
- misappropriation of benefits and/or the use of the person's money by other members of the household or by care staff
- fraud or intimidation in connection with wills, property or other assets.

National elder abuse incidence study

The National Elder Abuse Incidence Study, whose aim was to establish the numbers of older people suffering abuse or neglect, was a landmark American study.

The following is a summary of their findings:

- An incidence rate of 1.6 percent was found.
- Family members were the most common perpetrators of elder abuse.
- The incidence of abuse and/or neglect increased with increasing age and was more common in women and in elders who were unable to care for themselves.

- The findings of the study supported the validity of the iceberg theory of elder abuse, which argues that the identified cases represent only a partial and incomplete picture of prevalence or incidence of elder abuse; while the most visible types of abuse and neglect may be reported, a large number of incidents go unidentified and unreported.
- The study identified social isolation as a factor which may both hinder the detection and increase the risk of abuse and neglect.
- Educating health professionals and caregivers in how to recognise and report the signs and symptoms of elder abuse and neglect was identified by the report as paramount.

WHAT ARE THE EFFECTS OF ELDER ABUSE?

Daichman (2005, p. 327) refers to seminal research, which examined the effects of elder abuse on health: 'when they compared mortality rates of the non-abused and the abused, they found that, by the thirteenth year following the study's initiation, 40 percent of the non-reported (i.e. non-abused, non-neglected) group were still alive and only 9 percent of the physically abused or neglected elders. After controlling for all the possible factors that might affect mortality (e.g. age, gender, income, functional status, cognitive status, diagnosis, social supports, etc.) and finding no significant relationships, the researchers speculated that mistreatment causes extreme interpersonal stress that may confer an additional death risk'. These findings reflect the consequences of abuse, which is not just psychological, as is often thought, but also has physical implications, such as stress and distress. Elder abuse is now recognised to be more widespread than previously thought.

We leave our discussion of abuse, its factors and characteristics to examine another aspect – that of the experiences of those victimised by abuse. Here we will take a more intimate look at theories and research within psychology that attempts to shed light on the experiences of survivors, we will explore the search for meaning that can accompany trauma and abuse. First though we will overview post-traumatic stress disorder, which acknowledges the impact of experiencing or witnessing life-threatening experiences.

TRAUMA

As well as the aetiology (causes) and factors associated with abuse, it is important to consider the effects that abuse can have upon an individual. One such effect is post-traumatic stress disorder (PTSD). The history of PTSD is interesting. It was first seen as a syndrome in American soldiers returning from the Vietnam War. Initially there was scepticism regarding the existence of a cluster of behaviours which were triggered by a traumatic event. There was also reluctance on the part of the American administration to recognise that these soldiers had suffered psychological anguish through participation in the war. Now, of course, it is a recognised syndrome. The range of traumas that can trigger it has been widened to include not just war, but also rape, and any event where an individual's ability to recover is affected. Of course, it is important to realise that we all experience events that are upsetting and to be saddened by them is quite normal. PTSD is different in that the person continues to be affected by it for a length of time.

Post-traumatic stress disorder

PTSD is a psychiatric disorder that can occur in people who have experienced or witnessed life-threatening events, such as natural disasters, serious accidents, terrorist incidents, war or violent personal assaults, such as rape. People who suffer from PTSD often relive the experience as flashbacks or nightmares, have difficulty sleeping and feel detached or estranged. The history of PSTD is an interesting insight into how we categorise mental health. The disorder is a relatively recent addition to the Diagnostic and Statistical Manual (DSM), following the development of psychiatric difficulties in Vietnam veterans.

Four major symptoms commonly occur in this anxiety disorder:

- The person experiences severe symptoms of anxiety, arousal and distress that were not present before the trauma.
- The person relives the trauma recurrently in flashbacks, dreams and fantasy.
- This happens when sudden, vivid memories, accompanied by painful emotions, take over the person's attention. Flashbacks may be so strong that individuals feel as though they are actually reliving the traumatic experience or seeing it unfold before their eyes or in nightmares.
- The person becomes numb to the world and avoids stimuli that remind them of the trauma.
- After events where others have been killed, the person may experience extreme guilt about surviving the catastrophe when others did not.

PTSD usually appears within three months of the trauma, but sometimes later. Some will try to self-medicate with alcohol or drugs to dull or ease the pain and trauma.

TREATMENT

Cognitive behaviour therapy focuses on correcting the painful and intrusive patterns of behaviour and thought, by teaching people with PTSD relaxation techniques and examining (and challenging) the mental processes that are causing the difficulty. Psychodynamic psychotherapy focuses on helping the individual examine personal values and how behaviour and experience during the traumatic event affected them. Exposure therapy uses careful, repeated, detailed imagining of the trauma (exposure) or progressive exposures to symptom 'triggers' in a safe, controlled context to help the survivor face and gain control of the fear and distress that was overwhelming during the trauma. In some cases, trauma memories can be confronted all at once (flooding).

For others, it is preferable to work up to the most severe trauma gradually or by taking the trauma one piece at a time (desensitisation).

In focus: Trauma and the search for meaning

The aim of this section is to illustrate the many aspects that may be considered in how a person makes sense or 'meaning' from the trauma they have suffered. Hopefully, this will enable you to gain an appreciation of the mechanisms that create meaning; the meaning an individual who has suffered a trauma possibly creates; and finally perhaps to reflect and challenge any assumptions you may hold.

DEFINITION OF SCHEMA

Fiske and Taylor (1984) define a schema as a 'cognitive structure that represents organized knowledge about a given concept or type of stimulus' (p. 140).

- Fiske and Taylor further maintain that schemas tend to be resistant to change and people are more likely to modify incoming information to fit the existing schema rather than modify the schema in response to new and challenging information. Compared to Piaget's type of schema (see Chapter 4), the schemas referred to here are of a higher order and form the essence of how we view ourselves, others and the world around us.
- Janoff-Bulman (1992, p. 5) refers to these schemas as 'global' theories or assumptions that people hold about themselves and their world. These schemas, or conceptual systems, guide and inform our actions and perceptions. Further, we operate on the basis of 'these assumptions without even being aware or conscious of them' (Janoff-Bulman & Frantz, 1997, p. 97).

When incoming information so greatly challenges an individual's existing conceptual system or 'assumptive world' that it cannot be 'assimilated' or 'accommodated', the potential for trauma exists, as this information continues to be stored in active consciousness. Janoff-Bulman eloquently explains how this occurs:

> Traumatic life events force survivors to confront questions of meaning in their lives. These questions are posed with an intensity and immediacy that reflect the overwhelming power of meaning-related concerns in the aftermath of extreme negative events. Survivors are struck by the extent to which meaning, in its many guises, had typically been assumed and taken for granted in their lives. Now their traumatic experience compels them to re-examine these earlier, easy assumptions. (p. 12)

MEANING DEFINED

Meaning can be broadly defined in various ways to include purpose, intent, order, interpretation and significance. Within the fundamental assumptions framework are three core assumptions:

- the world is benevolent
- the world is meaningful
- the self has worth.

WHAT HAPPENS WHEN TRAUMA OCCURS?

Victims of trauma are plagued by a double dose of fear and anxiety as both their internal and external worlds are assaulted. Internally, they experience the disintegration of basic assumptions, which had provided psychological stability and coherence in a complex world. The survivor's inner world is now a state of dramatic upheaval, and is no longer able to provide a trustworthy road map for negotiating daily life.

As a result, the external world is now perceived as frightening. Survivors realise all too vividly the possibility of their own annihilation. They can no longer assume that their own self-worth and precautionary behaviours will protect them, for randomness and arbitrariness now characterise the workings of the universe. Old certainties and securities are gone. They are intensely aware that bad things can happen to them. The world no longer makes sense, and this realisation is devastating. As Ernest Becker writes in *The Denial of Death* (p. 63), it is terrifying 'to see the world as it really is. ... It makes routine, automatic, secure, self-confident activity impossible. ... It places a trembling animal at the mercy of the entire cosmos and the problem of the meaning of it'.

The self is good – belief in a just world

One of the three core assumptions outlined by Janoff-Bulman is that the self is good. When a traumatic event occurs, this can prompt an individual to question this: 'If I was a good person surely this would not have happened to me?' Further, others may reinforce this view, thus increasing the distress of the victim.

The expression 'Belief in a Just World' (BJW) was coined by Lerner in 1965, and refers to the belief that good things happen to good people and conversely bad things happen to bad people; that is, you get what you deserve. Lerner and Miller captured the essence of the 'Belief in a Just World' theory as follows:

> Individuals have a need to believe that they live in a world where people generally get what they deserve. The belief that the world is just enables the individual to confront his physical and social environment as though they are stable and orderly. Without such a belief it would be difficult for the individual to commit himself to the pursuit of long-range goals or even to the socially regulated behaviour of day to day life. Since the belief that the world is just serves such an important adaptive function for the individual, people are very reluctant to give up this belief, and they can be greatly troubled if they encounter evidence that suggests that the world is not really just or orderly after all (pp. 1030–31, in Furnham, 2003, p. 796).

It has been found that BJW is cross-culturally generalisable and stable across the life span. Belief in a Just World is seen as a bedrock in many religions, thus the cultural values of a society impact both on the victim and those around them. If a society has a high BJW, this can increase the distress of trauma victims, as their fundamental assumptions are even more greatly challenged; and the negative reaction of others towards the victim increases, again further increasing the victim's suffering.

'Creeping determinism', also known as '**hindsight bias**', is a phenomenon identified by psychologist Baruch Fischhoff, where once people know the outcome of events they overestimate the likelihood of that outcome. Victimisation demonstrates that, contrary to 'Belief in a Just World', bad things do happen to people who don't 'deserve' them; therefore, by default, 'it could happen to us, too'. So we search for any reasoning that explains why a traumatic event happens and in blaming the victims we can rest easily in our just, benevolent world.

Within a cultural context Wasco claims that these assumptions are not necessarily transferable to ethnic minorities and other marginalised groups. Wasco (2003) claims that 'these theories operate on the assumption that all non-traumatised people believe that the world is basically a safe, just, and predictable place and that trauma disrupts victims' assumptions about themselves, others, and the world' (p. 313). Wasco includes working-class people, immigrant and refugee peoples, women and children exposed to violence and abuse as individuals who never had an opportunity to establish Janoff-Bulman's three core assumptions.

PATHOLOGY OF THE SELF

Pathology of the self is considered by many trauma experts to be the central negative reaction in trauma victims (Aarts and Op Den Velde, 1996, p. 371). Pathology of the self refers to a shattering of the self in trauma victims. When shattering occurs it can form a split into so-called 'good' and 'bad' self-representations. Focus of treatment is towards the reintegration of the self and a restoration of the sense of self in trauma survivors.

POST-TRAUMATIC THERAPY – THE SEARCH FOR MEANING

Ochberg (1995) refers to the search for meaning in relation to post-traumatic therapy. The principles underpinning this therapy include the view that 'every individual has a unique pathway to recovery after traumatic stress' (p. 246). This principle highlights the interesting and relatively unique position held by PTSD within psychopathology, where the symptomology is the main focus of investigation and treatment. Ochberg (p. 261) describes the 'individualised search for meaning' in the wake of shattered assumptions and offers Viktor Frankl, a famous Viennese psychiatrist, as an example of such an individual. Janoff-Bulman and Frantz (1997), when discussing survivors of trauma, recognise the role of 'secondary control' over future victimisation; that is, the idea that they can cope with whatever comes their way. Secondary control can be framed another way as a belief in one's own personal strength, and this can help alleviate the apparent meaninglessness of the world following the shattering of an individual's 'assumptive world'. Also, with the increased sense of vulnerability and senselessness can spring forth a heightened appreciation of life and meaning in even the most banal and mundane experiences, and especially with respect to family and friends.

SUMMARY

So we end this chapter exploring the effect of trauma on survivors by looking at how, on an intrapersonal level, trauma and abuse may lead to a questioning of meaning, be it of self or the world in general. We have seen how certain groups are especially vulnerable to being mistreated and the associated factors. As in other chapters, defining abuse is complex and challenges particularly social workers, where safeguarding others is a core element of their work. Finally we've seen how the ecological approach offers a framework within which the many layers of influences from immediate to more distal can be understood.

chapter

10 SOCIAL PSYCHOLOGY - B=F(P,E)

CHAPTER OUTLINE

Man is biologically predestined to construct and to inhabit a world with others.

– Berger and Luckmann, *The Social Construction of Reality*, 1967

INTRODUCTION

Lewin's famous equation captures the concept that our behaviour reflects, and is a function of, environment. Sociological perspectives consider the role of society and its effects. Social psychology is often seen as a crossover between psychology and sociology, an interdisciplinary bridge between the two. The field of social psychology studies how people influence our behaviour (social influence), how we think about and perceive our social world (social thinking and social perception) and how we behave towards other people (social relations). Social psychology can help to explain why people succumb to conditions of oppression and can teach us to collaborate with others. Social Psychology thus has the potential for applications in the field of social work, where social phenomena such as prejudice and discrimination are of concern; further, it acknowledges the relationship between attitude and behaviour that is fundamental in agitating for social change and justice.

DEFINITION OF SOCIAL PSYCHOLOGY

The field of social psychology studies:

- how other people influence our behaviour (social influence),
- how we think about and perceive our social world (social thinking and social perception),
- how we behave towards other people (social relations).

In Philip Zimbardo's APA presidential address, he reflected on the capacity of social-psychological knowledge to offer a more positive contribution to social welfare and social life (Zimbardo, 2004). Pancer (1997) argues that social psychology within psychology (as opposed to sociology) has become increasingly asocial (disinterested in society or social practices), focusing specifically on mainstream social psychology in North America, which continues to dominate the field despite efforts to devise alternatives. This is in contrast to the 'reform-oriented aspirations' of social psychology's pioneers, such as Lewin, who wished to make the discipline socially useful. Pancer concludes that modern social psychology has adopted approaches that do little to advance human welfare. He claims that this is in part due to the influence of the 'cognitive revolution', which is increasingly dominant. Pancer advocates for a 'redirected, critical social psychology' which can help to elucidate why people acquiesce to conditions of oppression and teach us to collaborate with others.

Social psychology thus has the potential for applications in the field of social work if we envision Pancer's clarion call. Certainly, social phenomena, such as prejudice and discrimination, must be of concern to those interested in social justice. Later in this chapter we will consider prejudice from a social psychology perspective; this perhaps is a good time for you to reflect on what prejudices you hold and whether these belief systems affect your treatment of others in the form of discrimination.

Some figures in social psychology

Gordon Allport is recognised as one of the founders of social psychology. He wrote the seminal *Handbook of Social Psychology* (1954, p. 5) and in it defined social psychology as:

> an attempt to understand and explain how the thought, feeling, and behaviour of individuals are influenced by the actual, imagined, or implied presence of other human beings.

Kurt Lewin was an early leader of group dynamic research and is regarded by many as the founder of modern social psychology. Lewin's equation, $B = f(P,E)$, stipulates that behaviour is a function of the person and environment, and he advocated 'action research', applying this equation and scientific methods to address social problems such as prejudice and group conflict.

SOCIAL CONSTRUCTIONISM

In Chapter 1, social constructionism was outlined as an important approach embraced within psychology to make sense of our experiences and their origins. 'Embraced' is a good term to use as this perspective has its roots within a more sociological paradigm. It is evidence of the growing recognition of external forces on individual development that psychology has welcomed social constructionism within its approaches. Social constructionism considers how factors such as context, language and relationships interplay, influencing people's outlook and views of the world. If we take the word 'construct', which means to 'build', and then add 'social' to it, we begin to see that this approach suggests that we build our knowledge of the world through our interactions with others including media and language. Thus social constructionism questions 'what is mental illness?', 'what is gender?', 'what is disability?' and how do we come to our understanding of such concepts? It becomes clear that we 'build' this knowledge influenced by context, language and relationships. In Chapter 6 on disability, we discussed how language can have a stigmatising effect; here we can see social constructionism at work. Language such as 'retardation' can influence our perception of a person with a learning disability. This is just one example among many. Constructionism is of particular importance to social work as it highlights the influence of cultural and social norms on attitudes and behaviour, which in turn feed into issues of equality and diversity.

Gergen is recognised as one of the leading and most influential figures in the post-modern approach to social constructionism. According to Hruby (2001, p. 54), Gergen defines social construction using the following four themes:

1. Understanding of the world is not derived by observation but by linguistic, cultural and historical contingencies.
2. 'Understanding is not automatically driven by the forces of nature, but is the result of an active, cooperative enterprise of persons in relationship.'
3. 'The degree to which a given form of understanding prevails ... is not fundamentally dependent on the empirical validity of the perspective in question, but on the vicissitudes of social processes (e.g., communication, negotiation, conflict, rhetoric).'
4. Negotiated understandings are a form of social action and as such are integrated with all other human activities; an idea with profound implications for the analysis of the metaphors and assessments used in psychology, and more generally in social science.

Social constructionism emphasises how contextual, linguistic and relational factors combine to determine the kinds of human beings that people will become and how their views of the world will develop. Knowledge is negotiated between people within a given context and time frame. Thus all knowledge and even personhood itself is fleeting. Psychological constructs, such as personality, are viewed very differently than in the social-constructionist approach, which sees 'personality' as a socially constructed idea rather than something inherently 'intrapsychic' or within the person. Many would use the term 'identity' rather than 'self ' or 'personality', emphasising the idea that we each have multiple selves which are situated within the boundaries of culture, context and language.

Social constructionism proposes that reality is socially negotiated. This leads to questions such as 'what is mental illness?' or 'what is disability?', fundamentally every construct or concept is informed or constructed by social knowledge. If we take the example of IQ, racial differences in intelligence have been 'found'. This belief was created by others and accepted as such. Of course, the difficulty is that 'intelligence' is also a construct; what is perceived as 'intelligence' in the West would be different in another part of the world. Who decides what 'intelligence' is anyway? And yet we all are influenced by, and create, constructions in almost every facet of our lives. This also explains how we can challenge social constructions; for example, of disability. Fifty years ago the view of disability was different to the one we have now, capturing the idea that it is fleeting, culturally situated and subject to change.

THINK ABOUT IT!

How might social construction inform social work practice? One element is to start with where the client 'is'; social constructionism asks us to understand how the client views the world and their situation. Identify how you may do this and what aspects (culture, language or identity) you believe are most helpful in doing so. Another aspect is how social constructionism may inform the approaches we use to support clients; it lends itself well to solution-focused approaches and narrative therapy. Investigate these approaches and determine how they marry with the social constructionism perspective.

SYMBOLIC INTERACTIONISM

Symbolic interaction can best be understood as a framework whose general proposition holds that self reflects society and organises social behaviour. Further, society can be viewed as a web of communication or 'symbolic interaction', conducted through meanings developed in a person's interdependent activity. Society is created and recreated as individuals interact. Both society and individual derives from interaction: each presupposes the other.

Three assumptions characterise this perspective:

1. Adequate accounts of behaviour must reflect the perspectives of the 'actors' engaged in that behaviour and cannot rest on the perspective of observers alone.
2. Priority is assigned to social interaction with respect to the emergence of both social organisation and the individual: 'In the beginning there is society.' This assumption differentiates symbolic interactionism from social psychological approaches used by psychologists *giving priority to the individual*.
3. The self, people's reflexive responses to themselves, links societal processes to social interactions and behaviours.

Goffman and symbolic interactionism

We discussed symbolic interactionism (SI) in Chapter 3 and how it influences the interpersonal and communication process. Here we are going to look at it within a social psychological perspective. Slattery (2003) points to differences between symbolic interactionism (SI) and the work of Erving Goffman. Whereas SI tries to examine how people create or negotiate their self-images, Goffman focuses on how society forces people to present a certain image of themselves. As such, we are forced to switch back and forth between many complicated roles. Goffman seeks to explore and explain social action in respect of its meaning for others rather than focusing on the causal aspects. It is the relationship between social order, social interaction and the self – the interrelationship between society at large and everyday social intercourse – that is important to Goffman, whose interest lies in illustrating a more sociological account of the individual in an effort to analyse the distinction between the self as a character and the self as social actor, maintaining an image of self in various situations.

In Goffman's interpretations, the self is multifaceted, putting on whatever social mask is needed for different situations. Goffman's work on **labelling** highlighted not just the way people react to being labelled but also how the process of labelling can create 'abnormal behaviours'. His seminal work, *Asylums*, illustrates this phenomenon; in being labelled or, more negatively, stigmatised as 'insane' or 'sick', the individual's self-image began to change, leaving them feeling abnormal and reducing the likelihood of their recovery and their ability to recover. The result was that the individual adopted a new self-image and personality that kept them insulated from 'normal' society; for example, patients in mental health facilities or homeless people in a refuge. The labelling had a self-fulfilling prophecy where the stigmatised person became the image created for them by the label; thus, if labelled as deviant and antisocial, the person would eventually adopt such a persona. This finding had serious implications for those who work with patients and clients, especially in the social work arena.

Goffman's work on asylums was one of the first sociological examinations of the social situation of mental patients, the hospital world as subjectively experienced by the patient. His ideas were based on the use of the 'total institution model' and were not just confined to mental hospitals. Prisons, concentration camps, monasteries, orphanages and military organisations were also considered institutions. As Weinstein (1982, p. 268) relates; 'total institutions are places of residence and work where a large number of individuals are cut off from the wider society for a period of time. There is a fundamental split between a large managed group (inmates) and a small supervisory staff. Human needs are handled in a bureaucratic and impersonal way. The social distance between the inmates and staff is great, and each group tends to be hostile toward the other.' Weinstein relays Goffman's description of the 'inmate world' of the total institution. Upon entering the establishment, processes are set in motion to destroy the inmate's old self and create a new self. The person is dispossessed from normal social roles, stripped of their usual identities. The inmate undergoes a denial and shaming of self via physical and social abuse. Contacts with outside persons are limited and inmates cannot prevent their visitors from seeing them in humiliating circumstances.

THINK ABOUT IT!

As a practitioner, does your experience of residential unit placements resemble Goffman's description of the 'total institution'? Do any similarities exist? What steps can be taken to minimise the potential of residential care settings, such as nursing homes, coming to resemble the 'total institution' described by Goffman?

'LIKE A PRISON!'

Homeless women's narratives of surviving shelter

De Ward and Moe (2010) examine how the bureaucracy and institutionalisation within a homeless shelter fit various tenets of Goffman's (1961) 'total institution', particularly with regard to systematic deterioration of personhood and loss of autonomy. Women's experiences as shelter residents are explored via differing types of survival strategies: submission, adaptation and resistance.

Upon entering the shelter the women's familial leadership roles were usurped by staff authority. Subsequently, both mothers and their children were subjected to the rules and discipline of the shelter. Prior research on homeless women's shelter experiences confirms these elements of the total institution. For example, Stark (1994) cites the loss of respect experienced by parents from their children within shelter institutions. More specifically, Breese and Feltey (1996) found that the privacy, freedom and control women had within their homes, and lives in general, were drastically compromised upon entering a shelter. Becoming homeless and accepting space within a shelter institution were equated with forsaking the 'privileges' that housed people take for granted. So, while shelters are distinct from institutions, such as prisons and some mental health hospitals, wherein people are confined against their will and are not free to leave, there is an element of coercion within them. While women were free to leave, this 'freedom' was mitigated by the consequences of living homeless on the streets or otherwise without secure access to shelter, food and clothing. To put oneself, and in many instances one's children, in such perilous circumstances is not a realistic 'choice' per se. The safety of the shelter, regardless of its bureaucratic nature, becomes the most pragmatic and reasonable means of survival. (De Ward and Moe, 2010, pp. 121–2)

It is worrying that a place which is meant to be a refuge and offer safety can potentially disempowered and institutionalise individuals attempting to regain their freedom and autonomy.

THINK ABOUT IT!

Identify others areas or places which are potential 'total institutions' and that can strip autonomy. Prisons are an obvious example, but what about other types of 'shelters' or support centres: nursing homes or homeless shelters perhaps?

How would you address the issues raised by the women in this study such as their roles being usurped by staff? What other measures would you consider to reduce the likelihood of institutionalisation occurring?

SOCIAL COGNITION

Cognition, as we saw in Chapters 4 and 5 refers to, at its simplest, 'thinking skills'. We saw how Piaget and Vygotsky suggested children acquire cognitive capacities, the former emphasising more maturational and internal mechanisms, Vygotsky highlighting the role of social influence. Cognition includes language development, as well as reasoning, memory and problem-solving; however, we should not think of cognition as purely linked to academic pursuits such as algebra in school. How we feel, our beliefs, our sense of who we are and of others, how we make sense of the world, all have a cognitive component. The following section looks at one branch of cognitive theory, that of social cognition. Mirroring Vygotsky's assertion that social and cultural influences shape how we think, these theories further develop this idea. Their emphasis of the role of social justifies their inclusion in this chapter. Although stigma, social norms and roles have a clear 'social' component, it is important to recognise that these experiences need to be processed and thus shape our thinking. The first theory we will consider is Dodge's Social Information Processing (SIP) model.

Dodge's model of social information processing

Dodge's (1986) five-step model of social information processing, seeks to explain the cognitive mechanisms utilised in interpreting and responding to social situations. According to Crick and Dodge (1994, p. 74) 'social cognitions are the mechanisms leading to social behaviours that, in turn, are the bases of social adjustment evaluations by others'. The model describes cognitive steps thought necessary to children's appropriate and competent action in social situations, namely:

1. encoding social cues,
2. interpreting behaviour,
3. generating alternative responses,
4. choosing a response after evaluating potential consequences of alternatives, and
5. performing the chosen response.

> During Steps 1 and 2, encoding and interpretation of social cues, it is hypothesized that children focus on and encode particular cues in the situation and then, on the basis of those cues, construct an interpretation of the situation (e.g., an inference about the intent of a peer with whom the child is interacting). During Steps 3 and 4, it is proposed that children access possible responses to the situation from long-term memory, evaluate those responses, and then select the most favourable one for enactment (ibid.).

Dodge's general model of the role of cognition in social behaviour can be applied to social behaviours. Most often studied is its role in aggressive behaviour. SIP theory gives an insight into how children make decisions in social interactions; the decisions they make are influenced by their previously learning experiences, intrapsychic (within the individual) aspects, such as temperament, and the specifics of the situation. As we saw there are distinct steps within the process of social information processing, and research has suggested that the more 'steps' an individual struggles with, the more aggressively they will behave.

In terms of its relevance to social work, Crick and Dodge (1994, p. 75) suggest that as '... the model describes specific processes that can be taught to children, it has served as an important guide for those engaged in intervention with socially maladjusted children'. Another theory that attempts to integrate cognition in illuminating social processes such as behaviour, stereotypes and stigma is Developmental Intergroup Theory.

THINK ABOUT IT!

According to Dodge's model, the initial steps taken by an individual are to interpret or assess the social situation and any cues present. Let's apply this to aggressive behaviour using the following example.

> *Leon is 18 years old and grew up in a home where there was violence directed towards him, his younger sibling and his Mum by her boyfriend. In school, Leon often got into fights with other kids and his teachers reported that he was quick to temper and to escalate situations. He has recently been arrested for a serious assault, where he attacked a younger youth who he believed had 'disrespected' him.*

Using Dodge's suggestion that how we interpret or assess social cues affects our behaviour, how would you explain Leon's behaviour within this approach? Arguably, Leon is quicker to interpret social situations as threatening than others would be and thus to react aggressively. Using this model how would you apply it to other types of behaviour; for example, could children who have been sexually abused interpret social cues differently to children who have not been victims? Can this model also explain prosocial behaviour? How would that fit within the SIP model?

Of course, as you have seen, there are many explanations offered in attempting to explain the same behaviour, and we will see this again when we explore aggressive and prosocial behaviour at the end of the chapter. Nonetheless, social cognition makes intuitive sense in marrying how we think and behave. The next theory we are going to consider has its roots in intergroup theory and tackles the development of stereotypes, stigma and discrimination.

DEVELOPMENTAL INTERGROUP THEORY

Developmental Intergroup Theory (DIT) was developed (Bigler & Liben 2007) as a theoretical model examining the development of social stereotype and stigma in childhood. Stigma (O'Driscoll et al., 2012) is arguably an encompassing umbrella containing stereotypes, prejudice and discriminatory behaviour. The existence of stigma and prejudice in adults is well documented towards various groupings (e.g., race, gender and mental health) and theories have been advanced to explain such phenomena, including intergroup theory and lay theory. Increasing attention is now being turned towards the acquisition and development of stigma in children and adolescents. DIT builds on the role of intergroup relations through aligning this approach with that of cognitive-developmental theory in considering the mechanisms at play in the development of stigma across childhood.

According to DIT, four basic processes are involved in the formation and maintenance of social stereotypes and prejudice;

1. the **establishment** of the psychological salience (distinct aspects) of person attributes,
2. the **categorisation** of encountered individuals by salient dimensions,
3. the **development** of stereotypes and prejudice concerning salient social groups and
4. the **application** of a stereotype filter to encountered individuals.

DIT contends that children will apply categorisation processes in environments where social group membership is salient (noticeable), resulting in the likelihood of stereotypes and prejudices. Group size also plays a role in increasing the likelihood of stereotypes as smaller (minority) groups are more distinctive than larger groups, reflecting DIT roots in intergroup theory. According to Hilliard and Liben (2010, p. 1787) 'Developmental intergroup theory views the emergence of social stereotypes in children through constructivist lenses...thus children are thought to be active agents in processing social stimuli'.

Research has focused on the emergence of prejudice. Bigler and Liben (2007) suggest that by the age of four children already possess prejudices. Some research (Raabe & Beelman 2011) has attempted to explore the developmental progression of prejudice and found that there is a peak in prejudice between 5 and 7 years followed by a mild decrease until late childhood. They conclude this trend highlights that systemic changes occur during childhood yet none exist in adolescence, thus indicating the stronger influence of social context on prejudice with increasing age. Raabe and Beelman (2011, p. 1717) conclude that '... early childhood is a sensitive period for the formation of implicit prejudice in which children are more susceptible to contextual influences'.

THINK ABOUT IT!

If childhood is a sensitive period for the acquisition of prejudice, suggest interventions that would discourage this and promote equality and diversity. Justify your ideas.

Later in the section overviewing stigma, stereotypes and prejudice, the stigmatisation of anorexia nervosa, a mental illness with the highest mortality rate, will be discussed to illustrate the mechanisms at play within its stigmatisation. Social influence is powerful, as we will see, and involves social norms and roles, conformity and obedience, further highlighting the fundamental role of social in individual feeling, thinking and behaviour.

Social norms and roles

Social norms are the shared expectations about how people should think, feel and behave, and they are the cement that binds social systems together. Some norms are formal laws, others are unspoken. Either way, they exert a huge influence upon our daily lives.

A social role consists of a set of norms that characterise how people in a given social position ought to behave. The roles of 'police', 'doctor' and 'spouse' carry different sets of behaviour expectations.

Norms and roles can influence behaviour so strongly that they compel a person to act uncharacteristically. The 'guards' in the Stanford Prison study were well-adjusted students, yet norms related to the role of 'guard' and to concepts of crime and punishment seemed to override their values, leading to dehumanising treatment of the prisoners.

SOCIAL ROLES – STANFORD PRISON EXPERIMENT

The Stanford Prison experiment (SPE) aimed to examine social roles in order to research the power of the immediate social situation in individuals' behaviour. Philip Zimbardo designed a mock prison in the basement of Stanford University and placed an advertisement looking for volunteers to participate in his research. Twenty-four male volunteers were selected: 12 guards and 12 prisoners. These volunteers were judged to be emotionally stable and with no prior history of criminal behaviour. Zimbardo told the 'wardens' that they were allowed to run the prison as they saw fit; there was only one rule: that there was to be no physical punishment. The wardens were dressed in military-style clothing and mirrored sunglasses to limit eye contact, and were given wooden batons. Those volunteers assigned to the 'prisoner' role were told to stay at home and wait to be called. Then their homes were raided and they were arrested by real policemen (the local police force had agreed to cooperate with the research); they were finger-printed and stripped. They were then transported to the 'prison', where they were to spend the next 2 weeks during the experiment. The prisoners were dressed in smock-like clothing, given identity numbers rather than their names and were supplied with a basic mattress and plain food. As you can see, great efforts were made to make the experiment as lifelike as possible. What happened next was quite shocking, as Zimbardo and Haney (1998, p. 709) recount:

> Otherwise emotionally strong college students who were randomly assigned to be mock-prisoners suffered acute psychological trauma and breakdowns. Some of the students begged to be released from the intense pains of less than a week of merely simulated imprisonment, whereas others adapted by becoming blindly obedient to the unjust authority of the guards. The guards, too – who also had been carefully chosen on the basis of their normal- average scores on a variety of personality measures, quickly internalized their randomly assigned role. Many of these seemingly gentle and caring young men, some of whom had described themselves as pacifists or Vietnam War 'doves,' soon began mistreating their peers and were indifferent to the obvious suffering that their actions produced. Several of them devised sadistically inventive ways to harass and degrade the prisoners, and none of the less actively cruel mock-guards ever intervened or complained about the abuses they witnessed. Most of the worst prisoner treatment came on the night shifts and other occasions when the guards thought they could

> avoid the surveillance and interference of the research team. Our planned two-week experiment had to be aborted after only six days because the experience dramatically and painfully transformed most of the participants in ways we did not anticipate, prepare for, or predict.

What appears to be clear from this study is that if individuals are placed in defined roles they will behave accordingly. Many criticisms of this piece of research have been raised, including ethical ones, and there were also issues regarding the volunteers. Carnahan and McFarland (2007, p. 603) have suggested that it was participant self-selection that led to the cruelty witnessed in the Stanford Prison Experiment (SPE). The authors set out to investigate 'whether students who selectively volunteer for a study of prison life possess dispositions associated with behaving abusively'. Following the original experiment volunteers were recruited through an advertisement; the recruits were assessed by Carnahan and McFarland and were found to possess significantly higher scores on '... measures of the abuse, elated dispositions of aggressiveness, authoritarianism, Machiavellianism, narcissism, and social dominance and lower on empathy and altruism, two qualities inversely related to aggressive abuse'.

Rejecting criticism of their study, Zimbardo and Haney (1998, p. 710) argue that it was the situation, not the psychological makeup of the recruits, that caused the behaviour, 'the negative, anti-social reactions observed were not the product of an environment created by combining a collection of deviant personalities, but rather the result of an intrinsically pathological situation which could distort and rechannel the behaviour of essentially normal individuals. The abnormality here resided in the psychological nature of the situation and not in those who passed through it.' Regardless of what viewpoint you choose to take, this piece of research is considered relevant, including in discussions regarding American soldiers' behaviour in Abu Ghraib, which saw the torture and humiliation of prisoners by their guards.

THINK ABOUT IT!

Social roles consist of a set of norms and behaviour expectations dependent on the social position held. Identify the behaviour expectations that may exist for social workers. What roles do clients hold and what are your behaviour expectations for a young single mother, drug addict, elderly person with dementia or an individual with a disability? Once you have considered your expectations explore how this may impact on how you interact and communicate with that particular client. How do the social roles some clients may hold of social workers affect their expectations and influence the interactions they may have? Suggest how to challenge negative beliefs and promote positive expectations among different clients.

We can see how social roles influence others' perceptions and beliefs about different groups within society, including social workers, psychologists and the police. Norms are part of social roles and affect behaviour but only if people conform to them. For example, the police by the very nature of their remit and work require conformity to the laws of the land. Teachers are another group that require a high level of conformity.

The following section considers the mechanisms that influence conformity from a social psychological perspective.

Conformity and obedience

Norms can influence behaviour only if people conform to them. Without conformity – the adjustment of individual behaviours, attitudes and beliefs to a group standard – some suggest we would have social chaos. Two main hypotheses have been suggested as to why people conform:

- *Normative social influence* – we conform to obtain rewards that come from being accepted by other people, while at the same time avoiding their rejection.
- *Informational social influence* – we may conform to the opinions and behaviours of other people because we believe they have accurate knowledge and what they are doing is 'right'.

SOLOMAN ASCH'S (1951, 1956) CONFORMITY EXPERIMENTS

In Asch's experiments on factors that influence conformity, the following factors were found to be of most influence:

1. **Group size**: conformity increased from about 5 to 35 percent as group size increased from one to four individuals, but, contrary to common sense, further increases in group size did not increase conformity.
2. **Presence of a dissenter**: When one individual (according to the plan) disagreed with the others, this greatly reduced real participants' conformity. Apparently when someone dissents, this person serves as a model for remaining independent from the group.

OBEDIENCE TO AUTHORITY – MILGRAM'S STUDY

Milgram's study (1974) of the dilemma of obedience, when conscience confronted Malevolent Authority, demonstrates the familiar cry of 'I was only following orders'. The gist of the study was that participants were instructed to administer electric shocks to other people even though they screamed and begged for them not to. Sixty-five percent of participants obeyed the instructor's orders.

Factors that influence destructive obedience

- remoteness of the victim
- closeness and legitimacy of the authority figure
- cog in a wheel syndrome
- personal characteristics.

Milgram concluded that 'often, it is not so much the kind of person a man is as the kind of situation in which he finds himself that determines how he will act' (1974, p. 205). While it can be easy to see these experiments as being of little relevance to social work practice but how often have individuals acted on the orders of others, such as in a gang?

Cyber-bullying is an issue that is increasing and causes terrible suffering to others; it is explained particularly by the remoteness of the victim, which dehumanises them to the bully. Much of what is posted would not be so quickly said face to face, where the reaction can be seen, acting as a brake on this type of behaviour. In the recent years 2011 and 2013 we have seen serious riots occur with loss of life and serious damage caused; the following may offer one possible explanation for crowd behaviour and appears to support Milgram's conclusion that situation influences how a person acts.

Crowd behaviour and deindividuation

In New York several years ago, a man was perched on the ledge of a building threatening to jump. A crowd of nearly 500 people gathered below chanted at him to jump. Leon Mann (1981) found that in 10 of 21 cases where a person threatened to jump, the crowd had encouraged the person to jump.

A process of deindividuation, where a loss of individuality leads to disinhibited behaviour, has been implicated. This process has been applied to diverse types of anti-social behaviour, from cheating and stealing to riots and acts of genocide. Key to deindividuation is the anonymity to outsiders; conditions which make an individual less identifiable to people outside the group reduce feelings of accountability. Here we see the loss of individual will and identity, and identity is implicated in another area of social psychology we are going to explore later, Sherif's *Robber Cave Experiment*. This research is considered important in the history of social identity theory as it illustrated how inter-group conflict was caused by competition or incompatible goals. As you will see, a group of boys were divided into two groups and given new identities. In-group bias occurred as a result of this categorisation and demonstrates how people with very minimal identifications will discriminate in favour of the in-group. Discrimination falls within a rubric of stereotype and prejudice and illustrates the relationship between attitudes and behaviour. Before examining this we will examine aspects of stigma, including the stigmatisation of anorexia nervosa.

STIGMA AND PREJUDICE

Stigma is an umbrella term referring to stereotypes, prejudice and discriminatory behaviour. Stereotypes are cognitive schemas or beliefs about members of a social group, while prejudices reflect aversive attitudes affecting behaviour towards the target person or group (Hinshaw & Stier, 2008).

Social Identity Theory

Within Tajfel's *Social Identity Theory*, it is argued (Tajfel, 1981) that stereotypes serve three types of function:

- social causality – (scapegoating)
- social justification
- social differentiation.

Stereotype and identity, as we can see, are linked, as is stereotype, to prejudice and stigmatisation. The following piece examines the stigmatisation of a mental illness, anorexia nervosa, and illustrates these linkages, including stereotypes and the role of attributions associated with it.

A CASE STUDY OF STIGMATISATION – ANOREXIA NERVOSA

Anorexia nervosa is an eating disorder characterised by extreme weight loss, fear of gaining weight, distorted body image and amenorrhoea. Stigmatisation of mental illness has been widely documented with much research directed towards conditions such as depression, anxiety and schizophrenia. Although anorexia nervosa (AN) retains the highest mortality rate among mental illnesses (Agras et al. 2004), relatively little research (Stewart et al. 2006) has focused upon the stigmatisation of this condition and other eating disorders such as bulimia nervosa (BN). Early research conducted by Crisp (2005) involving nationwide surveys found that individuals with eating disorders (ED) were held more to blame for their condition than other mental illness. Research has confirmed Crisp's early findings that attitudes towards eating disorders tend to be quite negative (Stewart et al. 2006; Crisafulli et al. 2010). When anorexia nervosa is compared to other conditions, results confirm the negative perception that AN appears to evoke. Stewart et al. (2006) explored attributions and themes towards healthy individuals, those with AN, individuals with asthma and those with schizophrenia. Findings include the most negative evaluations of personal characteristics attributed to those with AN; further, those with AN were believed to be most to blame for their condition. Underlying these perceptions was the belief that those with AN were 'best able to pull themselves together' and that attention-seeking was another factor in the maintenance of their illness. Interestingly, and supportive of blame attributions, biological factors were believed to be least relevant in anorexia nervosa.

Stewart et al. (2008, p. 311) conducted further similar research presenting AN along with schizophrenia and mononucleosis. Characteristics attributed to targets were less positive for AN than the targets with schizophrenia and mononucleosis; participants reported greater discomfort interacting with the target with AN compared to the targets with depression and mononucleosis. Roehrig and McLean (2010) in their study compared eating disorders and depression, and found that participants viewed those with ED as more fragile, more responsible for their condition and more attention seeking. The role of control emerged as did envy, with some participants admitting to admiring certain aspects of ED. Mond et al. (2006, p. 519) found elements of 'envy' in their findings, reporting 'negative attitudes were apparent in responses to items addressing self-centredness and social distance. In addition, many participants had at some stage thought that it "might not be too bad" to have the problem described'.

Crisafulli et al. (2010) attempted to explore the role of aetiology (causes) in influencing the stigmatisation of AN, presenting three explanations including that of biology, socio-cultural factors and an interaction of both. The authors found that those presented with biological explanations of AN exhibited the least stigma, while those offered social cultural explanations showed the most. The authors concluded their findings were in line with attribution theory. The role of belief is thus fundamental to gaining greater insight into the mechanisms at play in the acquisition, development and maintenance of stigma towards eating disorders. Stereotypes of individuals with AN echoing 'responsibility and control' are recurrent, as confirmed by research findings (Holliday et al. 2005; Stewart, 2008). Stewart et al. (2006, p. 320) comments, 'Negative perceptions of a person with AN fell into stigma categories of self-attribution and responsibility' and further 'if AN is attributed to self-control, then blame for the illness may fall squarely with the afflicted individual' (ibid., 321). Crisp (2005, p. 151) confirms the existence of this negative perception in his findings and reflects, 'the same proportion of the public also report perceiving people with eating disorders as "self-inflicted." They "have only themselves to blame" and "could pull themselves together." This is a second damming judgement for the sufferer. It implies moral and other personality weaknesses and is also embedded in the controversial issue of whether, as humans, we have "choice" or whether our actions are "predetermined".' It is arguable that the issue of 'choice' plays an important role in attitude formation and stigmatisation of AN.

Ebneter et al. (2011), exploring the role of belief systems, such as just world and causal, in the stigmatisation of eating disorders and obesity, found that stronger just world beliefs were associated with higher levels of stigma towards all three eating disorders (AN, BN and binge eating disorder), as well as obesity. Further, greater attributions of individual responsibility for the development of the conditions increased stigmatising attitudes. Two factors were thus identified as involved in contributing to stigma; 'just world belief', that peoples misfortunes are deserved, and a belief that eating disorders are 'controllable'.

Here we can see the role of many different factors in the formation of stereotypes and stigma towards anorexia nervosa. If a biological explanation is presented then less stigmatising attitudes are witnessed. We see a stereotype evolve rooted in the idea of choice and free will; a person with AN possesses those and therefore 'chooses' to be ill. The Belief in a Just World (BJW), which is a cross-cultural construct, can be seen here again (see Chapter 9 for a more in-depth discussion on BJW), influencing attitude formation towards mental illness. It is interesting to note how this concept seems so prevalent across so many cultures. What we can glean is the complexity of stigma, how we form stereotypes, how we are influenced by social and cultural artefacts and constructs and the potentially negative impact such stereotypes and attitudes elicit. Stigma is but one element when we look at the relationship between attitudes and behaviour. We shall discuss another aspect, that of prejudice.

PREJUDICE

What is prejudice? Is it a social phenomenon with cognitive, affective and behavioural components, or rather is prejudice an affective component, stereotyping the cognitive part, and discrimination a behavioural response, with all three components making up the whole? Personally, I prefer the latter approach to considering prejudice.

Research in the area of prejudice began in earnest in the 1940s and 1950s and was characterised by an emphasis on the individual in the creation and perpetuation of prejudice. The authoritarian personality theory emphasised the individual, reflecting the popularity of Freud, and was influenced by the anti-Semitism witnessed to such great degree in the Holocaust. It maintained that prejudice was the result of a parenting style rather than a class model, even though it maintained that working-class parents with aspirations towards middle-class conventions demanded blind submission to authority and adherence to convention and tradition. Children brought up under this parenting style became adults who internalised this hostility and directed it against any grouping viewed as non-traditional or different.

By the 1960s this approach had fallen from favour, to be replaced by the 'subtle racism' and 'dissociation' models. These models emphasised internal conflict between the consciousness and unconsciousness and between culturally learned and internalised values. Movement away from prejudice is the result of internalised egalitarian values triumphing over social learned responses. Another alternative has been advocated in an attempt to reduce prejudice, grounded in social change. This approach took a more cognitive, context-driven approach than its predecessors.

Categorisation became the key term in this approach to understanding the dynamics of prejudice. Categorisation has adaptive functions that have ensured its continuance;

the categorisation of people allows us to attempt to predict their behaviour quickly. Further, the categorisation of both people and objects has enabled us to make sense of and adapt to our environments. These positive aspects of categorisation, however, appear to have come at a price, as categorisation can lay the foundations for prejudice and, from that, discrimination. In his seminal book *The Nature of Prejudice,* Allport was at the forefront in arguing for the role of social categorisation in prejudice and its solution through constructive inter-ethnic contact. Allport further argued that the capacity to categorise was inherent and quite normal. As we categorised chairs as furniture, we would categorise people as 'in-group' and 'out-group', and go one step further into loving one or hating the other. This assertion of Allport's has remained popular, though modified over time.

The 'us–them' attitude, or 'in-group' and 'out-group', has been studied in laboratory experiments and it has been established that common biases occur. In-group favouritism refers to the tendency to prefer and attribute more positive characteristics towards members of the 'in-group' and conversely to attribute negative traits to the 'out-group'. Further, people display an 'out-group homogeneity bias'; in-groups can recognise diversity within their own group but consider members of 'out-groups' as all the same, ignoring that many sub-groups exist. For example, when we identify an individual as Asian we ignore the many subgroups of Asians that exist. If one has a negative bias towards the 'out-group', it is more likely that these perceived group biases will be attributed towards an individual of that group. Pettigrew (1979) found that when a stereotype is challenged, that is, a member of the 'out-group' is seen to behave in a way that is opposite to that of the stereotype, this will be written off as an exceptional case or down to luck. For example, if an individual has a stereotype of women as passive and weak and is then confronted by a strong and independent woman they are likely to describe the woman as a 'feminist'. In the case of Margaret Thatcher, a commentator contended that she had more 'male' genes to explain her position of power and strength. In doing this the general stereotype remains intact.

Motivational aspects have been considered as possible roots of prejudice. Fein and Spencer (1997, in Passer, 2001) suggested those with poor self-esteem use prejudice against others in order to enhance their own self-esteem. The term **'social-identity theory'** was coined to refer to this phenomenon. Another motivational factor considered was the realistic-conflict theory forwarded by Pettigrew. This view maintained that in times of economic hardship and scarcity intense competition for limited resources leads to prejudice.

Attempts to reduce prejudice

Fiske (1998) maintains that since the 1970s social psychological research has assumed the importance of information or the lack of it as a facilitator of prejudice. Certainly information can aid the breaking down of misinformed and negative stereotypes, but another approach taken to reduce prejudice has its origins arguably in Allport's work.

ALLPORT'S 'THE CONTACT HYPOTHESIS'

The contact hypothesis, as its name suggests, advocates contact to challenge negative and prejudicial stereotypes. Race is one of the most powerful categories an individual is placed in, and it is frequently the grounds upon which prejudice is formed. The contact hypothesis can be seen potently in the desegregation of schools in America in the 1950s. Until the 1954 judgment of the American Supreme Court that segregation violated African Americans' constitutional rights, black children had been segregated from white children. Testimony in the case from psychologists maintained that segregation was damaging the outcomes and self-esteem of African Americans, and further that it increased hostility and prejudice. Did contact decrease prejudice? Studies have been divided, although overall the results appear to be disappointing. Stephan's (1990, as cited in Paluck and Green, 2009) review of 80 evaluation studies of desegregation programmes involving African American and Caucasian children concluded that direct contact had not appeared to reduce prejudice. Only 13 percent reported a reduction in prejudice among whites while 53 percent actually reported an increase.

Several possible explanations could lie behind this result and need to be taken into account in attempting to reduce prejudice through the contact hypothesis. First, both groups should be of equal status, as this has been found effective in reducing prejudice. 'One-on-one' interactions by members from the groups challenge 'out-group homogeneity bias', as an individual often confronts the group stereotype that has been attached; sub-grouping is also more clearly recognised. When groups are forced to work together towards some common goal, results appear to suggest this to be effective in breaking down the stereotypes that lead to prejudice.

THE ROBBER CAVE EXPERIMENT

Sherif et al.'s (1961) research entitled 'The Robber Cave experiment' is an example of this principle at work and also arguably of the realistic conflict theory. A group of 11-year-old boys was divided by researchers into two groups, which were given the names 'the Eagles' and 'the Rattlesnakes'. While they lived in different cabins, the groups took part in activities together and were getting along well until an element of competition was introduced into the activities they were taking part in. Very quickly hostility and conflict began and prejudice was seen with members of both groups now refusing to form friendships with members from the other group. Researchers attempted to reduce this hostility and prejudice by increasing contact through activities, but increased contact was found to increase the hostility. Finally, hostility and prejudice was reduced by forcing both groups to cooperate in order to achieve mutually beneficial goals. This type of cooperative learning programme has found great favour in school settings.

Another approach theorised by social psychologists to reduce prejudice is that of 'interactive problem solving'. This has been applied in an attempt to reduce inter-group conflict and has been utilised in the new field of international conflict resolution. Both these approaches emphasise a more inter-group conflict approach in reducing prejudice.

THINK ABOUT IT!

These key questions will help you undertake an in-depth exploration of your own values and attitudes, both individually and within team or network discussions. To gain awareness, ask yourself:

Can I?

- Be comfortable sharing feelings and experiences about bias or discrimination?
- Stand back, examine and discuss objectively my own ethnicity and culture?
- Stand up for myself if a target of discrimination?
- Identify unfair and untrue images, comments and behaviours made about people from minority backgrounds?
- Identify and empathise with adults and children affected by discrimination and racism?
- Recognise, acknowledge and understand influences on children's attitudes and values from home, the childcare setting, community, media and the wider world?
- Identify and discuss what are acceptable and non-acceptable behaviours in the professional context, for example, discussion in relation to a child or family or among clients using the service?
- Recognise there are unequal power relations within society?
- Explain what prejudice, discrimination and racism mean?
- Understand the impact of prejudice, discrimination and racism on families and children?
- Recognise and explore any misinformation, stereotypes, prejudices I have learned?
- Recognise excuses or objections to avoid doing this work within myself and from others around me?

We are going to end this chapter with an overview of pro-social and aggressive behaviour. While this chapter relates to social psychology it seems fitting for other explanations to be outlined to give a more rounded picture of the many possible processes involved in what is a very socially grounded activity, that of behaviour. Hopefully, this will illustrate the totality and complexity of the varied and many influences that help form behaviour.

IN FOCUS: IS BEHAVIOUR THE PRODUCT OF ENVIRONMENT? AN EXPLORATION OF PROSOCIAL AND AGGRESSIVE BEHAVIOUR

Why do some people help others at great risk to themselves and for no apparent benefit, while others display aggressive and antisocial behaviours? Are genes to answer, the family environment we are raised in, our peer group or perhaps our culture? Many researchers have grappled with these issues. Both behaviours have very practical consequences and implications for our understanding of human nature and are relevant to social work.

What is prosocial behaviour?

The term refers to helping, caring, sharing, cooperation and sympathy (Hay 1994).

What processes or influences motivate prosocial behaviour?

The empathy-altruism hypothesis was proposed by C. Daniel Batson. Empathy refers to the ability to put oneself in the place of another and to share what that person is experiencing, while altruism relates to the desire to help another without concern for oneself.

Hoffman's model of the development of empathy

Hoffman (1987, cited in Schaffer, 1996, p. 271) devised four stages in the development of empathy:

Stage 1: *'Global empathy'*
begins at the start of first year and is characterised with the baby not seeing others as distinct and separate from themselves; therefore, the child behaves as though what has happened to another has actually befallen them.

Stage 2: *'egocentric empathy'*
starts in second year. The child is now aware that it is a separate entity but continues to internalise the other's state.

Stage 3: *'empathy for another's feeling'*
is found in children between the age of 2–3 years. The child now recognises that others have distinct feelings.

Stage 4: *'empathy for another's life condition'*
This is the final stage in the development of empathy and covers early childhood. Here affect (feelings) is twinned with mental representation of the other's general condition. Thus a concern for others in the form of an emotional response or a behaviour can be seen from the second year onwards.

Lois Murphy (1937) in her study of preschoolers and their interactions with peers maintained that these young children demonstrated more instances of selfish and aggressive behaviour than of sharing and helping behaviours. Piaget concluded that before the age of six children were not capable of caring about others. These findings have been discredited by recent researchers:

- Simner (1971) found that babies will cry in response to another baby crying.
- Rheingold, Hay, and West (1976) found that Children as young as 18 months old have been found to share toys with another without prompting or encouragement. Rheingold's belief that prosocial behaviours are a 'natural' behaviour contradicts the suggestion of egocentrism.
- Zahn-Waxler et al. (1979) produced a series of findings that children's prosocial tendencies are most obvious when another is distressed. At the beginning of the second year more attempts to comfort and ease suffering are witnessed in the form of patting and hugging, and by mid second year verbal incidence of comforting attempts are both evident and increasing in frequency.

While prosocial behaviour increases in frequency from birth to 2 years, Hay (1994) has argued that between the ages of 3–6 there is a decline in prosocial behaviour. However, Caplan and Hay (1989) observed that 3–5 year olds were upset by another child's distress yet did not attempt to help or alleviate this distress. When the children were questioned as to why they had not helped they responded that there was an adult present and that it was not up to them to help. This example would support Eisenberg's (1989) assertion that a more complex approach is needed when viewing prosocial behaviours at this stage and points to the influence of gender and situation.

The role of genetics, culture and family

GENETICS

While genetic influences can help explain acts of prosocial behaviour towards family members according to the *principle of kin selection* (Buck & Ginsberg, 1991), this does not give an insight into examples of this behaviour towards non-kin. Sociobiologists have suggested the *concept of reciprocal altruism*, that one helps another in the belief that this will increase the likelihood of help being received (Trivers, 1971). This obviously does not satisfactorily explain the differences in prosocial behaviour. Evidence has also been found in studies of identical twins and fraternal twins, pointing to the greater similarity of the behaviour in the former compared to the latter (Rushton et al. 1986).

CULTURE

Cultural differences have been proposed as an explanation in the development and individualisation of prosocial behaviours. Beatrice and John Whiting (1975) conducted studies of 3–10 year olds in six small communities in the Philippines, America, Mexico, India, Kenya and Okinawa. They found that Kenyan, Philippine and Mexican children scored highest on altruistic behaviours with the American children scoring lowest. A possible explanation for this result is that children from poorer backgrounds have more child minding and other responsibilities as the mother often has to work in the fields. These children can witness the importance and genuine contribution altruism makes to their survival and that of their family. American culture tends to be more individualistic and the importance of altruism is not as pressing. Hindus were found to feel more obligated to behave prosocially than their American counterparts (Miller et al. 1990), which gives another aspect to the cultural influence.

PARENTING

Studies by Zahn-Waxler et al. (1979) propose that parental type is closely associated with children's prosocial behaviour.

These instrumental types are:

- *Provision of clear rules and principles:* which maintains that if a parent explains a rule of behaviour the child is more likely to exhibit prosocial behaviour; for example, explaining to a child why it should not bite another is more likely to elicit a positive response than merely telling them not to do it.
- *Attributing prosocial qualities to the child:* suggests if a child is told that it is kind and so on then the child is more likely to internalise these characteristics as part of their own perceived personality.
- *Modelling by parent:* this is believed to be one of the most vital functions of parents and is almost common sense.

- *Empathic care giving to the child:* if parents are warm and responsive towards the child then the likelihood increases of the child displaying the same tendencies.

What is definitely evident is that there is no one formula that fits and explains prosocial behaviour entirely. The importance of peer group in the development of prosocial behaviours can be seen through programmes in schools that attempt to encourage this behaviour (Solomon et al. 1988). It has been found that girls exhibit more kindness than boys, although this can be partially accounted for by socialisation and expectation. What is becoming clear is that prosocial behaviour tends to stabilise in mid childhood.

AGGRESSIVE BEHAVIOUR

We focused on prosocial behaviour, exploring the different theoretical approaches to its understanding and also the possible influence of nature (biology, genetics) and nurture (culture) elements. We're going to investigate the opposite side of prosocial behaviour, aggressive behaviour. In recent times, there appears to be an increasing opinion forming that our society is becoming more violent, and particular concern has been voiced regarding the behaviours of pre-teens and adolescents. If aggression is a behaviour, how does that behaviour develop and manifest? These questions have been considered by psychologists with varying explanations suggested. Let's have a closer look.

Problems with defining aggression

To define aggression creates many difficulties, especially when dealing with *intentionality*. If a person does harm when under the influence of drugs compared to a soldier on the battlefield, is there a difference? If a child pulls a toy away from another because they want to play with it and the other child is hurt in the process, did the child intentionally mean to cause hurt? In studying aggression there appears to be a schism in how it is approached, whether aggression is defined by *intentionality* or by *result*.

Schaffer (1996, p. 279) suggests dividing the categories of aggression into:

1. hostile aggression, where the intention of the act is to harm another.
2. instrumental hostility could be used to define the example of the child and the toy, where the action is aggressive but the motivation is non aggressive.

Distinction is also useful, especially when dealing with gender difference between physical aggression and relational (relationships) aggression. Research into relational aggression is helpful in explaining the differences in levels of aggression between boys and girls and perhaps presenting a more complete picture of female aggression. Thus far, gender difference has been accredited to hormonal and socialisation differences. In the past, adult aggressive behaviours were studied without reference to childhood aggressive behaviours. It has now been proposed that aggressive behaviour in childhood can become stable and persist into adulthood. So let's consider some findings examining aggression in childhood:

- Facial expressions of anger have been observed in infants as young as three months old (Izard et al., 1995). Yet even at this young age gender differences have been reported, with boys more likely to express anger than girls. As the infant becomes older, an increase in verbal aggression is witnessed as the child is no longer confined to physical outbursts alone. This might explain the decrease that has been reported in preschool children.
- Hartup (1970) found a decrease in frequency of aggressive incidents in children between the ages of 4–7 years of age, although as previously stated this could be a reduction in instrumental aggression rather than in aggression per se.
- Aggression observed at six to ten years old correlates with aggression towards peers at ages 10–14 (Olweus, 1991). With respect to stability, several studies have reported that children who are perceived or believed to be aggressive by a certain age in childhood are more at risk of continuing to be aggressive in adulthood.

Eron studies

One of the most influential studies relating to the stability of aggression was carried out by Eron, sampling 600 eight year olds over 22 years. The children were first rated at 8 years of age, based on peer perception and their own perception of their aggression. Researchers contacted the sample again (modal age 19) and managed to re-interview 427 of the original cohort. Eron reported that one of the most impressive findings was the stability of the aggression over time and also noted that their intellectual ability was negatively related to aggressive behaviour. Finally, Eron and his team contacted the sample (modal age 30) and re-interviewed 295 in person and 114 by mail. They also interviewed the spouses and children of some of the sample. What they discovered was the continued stability of aggression but also, that as parents they were more likely to punish their children severely and be aggressive towards their spouses. Eron concluded that:

> *By the time the child is 8 years old, characteristic ways of behaving aggressively or non aggressively have already been established.*

Farrington (1991) supports this study through his similar research in England and found that with males aggressiveness in mid childhood was an important predictor of antisocial activities in adulthood.

THEORIES

Many theories and approaches have been forwarded in an attempt to shed light on the determinants of aggressive behaviour, here we will overview the more popular ones.

Temperament and emotional regulation

Children who are reported by their parents as having difficult temperaments are more likely to experience behavioural problems and aggression (Kingston & Prior, 1995).

Naturally, the parent–child relationship would have to be factored into the parents' perception that their child was difficult.

Ethological

Lorenz's ethological theory posits that humans are inherently or naturally aggressive and have learned ways to control these tendencies. Lorenz emphasised the evolutionary value of aggressiveness with regard to survival. Kalikow (2000) outlines that in *On Aggression* (1966) Lorenz claimed that intraspecies aggression, normally an adaptive phenomenon in animals, has turned deadly in humans because our development of new weapons that can kill at a distance has outrun our innate inhibitions against killing.

Cognitively

It has argued that aggressive children have a greater inability to solve problems on a cognitive level and also to understand others' intentions and motives, resulting in an inappropriate aggressive response. As discussed earlier, Dodge and Crick's *Social Information Processing* theory remains popular in attempts to explain cognitive process in aggression.

Parenting and family environment

The family environment and relationship, as witnessed with Eron's findings, plays an influential role in the development of aggressiveness. Several types of parenting have been associated with increased levels of aggression in children.

OLWEUS (1980) TYPES OF PARENTING STYLES

Dan Olweus (cited in Schaffer, 1996, p. 287) identified several parenting styles, which he proposed were implicated in children's aggression:

Rejection by parents
Suggests that adolescent boys whose mothers are indifferent or fully reject them behave more aggressively. The mother's indifference is reflected in a lack of praise and a lack of interest in the youth's attempt to develop self-control.

Parental permissiveness
When a parent does not set limits of behaviour and maintain them the boy feels he can behave as he wishes with apparent parental approval. Olweus found a strong relationship between a high incidence of aggression coupled to a high degree of laxness on the mother's part.

Parental modelling of aggression
Children imitate and learn behaviours from their parents, including aggression. Aggression has been traced across three generations (Eron study).

Culture

Cultural factors have a part to play in the development of aggression and its maintenance. The Great Whale River Eskimos place emphasis on peace and abhorrence of violence and aggressiveness, and this is reflected in their child-rearing practice, where they actively discourage aggressive behaviour (Honigmann, 1954). Whilst in other cultures and sub-cultures toughness and aggressiveness are behaviours often revered and encouraged.

WHAT DO YOU THINK?

While we may think of culture or ethnic group defined as difference in geographical origins, languages and belief systems, could it be argued that sub-cultures exist and that for young people living in a socially and economically deprived area their immediate ethnic group and beliefs might not be as powerful or influential as that of the sub-group they belong to (such as a gang affiliation)? If research has found that culture and subcultures are important in the development and maintenance of aggressive behaviour, what implication does that have for social workers and their practice?

We are going to consider explanations more firmly grounded within a sociological paradigm, as behaviour is not just individual but a social activity that affects wider society.

Factors that can influence behaviour – a sociological perspective

BYSTANDER INTERVENTION

One of the best known phenomena in social psychology, 'Bystander Effect' was devised by Darley and Latane (1968) in the aftermath of the murder of Kitty Genovese. Kitty Genovese arrived home to the block of apartments where she lived in New York. There, she was attacked for over half an hour. Despite her screams for help and the fact that allegedly 38 witnesses admitted to hearing her screams, it took 30 minutes before anyone called the police. This tragic case illustrated what has come to be known as the 'bystander effect'; the more people are present, the less likely an individual is to act, the inference being that they are waiting or expect another to act instead. Maybe you've heard radio announcements warning of gas leaks on the street? In the ad you are asked to phone and, 'don't expect that someone else will'. This message highlights the phenomenon that people are less likely to act if others are present; further, the more people are present, the less likely it is that an individual will act themselves.

SOCIAL-LEARNING

If you recall in Chapter 4, Bandura's theory of social learning was examined, where Bandura focused on the development of aggression from a social learning approach. In his study of hyper-aggressive boys, Bandura suggested that children's aggression was imitated from those they admire. Further research confirmed to Bandura that we learn to aggress through social learning; that is, through modelling by others. Bandura found that parental modelling of aggressive behaviours played a significant role in the familial transmission of aggression.

Bandura's interest lay in the role of violence on television in the development of aggression and has very practical implications with regard to violence on television, video games and films. Much of Bandura's research demonstrates the relationship between children observing aggression and copying. Yet interestingly, Schuck et al. (1971) found that after interactions with violent media girls showed a decrease in aggressive tendency, whereas in boys an increase was noted.

THE BOBO EXPERIMENT

In order to test his idea that children copy and imitate violence, Bandura designed an experiment to clarify the processes governing observational learning. In basic terms, children watched a programme where an adult continually hit a life-size doll (Bobo doll). The children were then left in a room with a Bobo doll and their behaviour was observed. It was found that the majority of children copied what they had previously seen on the television; they hit the Bobo doll as they had seen the adult do. This confirmed for Bandura the relationship between violence on television and its imitation by children.

Bandura identified four major effects of exposure to televised violence. It can

- teach novel aggressive styles of conduct
- weaken restraints over interpersonal aggression by legitimising, glamorising, and trivialising violent conduct
- desensitise and habituate viewers to human cruelty, and
- shape public images of reality.

Bandura relates that the television industry launched an attack on his findings and the suggestion that television was responsible for encouraging violence and aggressive behaviour in children. This issue was taken so seriously that American Congress held a special committee to examine the issue in closer detail (*Surgeon General's Scientific Advisory Committee on Television and Social Behavior,* 1972*).* Because this is such a pertinent issue, especially with the increased television viewing of children and access to video games (some quite violent), we're going to delve into the topic a little more.

The role of Media in Violence

- 60–70 percent of all TV programmes contain violence
  - 70–80 percent show no remorse, criticism or penalty for the violence
- By the time the average American child graduates from elementary school they have witnessed:
  - More than 8000 murders
  - More than 100,000 other acts of violence (e.g., assaults, rape)
- More recently, video games have become kids' favourite form of media
  - 90 percent of kids age 2–17 play regularly
- Majority of popular games are violent

The American Psychological Association outlines the following issues they identify in the role of television and video games in aggression.

- Decades of social science research reveals the strong influence of televised violence on the aggressive behaviour of children and youth.

- Psychological research reveals that the electronic media play an important role in the development of attitude, emotion, social behaviour and intellectual functioning of children and youth.
- There appears to be evidence that exposure to violent media increases feelings of hostility, thoughts about aggression, suspicions about the motives of others, and demonstrates violence as a method to deal with potential conflict situations.
- Perpetrators go unpunished in 73 percent of all violent scenes, and therefore teach that violence is an effective means of resolving conflict. Only 16 percent of all programmes portrayed negative psychological or financial effects, yet such visual depictions of pain and suffering can actually inhibit aggressive behaviour in viewers.
- Comprehensive analysis of violent interactive video game research suggests such exposure
  a. increases aggressive behaviour,
  b. increases aggressive thoughts,
  c. increases angry feelings,
  d. decreases helpful behaviour, and,
  e. increases physiological arousal.
- Studies further suggest that sexualised violence in the media has been linked to increases in violence towards women, rape myth acceptance and anti-women attitudes. Research on interactive video games suggests that the most popular video games contain aggressive and violent content; depict women and girls, men and boys, and minorities in exaggerated stereotypical ways; and reward, glamorise and depict as humorous sexualised aggression against women, including assault, rape and murder.
- The characteristics of violence in interactive video games appear to have similar detrimental effects as viewing television violence; however, based upon learning theory (Bandura, 1977; Berkowitz, 1993), the practice, repetition and rewards for acts of violence may be more conducive to increasing aggressive behaviour among children and youth than passively watching violence on TV and in films. With the development of more sophisticated interactive media, such as virtual reality, the implications for violent content are of further concern, due to the intensification of more realistic experiences, and may also be more conducive to increasing aggressive behaviour than passively watching violence on TV and in films.
- Studies further suggest that videogames influence the learning processes in many ways more than in passively observing TV:
  a. requiring identification of the participant with a violent character while playing video games,
  b. actively participating increases learning,
  c. rehearsing entire behavioural sequences, rather than only a part of the sequence, facilitates learning, and
  d. repetition increases learning.

This synopsis doesn't outline methodological or other weaknesses of the research that was considered in drafting these points; as always, when reading any finding one should use a critical eye. However, many psychologists would feel strongly that there is a plethora of evidence illustrating the powerful link between media and violence. Sometimes I can't help but feel that it is common sense; surely it is not a good idea for children and teens to watch and interact with violent games detached from any kind of reality. With the increasing popularity of games such as Grand Theft Auto, which includes having sex with prostitutes and then murdering them and stealing money back, what kind of message are we sending out? I think it's only fair that I am clear that I support the position taken by the APA, so I can be accused of bias in this issue. Although, of course, aggression as with all things, is a complex issue with many different factors at play, nonetheless the role of media as a powerful factor is difficult to dispute. There are those who feel that the relationship is exaggerated and this is harmless entertainment, fun – naturally it is up to you what you think is the relationship between TV and video games and aggression. Look at evidence and weigh it up in deciding your opinion.

FURTHER READING

The following link outlines the research referenced in outlining the points the APA have addressed:

www.apa.org/about/policy/interactive-media.pdf

www.google.ie/webhp?sourceid=chromeinstant&rlz=1C1WLXB_enIE557IE557&ion=1&espv=2&ie=UTF-8#q=media+violence+site:apa.org

SUMMARY

In this chapter, social psychology is described as studying social influence, thinking and behaviour. Issues such as prejudice, discrimination and social roles have an immediate relevance in the field of social work. A study of some of the concepts addressed in this chapter should provide an opportunity to reflect on how we perceive others and relate to them: how attitudes are formed and stereotypes emerge. If we recognise the larger social and cultural element then we can advocate to change perceptions. Social roles and the expectations that accompany them are incredibly important to social work as they affect the relationship and dynamic between social worker and clients and aid a greater awareness of the influence of social roles within the client's life too. This chapter, marking the end of the book, deliberately ended with an overview of aggressive and prosocial behaviour, diametrically opposite to each other, one promoted and the other shunned. An overview of all the different aspects we have met throughout the book merged to offer a more global and rounded lens to consider these behaviours. It is up to you if you're more drawn to biological explanations or those rooted from a more social-cultural approach, and it may be a bit of everything! Regardless, hopefully, this book has raised more questions for you to consider and engage with than it has offered answers. What is clear is that no easy answers exist.

REFERENCES

Aarts, P. and Op den Velde, W., 'Prior traumatization and the process of aging: Theory and clinical implications' in B. A. van der Kolk et al. (eds.), *Traumatic Stress: The Effects of Overwhelming Experience on Mind, Body, and Society*, New York: Guilford 1996.

Abkarian, G. G., 'Communication effects of prenatal alcohol exposure', *Journal of Communication Disorders*, 25 (1992), 221–40.

Abramson, L. Y., Seligman, M. E. P. and Teasdale, J. D., 'Learned helplessness in humans: Critique and reformulation', *Journal of Abnormal Psychology*, 87 (1978), 32–48.

Agras, W. S., Brandt, H. A., Bulik, C. M., Dolan-Sewell, R., Fairburn, C. G., Halmi, K. A., et al., 'Report of the National Institutes of Health Workshop on overcoming barriers to treatment research in anorexia nervosa' *International Journal of Eating Disorders*, 35 (2004), 509–21.

Ainsworth, M. D. S., Blehar, M. C., Waters, E. and Wall, S., *Patterns of Attachment: A Psychological Study of the Strange Situation*, Hillsdale, NJ: Erlbaum 1978.

Algood, C. L., Harris, C. and Hong, Jun Sung. 'Parenting Success and Challenges for Families of Children with Disabilities: An Ecological Systems Analysis', *Journal of Human Behavior in the Social Environment*, 23:2, 2013, 126–36.

Allen, G. and Duncan-Smith, I., 'Early intervention: Good parents, great kids, better citizens. Published jointly by the Centre for Social Justice and the Smith Institute, 2008; www.centreforsocialjustice.org.uk/UserStorage/pdf/Pdf%20reports/EarlyInterventionFirstEdition.pdf accessed 11 March 2015.

Allport, G., *Handbook of Social Psychology*, Worcester, MA: Clark University Press 1954.

Allport, G., *The Nature of Prejudice*, Reading, MA: Addison-Wesley 1954; 1979.

American Psychiatric Association. DSM 5 – Autism Spectrum Disorder Factsheet. http://www.dsm5.org/Documents/Autism%20Spectrum%20Disorder%20Fact%20Sheet.pdf

American Psychiatry Association, *Diagnostic and Statistical Manual of Mental Disorders DSM-IV-TR*, 4th ed., APA 2000.

Anthony, E. J. (1974). The syndrome of the psychologically invulnerable child. In E. J. Anthony & C. Koupernik (Eds.), *The child in his family: Children at psychiatric risk* (pp. 529–545). New York: Wiley

Asch, S. E., 'Effects of group pressure upon the modification and distortion of judgment' in H. Guetzkow (ed.), *Groups, Leadership and Men*, Pittsburgh, PA: Carnegie Press 1951.

Asch, S. E., 'Studies of independence and conformity: A minority of one against a unanimous majority', *Psychological Monographs*, 70 (1956) (Whole no. 416).

Atkinson, J. W., 'Motivational determinants of risk-taking behavior' (1957) in *Personality, Motivation, and Action: Selected papers*, New York: Praeger 1983.

Ayuso-Mateos, J. L., Pereda, A., Dunn, G., Vazquez-Barquero, J. L., Casey, P., Lehtinen, V., Dalgard, O., Wilkinson, G. and Dowrick, C., 'Predictors of compliance with psychological interventions offered in the community', *Psychological Medicine*, 37(5) (2007), 717–25.

Babyak, M. A., Blumenthal, J. A., Herman, S., Khatri, P., Doraiswamy, P. M., Moore, K. A., Craighead, W. E., Baldewicz, T. T. and Krishnan, K. R., 'Exercise treatment for major depression: Maintenance of therapeutic benefit at 10 months', *Psychosomatic Medicine*, 62 (2000), 633–38.

Bandura, A., 'Autobiography' in M. G. Lindzey and W. M. Runyan (eds.), *A History of Psychology in Autobiography*, Vol. IX, Washington, DC: American Psychological Association 2006.

Bandura, A., 'The evolution of social cognitive theory' in K. Smith and M. Hitt (eds.), *Great Minds in Management: The Process of Theory Management*, Oxford: Oxford University Press 2001.

Bardone, A. M., Moffitt, T. E., Caspi, A., Dickson, N. and Silva, P. A., 'Adult mental health and social outcomes of adolescent girls with depression and conduct disorder', *Development and Psychopathology*, 8(4) (1996), 811–29.

Baron-Cohen, S., *The Essential Difference: The Extreme Male Brain*, London: Penguin 2004.

Barter, C., 'Children and young people who harm others', *Child Abuse Review*, 22(4) (2013), 227–31.

Baumrind, D., 'Effects of authoritative parental control on child behavior', *Child Development*, 37(4) (1966), 887–907.

Beardslee, W. R., 'The role of self-understanding in resilient individuals: The development of a perspective', *American Journal of Orthopsychiatry*, 59 (1989), 266–278.

Beck, A.T. *Cognitive Therapy of Depression*, Guildford Press 1976.

Beck, A. T., Rush, A. J., Shaw, B. F. and Emery, G., *Cognitive Therapy of Depression,* New York: Guilford 1979.

Beck, A. T., 'Cognitive therapy of depression: New perspectives' in P. J. Clayton and J. E. Barrett (eds.), *Treatment of Depression: Old Controversies and New Approaches*, New York: Raven Press 1983.

Becker, E., *The Denial of Death,* New York: Free Press 1973.

Becker, A. E., Burwell, R. A., Gilman, S. A., Herzog, D. B. and Hamburg, P. 'Eating behaviours and attitudes following prolonged exposure to television among ethnic Fijian adolescent girls', *British Journal of Psychiatry*, 180 (2002), 509–14.

Beecher, B., 'The medical model, mental health practitioners, and individuals with schizophrenia and their families', *Journal of Social Work Practice,* 23(1) (2009), 9–20.

Bennett, M., 'Socialisation', in B. Hopkins (ed.), *The Cambridge Encyclopedia of Child Development*, Cambridge University Press 2005.

Bennett,D. S., Bendersky, M. and Lewis,M., 'Antecedents of emotion knowledge: Predictors of individual differences in young children', *Cognition & Emotion*, 19(3) (2005), 375–96.

Benson, C., 'The unthinkable boundaries of self: The role of negative emotional boundaries for the formation, maintenance, and transformation of identities' in R. Harré and F. M. Moghaddam (eds.), *The Self and Others: Positioning Individuals and Groups in Personal, Political and Cultural Contexts,* Westport, CT: Praeger 2003.

Berger, P. L. and Luckmann, T., *The Social Construction of Reality: A Treatise in the Sociology of Knowledge,* New York: Anchor 1967.

Best, D., Day, E., McCarthy, T., Darlington, I. and Pinchbeck, K., 'The hierarchy of needs and care planning in addiction services: What Maslow can tell us about addressing competing priorities?', *Addiction Research and Theory*, 16(4) (2008), 305–7.

Bigler, R. S. and Liben, L. S., 'Developmental intergroup theory explaining and reducing children's social stereotyping and prejudice', *Current Directions in Psychological Science*, 16(3) (2007), 162–6.

Bishop, S. and Leadbeater, B., 'Maternal social support patterns and child maltreatment: Comparison of maltreating and nonmaltreating mothers', *American Journal of Orthopsychiatry*, 69 (1999), 172–81.

Black, M. M., 'The roots of child neglect' in R. M. Reece (ed.), *Treatment of Child Abuse: Common Ground for Mental Health, Medical, and Legal Practitioners*, Baltimore, MD: Johns Hopkins University Press 2000.

Blatt, S. J. and Zuroff, D. C., 'Interpersonal relatedness and self-definition: Two prototypes for depression', *Clinical Psychology Review*, 12 (1992), 527–62.

Blyth, D. and Traeger, C., 'Adolescent self-esteem and perceived relationships with parents and peers' in S. Salzinger, J. Antrobus and M. Hammer (eds.), *Social Networks of Children, Adolescents and College Students*, Hillsdale, NJ: Erlbaum Associates 1988.

Bowlby, J., 'Maternal care and mental health', World Health Organization Monograph (1951) (Serial No. 2).

Bowlby, J., *Attachment and Loss*, Vol. 2., London: Hogarth 1980.

Boyd, D. and Bee, H., *Life span Development*, 4th ed., New York: Allyn and Bacon 2005.

Bracken, P. and Thomas, P., 'From Szasz to Foucault: On the Role of Critical Psychiatry', *Philosophy, Psychiatry, & Psychology*, 17(3) (2010), 219–28.

Bracken, P. and Thomas, P. *Postpsychiatry: a new direction for mental health* 2001.

Brown, J., O'Donnell, T. and Erooga, M., 'Sexual abuse: a public health challenge. NSPCC', 2011; http://www.nspcc.org.uk/services-and-resources/research-and-resources/sexual-abuse-public-health/

Brown, J., O'Donnell, T. and Erooga, M., *Sexual Abuse: A Public Health Challenge*, London: NSPCC. 2011; http://www.nspcc.org.uk/Inform/resourcesforprofessionals/sexualabuse/evidence-review-pdf_wdf87818.pdf

Breese, J. R. and Feltey, K. M., 'Role exit from home to homeless', *Free Inquiry in Creative Sociology*, 24 (1996), 67–76.

Brewin, C. and Andrews, B., 'Psychological defence mechanisms: The example of repression', *The Psychologist,* Special Issue: Freud in a Modern Light, 13(12) (2000), 615–17.

Bronfenbrenner, U., *The Ecology of Human Development*, Cambridge, MA: Harvard University Press 1979.

Brooker, D., 'What is person-centred care in dementia?', *Reviews in Clinical Gerontology*, 13 (2004), 215–22.

Brooks-Gunn, J., Petersen, A. C. and Eichorn, D., 'The study of maturational timing effects in adolescence', *Journal of Youth and Adolescence*, 14(3) (1985), 149–61.

Bruch, H., Czyzewski D. and Suhr, M. A., *Conversations with Anorexics*, New York: Basic Books 1988.

Buck, R. and Ginsburg, B. E., 'Emotional communication and altruism: The communicative gene hypothesis' in M. Clark (ed.), *Altruism: Review of Personality and Social Psychology,* Vol. 12, Newbury Park, CA: Sage 1991.

Bugental, J., 'The third force in psychology', *Journal of Humanistic Psychology*, 4(1) (1964), 19–25.

Buskist, W. and Miller, H., 'The analysis of human operant behavior: A brief census of the literature, 1958–1981', *The Behavior Analyst*, 5 (1982), 137–41.

Buss, A. H. and Plomin, R., *Temperament: Early Developing Personality Traits*, Hillsdale, NJ: Erlbaum 1984.

Cain, D. J., 'Advancing humanistic psychology and psychotherapy: Some challenges and proposed solutions', *Journal of Humanistic Psychology*, 43(3) (2003), 10–41.

Caplan, M. Z. and Hay, D. F. 'Preschoolers' responses to peers' distress and beliefs about bystander intervention', *Journal of Child Psychology and Psychiatry and Allied Disciplines*, 30(2) (1989), 231–42.

Carnahan, T. and McFarland, S., 'Revisiting the Standford Prison Experiment: Could self-selection have led to the cruelty?', *Personality and Social Psychology Bulletin*, 33(5) (2007), 603–14.

Carr, A., *The Handbook of Clinical and Adolescent Clinical Psychology: A contextual approach*, New York, Brunner-Routledge 2003.

Carr, A., *Positive Psychology: The Science of Happiness and Human Strengths*, London: Brunner-Routledge 2004.

Carr, A., 'Effectiveness of Psychotherapy', 2007; http://www.psychotherapy- ireland.com/wp-content/uploads/2007/09/recommendations.pdf.

Carr, A. and Byrne, J., 'Psychosocial profiles of Irish children with conduct disorders, mixed disorders of conduct and emotion and emotional disorders' in A. Carr (ed.), *Clinical Psychology in Ireland: Empirical Studies of Problems and Treatment Processes in Children and Adolescents*, Vol. 3, New York: Edwin Mellen 2000.

Carter, R., *Mapping the Mind*, London: Phoenix Publishers 1998.

Carter, R., *The Brain Book*, London: Dorling Kindersley 2009.

Cattell, R. B. and Horn, J. L., 'Age differences in fluid and crystallized intelligence', *Acta Psychologica*, 26 (1967), 107–29.

Central Statistics Office, *Ageing in Ireland*, Dublin: Stationery Office 2007.

Cianciolo, A. T. and Sternberg, R. J., *Intelligence: A Brief History*, Malden, MA: Blackwell 2004.

Clarke, A. M. and Clarke, A. D. B., *Early Experience: Myth and Evidence*, London: Open Books, 1976.

Clulow, C., 'Marriage, partnership and adult attachment', *Sexual and Relationship Therapy*, 22(3) (2007), 291–294.

Cohen, D. J. and Volkmar, F. R., *Handbook of Autism and Pervasive Developmental Disorder*, 2nd ed., New York: John Wiley & Sons 1997.

Colby, A., Kohlberg, L., Gibbs, J. and Lieberman, M., 'A longitudinal study of moral judgment', *Monographs of the Society for Research in Child Development*, 48(1–2) (1983), Serial no. 200.

Commission on the Status of People with Disabilities, *A Strategy for Equality: Report of the Commission on the Status of People with Disabilities*, Stationery Office, Dublin 1996.

Connolly, G., Kennelly, S., Conroy, R. and Byrne, P., 'Teenage pregnancy in the Rotunda Hospital, 1992–1996, A review', *Irish Medical Journal*, 91 (1998), 209–12.

Coolican, H., *Research Methods and Statistics in Psychology*, 5th ed., London: Hodder Education 2009.

Corcoran, J., 'Strengths-based models in social work', *Oxford Bibliographies* in Social Work. doi: 10.1093/obo/9780195389678-0006, 2011

Corcoran,Jacqueline,Strengths-basedmodelsinsocialwork. http://www.oxfordbibliographies.com/view/document/obo-9780195389678/obo-9780195389678-0006.xml

Costello, L., *A Review of Children's Well-Being*, Dublin: Combat Poverty Agency 1999; http://www.combatpoverty.ie/publications/ ALiteratureReviewOfChildrensWellBeing_1999.pdf

Costa, P. and McCrae, R., 'A five-factor theory on the Rorschach', *Rorschachiana*, 27 (2005), 80–100.

Cournoyer, B., *The Social Skills Workbook*, London: Wadsworth 1991.

Cowie, H., Smith, P. and Blacks, M., *Understanding Children's Development*, 3rd ed., Oxford: Blackwell 2003.

Cozolino, L., *The Neuroscience of Psychotherapy: Building and Rebuilding the Human Brain*, New York: W. W. Norton 2002.

Crain W. C., *Theories of Development: Concepts and Applications*, London: Prentice-Hall 1985.

Crick, N. R. and Dodge, K. A., 'A review and reformulation of social information-processing mechanisms in children's social adjustment', *Psychological Bulletin*, 115(1) (1994), 74.

Crisafulli, M. A., Thompson-Brenner, H., Franko, D. L., Eddy, K. T. and Herzog, D. B., 'Stigmatization of anorexia nervosa: characteristics and response to intervention' *Journal of Social and Clinical Psychology*, 29(7), (2010) 756–70.

Crisp, A., 'Stigmatization of and discrimination against people with eating disorders including a report of two nationwide surveys', *European Eating Disorders Review*, 13(3) (2005), 147–52.

Crockett, L. and Petersen, A., 'Pubertal status and psychological development: Findings from early adolescence studies' in R. M. Lerner and T. T. Foch (eds.), *Biological-Psychosocial Interactions in Early Adolescence: A Life span Perspective*, Hillsdale, NJ: Erlbaum 1987.

Crosse, S., Kaye, E. and Ratnofsky, A., *A Report on the Maltreatment of Children with Disabilities*, Washington, DC: National Clearinghouse on Child Abuse and Neglect 1993.

Crowell, J. A. and Treboux, D., 'A review of adult attachment measures: implications for theory and research'. *Social Development*, 4 (1995), 294–327.

Curtiss, S., *Genie: A Psycholinguistic Study of a Modern Day 'Wild Child'*, London: Academic Press 1977.

Daichman, L. S., 'Elder abuse in developing countries' in M. Johnson (ed.), *The Cambridge Handbook of Age and Ageing*, Cambridge: Cambridge University Press 2005.

Damasio, A., *The Feeling of What Happens: Body and Emotion in the Making of Consciousness*, New York: Harcourt Brace 1999.

Daniel, B., Wassell, S. and Gilligan, R. *Child Development for Child Care and Protection Workers*. 2nd ed., London: Jessica Kingsley Publishers 2010.

Darley, J. M. and Latané, B., 'Bystander "apathy"', *American Scientist*, 57 (1969), 244–68.

Davidson, L., 'Philosophical foundations of humanistic psychology', *The Humanistic Psychologist*, 28(1–3) (2000), 7–31.

Davies, C. and Ward, H. *Safeguarding Children across Services*, London: Jessica Kingsley 2012.

De Maat, S., de Jonghe, F., Schoevers, R. and Dekker, J., 'The effectiveness of long-term psychoanalytic therapy: A systematic review of empirical studies', *Harvard Review of Psychiatry*, 17 (2009), 1–23.

De Raad, B. and Perugini, M. (eds.), *Big Five Assessment*, Göttingen, Germany: Hogrefe and Huber 2002.

De St. Aubin, E., McAdams, D. P. and Kim, T.-C. (eds.), *The Generative Society: Caring for future generations*, Washington, DC: American Psychological Association 2004.

De Ward, S. and Moe, A., 'Like a prison: Homeless women's narratives of surviving shelter', *Journal of Sociology and Social Welfare*, 37(1) (2010) 115–35.

De Wolff, M. S. and van Ijzendoorn, M. H., 'Sensitivity and attachment: A meta- analysis on parental antecedents of infant attachment', *Child Development*, 68 (1997), 571–91.

Dekovic, M. and Janssens, J. M., 'Parents' rearing style and child's sociometric status', *Developmental Psychology*, 28 (1992), 925–932.

Department for Work and Pensions., 'An evidence review of the drivers of child poverty for families in poverty now and for poor children growing up to be poor adults', 2014; https://www.gov.uk/government/uploads/system/uploads/attachment_data/file/285389/Cm_8781_Child_Poverty_Evidence_Review_Print.pdf

Department for Children, Schools and Families, HM Government. *Working Together to Safeguard Children: A guide to inter-agency working to safeguard and promote the welfare of children*, 2010. http://webarchive.nationalarchives.gov.uk/20130401151715/https://www.education.gov.uk/publications/eorderingdownload/00305-2010dom-en-v3.pdf

Department of Education., H5 Structural factors affecting children and families, 2012; https://www.gov.uk/government/uploads/system/uploads/attachment_data/file/268893/h5_structural_factors_affecting_children_and_families.pdf

Department of Education., 'Working together to safeguard children. A guide to inter-agency working to safeguard and promote the welfare of children', 2013; https://www.gov.uk/government/uploads/system/uploads/attachment_data/file/281368/Working_together_to_safeguard_children.pdf

Department of Health and Children, *Children First: National Guidelines for the Protection and Welfare of Children*, Dublin: Department of Health and Children 1999.

Department of Health and Children, *Working for Children and Families: Exploring Best Practice*, Dublin: Department of Health and Children, 2003

Department of Health. *A Sign of the Times: Modernising Mental Health Services for people who are Deaf*. 2002.

Department of Health., 'Mental Health and Deafness – Towards Equity and Access: Best Practice Guidance' 2005; http://www.dh.gov.uk/en/Publicationsandstatistics/Publications/PublicationsPolicyAn dGuidance/DH_4103995

Department for Work & Pensions, 'Office for Disability Issues', 2014; https://www.gov.uk/government/publications/disability-facts-and-figures/disability-facts-and-figures

Diaz-Laplante, J., 'Humanistic psychology and social transformation: Building the path towards a livable today and a just tomorrow', *Journal of Humanistic Psychology*, 47(1) (2007), 54–72.

Diggins, M., 'Teaching and learning communication skills in social work education: SCIE Guide 5', 2004; http://www.scie.org.uk/publications/guides/guide05/index.asp

Dodge K. A. 'A social information processing model of social competence in children', in: Perlmutter, M, ed. *Minnesota Symposium in Child Psychology*. Vol. 18. Hillsdale, NJ: Erlbaum 1986. pp. 77–125.

Doka, K. J. 'Living with life-threatening illness', Lexington, MA: Lexington Books, 1993.

Double, D. *What is critical psychiatry?* 2012; http://criticalpsychiatry.blogspot.ie/2012/04/what-is-critical-psychiatry.html)

Drewes, A., 'Bobo revisited: What the research says', *International Journal of Play Therapy*, 17(1) (2008), 52–65.

Dryden, W., 'Some reflections on rational beliefs' in M. Neenan and W. Dryden (eds.), *Rational Emotive Behaviour Therapy: Advances in Theory and Practice*, London: Whurr 1999.

Dubas, J. S., Graber, J. A. and Petersen, A. C., 'The effects of pubertal development on achievement during adolescence', *American Journal of Education*, 99 (1991), 444–60.

Ebneter, D. S., Latner, J. D. and O'Brien, K. S., 'Just world beliefs, causal beliefs, and acquaintance: Associations with stigma toward eating disorders and obesity' *Personality and Individual Differences*, 51(5) (2011), 618–22.

Eisenberg, N. and Mussen, P. *The roots of pro-social behaviour in children*. Cambridge: Cambridge University Press 1989.

Elder, G. H., 'Human lives in changing societies: Life course and developmental insights' in R. Cairns, G. H. Elder and E. J. Costello (eds.), *Developmental Science*, Cambridge: Cambridge University Press 2001.

Elkind, D., 'Egocentrism in adolescence', *Child Development*, 38 (1967), 1025–33.

Elkins, D., 'Why humanistic psychology lost its power and influence in American psychology: Implications for advancing humanistic psychology', *Journal of Humanistic Psychology*, 49(3) (2009), 267–91.

Ellis, B. J. and Garber, J., 'Psychosocial antecedents of variation in girls' pubertal timing: Maternal depression, stepfather presence, and marital and family stress', *Child Development*, 71 (2000), 485–501.

Eron, L. D., Walder, L. O. and Lefkowitz, M. M., *Learning of Aggression in Children*, Boston: Little Brown 1971.

Farrington, D. P., 'Childhood aggression and adult violence: Early precursors and later outcomes' in D. J. Pepler and K. H. Rubin (eds.), *The Development and Treatment of Childhood Aggression,* Hillsdale, NJ: Erlbaum 1991, 5–30.

Fein, S. and Spencer, S. J., 'Prejudice as self-image maintenance: Affirming the self through derogating others', *Journal of Personality and Social Psychology*, 73 (1997), 31–44.

Field, H. and Domangue, B., *Eating Disorders Throughout the Life span*, New York: Praeger 1987.

Finkelhor, D. *Child Sexual Abuse: New Theory and Research*, New York: Free Press 1984.

Fischoff, B., 'Hindsight foresight: The effect of outcome knowledge on judgement under certainity', *Journal of Experimental Psychology: Human Perception and Performance*, 1 (1975), 288–99.

Fiske, S., *Stereotyping, Prejudice, and Discrimination: The Handbook of Social Psychology,* Vol. 2, 4th ed., New York: McGraw-Hill 1998.

Fiske, S. T. and Taylor, S. E., *Social Cognition*, Reading, MA: Addison-Wesley 1984.

Fitzmaurice, E., *Applied Social Care*, 2nd ed., Dublin: Gill and MacMillan 2009.

Fitzpatrick, C. C., Fitzpatrick, P. E. and Turner, M. J., 'Profile of patients attending a Dublin adolescent antenatal booking clinic', *Irish Medical Journal*, 90 (1997), 96–7.

Fox, E. and Riconscente, M., 'Metacognition and self-regulation in James, Piaget, and Vygotsky', *Educational Psychology Review*, 20 (2008), 373–89.

Freud, S., *An Outline of Psychoanalysis: The Standard Edition of the Complete Psychological Works of Sigmund Freud,* Vol. 23, London: The Hogarth Press and the Institute of Psychoanalysis 1964.

Frith, U., *Autism: Explaining the Enigma*, Oxford: Blackwell 1996.

Furnham, A., 'Belief in a just world: Research progress over the past decade', *Personality and Individual Differences*, 34 (2003), 795–811.

Gardner, F. 'Social Work Students and Self-awareness: how does it happen?', *Reflective Practice*, 2.1 (2001), 27-40.

Gardner H., *Frames of Mind: The theory of multiple intelligence*, New York: Basic Books 1983.

Garmezy, N., 'Stressors of childhood' in N. Garmezy and M. Rutter (eds.), *Stress, Coping and Development in Children*, New York: McGraw-Hill 1983, 43–84.

Garnefski, N. and Arends, E., 'Sexual abuse and adolescent maladjustment: Differences between male and female victims', *Journal of Adolescence*, 21 (1998), 99–107.

Geldard, K. and Geldard, D., *Practical Counselling Skills*, London: Palgrave Macmillan 2005.

Giedd, J., 'What makes teens tick?' *Time,* 10 May, 2004.

Giles, Bridget (ed.), *Social Psychology*, London: Grange Books 2002.

Gilligan, R., 'Family support and child welfare: Realising the promise of the Child Care Act' in H. Ferguson and P. Kenny (eds.), *On Behalf of the Child: Child Welfare, Child Protection and the Child Care Act*, Dublin: Farmer 1995.

Gilligan, R., 'Promoting resilience in children in long-term care: The relevance of roles and relationships in the domains of recreation and work', *Journal of Social Work Practice*, 22(3) (2008), 37–50.

Glaser, B. G. and Strauss, A. L. *Awareness of dying*. Transaction Publishers, 1966.

Glaser, B. and Strauss, A. *Time for Dying*. Chicago: Aldine. London: Weidenfeld and Nicholson, 1968.

Glass, G., 'Primary, secondary and meta-analysis of research', *Educational Researcher*, 5 (1976), 3–8.

Goffman, E., *Asylums: Essays on the Social Situation of Mental Patients and Other Inmates*, New York: Doubleday Anchor 1961.

Government of Ireland, *Disability Act 2005* (2005a); http://www. oireachtas.ie/documents/bills28/acts/2005/a1405.pdf [Accessed 6.1.2015].

Grant, G., Goward, P., Richardson, M. and Ramcharan, P. (eds.), *Learning Disability: A Life Cycle Approach to Valuing People*, Maidenhead: Open University Press 2005.

Greening, T., 'Five basic postulates of humanistic psychology', *Journal of Humanistic Psychology*, 47 (2007), 1.

Griffin, S. and Shevlin, M., *Responding to Special Educational Needs: An Irish Perspective*, Dublin: Gill and Macmillan 2007.

Gross, R., *Psychology: The Science of Mind and Behaviour*, 6th ed., London: Hodder Education 2009.

Guralnick, M. J. (ed.) *The Effectiveness of Early Intervention*, Baltimore: P.H. Brooks 1997.

Hall, D., 'Technical note: Extreme deprivation in early childhood', *Journal of Child Psychology and Psychiatry*, 26(5) (1985), 825.

Harter, S., 'Causes, correlates and the functional role of global self-worth: A life- span perspective' in R. J. Sternberg and J. Kolligian (eds.), *Competence Considered*, New Haven, CT: Yale University Press 1990.

Hartman, D., 'Oppositional defiant disorder', 2007; http://www.sess.ie/categories/ emotional-disturbance-and/or-behavioural-problems/oppositional-defiant-disorder [Accessed 17.6.2010].

Hartup, W.W. 'Peer interaction and social organization', in P. H. Mussen (Ed.), *Carmichael's manual of child psychology* Vol. 2. (3rd edn.). New York: Wiley, 1970.

Hay, D. F., 'Prosocial development', *Journal of Child Psychology and Psychiatry*, 35 (1994), 29–71.

Health Service Executive, *Protecting Our Future*, Dublin: Stationery Office 2002.

Herbert, M., *Typical and Atypical Development: from Conception to Adolescence*, Oxford: BPS Blackwell 2006.

Herrnstein, R. J. and Murray, C. *The bell curve: The reshaping of American life by differences in intelligence*, New York: Free 1994.

Hetherington, E. M. and Parke, R. D., *Child Psychology: A Contemporary Viewpoint*, 5th ed., New York: McGraw-Hill 1999.

Hilliard, L. J. and Liben, L. S., 'Differing levels of gender salience in preschool classrooms: Effects on children's gender attitudes and intergroup bias', *Child Development*, 81(6) (2010), 1787–98.

Hinshaw, S. P. and Stier, A. Stigma as related to mental disorders. *Annual Review of Clinical Psychology*, 4 (2008), 367–93.

Hodapp, R. and Dykens, E., 'Intellectual disabilities and child psychiatry: looking to the future', *Journal of Child Psychology and Psychiatry*, 50(1–2) (2009), 99–107.

Hoffman, M., 'The origins and development of empathy', *Motivation and Emotion,* 14(2) (1990), 75–80.

Hogan, D. M., *The Social and Psychological Needs of Children of Drug Users: Report on an Explanatory Study*, Trinity College Dublin: The Children's Centre 1997; https://www.tcd.ie/childrensresearchcentre/assets/pdf/Publications/social&psychological.pdf

Holliday, Joanna, et al. 'Perceptions of illness in individuals with anorexia nervosa: A comparison with lay men and women', *International Journal of Eating Disorders* 37.1 (2005), 50–6.

Holt, S., Manners, P. and Gilligan, R., *An Evaluation of the Naas Child and Family Project: A Springboard Initiative*, Kildare Youth Services and South Western Health Board 2002.

Holzman, L., 'Critical psychology, philosophy and social therapy', 2011; http://eastsideinstitute.org/wp-content/uploads/2014/05/HumanStudiesFinal.pdf

Honigmann, I. and Honigmann, J., 'Child-rearing patterns among the Great Whale River Eskimo' (1954) in H. R. Schaffer (ed.), *Social Development*, Oxford: Blackwell 1996.

Horkan, M. and Woods, A., *This Is Our World: Perspectives of Some Elderly People on Life in Suburban Dublin*, Report no. 12, National Council for the Aged, 1986; http://www.ncaop.ie/publications/research/reports/This_Is_Our_World12.pdf [Accessed 11.9.2007].

Horwath, J. *Child Neglect: Identification and assessment*, Hampshire: Palgrave MacMillan 2007.

Hruby, G., 'Sociological, postmodern, and new realism perspectives in social constructionism: Implications for literacy research', *Research Reading Quarterly*, 36(1) (2001), 48–62.

Improving Access to Psychological Therapies, IAPT. *Black and Minority Ethnic (BME) Positive Practice Guide*. Dept. of Health, 2009; http://www.iapt.nhs.uk/silo/files/black-and-minority-ethnic-bme-positive-practice-guide.pdf

International Federation for Social Workers. *Social Work Principles*. http://ifsw.org/policies/human-rights-policy/ (1996)

Irish College of Psychiatrists, *A Better Future Now: Position Statement on Psychiatric Services for Children and Adolescents in Ireland*, 2005; http://www.rcpsych.ac.uk/ files/pdfversion/op60.pdf [Accessed 12.7.2010].

Irwin, L. G., Siddiqi, A. and Hertzman, C. *A powerful equalizer final report for the world health organization's commission on the social determinants of health*. 2007; http://www.who.int/social_determinants/resources/ecd_kn_report_07_2007.pdf

Izard,C. E., Fantauzzo, C. A., Castle, J. M., Haynes, O. M., Rayias, M. F. and Putna, P. H. 'The ontogeny and significance of infants' facial expressions in the first nine months of life', *Developmental Psychology*, 31 (1995), 997–1013.

Jablensky, A., Sartorius, N., Ernberg, G., Anker, M., Korten, A., Cooper, J. E., Day, R. and Bertelsen, A., 'Schizophrenia: manifestations, incidence and course in different cultures. A world health organization ten-country study' in *Psychological Medicine Monograph Supplement* 20, Cambridge: Cambridge University Press 1992.

Jahoda, M., *Current Concepts of Positive Mental Health*, New York: Basic Books 1958.

James, A. E. *The syndrome of the psychologically invulnerable child*. 1974.

Janoff-Bulman, R., *Shattered Assumptions: Towards a New Psychology of Trauma*, New York: Free Press 1992.

Janoff-Bulman, R. and Frantz, C. M., 'The impact of trauma on meaning: From meaningless world to meaningful life' in M. Power and C. Brewin (eds.), *The Transformation of Meaning in Psychological Therapies: Integrating Theory and Practice*, Chichester, Sussex: John Wiley & Sons 1997.

Jay, A. (2014), Independent Inquiry into Child Sexual Exploitation in Rotherham, 1997–2013; http://www.rotherham.gov.uk/downloads/file/1407/independent_inquiry_cse_in_rotherham

Kagan, J., Reznick, J. S. and Snidman, N., 'Biological basis of childhood shyness', *Science*, 240(4849) (1988), 167–71.

Kalikow, T. J., 'Konrad Lorenz' in Alan E. Kazdin (ed.), *Encyclopedia of Psychology*, Vol. 5, Washington, DC: American Psychological Association 2000.

Karau, S. J., 'Deindividuation' in A. E. Kazdin (ed.), *Encyclopedia of Psychology*, Vol. 2, Washington, DC: American Psychological Association 2000.

Kastenbaum, R., *The Psychology of Death*. 3rd ed., New York: Springer Publishers 2000.

Kelly, B. D., 'Penrose's law in Ireland: An ecological analysis of psychiatric inpatients and prisoners', *Irish Medical Journal*, 100(2) (2007), 373–4.

Keogh, M. (2012). *Training on the Inclusion of Persons with Disabilities in EU Development Cooperation, Module 1: Setting the stage: Why disability inclusive development and what does it mean?* :///C:/Users/user/Downloads/module_1.pdf [Accessed 8.4.2015].

Kingston, L. and Prior, M., 'The development of patterns of stable, transient and school-age aggressive behavior in young children', *Journal of American Academy of Child and Adolescent Psychiatry*, 34 (1995), 348–58.

Kirk, S., Gallagher, J. J., Coleman, M. R. and Anastasiow, N., *Educating Exceptional Children*, Boston: Houghton Mifflin 2000.

Klein, M., 'The mutual influences in the development of ego and id', *Psychoanal Study Child*, 7 (1952), 51–3.

Kolb, B. and Whishaw, I. Q., *Fundamentals of Human Neuropsychology*, 5th ed., New York: Freeman-Worth 2003.

Kohlberg, L., 'Moral stages and moralisation: The cognitive developmental approach',. in T. Lickona (ed.), *Moral Development and Behaviour: Theory, Research and Social Issues*, New York: Holt 1976, 31–53.

Kübler-Ross, E., *On Death and Dying*, London: Routledge 2005.

Kuhn, D., Nash, S. C. and Brucken, L., 'Sex role concepts of two- and three-year-olds', *Child Development*, 49 (1978), 445–51.

Lahey, B. B., Loeber, R., Burke, J. and Rathouz, P. J., 'Adolescent outcomes of childhood conduct disorder among clinic-referred boys: Predictors of improvement', *Journal of Abnormal Child Psychology*, 30(4) (2002), 333–48.

Laing, R. D. *The Politics of Experience*, New York: Ballantine 1968.

Lalor, K. and Share, P., *Applied Social Care: An Introduction for Students in Ireland*, Dublin: Gill and Macmillan 2009.

Larson, K. 'A research review and alternative hypothesis explaining the link between learning disability and delinquency', *Journal of Learning Disability*, 21(6), [1988], 357–69.

Larson, R., 'Toward a psychology of positive youth work', *American Psychologist*, 55(1) (2000), 170–83.

Latané, B. and Darley, J. M., 'Group inhibition of bystander intervention in emergencies', *Journal of Personality and Social Psychology*, 10 (1968), 215–21.

LeClerc, G., 'The self-actualization concept: A content validation', *Journal of Social Behaviour and Personality*, 13(1) (1998), 69–84.

Lee, B. J. and Goerge, R. M., 'Poverty, early childbearing, and child maltreatment: A multinomial analysis', *Child and Youth Services Review*, 21(9–10) (1999), 755–80.

Lefevre,M., Tanner, K. and Luckock, B., 'Developing social work students' communication skills with children and young people: a model for the qualifying level curriculum' *Child and Family Social Work*, 13(2) (2008), 166–76.

Lerner, M. J., 'Evaluation of performance as a function of performer's reward and attractiveness', *Journal of Personality and Social Psychology*, 1 (1965), 355–60.

Levinson, D., 'A conception of adult development', *American Psychologist*, 41(1) (1986), 3–13.

Lewis-Beck, M. S., Bryman, A. and Liao, T. F., *The Sage Encyclopedia of Social Science Research Methods*, London: Sage, 2003.

Linden, M. and Kristiansen, I. Guidelines on service provision for families of children with acquired brain injury (ABI): An international perspective', 2013; http://www.internationalbrain.org/guidelines-on-service-provision-for-families-of-children-with-abi/

Lindon, J. *Understanding children's play*. Nelson Thornes, 2001.

Loewenthal, D., Mohamed, A., Mukhopadhyay, S., Ganesh, K. and Thomas, R., 'Reducing the barriers to accessing psychological therapies for Bengali, Urdu, Tamil and Somali communities in the UK: some implications for training, policy and practice', *British Journal of Guidance & Counselling*, 40(1) (2012), 43–66.

Luthar, S. and Zigler, E., 'Vunerability and competence: A review of research on resilience in childhood', *American Journal of Orthopsychiatry*, 61(1) (1991), 1–22.

MacLeod, J., *An Introduction to Counselling*, London: Open University 2003.

Madden, D. *The Relationship Between Low Birthweight and Socioeconomic Status in Ireland.* UCD Centre For Economic Research Working Paper Series 14, 2012; http://www.ucd.ie/t4cms/WP12_14.pdf [Accessed on 12th August 2012]

Magnusson, D., Stattin, H. and Allen, V. L., 'Biological maturation and social development: A longitudinal study of some adjustment processes from mid adolescence to adulthood', *Journal of Youth and Adolescence*, 14(4) (1985), 267–83.

Maldonado, J. R., Butler, L. D. and Spiegel, D., 'Treatments for dissociative disorders' in P. E. Nathan and J. M. Gordon (eds.), *A Guide to Treatments that Work*, New York: Oxford University Press 1998.

Malim, T. and Birch, A., *Research Methods and Statistics* (Introductory Psychology Series), London: Palgrave Macmillan 1997.

Malina, R. M., Bouchard, C. and Bar-Or, O., *Growth, Maturation and Physical Activity*, 2nd ed., Human Kinetics Europe 2004.

Mann, L., 'The baiting crowd in episodes of threatened suicide', *Journal of Personality and Social Psychology*, 41(4) (1981), 703–9.

Marcia, J., 'Identity in adolesence' in J. Adelson (ed.), *Handbook of Adolescent Psychology*, New York: Wiley 1980.

Maslow, A., 'A theory of human motivation', *Psychological Review*, 50 (1943), 370–96.

Maslow, A., 'Humanistic science and transcendent experiences', *Journal of Humanistic Psychology*, 5 (1965), 219–27.

Maslow, A., *Motivation and Personality*, 3rd ed., New York: Harper & Row 1970.

Masten, A. S., 'Ordinary magic: Resilience processes in development', *American Psychologist*, 56 (2001), 227–38.

Mayock, P., Bryan, P., Carr, N. and Kitching, K., *Supporting LGBT Lives: A Study of Mental Health and Well-being of Lesbian, Gay, Bisexual and Transgender People*. Published by the Gay and Lesbian Equality Network (GLEN) and BeLong to Youth Service 2009.

McAvoy, H., Sturley, J., Burke, S. and Balanda, K., 'Unequal at birth: Inequalities in the occurrence of low birthweight babies in Ireland', The Institute of Public Health in Ireland, 2006; http://www.publichealth.ie/index.asp?locID=489 anddocID=689 [Accessed 1.6.2010].

McKay, S., 'Ireland and rape crises' in W. Balzano and M. Sullivan (eds.), *The Irish Review*, 35 (Summer 2007), 92–9.

McNicholas,F., Lydon, A., Lennon, R. and Dooley, B., 'Eating concerns and media influences in an adolescent context', *European Eating Disorders Review*, 17 (2009), 208–13.

McPherson, K., Kerr, S., McGee, E., Cheater, F. and Morgan, A., *The Role and Impact of Social Capital on the Health and Wellbeing of Children and Adolescents: a systematic review*, 2013.

Meekosha, H. and Shuttleworth, R., 'What's so 'critical' about critical disability studies?', *Australian Journal of Human Rights*, 15(1) (2009), 47–75.

Meltzoff, A. and Moore, M., 'Imitation of facial and manual gestures by human neonates', *Science*, 198 (1977), 75–8.

Meltzoff, A. and Moore, M., 'Infant imitation and memory: nine month olds in immediate and deferred tasks', *Child Development*, 59 (1988), 217–25.

Mental Health Commission, *Code of Practice: Guidance for persons working in mental health services with people with intellectual disabilities*, 2009; http://www.mhcirl.ie/Mental_Health_Act_2001/Mental_

Health_Commission_ Codes_of_Practice/People_with_Intellectual_Disabilities/Code_of_Practice_Guidance_for_Persons_working_in_Mental_Health_Services_with_People_with_Intellectual_Disabilities.pdf.

Mental Health Commission., 'The human cost: an overview of the evidence on economic adversity and mental health and recommendations for action', Dublin (2011).

Milgram, S., *Obedience to Authority: An experimental view*, London: Harper Collins 1974.

Miller, J. G., Bersoff, D. M. and Harwood, R. L., 'Perceptions of social responsibilities in India and in the United States: Moral imperatives or personal decisions?', *Journal of Personality and Social Psychology*, 58 (1990), 33–47.

Miller, P., *Theories of Developmental Psychology*, 4th ed., New York: Worth Publishers 2002.

Mond, J. M., Robertson-Smith, G. and Vetere, A., 'Stigma and eating disorders: Is there evidence of negative attitudes towards anorexia nervosa among women in the community?' *Journal of Mental Health*, 15(5) (2006), 519–32.

Monteith, Margo, 'Self-regulation of prejudiced responses: Implications for progress in prejudice-reduction efforts', *Journal of Personality and Social Psychology*, 65(3) (1993), 469–85.

Moody, H., 'Ethical dilemmas in old age care' in Johnson, M., ed., *The Cambridge Handbook of Age and Ageing*, Cambridge: Cambridge University Press 2005.

Morrison, T. Emotional Intelligence, Emotion and Social Work: Context, Characteristics, Complications and Contribution. *The British Journal of Social Work*, 37(2) (2007), 245–63.

Morse, B. A., 'Fetal Alcohol Syndrome in the Developing Child', paper presented at the Fetal Alcohol Syndrome and Other Congenital Alcohol Disorders: A National Conference on Surveillance and Prevention, Centers for Disease Control, Atlanta, GA, 1991.

Mraovick, L. and Wilson, J., 'Patterns of child abuse and neglect associated with chronological age of children living in a midwestern county', *Child Abuse and Neglect*, 23(9) (1999), 899–903.

Mrazek, P. and Mrazek, D., 'Resilience in child maltreatment victims: A Conceptual exploration', *Child Abuse and Neglect*, 11 (1987), 357–66.

Munro, E., 'The Munro review of child protection: final report, a child-centred system CM, 8062. The Stationery Office, London', 2011; https://www.gov.uk/government/uploads/system/uploads/attachment_data/file/175391/Munro-Review.pdf

Murphy, L. *Social Behavior and Child Personality.* New York: Columbia University Press 1937.

Murray Parkes, C. *Bereavement*, London: Penguin 1998.

Music, G., *Nurturing Natures: Attachment and Children's Emotional, Sociocultural and Brain Development*, London: Psychology Press 2011.

Nagy, M., 'The child's theories concerning death', *The Pedagogical Seminary and Journal of Genetic Psychology*, 73(1) (1948), 3–27.

Nanson, J. L., Hiscock, M., 'Attention deficits in children exposed to alcohol prenatally', *Alcoholism: Clinical and Experimental Research*, 14 (1990), 656–61.

Nasser, M., 'The rise and fall of the anti-psychiatry movement', *The Psychiatrist*, 19(12) (1995), 743–6.

National Children's Bureau, *Promoting the Health and Well-being of Young People in Supported Housing: A Practical Guide and Training Manual*, National Children's Bureau 2006.

National Institute of Mental Health 'Schizophrenia' 2009; http://www.nimh.nih.gov/health/publications/schizophrenia/schizophrenia-booket-2009_34643.pdf

Nevin, J., 'Analyzing Thorndike's law of effect: the question of stimulus-response bonds', *Journal of the Experimental Analysis of Behaviour*, 72 (1999), 447–50.

Nixon, L., Greene, S. and Hogan, D., 'Concepts of family among children and young people in Ireland', *The Irish Journal of Psychology*, 27(1–2) (2006), 79–87.

NSPCC. *Physical Abuse in High Risk Families: An Introduction to Our Work.* 2012.

O'Brien, M., Alldred, P. and Jones, D. (1996), 'Children's constructions of family and kinship' in J. Brannen and M. O'Brien (eds.), *Children in Families: Research and Policy*, London: Falmer Press 1996.

O'Donovan, M.-A. and Doyle, A., 'Measure of Activity and Participation (MAP): Participation and ageing: The experience of people 'on the NPSDD', *MAP Bulletin*, 4, 2009; http://www.hrb.ie/uploads/tx_hrbpublications/MAPBulletinIssue4.pdf.

O'Driscoll, C., Heary, C., Hennessy, E. and McKeague, L., 'Explicit and implicit stigma towards peers with mental health problems in childhood and adolescence', *Journal of Child Psychology and Psychiatry*, 53(10) (2012), 1054–62.

Ochberg, F., 'Post-traumatic Therapy' in G. Everly, and J. Lating (eds.), *Psychotraumatology*, London: Plenum Press 1995.

Okumura, Y., Tanimukai, S. and Asada, T., 'Effects of short-term reminiscence therapy on elderly with dementia: A comparison with everyday conversation approaches', *Psychogeriatics*, 8 (2008), 124–33.

Olweus D. 'Familial and tempermental determinants of aggressive behaviour in adolescent boys: A causal analysis', in Schaffer, H. R. *Social Development*, Blackwell Publishing: Oxford 1996.

Paluck, E. L. and Green, D. P., 'Prejudice reduction: What works? A critical look at evidence from the field and the laboratory', *Annual Review of Psychology*, 60 (2009), 339–67.

Pancer, M., 'Social psychology: The crisis continues' in Dennis Fox and Isaac Prilleltensky (eds.), *Critical Psychology: An Introduction*, Thousand Oaks, CA: Sage 1997.

Papalia, D. E., Olds, S. W. and Feldman, R. D., *Human Development*, 10th ed., New York: McGraw-Hill 2005.

Passer, M. and Smith, R., *Psychology: Frontiers and Applications*, New York: McGraw-Hill 2001.

Pavee Point Travellers' Centre., *Our Geels–All Ireland Traveller Health Study*, 2010; http://www.paveepoint.ie/resources/our-geels-all-ireland-traveller-health-study/

Pearson, E. and Podeschi, R., 'Humanism and individualism: Maslow and his critics', *Adult Education Quarterly*, 50(1) (Fall 1999), 41–55.

Perry, B. and Szalavitz, M. *The Boy The Boy Who Was Raised As a Dog: And Other Stories from a Child Psychiatrist's Notebook - What Traumatized Children Can Teach Us About Loss, Love, and Healing*, New York: Basic books 2008.

Peterson, C. and Seligman, M., *Character Strengths and Virtures: A Handbook and Classification*, Washington, DC: Oxford University Press 2004.

Pettigrew, T. F., 'The ultimate attribution error: Extending Allport's cognitive analysis of prejudice', *Personality and Social Psychology Bulletin*, 5(4) (1979), 461–76.

Pipher, M., *Reviving Ophelia: Saving the Selves of Adolescent Girls*, New York: Ballantine Books 1994.

Pope, K. and Tabachnick, B., 'Therapists as patients: A national survey of psychologists' experiences, problems and beliefs', *Professional Psychology: Research and Practice*, 25(3) (1993), 247–58.

Raabe, T. and Beelmann, A., 'Development of ethnic, racial, and national prejudice in childhood and adolescence: A multinational meta-analysis of age differences', *Child Development*, 82(6) (2011), 1715–37.

Radke-Yarrow, M., Cummings, E. M., Kuczinsky, L. and Chapman, M., 'Patterns of attachment in two- and three-year-olds in normal families and families with parental depression', *Child Development*, 56 (1985), 884–93.

Revelle, W., 'Personality structure and measurement: The contribution of Raymond Cattell', *British Journal of Psychology*, 100 (2009), 253–7.

Rheingold,H. L., Hay, D. F. and West, M. J. 'Sharing in the second year of life', *Child Development*, 47 (1976), 1148–58.

Richardson, G., 'The metatheory of resilience and resiliency', *Journal of Clinical Psychology*, 58(3) (2002), 307–21.

Robbins, B., 'What is the good life? Positive psychology and the renaissance of humanistic psychology', *The Humanistic Psychologist*, 36 (2008), 96–112.

Robinson, L. *Cross-cultural Child Development for Social Workers: an Introduction*, London: Palgrave 2007.

Roberts, B. W. and Del Vecchio, W. F., 'The rank-order consistency of personality traits from childhood to old age: A quantitative review of longitudinal studies', *Psychological Bulletin*, 126 (2000), 3–25.

Roberts, J. and Dicenso, A., 'Identifying the best research design to fit the question: Part 1: quantitative designs', *Evidenced-based Nursing*, 2 (1999), 4–6.

Rochat, P., 'Origins of self-concept' in G. Bremner and A. Fogel (eds.), *Blackwell Handbook of Infant Development*, Oxford: Blackwell 2001.

Roehrig, J. P. and McLean, C. P., 'A comparison of stigma toward eating disorders versus depression' *International Journal of Eating Disorders*, 43(7) (2010), 671–4.

Rogers, Carl, *On Becoming a Person*, Boston: Houghton Mifflin 1961.

Rolfe, G. and Cutcliffe, J., 'Post-psychiatry: good ideas, bad language and getting out of the box', *Journal of Psychiatric and Mental Health Nursing*, 13 (2006), 619–25.

Rolland, J.-P., 'Cross-cultural generalizability of the five-factor model of personality' in R. R. McCrae and J. Allik (eds.), *The Five-Factor Model of Personality Across Cultures*, New York: Kluwer Academic/Plenum 2002.

Rosario, M., Schrimshaw, E. and Hunter, J., 'Different patterns of sexual identity development over time: implications for the psychological adjustment of lesbian, gay and bisexual youths', *Journal of Sex Research*, 48(1) (2011), 3–15.

Rosenberg, M., 'Self-concept and psychological well-being in adolescence' in R. L. Leahy (ed.), *The Development of the Self*, Orlando, FL: Academic Press 1985.

Rosenhan, D. L., `On Being Sane in Insane Places', *Science*, 179(4070) (1973), 250–8.

Ross, L., & Kavanagh, D. (2013). David L. Rosenhan (1929–2012), *American Psychologist*, 68(6) , 469.

Rushton, J. P., Fulker, D. W., Neale, M. C., Nias, D. K. B. and Eysenck, H. J., 'Altruism and aggression: The heritability of individual differences', *Journal of Personality and Social Psychology*, 50 (1986), 1192–8.

Rutter, M. and Bartak, L., 'Special education treatment of autistic children: A comparative study: I. Follow-up findings and implications for services', *Journal of Child Psychology and Psychiatry*, 14 (1973), 241–70.

Rutter, M. 'Psychosocial resilience and protective mechanisms', *American Journal of Orthopsychiatry* 57.3 (1987), 316.

Rutter, M., 'Pathway from childhood to adult life', *Journal of Child Psychology and Psychiatry*, 30 (1989), 23–51.

Rutter, M., 'Practitioner review: Routes from research to clinical practice in child psychiatry: Retrospect and prospect', *Journal of Child Psychology and Psychiatry*, 39(6) (1998), 805–16.

Rutter, M., 'Resilience concepts and findings: Implications for family therapy', *Journal of Family Therapy*, 21 (1999), 119–44.

Rutter, M., Bailey, A., Simonoff, E. and Pickles, A., 'Genetic influences in autism' in D. J. Cohen and F. R. Volkmar (eds.), *Handbook of Autism and Pervasive Developmental Disorders*, 2nd ed., New York: Wiley (1997).

Rutter, M. and the English and Romanian Adoptees (ERA) study team, 'Developmental catch-up, and deficit, following adoption after severe global early privation', *Journal of Child Psychology and Psychiatry*, 39(4) (1998), 465–76.

Sabates, R. and Dex, S. Multiple risk factors in young children's development. Centre for Longitudinal Studies, 2012; file:///C:/Users/user/Downloads/WP%202012-1%20Multiple%20risk%20factors%20in%20young%20children's%20development%20-%20SABATES,%20R%20AND%20DEX,%20S.pdf

Saleebey, D., *The Strengths Perspective in Social Work*, New York: Allyn & Bacon 2009.

Schaffer, H. R., *Social Development*, Oxford: Blackwell 1996.

Schaie, K. W. and Willis, S. L., 'A stage theory model of adult cognitive development revisited' in R. Rubenstein, M. Ross and M. Kleban (eds.), *The Many Dimensions of Ageing: Essays in Honor of M. Powell Lawton*, New York: Springer 2000.

Schilling, R. and Schinke, S., 'Personal coping and social support for parents of handicapped children', *Child and Youth Services Review*, 6 (1984), 195–206.

Schlundt, D. G. and Johnson, W. G., *Eating Disorders: Assessment and Treatment*, Boston: Allyn and Bacon 1990.

Schorr, L. and Marchand, V., 'Pathway to the prevention of child abuse and neglect', 2007; http://www.dss.cahwnet.gov/cdssweb/entres/pdf/Pathway.pdf [Accessed 11.7.2010].

Schuck, S. Z. et al., 'Sex differences in aggressive behaviour subsequent listening to a radio broadcast of violence' *Psychological Reports*, 28(3) (1971), 931–6.

Sedlak, A. and Broadhurst, D., *Third National Incidence Study of Child Abuse and Neglect: Final report*, Washington, DC: US Government Printing Office 1996.

Seligman, M., *Helplessness: On depression, development, and death*, New York: Freeman 1992.

Seligman, M. and Csikszentmihalyi, M., 'Positive psychology: An introduction', *American Psychologist*, 55 (2000), 5–14.

Shaffer, D. R., *Developmental Psychology: Childhood and adolescence*, 4th ed., Pacific Grove, CA: Brooks/Cole 1999.

Shaver, P. and Mikulincer, M., 'New directions in attachment theory and research', *Journal of Social and Personal Relationships*, 27(2) (2010), 163–72.

Sherif, M., Harvey, O. J., White, B. J., Hood, W. R. and Sherif, C. W., *Intergroup Conflict and Cooperation: The Robbers Cave experiment*, Norman: University of Oklahoma Book Exchange 1961.

Simner, M. L. 'Newborn's response to the cry of another infant', *Developmental Psychology*, 5 (1971), 136–50.

Singh, N. A., Clements, K. M., Fiattarone, M. A., 'A randomized controlled trial of progressive resistance training in depressed elders', *Journal of Gerontology*, 52 (1997), 27–35.

Skinner, B. F., 'A brief survey of operant conditioning', http://www.bfskinner.org/BFSkinner/SurveyOperantBehavior_files/A_brief_survey_of_operant_behavior.pdf [Accessed 6.6.2010].

Skinner, B. F., *The Behaviour of Organisms: An experimental analysis*, New York: Appleton 1938.

Skinner, B. F., *Science and Human Behavior*, New York: Macmillan 1953.

Skinner, D. and Weisner, T., 'Sociocultural studies of families of children with intellectual disabilities',. *Mental Retardation & Developmental Disabilities Research Reviews*, 13 (2007), 302–12. http://www.tweisner.com/yahoo_site_admin/assets/docs/Skinner_Weisner_2007.239124837.pdf

Skuse, D., 'Extreme deprivation in early childhood – I. Diverse outcomes for three siblings from an extraordinary family', *Journal of Child Psychology and Psychiatry*, 25(4) (1984), 525–41.

Skuse, D., 'Extreme deprivation in early childhood – II. Theoretical issues and a comparative review', *Journal of Child Psychology and Psychiatry*, 25(4) (1984), 543–72.

Slattery, M., *Key Ideas in Sociology*, UK: Nelson Thornes 2003.

Smith, P., Cowie, H., Blades, M., *Understanding Children's Development*, 4th ed., London: Blackwell 2003.

Solomon, D., Watson M., Delucchi K. L., Schaps, E. and Battistich, V. 'Enhancing Children's Prosocial Behavior in the Classroom', *American Educational Research Journal*, 25(4) (1988), 527–54.

Stark, L. R., 'The shelter as "total institution"', *American Behavioral Scientist*, 37 (1994), 553–62.

Stewart, M. C., Keel, P. K. and Schiavo, R. S., 'Stigmatization of anorexia nervosa' *International Journal of Eating Disorders*, 39(4) (2006), 320–5.

Stewart, Maria-Christina, et al. 'Stereotypes, prejudice and discrimination of women with anorexia nervosa', *European Eating Disorders Review* 16.4 (2008), 311–18.

Steiner, Jean-François, *Treblinka*, New York: Plume 1966.

Sternberg, R. J., *The Triarchic Mind: A New Theory of Human Intelligence*, New York: Viking 1988.

Stoltenborgh, M., Bakermans-Kranenburg, M. J., van IJzendoorn, M. H. and Alink, L. A. 'Cultural-geographical differences in the occurrence of child physical abuse? A meta-analysis of global prevalence', *International Journal of Psychology*, 48(2) (2013), 81–94.

Stratton, K., Howe, C. and Battaglia, F. (eds.), Institute of Medicine, Fetal Alcohol Syndrome: Diagnosis, Epidemiology, Prevention, and Treatment, Washington, DC: National Academy Press 1996.

Sunderland, M., *The Science of Parenting*, London: Dorling Kindersley 2006.

Szasz, T., *The Myth of Mental Illness: Foundations of a Theory of Personal Conduct*, New York: Harper Row 1974.

Tajfel, H. *Human groups and social categories: Studies in social psychology*, CUP Archive 1981.

Talbot, J., 'Prisoners' voices: Experiences of the criminal justice system by prisoners with learning disabilities and difficulties' 2008; http://www.prisonreformtrust.org.uk/Portals/0/Documents/No%20One%20Knows%20report-2.pdf

Talerico, K., 'Person-centred approach: An important approach for 21st century health care', *Journal of Psychosocial and Mental Health Services*, 14(11) (2003), 14.

Target, M., Fonagy, P. and Shmueli-Goetz, Y., 'Attachment representations in school-age children: the development of the child attachment interview (CAI)', *Journal of Child Psychotherapy*, 29(2) (2003), 171–86.

Teater, B. *An introduction to applying social work theories and methods*, Open University Press: McGraw-Hill Education 2010.

Thomas, A. and Chess, S., 'The New York longitudinal study: From infancy to early adult life', in R. Plomin and J. Dunn (eds.), *The Study of Temperament: Changes,*

Continuities and Challenges, Hillsdale, NJ: Erlbaum 1986.

Thomas, A. and Chess, S., *Temperament and Development*, New York: Brenner & Mazel 1977.

Thomas, C., 'How is disability understood? An examination of sociological approaches', *Disability & Society*, 19(6) (2004), 569–83.

Thomas, D., Leicht, C., Hughes, C., Madigan, A. and Dowell, K., 'Emerging practices in the prevention of child abuse and neglect', 2003; http://www. childwe lfare.gov/preventing/programs/whatworks/report/report.pdf [Accessed 10.8.2010].

Tiet, Q. Q., Bird, H. R. and Davies, M., 'Adverse life events and resilience', *Journal of the American Academy of Child and Adolescent Psychiatry*, 37 (1998), 1191–200.

Timimi, S. and Taylor, E., 'ADHD is best understood as a cultural construct', *British Journal of Psychiatry*, 184 (2004), 8–9. http://bjp.rcpsych.org/content/bjprcpsych/184/1/8.full.pdf

Tjeltveit, C., 'There is more to ethics than codes of professional ethics: Social ethics, theoretical ethics and managed care', *The Counselling Psychologist*, 28(2) (2000), 242–52.

Trivers, R. L., 'The evolution of reciprocal altruism', *Quarterly Review of Biology*, 46 (1971), 35–57.

Trevithick, P. *Social Work Skills: A Practice Handbook*, Buckingham: Open University Press 2000.

Tzeng, O., Jackson, J. and Karlson, H., *Theories of Child Abuse and Neglect: Differential Perspectives, Summaries, and Evaluations*, New York: Praeger 1991.

United Nations Children's Fund and World Health Organization. *Low Birth Weight: Country, regional and global estimates*. New York: UNICEF, 2004.

UNICEF. 'Hidden in plain sight. A statistical analysis of violence against children', 2007; http://files.unicef.org/publications/files/Hidden_in_plain_sight_statistical_analysis_EN_3_Sept_2014.pdf

Valentino, K.; Cicchetti, D.; Toth, S. L. and Rogosch, A., 'Mother–child play and maltreatment: A longitudinal analysis of emerging social behavior from infancy to toddlerhood', *Developmental Psychology*, 47(5) (2011), 1280–94.

Van Ijzendoorn, M. H. and Kroonenberg, P. M. 'Cross-cultural patterns of attachment: A meta-analysis of the strange situation', *Child Development* (1988): 147–56.

Vygotsky, L. S., *Mind and Society: The Development of Higher Psychological Processes*, Cambridge, MA: Harvard University Press 1978.

Walker, J., 'Communication and social work from an attachment perspective', *Journal of Social Work Practice*, 22(1) (2008), 1–22.

Waller, M., 'Resilience in an ecosystemic context: Evolution of the concept', *American Journal of Orthopsychiatry*, 71(3) (2001), 290–7.

Wasco, S. M., 'Conceptualizing the harm done by rape: Applications of trauma theory to experiences of sexual assault', *Trauma, Violence, and Abuse*, 4 (2003), 309–22.

Watson, J. and Rayner, R., 'Conditioned emotional reactions' (1920); http://psychclassics.yorku.ca/Watson/emotion.htm [Accessed 14.8.2010]

Weber, J. A. and McCormick, P., 'Alateen members and non-members understanding of alcoholism', *Journal of Alcohol and Drug Education*, 37(3) (1992), 74–84.

Weinstein, R., 'Goffman's asylums and the social situations of mental patients', *Orthomolecular Psychiatry*, 11(4) (1982), 267–74.

Werner, E. E., 'Risk, resilience, and recovery: Perspectives from the Kauai longitudinal study', *Development and Psychopathology*, 5 (1993), 503–15.

Whitehead, M. and Dahlgren, G., 'Concepts and principles for tackling social inequities in health: Levelling up Part 1', *World Health Organization: Studies on Social and Economic Determinants of Population Health*, 2, 2006; http://www.euro.who.int/__data/assets/pdf_file/0018/103824/E89384.pdf

Whiting, B. and Whiting, J., *Children of Six Cultures*, Cambridge, MA: Harvard University Press 1975.

WHO., 'Early childhood development and disability: discussion paper', 2012; www.who.int/disabilities/publications/other/ECDD_final_word.doc

Wilkes, G., 'Introduction: A second generation of resilience research', *Journal of Clinical Psychology*, 58(3) (2002), 229–32.

Wilkins, D., 'Disorganised attachment indicates child maltreatment: how is this link useful for child protection social workers?', *Journal of Social Work Practice: Psychotherapeutic Approaches in Health, Welfare and the Community*, 26(1) (2012), 15–30.

Windholz, G., 'Pavlov, psychoanalysis, and neuroses', *Pavlovian Journal of Biological Science*, 25(2) (1990), 48–52.

Woolhead, G., Tadd, W., Boix-Ferrer, J., Krajcik, S., Schmid-Pfahler, B., Spjuth, B., Stratton, D. and Dieppe, S., '"Tu" or "vous?" A European qualitative study of dignity and communication with older people in health and social care settings', *Patient Education and Counseling*, 61 (2006), 363–71.

World Health Organization, *The Ottawa Charter for Health Promotion*, 1986; http://www.who.int/healthpromotion/conferences/previous/ottawa/en/index.html [Accessed 14.6.2010].

World Health Organization, *Promoting Mental Health: Concepts, emerging evidence and practice*, Geneva: WHO, 2005; http://www.who.int/mental_health/ evidence/MH_Promotion_Book.pdf [Accessed 11.7.2010].

World Health Organization, *Child Maltreatment*, 2010; http://www.who.int/topics/child_abuse/en/ [Accessed 15.8.2010].

World Health Organisation. *Mental Health and Development Targeting People with Mental Health Conditions as a Vulnerable Group*, 2010; http://whqlibdoc.who.int/publications/2010/9789241563949_eng.pdf?ua=1

World Health Organisation (2012). *Risks to mental Health: An overview of vulnerabilities and risk factors.* Background paper by WHO Secretariat for the development of a comprehensive mental health action plan.

Wyatt, R. C. and Livson, N., 'The not so great divide? Psychologists and psychiatrists take stands on the medical and psychosocial models of mental illness', *Professional Psychology: Research and Practice*, 25 (1994), 120–31.

Zahn-Waxler, C., Radke-Yarrow, M. and King, R. A., 'Child-rearing and children's prosocial initiations toward victims of distress', *Child Development*, 50 (1979), 319–30.

Zigler, E. F. and Finn-Stevenson, M., 'Applied developmental psychology', in M. H. Bornstein and M. E. Lamb (eds.), *Developmental Psychology: An Advanced Textbook*, 4th ed., Mahwah, NJ: Earlbaum 1999.

Zimbardo, P. and Haney, C., 'The past and future of American prison policy: Twenty-five years after the Stanford Prison Experiment', *American Psychologist*, 53(7) (1998), 709–27.

Zimbardo, P. G., 'Does psychology make a significant difference in our lives?', *American Psychologist*, 59 (2004), 339–51.

INDEX